INTERNATIONAL RELATIONS

INTERNATIONAL RELATIONS

BRIEF EDITION

ERIC B. SHIRAEV
GEORGE MASON UNIVERSITY

VLADISLAV M. ZUBOK
LONDON SCHOOL OF ECONOMICS

NEW YORK   OXFORD
OXFORD UNIVERSITY PRESS

Oxford University Press is a department of the University of Oxford. It furthers the University's objective of excellence in research, scholarship, and education by publishing worldwide.

Oxford New York
Auckland   Cape Town   Dar es Salaam   Hong Kong   Karachi
Kuala Lumpur   Madrid   Melbourne   Mexico City   Nairobi
New Delhi   Shanghai   Taipei   Toronto

With offices in
Argentina   Austria   Brazil   Chile   Czech Republic   France   Greece
Guatemala   Hungary   Italy   Japan   Poland   Portugal   Singapore
South Korea   Switzerland   Thailand   Turkey   Ukraine   Vietnam

For titles covered by Section 112 of the US Higher Education Opportunity Act, please visit www.oup.com/us/he for the latest information about pricing and alternate formats.

Published in the United States of America by
Oxford University Press
198 Madison Avenue, New York NY 10016
http://www.oup.com

Library of Congress Cataloging-in-Publication Data

Shiraev, Eric, 1960-
    International relations / Eric B. Shiraev, George Mason University, Vladislav M. Zubok,
London School of Economics. — Brief ed.
        pages cm
    Includes bibliographical references and index.
    ISBN 978-0-19-976556-0
    1. International relations. I. Zubok, V. M. (Vladislav Martinovich) II. Title.
    JZ1242.S555   2014
    327—dc23
                                                                                2013020426

9 8 7 6 5 4 3 2 1
Printed in the United States of America on acid-free paper

Brief Contents

Contents

CHAPTER 3 Alternative Views 79

CHAPTER 9   Humanitarian Challenges 293

Preface

W E WROTE THIS BRIEF BOOK TO ADDRESS A NEW GEN-ERATION OF STUDENTS WHO HAVE UNPRECEDENTED ACCESS TO GLOBAL INFORMATION YET LACK THE background to fully understand and evaluate it. Statistics, video clips, tweets, maps, eyewitness reports, scholarly articles, and biographies—all are just a click away. But how can we effectively navigate through this wealth of data and opinions? We wanted to guide students through this information by paying special attention to the rigorous, critical evaluation of facts and by discussing several frameworks of analysis—at least two major tasks in teaching international relations today.

With that in mind, we designed this book to offer a consistent framework, one that helps students approach the field of international relations with an engaged, serious mindset and a critical eye. This brief edition of *International Relations* retains the most distinctive features of the comprehensive edition while covering the major themes and discussions in a more concise way. Like a handbook to the field, in this book we steer students through major international issues, offer contending approaches, and consider real-world applications of analysis. The educational tools we have built into this book will equip students not only with facts and concepts for a solid background but also with the skills for critical thinking. Students will learn to distinguish opinions from scholarly concepts, superficial judgments from theory-guided reasoning. We tell students that the complexities of today's world are not likely to fit a single approach. We encourage them, with the help of case studies and questions, to cross the boundaries of research traditions and think independently.

A Consistent Learning Framework

The consistent chapter outline centers on three basic questions: (1) what do we study, (2) how do we study it, and (3) how do we apply it? Every chapter follows this format so that students know what to expect.

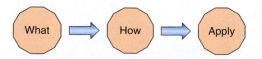

1. **What do we study?** In an engaging opening case in every chapter we introduce the chapter's main theme. Following this case, we present chapter learning objectives to focus students on the essential information to look for. Next we cover basic concepts and definitions, key facts and developments, and major international problems related to the chapter's theme.

2. **How do we study it?** In the second section of each chapter we present the main frameworks and approaches used to analyze these facts, events, and problems. The book reflects a wealth of conceptual discussions, including the growing prominence of alternatives to realism and liberalism. Through real issues, case studies, and frequent questions, in this book we help students cut across research traditions to look for their own answers. In the process, students will see that any single approach or model cannot in itself explain the complexities of today's world.

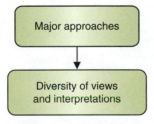

3. **How do we apply it?** In the third section of each chapter, we show students how to apply these approaches in individual, state, and global contexts. In an extended, chapter-ending application called "Past, Present, and Future," we consider a new case in depth. This case concludes the discussion of applications by focusing on real-life ramifications and posing new questions.

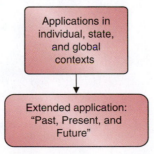

A Guide to Critical Thinking

We introduce the critical thinking approach in Chapter 1 and then apply it in every chapter. Rather than merely presenting facts and theories of international relations, we show students how to explain and evaluate them critically. Emphasis on critical thinking helps students achieve at least two goals. First, it shows them how to extract more valuable, complex information from apparently simple facts or research data. Second, it teaches them to be informed skeptics.

Several features of the text include a critical-thinking component:

DEBATE > WHY HAS OBAMA ENGAGED IN SEVERAL ARMED CONFLICTS?

Few state leaders support war as the only security option, whereas even the most passionate advocates of peace often see preparations for war as vital security measures. Domestic critics of President Obama before he took office often charged him of being dovish. Indeed, Obama was very critical of Washington's military engagements overseas and moved to reduce nuclear weapons (Parker, 2010). But Obama did not withdraw immediately from Iraq and even increased U.S. military presence in Afghanistan in 2010. Moreover, in 2011, he intensified missile strikes against suspected terrorists in several counties and ordered military operations against the Qaddafi regime in Libya.

WHAT'S YOUR VIEW?
Does Obama's attitude toward armed conflicts seem reasonable and consistent to you? Do you think he succeeded in finding a good balance between seeking peace and relying on military force?

@ Book review: "In Bob Woodward's 'Obama's Wars,' Neil Sheehan sees parallels to Vietnam." Find more on the companion website.

"Debate" boxes include "What's Your View?" sections, asking students to consider their own views on controversial questions and issues.

CASE IN POINT > *Diplomatic Efforts in an India-Pakistan Conflict*

In December 2001, in the wake of a terrorist attack on India's parliament by Pakistan-based militant groups, India and Pakistan amassed over a million troops on the Indo-Pakistani border. These countries had gone to war several times before, the last time in 1971. Now they threatened each other with nuclear missiles. The entire international community joined urgent efforts to avoid what appeared to be imminent violence. After weeks of relentless diplomatic talks, the standoff eased out, and reciprocal concessions began. Pakistan's leaders promised to stop cross-border infiltrations of civilian combatants into Indian-controlled Kashmir. India, in exchange, withdrew its navy from the North Arabian Sea and lifted the over-flight ban imposed on Pakistani commercial jets. India also agreed to upgrade diplomatic ties with Islamabad. Indo-Pakistani relations remain tense and difficult, but international diplomacy proved its efficacy in easing military threats.

CRITICAL THINKING
Why did diplomacy work in this particular conflict but fail in others, such as during the conflict between the United States and Iraq in 2003? Compare these two conflicts by paying attention to (1) the willingness of the involved governments to communicate with each other and (2) the ability of the international community to influence the conflicting sides. Can you think of other, more contemporary conflicts that lead to a peaceful resolution because of diplomatic efforts?

"Case in Point" boxes, in which we examine current or historical events and issues, contain Critical Thinking questions that ask students to think deeply about the cases discussed. These questions make excellent prompts for class discussion or writing assignments.

Critical Thinking

- Compare and contrast the realist, liberal, constructivist, and alternative perspectives on security.
- Explain two applications of security policies at each of the following levels: individual decisions, government politics, and global developments.
- Give an example of a security policy you consider effective and one you consider ineffective. Explain your choices.

Critical Thinking questions within **"Visual Reviews"** at the end of every chapter prompt students to think further about the chapter's key topics and conclusions.

Examples and Cases:
Connecting Context, Examples, and Real-World Applications

We know from experience that students need substantial context to fully understand contemporary issues and to see the relevance of an analytical framework. We therefore provide abundant examples throughout the book, many examining parallels between past and present yet considering the limits of historical analogies. This carefully integrated context not only gives students a way to frame information and make connections but also helps correct misconceptions.

Three features in particular demonstrate the kinds of examples and cases we provide throughout:

Each chapter begins with a vivid historical example that includes several framing questions.

"Case in Point" boxes feature brief, practical examples from the past and the present to illustrate the relevance of the chapter's concepts.

CASE IN POINT > *The End of a French-German Obsession: Alsace-Lorraine*

Crossing the border between France and Germany today is hardly noticeable. It wasn't in the past. Consider the case of Alsace-Lorraine, a relatively small territory that Germany and France contested for centuries in several bloody wars (see Map 1.1). France consolidated its sovereignty over the territory during the revolution of the end of the 18th century. After the war of 1871, the newly formed German Reich annexed Alsace-Lorraine. In 1919, after Germany lost in World War I, France reclaimed its sovereignty over the territory. Not for long. After Germany attacked France in 1940, the residents of the region became citizens of Hitler's Third Reich. Only in 1944, after the British-American troops defeated the Nazis, did Alsace-Lorraine join France one last time.

It is only appropriate that after many years of disputes and violence, Strasbourg, the principal city in this region, became the official seat of the European Parliament where representatives from France, Germany, and other member-states jointly discuss and resolve common issues of the united continent.

CRITICAL THINKING
Later in this book we will learn about territorial conflicts that are causing international tensions. India and Pakistan, Armenia and Azerbaijan, China and Japan, Argentina and the United Kingdom, and many other countries are dealing with their unresolved territorial disputes. Why is there so much tension over territories? Some might think the answer to this question is

obvious: The disputed territories have natural resources, and this is what countries care about above all. Although resources play a big role in territorial conflicts, could you suggest other reasons contributing to such disputes? Consider issues such as a country's concern for its "prestige," the importance of a territory for a people's national identity, pressures of domestic political forces, and the impact of public opinion. Imagine for the sake of the argument that Mexico asked the United States to return—as a sign of a good gesture—some small territories of California and New Mexico that previously belonged to Mexico. How do you think the United States would react to this request?

MAP 1-1 Alsace-Lorraine

The extended analytical cases called "Past, Present, and Future" at the end of every chapter feature detailed accounts of noteworthy developments from the past several decades. In each one we consider critical assessments and address three interconnected questions:

What is this case about? → What are this case's applications? → What new questions about international relations does this case bring up?

Summary of Features

After reading this chapter, you should be able to:

Learning Objectives

▶ define terrorism, explaining its logic, strategies, and methods;
▶ explain how states, international organizations, and the entire global system deal with the challenge of terrorism;
▶ distinguish among different views of terrorism and counterterrorist policies; and
▶ apply your knowledge about terrorism and counterterrorism at three levels of analysis.

What Do We Study?

Most states agree that problem of international terrorism needs immediate attention. They only disagree as to how terrorism can be defeated. Journalists and security experts debate definitions and policies to deal with terrorism. Governments and international organizations have committed huge resources to study, understand, and combat it. Thousands of people have died. Many areas of our lives, including public safety procedures and international travel, have been altered. In this chapter we will define terrorism, examine its historical roots, discuss counterterrorism, and critically examine various views of terrorism and counterterrorism.

Terrorism and Counterterrorism

Terrorism is violence by nonstate actors, such as individuals or groups, to achieve radical political goals. Terrorism is thus a form of *political radicalism*—ideas and methods to produce rapid, dramatic change in the social or political order. Terrorism can be state sponsored, in that a foreign government can provide financial, military, or logistical support to terrorists to further its policy goals. Yet in essence it remains a nonstate phenomenon.

Chapter-opening cases provide vivid examples that set the stage for the chapter and pose framing questions.

Learning Objectives focus students on the key information to look for in each chapter. These are echoed in the Critical Thinking section of the Visual Review at the end of the chapter.

DEBATE > WHO ARE PATRIOTS AND NATIONALISTS?

The labels "nationalist" and "patriot" are often confusing. Just what does it mean to be a Korean, Mexican, or American patriot? In public discourse, as research shows, to be a "patriot" has always been more suitable than to be a "nationalist" (Kosterman and Feshbach, 1989). "Patriotic" behavior is sometimes associated with agreeing with a majority. Moreover, the terms

nationalist, *patriot*, *patriotic*, or *unpatriotic* are often deliberately misused to boost one's popularity and scorn political opponents.

WHAT'S YOUR VIEW?
Do you think it is patriotic to support your country's leaders unconditionally and at all times? Why or why not? When do you think it can be patriotic to criticize your

country's policies and its leaders? Give an example of an unpatriotic statement or behavior.

@ You can easily search for the media's interpretation of "unpatriotic" acts or statements—for example, "Fox Accuses Google of Being Unpatriotic" by Chris Matyszczyk (June 2012). See the companion website.

In "Debate" boxes we ask students to consider their own views on a controversial question. In these boxes we also point to online resources for further research on the topic.

Environmental pollution and trash scattered in the crowded Makoko neighborhood of Lagos, Nigeria. Although megalopolises grow rapidly, in the countries where governments are inefficient and economic infrastructure is poor, acute environmental problems are inevitable.

▶ Define a humanitarian intervention.
▶ What is a pandemic?
▶ Who are the *internally displaced*?
▶ What is human trafficking?

CHECK YOUR KNOWLEDGE

"Check Your Knowledge" questions appear throughout, checking student comprehension at key points in the text.

In "Past, Present, and Future" sections we conclude each chapter's narrative by applying the material to both classic and contemporary cases (such as the Cuban missile crisis, "misperceptions and realities" in the war on terror, and "celebrity interventions" in humanitarian issues).

An icon in the margin and in "Debate" boxes indicates that relevant readings or links are available on the companion website, www.oup.com/us/shiraev.

Key terms are boldfaced, listed at the end of each chapter, and defined in the glossary at the back of the text.

Bulleted chapter summaries recap key points at a glance.

In "Visual Reviews" at the end of each chapter we map out the key concepts according to each chapter's consistent structure: (1) what do we study, (2) how do we study it, and (3) how do we apply it, followed by Critical Thinking questions that reflect the chapter learning objectives.

Bulleted chapter summaries recap key points at a glance.

In an appendix on IR careers we provide descriptions of the major career categories as well as resources for finding positions in the field of IR.

Organization and Coverage

The book contains nine chapters and is divided into three parts:

• In **Part I, Studying International Relations** (Chapters 1–3), we introduce the field. We offer key definitions, introduce essential facts, and describe major methods used in this field. Main actors, including states, international governmental organizations, and nongovernmental organizations are introduced in the section. In this section we also present the major approaches to international relations—realism, liberalism, and constructivism—as well as several alternative approaches, including conflict theories, feminism, and political psychology.

- In **Part II, Three Facets of International Relations** (Chapters 4–6), we discuss three major, classic facets of international relations: international security, international law, and international political economy. We discuss main concepts, including international security, war, economic policy, free trade, territoriality, universal jurisdiction, and human rights—to name a few—in this section.

- In **Part III, Twenty-First Century Challenges** (Chapters 7–9), we explore domestic and global challenges of today's world that are likely to continue into the future. These topics include terrorism and nonstate violent radicalism, global environmental problems, and humanitarian challenges. In the concluding section of the book we provide critical evaluations of various predictions about the future of international relations.

After Chapter 1, in which we introduce the discipline and the critical-thinking approach, we provide two full chapters on main approaches: realism and liberalism (Chapter 2), and alternative views (Chapter 3). The next three chapters cover the issues of international security (Chapter 4), international law (Chapter 5), and international political economy (Chapter 6). We give special attention to terrorism (Chapter 7) as well as to environmental and humanitarian challenges and their solutions (Chapters 8 and 9). A brief Conclusion serves as a capstone for the book and is essentially an extended exercise, guiding students in making predictions about the future of international relations.

Supplements

Oxford University Press offers instructors and students a comprehensive ancillary package for qualified adopters of *International Relations*.

- **Companion Website at www.oup.com/us/shiraev**
  - For instructors, this site includes the teaching tools described below, available for immediate download. Contact your local OUP sales representative for access.
  - For students, the companion website includes a number of study tools, including learning objectives, key-concept summaries, quizzes and essay questions, Web activities, and Web links.
- **Instructor's Resource Manual with Test Item File**
  - The Instructor's Resource Manual includes chapter objectives, a detailed chapter outline, lecture suggestions and activities, discussion questions, video resources, and Web resources. Available on the Instructor's Resource CD or as a download from the Web at **www.oup .com/us/shiraev**.
  - The Test Item File includes over 7,000 test items, including multiple-choice, short-answer, and essay questions. Questions are identified as factual, conceptual, or applied; and correct answers are keyed to the text pages where the concepts are presented.

- **Computerized Test Bank**—Using the test authoring and management tool Diploma, the computerized test bank that accompanies this text is designed for both novice and advanced users. Diploma enables instructors to create and edit questions, create randomized quizzes and tests with an easy-to-use drag-and-drop tool, publish quizzes and tests to online courses, and print quizzes and tests for paper-based assessments. Available on the Instructor's Resource CD.
- **PowerPoint-Based Slides**—Each chapter's slide deck includes a succinct chapter outline and incorporates relevant chapter graphics. Available on the Instructor's Resource CD or as a download from the Web.
- **Instructor's Resource CD**—This resource puts all of your teaching tools in one place. The CD includes the Instructor's Resource Manual with Tests, the Computerized Test Bank, the PowerPoint-based slides, and the graphics from the text.
- **CNN Videos**—Offering recent clips on timely topics, this DVD provides up to 15 films tied to the chapter topics in the text. Each clip is approximately 5–10 minutes in length, offering a great way to launch your lectures. Contact your local OUP sales representative for details.
- **Ebook**—This text is also available as a CourseSmart Ebook (978-0-19-933630-2).
- **Facebook page**—Regular updates, links, and discussions relevant to the textbook can be found at: https://www.facebook.com/International RelationsTextbook
- **Course Cartridges** are also available.

To order the Instructor's Resource CD, CNN Videos, Ebook, or Course Cartridges, or to arrange for a packaging option (see details following), please contact your Oxford University Press sales representative at (800) 280–0280.

Packaging Options

Adopters of *International Relations* can package **ANY** Oxford University Press book with the text for a 20 percent savings off the total package price. See our many trade and scholarly offerings at **www.oup.com**, then contact your local OUP sales representative to request a package ISBN. **In addition, the following items can be packaged with the text for free:**

- *Oxford Pocket World Atlas*, **Sixth Edition**—This full-color atlas is a handy reference for international relations students (package ISBN 978-0-19-935648-5).
- *Very Short Introduction* Series—These very brief texts offer succinct introductions to a variety of topics. Titles include *Terrorism*, Second Edition, by Townshend (package ISBN 978-0-19-937348-2), *Globalization*, Third Edition, by Steger (package ISBN 978-0-19-937350-5), and *Global Warming*, Second Edition, by Maslin (package ISBN 978-0-19-937349-9), among others.
- *Now Playing* **Video Guide**—Through documentaries, feature films, and You-Tube videos, *Now Playing: Learning Global Politics Through Film* provides video examples of course concepts to demonstrate real-world relevance. Each video is accompanied by a brief summary and 3–5 discussion questions. Qualified adopters will also receive a Netflix subscription that enables them to show

students the films discussed in the *Now Playing* guide. Please use package ISBN 978-0-19-935643-0 to order.

• *The Student Research and Writing Guide for Political Science*—This brief guide provides students with the information and tools necessary to conduct research and write a research paper. The guide explains how to get started writing a research paper, describes the parts of a research paper, and presents the citation formats found in academic writing. Please use package ISBN 978-0-19-935645-4 to order.

Acknowledgments

Invaluable contributions, help, and support for the brief edition of this book came from many individuals. We are grateful for the insightful feedback and critical advice of colleagues and reviewers, the thorough efforts of research assistants, and the patience and understanding of family members. We also take this opportunity to acknowledge the tremendous support we received at virtually every stage of this project's development from the team at Oxford University Press. Executive Editor Jennifer Carpenter championed this project from the start; Associate Editor Maegan Sherlock arranged reviews, saw to the details, and kept the project on schedule; Development Editor Lauren Mine provided constant support and good ideas during the writing stage; and Production Editor Theresa Stockton guided the book through production.

Special thanks to William Wohlforth from Dartmouth University; Mark Pollack, Richard Immerman, and Petra Goedde from Temple University; Mark Kramer and Mary Sarotte from Harvard University; Norman Naimark, David Holloway, and Mikhail Bernstam from Stanford University; Thomas Blanton from the National Security Archive; William Taubman from Amherst College; Odd Arne Westad and Mike Cox from the London School of Economics; John Ikenberry from Princeton University; Ted Hopf from the National University of Singapore; David Sears from UCLA; James Sidanius from Harvard University; David Levy from Pepperdine University; Peter Stearns, Bob Dudley, and Priscilla Regan from George Mason University; Cheryl Koopman from Stanford University; Philip Tetlock from the University of Pennsylvania; Christian Ostermann, Robert Litwak, and Blair Ruble from the Woodrow Wilson Center; Andrew Kuchins from the Center for Strategic and International Studies; Alan Whittaker from the National Defense University; and Scott Keeter from the Pew Research Center for inspiring us early and throughout our careers.

We received constant help, critical advice, and validation from our colleagues and friends in the United States and around the world. We express our gratitude to Hohn Haber, Mark Katz, Ming Wan, Colin Dueck, Dimitri Simes, Paul Saunders, Henry Hale, James Goldgeier, Eric John, Eric McGlinchey, Peter Mandaville, Barbara Saperstone, Jason Smart, Richard Sobel, Henry Nau, Martijn Icks, Stanislav Eremeev, Konstantin Khudoley, and Vitaly Kozyrev. A word of appreciation to Olga Chernyshev, Elena Vitenberg, Michael Zubok, John and Judy Ehle, Dmitry Shiraev, Dennis Shiraev, and Nicole Shiraev. We can never thank them enough.

We also thank the reviewers commissioned by Oxford University Press for the comprehensive edition of this text, as well as the following reviewers of this brief edition, for their insightful and valuable comments:

Victor Asal, State University of New York at Albany

Abdalla Battah, Minnesota State University, Mankato

Dylan Bennett, University of Wisconsin-Washington County

Austin Carson, The Ohio State University

Suheir Daoud, Coastal Carolina University

Jose de Arimateia da Cruz, Armstrong Atlantic State University

Daniel Friedheim, Drexel University

Nathan Gonzalez, California State University, Long Beach

Gregory Granger, Northwestern State University of Louisiana

Eric A. Heinze, University of Oklahoma

Marcus Holmes, Fordham University

Lisa Kissopoulos, University of Cincinnati Clermont College

Tobias Lanz, University Of South Carolina–Columbia

Jeffrey Lewis, Cleveland State University

Patrice McMahon, University of Nebraska—Lincoln

Andrea Neal-Malji, University of Kentucky

James Rae, California State University, Sacramento

Christopher J. Saladino, Virginia Commonwealth University

We would be remiss if we did not express a word of gratitude to the administration, faculty, staff, and students at our academic institutions where we have consistently been provided with an abundance of encouragement, assistance, and validation.

The journey continues.

Eric Shiraev and Vladislav Zubok

WASHINGTON, DC—LONDON—PHILADELPHIA—ROME—MOSCOW

To the Student

Imagine that to study international relations you have obtained the power to travel back in time and space. How far back and where would you go? Would you pick a seat in a crowded room among revolutionary conspirators? Would you be a fly on the wall in the White House, listening to a president's top-secret discussion with a foreign leader? Would you like to be present at the peace conference in Yalta in 1945, watching how Franklyn Roosevelt, Joseph Stalin, and Winston Churchill decided the future of the world? Or would you prefer to climb atop the Berlin Wall on November 9, 1989, to chip off a chunk of this monstrous barrier, the symbol of the Cold War? Would you rather be among the few physicians contemplating Doctors Without Borders in 1971? Or maybe you would like to attend the NATO meeting when a decision to bomb Libya was made in 2011?

Too many choices, too many people. . . . But even if you saw everything you wanted and met everybody you planned, what exactly could you learn from that experience? And what lessons could you draw when everything in the world is so rapidly changing? During just the last two decades, the world has witnessed the September 11 attacks, two wars launched by the United States, the birth of several new sovereign states, the rapid growth of economic superpowers in Asia and Latin America, the global financial crisis, and the turbulent revolutions in the Middle East. As you are reading these pages, something highly important is likely to be happening in some part of the world. Is it feasible to draw any serious lessens from a kaleidoscope of rapidly unfolding events, let alone study something that happened ten years, twenty years, or even longer ago?

We believe such valuable lessons exist and that we need to study them and study carefully. Reliable knowledge of international relations takes more than observing things unfolding at this hour. Experts in international politics do more than register a perpetual chain of events. They *analyze* the inner logic of these events. Therefore, we will need serious analysis, or the breaking up of something complex into smaller parts, to comprehend their important features and interactions.

And even this is not enough. If you want to become a successful professional dealing with international relations—a politician or diplomat, researcher or military officer, blogger or college professor, lawyer or president—you cannot focus merely on analysis of events without understanding their context. How would you know which events to analyze and what their significance is? Which news stories deserve immediate action—and what action? To answer these questions, you will have to gain a broader knowledge about international relations. To make conclusions, you have to study, analyze, and generalize not only the headlines popping up on the screen of your mobile device but also the rich database of facts, opinions, and theories accumulated over the years. You will need to familiarize yourself with some general "rules" and patterns of international behavior as well as exceptions to these rules: for example, the ways countries, leaders, and international organizations like the United Nations are likely to act and the ways they almost never act.

The more you become educated about international relations, the more you will realize that there are many things you don't know. This awareness of the limitations of your knowledge will be a sign that you are mastering the science of international relations—that you are ready to patiently test your conclusions against the stubborn realities of this ever-changing, complex world.

Now back to your earlier choices: did you pick the most outstanding events or individuals to meet? What questions will you ask? What lessons do you think you may learn by observing these events and conversing with these individuals? Consider your answers as your entry-level contribution to the studies of international relations. Welcome to the journey!

Maps of the World

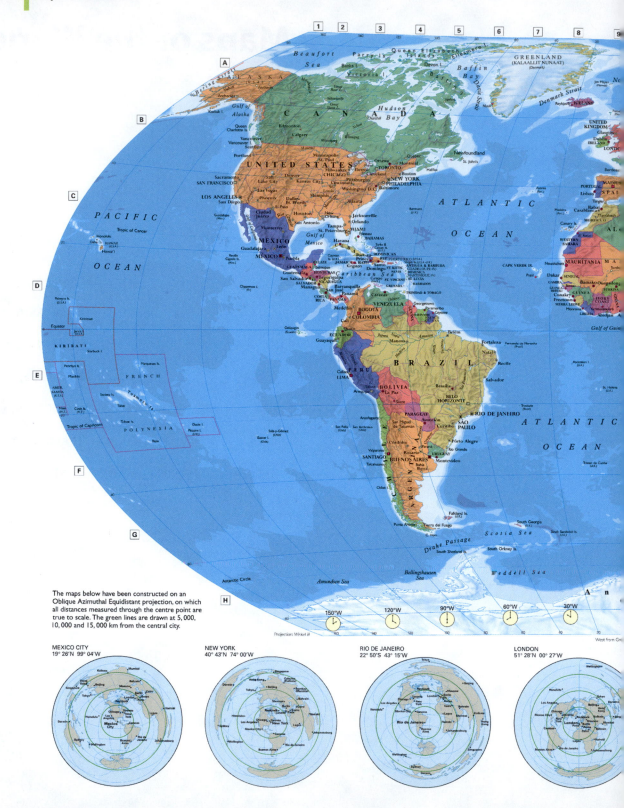

The maps below have been constructed on an Oblique Azimuthal Equidistant projection, on which all distances measured through the centre point are true to scale. The green lines are drawn at 5,000, 10,000 and 15,000 km from the central city.

MEXICO CITY
19° 26'N 99° 04'W

NEW YORK
40° 43'N 74° 00'W

RIO DE JANEIRO
22° 50'S 43° 15'W

LONDON
51° 28'N 00° 27'W

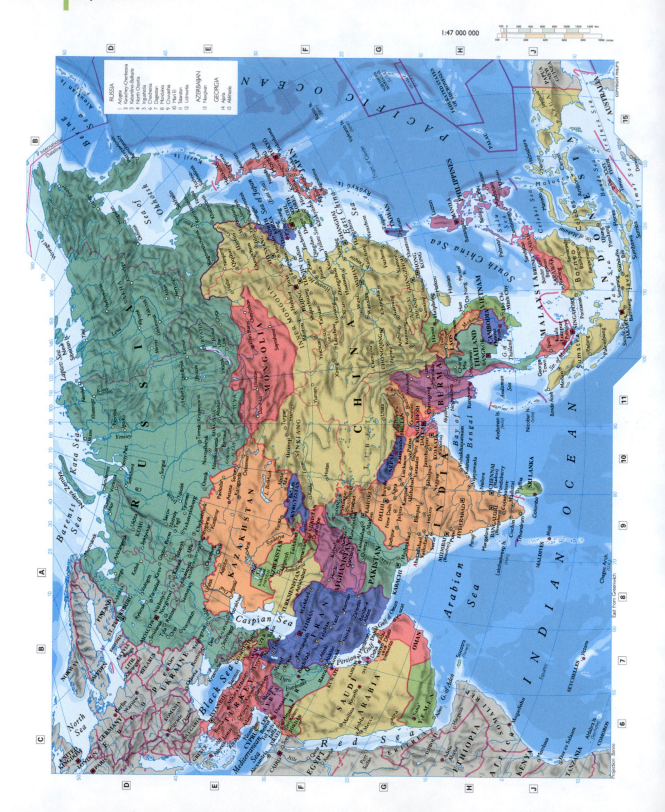

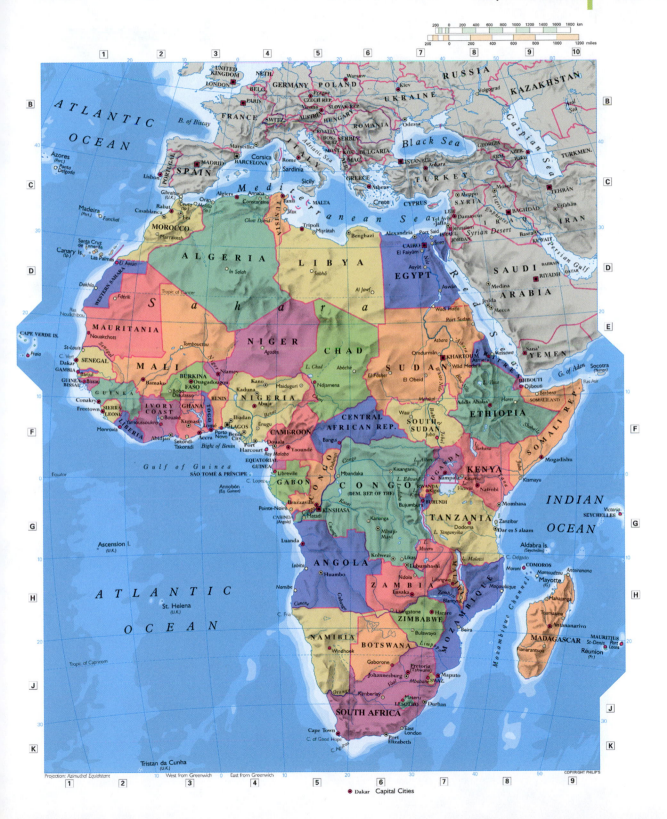

Dakar Capital Cities

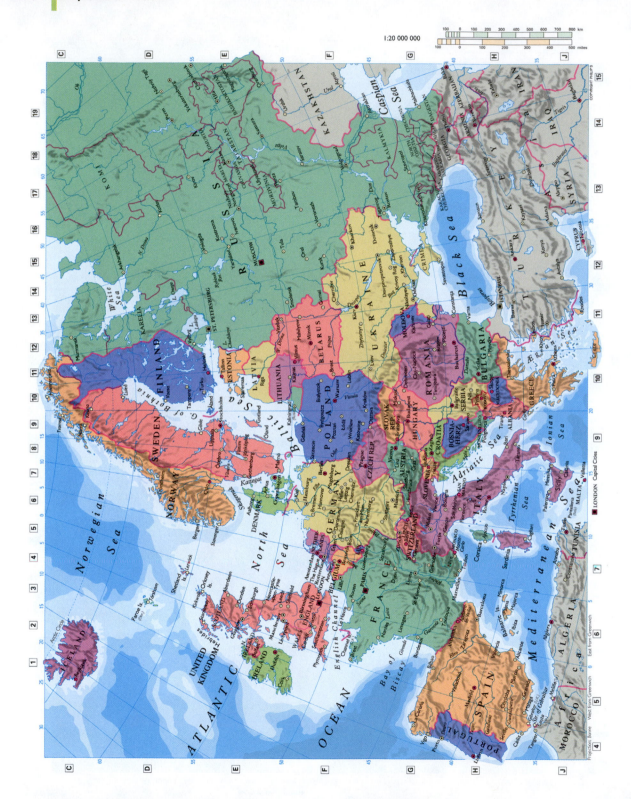

1:35 000 000

Projection: Bonne   ■ MÉXICO Capital Cities

1:35 000 000

100   0   200   400   600   800   1000   1200   1400 km
100   0   200   400   600   800   1000 miles

Projection: Lambert's Azimuthal Equal Area

■ LIMA Capital Cities

COPYRIGHT PHILIP'S

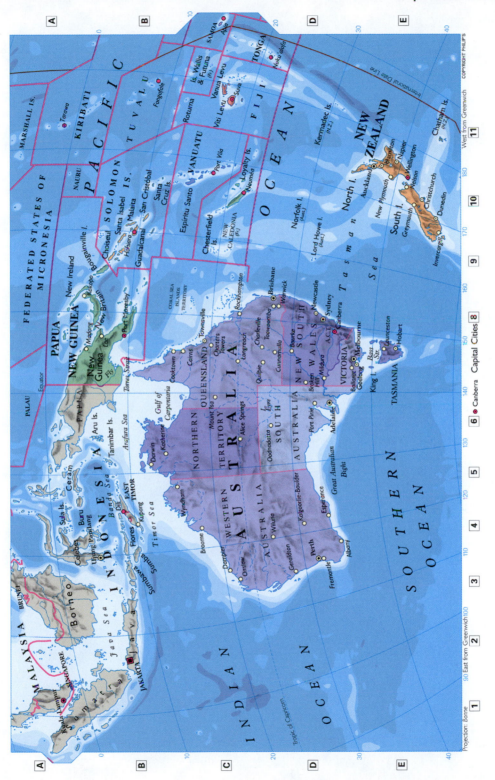

INTERNATIONAL RELATIONS

CHAPTER

1

Until recently, Cubans could not leave their country. Now things are changing. Cuban dissident blogger Yoani Sanchez has her documents checked at passport control before leaving Cuba to travel to Brazil and other countries in 2013. People today travel and migrate from one place to another on a scale previously unknown in human history. How has such freedom of global travel affected international relations?

Introducing International Relations

It is possible to live in peace.
  —MAHATMA GANDHI (1869–1948)

W E LIVE IN A FASCINATING AND RAPIDLY CHANGING WORLD. CONSIDER THE FOLLOWING:

- Not long ago, the European Union was the best example of an economically successful and stable regional organization. Today, many are asking if this union will survive the decade.
- In 2010, it seemed that corrupt dictators would govern the Arab countries of the Middle East and North Africa for many years to come. Yet the beginning of the Arab Spring one year later turned the entire region into an area of change and instability.
- Thirty years ago, textbooks published in the United States identified Soviet nuclear threats as the major challenge to international peace. What are today's greatest security challenges?

Even the most permanent-seeming aspects of international relations cannot be taken for granted. People today travel and migrate from one place to another on a scale previously unknown in human history. The Internet and social networks such as Facebook and Twitter bring billions of people together across national borders and have helped many people challenge authoritarian governments. How can we predict what the world will be like ten or twenty years from now?

In this book, we contrast traditional and novel views of international relations. We also reflect on current global and local processes, though of course we do not possess ultimate wisdom to explain them definitively. Some experts call today's world "flat," no longer divided into the superior West and "the rest." Others, on the contrary, warn about the deep divisions between the countries of the prosperous and arrogant "North" and the poor and desperate "South." Some believe that today's environmental problems are more important than the issues of borders, wars, and state security. Their opponents insist that borders, wars, and nuclear weapons will not disappear and require constant attention.

We want to include as many views as possible to show that the world is a diverse, dynamic place. We will see that international relations involves not only big states like the United States and China but also, critically, nonstate or intergovernmental organizations like the European Community or the United Nations. We will see, too, how their roles are changing in an era of globalization. We will see the urgency of studying international relations in a world facing matters of war, the environment, poverty, human rights, and other pressing issues. Welcome to the field of international relations.

Learning Objectives

After reading this chapter, you should be able to:

- ▶ define international relations as a discipline;
- ▶ identify major actors and decision makers in international relations and the main areas in which they interact;
- ▶ recognize major challenges and problems the world is facing today;
- ▶ understand the methodology of international relations and the ways critical thinking might be applied to study and analyze information; and
- ▶ apply the knowledge you gathered in this chapter to a critical analysis of a case related to war and democracy.

What Do We Study, and Why? The Field of International Relations

To study **international relations (IR)** is to examine interactions among states and the international activities of nonstate organizations. These interactions take many forms. They may be negotiations about territorial disputes, migration of people across borders, trade agreements, charitable activities, court decisions about an international criminal gang, or food deliveries to the population of a country suffering from a natural disaster. *International relations* can also refer to the foreign affairs of states and of intergovernmental (IGOs) and nongovernmental (NGOs) organizations.

What Is International Relations?

International relations is both an academic and an applied field because it seeks to understand the realities of today's world as well as to suggest solutions to the world's many problems. Even an abridged list of the issues related to international relations can be overwhelming, but several topics remain prominent year after year. We can group these into three main areas: (1) international politics, (2) international political economy, and (3) international law.

International politics is the analysis of how states pursue and protect their interests. Countries naturally try to secure their borders and to reduce outside threats and aggressions, and one of the most important topics in relations among states is the issue of war and peace. Typically, in today's world, most countries try to avoid the use of military force and act through diplomacy. At the same time, however, military confrontations continue. War has been part of international politics for centuries.

International relations also revolves around economic, financial, and trade issues. Countries buy and sell their resources and products, offer and accept financial assistance, and support or block certain economic transactions with other countries. The study of complex interactions of international economic and political factors is called **international political economy**. Economic and security issues are interconnected and affect all areas of international relations. For example, oil and gas as energy sources have become significant factors in world's politics.

International law, the third main area of study, is about mutually agreed formal rules and regulations concerning interactions among states, institutions, organizations, and individuals involved in international relations. As we will see later in this book, international law is effective only as long as countries recognize and follow it; there is no a supreme power above states to enforce it.

The field of international relations differs from comparative politics, which focuses more on comparing political systems rather than on how they interact. Yet the interests of both disciplines frequently overlap. Moreover, the study of international relations has become increasingly multidisciplinary. A specialist in international relations nowadays should know the basics of fields such as government, economics, history, sociology, cultural studies, and military studies, to name a few. For instance, if you study the relations between Saudi Arabia and Iran, you have to know the history of the Arab Caliphates and of the Persian and Ottoman Empires. You have to understand the basic traditions of Islam, the official religion of these two countries. And you have to be familiar with oil politics, issues related to regional security, the changes happening in Muslim countries, and the directions of U.S. foreign policy. If we want to explain *why* certain events take place in today's world and *how* they affect our lives, we have to be ready to gather data from many fields. (See Figure 1.1.)

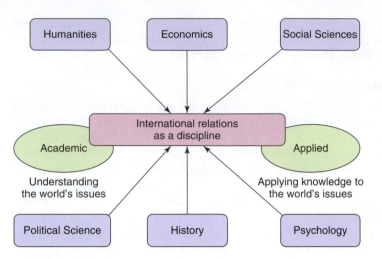

FIGURE 1-1 The field of international relations.

Let's now turn to a few simple questions. These only hint at the potential depth and scope of international relations as a discipline, but they may highlight a few educational or professional pursuits that interest you.

WHAT DOES THE UNITED NATIONS SECURITY COUNCIL DO? In 1945, the United States, the Soviet Union, and the United Kingdom, the victors of World War II, created a global international organization called the United Nations. Together with their war allies, China and France, they proposed a governing body of the United Nations—the Security Council. These five states became permanent members of this council, with the right to veto any decision voted by all other members of the United Nations. Ten temporary members also join the Security Council on a rotating basis, yet they have no veto power. Is the Security Council a democratic institution? There are almost 200 countries in the world today. Do you believe that the "big five" should lose their permanent status and veto power? Would it be a good idea to give other countries permanent membership on the Security Council? Which countries would you recommend?

When studying international relations, you will learn how the contemporary international system was built and that some countries have gained more power than others in various international organizations. You will also learn that it is desirable but often very difficult to conduct international affairs in a democratic way.

WHO DRAFTED THE CURRENT JAPANESE CONSTITUTION? In 1946, after defeat in World War II and occupation by American forces, Japan adopted a new constitution based on the principles of liberal democracy. The constitution, which survived for more than half a century, was drafted by American officers and legal scholars.

International relations provides lessons in how foreign powers make changes in other countries not only in times of war, but also in peace. Involvement into

The Security Council, the upper body of the United Nations, meets at its headquarters in New York in 2012. A permanent member of the Security Council may veto any UN resolution.

other countries' politics can be a success story, like in Japan, but also of tragic mistakes and spectacular blunders. Could you name them? By learning from such mistakes, we can hope to avoid them in the future.

IDENTIFY THE AUTHOR OF THIS REMARK: "WHETHER YOU LIKE IT OR NOT, HISTORY IS ON OUR SIDE. WE WILL BURY YOU."   That was Nikita Khrushchev, leader of the Soviet Union. He was speaking in 1956, and "you" meant Western countries. Russia then was building its own nuclear arsenal and challenging the nuclear supremacy of the United States by launching the first Sputnik, a space capsule. Khrushchev appeared to be threatening Western leaders. In reality, he meant to express a belief that Communism, as an economic and political system, would eventually prevail over American-style capitalism.

Examining the past and present status of international relations we will find examples of how words and their interpretations and misinterpretations affect foreign policies and the actions of world leaders.

HOW MUCH DOES IT COST TO PROTECT THE UNITED STATES FROM FOREIGN THREATS? Exact numbers are difficult to produce, and the reports are always dated. Back in 2012, the U.S. defense budget was close to $1 trillion. Out of this amount, $141 billion went to support veterans, and about $55 billion was spent to support foreign allies. About $56 billion was allocated to the Department of Homeland Security, and over $50 billion was spent on intelligence. The Defense Department received the biggest share. Keep in mind that military operations in Afghanistan and Iraq were funded through separate bills. Does Washington spend too much, too little, or just about right on protecting America? Is it better to be safe than sorry? Or maybe many foreign threats are simply exaggerated?

As you explore international relations, you will be able to form your own opinion about the costs of security and defense policies. You will also critically examine other factors and forces, different from defense and intelligence, that may contribute to peace and security in international relations.

The range of events and developments in international relations may appear too complicated and chaotic to understand. Yet there is logic in all these developments. To understand it, we have to examine some basic definitions.

Key Concepts

State sovereignty is a central concept in the study of international relations. A **state** is commonly defined as a governed entity with a settled population occupying a permanent area with recognized borders. **Sovereignty** refers to the independent authority over a territory. Let's consider these terms in some detail.

SOVEREIGNTY

A sovereign state, in theory, should make its decisions independently. There is no higher authority such as a foreign power or international organization telling a sovereign state what to do within its territory. India and Pakistan, for example, became sovereign states in 1947, after the United Kingdom, their former colonial ruler, had partitioned India and transferred power to local authorities in the two newly formed sovereign states.

Sovereignty refers to a territory and also to the allegiance of the people living on it. Territorial disputes, as history shows, frequently cause military confrontations. European states began to develop and protect sovereignty a few hundred years ago. In 1648, a handful of Christian kingdoms and principalities in Europe agreed that only they (and not the Roman Catholic Church) should determine religious identity of their subjects. After the 1800s, the most important markers of sovereignty became the ethnic identity of the people living on that territory. (At the time spoken language was the prime indicator of ethnic identity.) Disputes over territorial issues have always been common causes of international conflict. (See "Case in Point.")

International treaties and economic and military capacities of states support their sovereignty. Therefore, some states' sovereignty today may be strong, whereas others' remain weak. For instance, in Africa most state boundaries emerged as a result of colonization by Western powers within the last two hundred years. Politicians guided cartographers and ethnographers, mostly from Britain, France, Belgium, Portugal, Germany, and Italy, who drew state lines— often with a simple ruler. Some African governments, such as Central African Republic and Somalia, are unable to control their own territory efficiently, battling numerous warlords and rebel groups that challenge state power. Have you heard of Somaliland and Puntland? They declared independence from Somalia in the 1990s, but most other countries do not consider them independent states.

CASE IN POINT > *The End of a French-German Obsession: Alsace-Lorraine*

Crossing the border between France and Germany today is hardly noticeable. It wasn't in the past. Consider the case of Alsace-Lorraine, a relatively small territory that Germany and France contested for centuries in several bloody wars (see Map 1.1). France consolidated its sovereignty over the territory during the revolution of the end of the 18th century. After the war of 1871, the newly formed German Reich annexed Alsace-Lorraine. In 1919, after Germany lost in World War I, France reclaimed its sovereignty over the territory. Not for long. After Germany attacked France in 1940, the residents of the region became citizens of Hitler's Third Reich. Only in 1944, after the British-American troops defeated the Nazis, did Alsace-Lorraine join France one last time.

It is only appropriate that after many years of disputes and violence, Strasbourg, the principal city in this region, became the official seat of the European Parliament where representatives from France, Germany, and other member-states jointly discuss and resolve common issues of the united continent.

CRITICAL THINKING

Later in this book we will learn about territorial conflicts that are causing international tensions. India and Pakistan, Armenia and Azerbaijan, China and Japan, Argentina and the United Kingdom, and many other countries are dealing with their unresolved territorial disputes. Why is there so much tension over territories? Some might think the answer to this question is obvious: The disputed territories have natural resources, and this is what countries care about above all. Although resources play a big role in territorial conflicts, could you suggest other reasons contributing to such disputes? Consider issues such as a country's concern for its "prestige," the importance of a territory for a people's national identity, pressures of domestic political forces, and the impact of public opinion. Imagine for the sake of the argument that Mexico asked the United States to return— as a sign of a good gesture—some small territories of California and New Mexico that previously belonged to Mexico. How do you think the United States would react to this request?

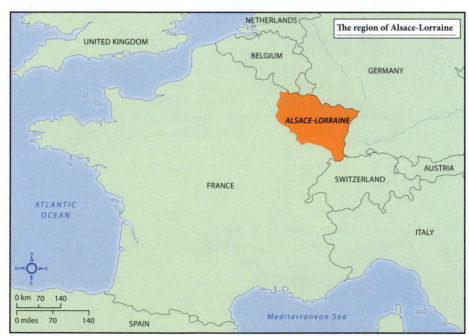

MAP 1-1 Alsace-Lorraine.

Demonstrators wave the flag of the self-declared republic of Somaliland as they hold a pro-independence rally in London in 2012. Most countries do not recognize Somaliland as a sovereign state.

According to the definition, sovereignty allows the state to claim that everything taking place inside its borders belongs to its **internal affairs**, and no outside authority may interfere in this state's activities. For centuries, sovereign states were expected to have armies, print their own money, and issue laws. This expectation is no longer accurate. States themselves can limit their own sovereignty and delegate authority to international organizations (such as the United Nations) or to international treaties. The members of the European Union, for example, voluntarily gave up on their currencies (such as marks, franks, liras, and pesos) to establish one common currency, the Euro. In studying international relations, you will find that sovereignty can be limited by other states or taken away forcefully. The ultimate violation of sovereignty is occupation by foreign powers. This happened in Afghanistan in 2001 and Iraq in 2003. Both states lost their sovereignty as a result of military actions taken by the U.S.-led coalitions against their governments. These states began to restore their sovereignty under foreign occupation.

NATIONS AND STATES

The terms *state*, *country*, and *nation* are often used interchangeably. In most cases, however, we prefer to speak about states, because the term *nation* has several meanings. We may think of a **nation** as a legal term or as a collective identity. In legal terms, about 193 countries in existence today (and the number is changing) consider themselves nations, recognized by other states. The term has the clearest meaning when it applies to a homogeneous country, usually populated by one ethnic group with no large ethnic minorities. For example, it is common to say the "Finnish nation," referring to people who live on the territory of Finland, speak the Finnish language, and have ancestors of the Finnish origin. The meaning of the "French nation" is more complicated. Until the early 1960s, Algerians were considered French nationals; Algeria in Africa was considered not a colony but a French "department" overseas. The war of Algerian independence, however, required French politicians, lawyers, and the general public to narrow the definition. Algeria and the majority of its Islamic population (Arabs, Berbers, etc.) became excluded from the "French nation." In contrast, some Algerian Christians (called *pieds-noirs*) and Jews resettled in France and were accepted as French (Shepard, 2006).

Many believe that nations can be "invented" or constructed even before they acquire a physical space and gain sovereignty over it. Kurdish nationalists in Turkey and Iraq often speak about *the Kurdish nation*, although there is no Kurdistan as a state. **Separatism** is advocacy of or attempts to establish a separate nation within another sovereign state. States almost always reject national separatism, seeing it as a grave threat to state sovereignty. In Turkey, the pursuit of Kurdish national identity is outlawed. China fights against separatism in its predominantly Muslim area Xinjian. The list of examples goes on.

CHECK YOUR KNOWLEDGE

▶ Define and explain state sovereignty.
▶ What is separatism? Is separatism always dangerous for international peace?
▶ Give two interpretations of the term *nation*.

Key Actors

People today cannot act like the citizens of ancient Greek and Roman city-states: they do not gather on a central square to vote on international trade agreements or foreign wars. Instead, they have representatives who possess the authority to deal with international affairs. These officials are either elected or appointed to represent a **state government** (which we may also call a *national government* or simply a *government*)—an institution with the authority to formulate and enforce its decisions within a country's borders.

STATE GOVERNMENT AND FOREIGN POLICY

State governments conduct **foreign policy**—actions involving official decisions and communications, public and secret—with other state governments, nongovernmental organizations, corporations, and international institutions. A country's foreign policy is usually directed by Ministries of Foreign Affairs through embassies or other official offices in foreign countries. **Diplomacy** is the practice of managing international relations by means of negotiations. In cases when formal diplomatic relations do not exist between two states, there may be informal channels of communication involving third parties, special emissaries, and even personal contacts.

For example, for many years Iran and the United States did not have official diplomatic relations. The embassy of Pakistan to the United States served as a mediator through a specially established "interests section." The content of foreign policy ranges from peace treaties to threats of force; from trade agreements to trade sanctions; from scientific, technical, and cultural exchange programs to visa and immigration policies. State governments usually prefer diplomatic means of interaction, but violence or a threat of it frequently backs diplomatic moves.

In today's developed democracies, all three branches of state government commonly participate in foreign policy, although their roles differ. Within the *executive branch*, government structures dealing with international relations include a ministry or department of foreign affairs. (In the United States, this is called the State Department; in India it is the Ministry of External Affairs; in the United Kingdom, it is the Foreign Office.) The *legislative branch* passes laws about the direction and handling of foreign policy. In many countries, parliaments ratify (or approve) international agreements signed by state executive leaders. In the United States, Congress allocates money to conduct foreign policy according to the Federal budget. Congress may also instantly finance specific policies or actions related to foreign policy.

The *judicial branch* is involved in foreign policy in several ways. For example, courts can make assessments of and about the applicability of certain international laws or agreements on the territory of the state. The courts also decide on claims submitted by foreign countries including businesses and private individuals. (In Chapter 5, we will discuss international law in more detail.) In some countries—in the United States and Russia, for example—their presidents have significantly more influence on foreign policy of their countries compared to the executive in the United Kingdom or the Netherlands. Differences between democratic and nondemocratic governments are also important, as we will see in every chapter. (See Figure 1.2.)

INTERGOVERNMENTAL ORGANIZATIONS

Besides sovereign states, another major player on the field of international relations is **intergovernmental organizations (IGOs)**. These are associations of several states such as the United Nations, formed in 1945 to increase the collective responsibility of its member states, keep peace through a voluntary collective effort, and serve as an authoritative mediator in international conflicts.

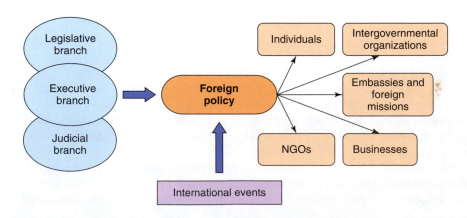

FIGURE 1-2 Foreign policy of a democratic state.

(We will learn about its role in Chapters 2 and 5.) Other IGOs are created for a combination of strategic and political purposes. We will see later how the North Atlantic Treaty Organization (NATO) led a military action against the Libyan government in 2011. Still other IGOs pursue primarily economic goals, like the Organization of Petroleum Exporting Countries (OPEC), which sets standards for how much oil member states should produce and sell on the global market. Of course, economic and political goals of IGOs are often interconnected.

International institutions are created to promote mutual security, create a climate of trust, monitor international treaties, and encourage financial stability and economic development. IGOs increase global accountability of individual states and, to some degree, limit their sovereignty. States receiving loans from international financial institutions, like International Monetary Fund (IMF), must modify their financial and economic policies according to some standards.

IGOs may suffer from corruption, incompetence, bureaucratic delays, political and ideological biases, and internal political disagreements, as we will discuss in Chapter 2. Yet their model of voluntary cooperation among states is playing an increasingly important role in international relations today.

NONGOVERNMENTAL ORGANIZATIONS

For centuries, only specially designated government officials and their staff were entrusted with steering foreign policy of their states. However, over several decades now, a growing set of nongovernmental actors plays an increasingly important role in foreign policy of many countries. **Nongovernmental organizations (NGOs)** are public or private interest groups attempting to influence

Laboratory workers sort tuberculosis test samples at a clinic for transmittable diseases funded by Médecins Sans Frontières (Doctors Without Borders) on the outskirts of Yangon, Myanmar, in 2012. Myanmar ranks among the lowest countries in nearly every category of health care funding.

foreign policy, raise international concerns about a domestic problem or domestic concerns about a global issue, and offer help in the solution of these problems. The NGOs we will study deal mostly with international issues. (There are also NGOs dealing with domestic problems.) NGOs today support environmental protection; relief programs in poor regions; and the distribution of medication, educational services, and other forms of humanitarian help. NGOs are usually the product of individual volunteer efforts or civic movements.

What explains the increased role of NGOs in today's world? In many democracies, government bureaucracies and political appointees are held more accountable to the public and their actions become more transparent with the help of the media. NGOs also grow stronger because democracies improve access to information related to foreign policy. For instance, the U.S. Freedom of Information Act (FOIA), strengthened in the 1970s by the U.S. Congress, led to the establishment of the National Security Archive by a group of investigative journalists, a public group that urges the U.S. government to declassify and release foreign policy-related information. This information, for example, became crucial in the public investigation of the so-called Iran-Contra scandal that broke out in 1986 and involved illegal foreign policy operations by some members of the Reagan administration.

A second reason for the new prominence of NGOs is globalization and the growing complexity of international problems. Even the most powerful government organizations cannot pay equal attention to every world's problem. After the end of the Cold War, for example, many Western powers were paying only limited attention to Africa. Hundreds of NGOs then responded by raising funds to address the spread of AIDS, small arms, and violence, along with the collapse of infrastructure and health services.

Finally, NGOs have benefitted from new communication and information technology. Because of the spread of technology, most governments, government-controlled media, and business elites cannot keep their long-established monopoly on printed information. Compared to corporate news organizations, NGOs are becoming increasingly attractive as reliable sources and analysts. The Internet enables NGOs to raise funds, solicit volunteers, and organize complex projects without relying on governmental bureaucracies.

CHECK YOUR KNOWLEDGE

▶ What is diplomacy?
▶ In democracies, which three branches of government commonly participate in foreign policy?
▶ What is the difference between NGOs and IGOs as international organizations?

Global Issues

Understanding international relations will provide you with analytical tools and confidence for explaining and addressing the significant problems of today and tomorrow. You will be better prepared to influence discussions about your

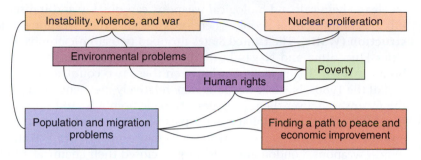

Why do we study international relations
and international politics?
To address the key challenges:

Instability, violence, and war

Nuclear proliferation

Environmental problems

Poverty

Human rights

Population and migration
problems

Finding a path to peace and
economic improvement

FIGURE 1-3 Why we study international relations.

country's foreign policy and build a more prosperous and stable world. What are the most significant challenges and issues that the world is facing today? What can be done to address these challenges? What role would you choose for yourself? Here we will mention just a few issues to get going. (See Figure 1.3.) We will revisit these issues in the following chapters.

INSTABILITY, VIOLENCE, AND WAR

Conflict and violence—internal as well as international—are major sources of instability. Violent conflicts disrupt international trade, damage the environment, and require substantial human and material resources. Instability, in turn, serves as a source of new conflicts and wars. Each war has its own origin, history, and consequences. Nevertheless, several important trends have emerged. Military dictatorships conducting brutal policies against their own population are likely to act violently against their neighboring states. Unstable or failing governments unable to exercise their basic functions are often prone to use radical and violent measures to defend themselves. Unsettled ethnic conflicts frequently result in violence and threaten international peace. Small radical groups, not affiliated with any state, can also cause international instability. They try to achieve their political goals by violence or threats of hostility against authorities or the civilian population. International terrorism has emerged as a threat to stability and a serious international problem as well, as we will see in Chapter 7.

There is no single or simple policy to prevent violent conflicts or to end them quickly. Would you agree that powerful countries have no other viable options except preserving stability by force? Stronger, more powerful states, in this view, can best maintain regional and global stability themselves. A range of preventive policies, including military action, should reduce the threats of instability and violence, including international terrorism. Or would you rather support the view that force cannot address the political and social causes of most conflicts? From this position, the international community should act to reduce poverty and injustice, and eliminate other causes of instability and violence. What specific measures would you propose to reduce violence in international relations? We look in depth at security in a global world in Chapter 4, and we address violence and injustice throughout.

WEAPONS OF MASS DESTRUCTION AND THEIR PROLIFERATION

Nuclear, chemical, and biological weapons can quickly and indiscriminately kill tens of millions of people. Therefore they are called **weapons of mass destruction (WMD).** The United States dropped two atomic bombs on Japanese cities Hiroshima and Nagasaki in 1945. The Soviet Union tested its atomic bomb in 1949. The nuclear race between these two countries lasted until the end of the 1980s. Nuclear weapons were relatively inexpensive to produce, but the means to deliver them (missiles, strategic bombers, and submarines) cost hundreds of billions of dollars. In the past, the Soviet Union, the United States, and the United Kingdom have worked on new types of chemical and bacteriological weapons. London and Washington closed their chemical and bacteriological labs in the 1960s. The Soviet Union, however, continued its secret chemical and bacteriological program out of bureaucratic inertia. The Soviets also mistrusted the West. Soviet scientists produced dangerous chemical weapons and stored viruses of plague and anthrax capable of killing the entire population of Western Europe and North America (Hoffman, 2010).

Today, chemical and bacteriological weapons are banned and their supplies destroyed. Only a few countries today openly possess nuclear weapons, including the United States, Russia, China, France, United Kingdom, India, and Pakistan. North Korea and Israel, as many experts believe, have nuclear weapons without declaring it, and South Africa had them but later destroyed them. Overall, the nuclear states have proved capable of restraining themselves and even agreeing in some cases to limit their nuclear arsenals.

However, one of the biggest concerns today remains **nuclear proliferation**— the spread of nuclear weapons, materials, information, and technologies. Why does it remain a serious challenge? For one thing, an unstable government could make frantic decisions costing millions of lives, or it could be too weak to protect its nuclear arsenals or prevent its scientists, in possession of secrets of WMD, from selling their knowledge to terrorist groups. The danger of such proliferation was strong after the sudden collapse of the Soviet Union. Some international terrorist groups believe today that their ultimate prize will be the possession of nuclear weapons.

How can the world address the danger of WMD and the nuclear danger in particular? Do you support global nuclear disarmament, which would mean that every state gives up its nuclear weapons? How can this be achieved? How can further proliferation of WMD be stopped? We will consider these questions and related arguments in Chapter 4.

ENVIRONMENTAL PROBLEMS

Environmental problems caused by human activities threaten human health and well-being. Industrial development, the rapid growth of urban areas, and increased consumption all play a role. We can think of two broad categories of environmental problems: *contamination* and *depletion*. The first includes pollution of the air, water, and soil. The second includes threats to forests, sources of fresh water, and many plants and animals. As a result, many governments have implemented programs to reduce pollution and conserve resources. They have opened national parks and restricted the use of land and water in their countries. Where governments are slow to act, NGOs frequently take the initiative.

Public opinion, NGOs, and international institutions are all important in persuading governments. However, there is no universal agreement on how to address such international environmental problems as global climate change. How do we keep our environment safe and at the same time guarantee economic development? There are no easy answers. International relations teaches us that every decision about the environment is a trade-off, and we discuss how to evaluate the gains and losses in Chapter 8.

POVERTY

Over two centuries ago, British scholar Thomas Robert Malthus pointed to a disequilibrium that threatened world stability. Food supplies, he wrote, cannot keep up with a growing population. This, he warned, would result in wars and violence. Today our planet has enough resources to supply every human being with food, water, and basic medical care. In the 1950s and 1960s, spectacular progress in agriculture, often called the *green revolution*, seemed to remove the danger of mass famine. Why then does poverty and famine persist in some parts of the world? According to the United Nations, today more than one billion people live on less than $1 per day. More than a quarter of the world's population does not have access to running water. Preventable infectious diseases continue to kill hundreds of thousands of children every year. In 2010 alone, malaria, a deadly infectious disease, killed approximately 900,000 children, mostly in Africa (WHO, 2012).

Can we significantly reduce poverty? Many argue for the benefits of free-market economies, like those in the United States and most Western countries. Here companies can form, people can purchase the goods they need, and prices rise or fall with relatively little government planning or regulation. Almost every prosperous country in today's world is a market democracy. But is that the whole story, and can it really address poverty and inequality? Critics argue that free-market principles work in some but countries but not others and that global poverty needs different approaches. What other solutions can you see as effective in solving world poverty? Would you, for example, support a global tax on wealthy countries to help the world's poor? If not, why? If yes, how high should this tax be? We will discuss the global economy and development in Chapters 3 and 6 and poverty in Chapter 9.

HUMAN RIGHTS

It has become increasingly accepted that human beings regardless of their origin or status have certain basic rights. International pressure grows on governments to protect their citizens threatened by the brutality of injustice, systematic violence, unlawful seizure of property, and physical abuse. However, for billions of people, access to justice, fair hearing of grievances, licensed lawyers, or binding contracts enforced by transparent courts are beyond their reach.

The Amazonian town of Acailandia, Brazil, produces pig iron. Brazil is fueled with charcoal from illegal felling of rainforests. The Brazilian Amazon, home to 60 percent of the world's forest and 20 percent of the Earth's oxygen, is threatened by rapid development.

In many parts of the world, property rights and civil rights are guaranteed only to small groups of people—commonly political, business, and government elites. The real power belongs to a few influential individuals whose power is likely to run through generations or has been obtained through force or dishonesty. Corruption, not the law, sets the criteria for right and wrong in many parts of the world.

Persecution continues today in many countries based on race, gender, ethnicity, religious beliefs, party affiliation, or sexual orientation. In the past, a totalitarian ideology was a major source of these violations. Ideologies such as Nazism, Fascism, and Communism have emerged as official policies in Germany, Italy, Soviet Union, the People's Republic of China, and Cuba. Racism was a governing ideology of South Africa and other countries. For the past few decades, these ideologies have been in decline, and yet violations of human rights continue. Although allowing some elements of freedom, the Chinese and Iranian governments do not think twice before jailing and executing people for political dissent. Many governments conceal violations of human rights behind the arguments of "cultural specificity," "traditions," and "values." In some African and Asian countries, women but not men can be brutally punished for adultery. The physical and sexual exploitation of children remains widespread. However, the world is far from agreeing on what rights should be considered universal and which are subject to cultural traditions.

Do you think the world should have a universal constitution that would clearly spell out the basic rights of people regardless of their nationality? If you disagree, explain why. If you agree, which rights do you want to see as universal and which international agency should enforce them? Chapters 5 and 9 explore the debates about international law and human rights.

POPULATION AND MIGRATION PROBLEMS

Population growth presents significant challenges. The world's population is about 7 billion now and is projected to grow to 8 billion by 2025. Overpopulation threatens the minimum conditions to sustain a reasonable quality of life. It can lead to serious health, environmental, and social problems. At the same time, many affluent countries are actually experiencing a decline in population, including Western Europe and Japan, and the results here, too, will be felt in the years ahead. Birth rates are declining in many Latin American and Asian countries.

A related topic is the movement of populations. Violence, hardship, or the threat of either can force people to move across state borders in search of better living conditions and jobs. Millions of people continue to be victims of involuntary migration: they are forced to move from their homes and often cross international borders for fear of their lives.

Do you believe that wealthy countries must assist other countries in solving their population problems? If yes, how? Do you think that to fight overpopulation, some countries should establish an official limit on the number of children a family could have? Do you believe that states should allow people to move across borders without restrictions? We will discuss the full range of these problems in Chapter 9.

FINDING A PATH TO PEACE AND ECONOMIC IMPROVEMENT

International relations as a discipline does not focus solely on threats and problems. One of the most important reasons we study international relations is to create a stable, healthy, and prosperous world. Informed opinion can be learned from success stories, and there are many examples of conflict resolution and sound political management. Here we mention just two.

In 1992, the Czech and Slovak leaders of Czechoslovakia discussed and reached an agreement to split the country and establish two independent states. Most partitions in the past resulted in mass casualties and destruction. But this case was a dramatic example of a peaceful separation. After the partition, both countries joined the European Union, and they remain close economic and political partners. Could other countries deal with separatist movements in a peaceful and civilized way, without resorting to violence? If these two ethnic groups achieved a peaceful separation, could others as well? We explore these questions in Chapters 3 and 7.

A second example is China. During the lifetime of one generation China evolved from an isolated and poor country into a second largest world economy. The government abandoned revolutionary slogans and encouraged entrepreneurship. Hundreds of millions of people have formed the middle class. China became an assertive player in international affairs. Can this country's economic model become a standard for the rest of the world to follow? In Chapter 6 and other places in the book we will explore this question in more detail.

Which other countries' positive experiences and policies do you think should become models for the world to follow? Which cases would you like to examine in detail in class?

Important political decisions lie ahead, with our future at stake. We will be returning to these and many other problems in every chapter. In the concluding section of the book, we will revisit them once more, as we ask you to consider what solutions your generation may find.

CHECK YOUR KNOWLEDGE

▶ What is nuclear proliferation?
▶ What are the main sources of regional and global instability?
▶ What proportion of the world's population does not have access to running water?
▶ What does the term "human rights" mean?

How Do We Study It?

The study of international relations includes three basic kinds of investigation. The first activity is informational: We gather facts to describe events and developments. The second is interpretive: We analyze the facts to explain why events take place. In this stage, we rely on concepts or schemes to organize and interpret what we know, and Chapters 2–3 take up some of the most important approaches, theories, and tools for studying international relations. The third activity is critical thinking: We look critically at the facts and their interpretations.

Gathering Information

Policy makers, their advisers, and researchers must all rely on information about countries, their actions, and their intentions. How do we gather unbiased information?

GOVERNMENTAL AND NONGOVERNMENTAL REPORTS

The Federal Reserve—the central banking system of the United States—submits a semiannual report to the Congress about the country's economic growth, inflation, and international trade. Foreign governments, international financial organizations, and individual investors from all countries eagerly await such reports to formulate and correct economic, trade, and investment policies.

Other statistical reports, too, contain facts related to foreign policies, economic production, finances, accomplishments, conflicts, and other relevant issues. Governments and nongovernmental organizations release periodic publications about the economy, defense, commerce, tourism, employment, education, and other developments. For example, The Center for Global Development, a nonprofit organization in Washington, DC, conducts research and publishes informational analyses about how rich countries' policies and their foreign aid impact people in the developing world.

How reliable are these reports? To judge their accuracy, we have to consider three factors. The first is the *self-interest* of the organization publishing a report. Even statistical publications can be distorted for political or other purposes. A second factor is the *professional prestige* of the institution providing a report. A high reputation is earned by accurate past publications. The third factor is *competition* from other sources of information: A competitive climate leads to

@ Go online to read the most recent reports and review the initiatives of The Center for Global Development related to foreign aid, migration, education, and global environmental issues.

Former World Bank President Robert Zoellick at a news conference in Beijing in 2012. He said that China would have difficulty sustaining its growth over the next two decades without substantial structural changes to its economy, financial system, and society. The Chinese government disagreed with his predictions.

higher-quality reports. Because of the complexity of today's world, statistical reports should be obtained from several sources.

In developing democracies or nondemocratic countries, the quality of reports may be in doubt because it is difficult to confirm their accuracy. For instance, before its collapse in 1991, the Soviet Union often released annual reports suggesting that it had been reducing its defense budget. In fact, defense spending grew significantly. Some nondemocratic governments deliberately distort statistics on the spread of HIV and violence against women. In democratic countries, in contrast, international sources and NGOs can more easily challenge official reports—and often do.

EYEWITNESS SOURCES

Professionals frequently use their own observations, or **eyewitness accounts**. Personal testimonies can offer success stories, reveal problems, disclose violations of international law, and describe political events. In some cases, they may be the only available source of information.

Investigative journalism has brought a new dimension to eyewitness reports. A journalist accredited by a news organization or working independently enters a foreign country or a zone of conflict (often without obtaining permission from local officials), conducts interviews, takes pictures, uploads them, and makes the information available to the world. Representatives of NGOs visit places where formally accredited journalists or diplomats are prohibited. Thanks to such reports, the world learned about violence in Chile in the 1970s; ethnic cleansing in Bosnia in the 1990s; human trafficking in contemporary Southeast Asia; and serious violations of human rights in Sudan, Somalia, and many other countries. Providing eyewitness accounts, however, can be risky. Reporters Without Borders, an international NGO, regularly posts reports about journalists imprisoned, persecuted, or killed for doing their job.

Government officials, especially when they retire, may provide information about their foreign-policy decisions, the reasoning behind their actions, and their interactions with foreign leaders. Political memoirs often include details previously unavailable even to experts. Beware though: People do not write memoirs to emphasize their mistakes. They want to show off their achievements. Even when witnesses try to describe facts truthfully, they almost inevitably put their spin on them.

COMMUNICATIONS

Official documents are often the best available sources on how states interact with each other. A *communiqué*, which is an official report about an international meeting, often provides clear and unambiguous information about the intentions, expectations, and actions of two or more states. Correspondence between state leaders is often helpful in understanding policy strategies. Letters exchanged between President Roosevelt and the Soviet leader Joseph Stalin during World War II reveal that these leaders carefully masked serious ideological disagreements to defeat Germany and to establish a postwar peace.

One tool for examining texts like these is **content analysis**—a research method that systematically organizes and summarizes both the *manifest* content (what was actually said or written) and the *latent* content (the hidden meaning) in speeches, interviews, television or radio programs, letters, newspaper articles, blogs, and other reports. For example, specialists have found that the more ideologically driven a U.S. president's speech is, the less sophisticated are the explanations of foreign policy (Tetlock, 2011).

Speeches and press conferences are also valuable sources of information because they articulate domestic political goals, such as public mobilization. British Prime Minister Winston Churchill, for example, delivered one of his most famous speeches in Fulton, Missouri, on March 9, 1946. He criticized the Soviet Union and hoped that his words would convince the American public and others of the dangers posed by international Communism.

Most government documents remain classified for years: usually states are interested in keeping their secrets away from the public as long as possible. In the United States, however, the FOIA allows any person, even a noncitizen, to submit a claim for declassification of state secrets, making them available to the public. NGOs use the FOIA to promote public knowledge and awareness about foreign policy as well as the government's sense of responsibility and accountability before the public. The *WikiLeaks* scandal of 2010—when tens of thousands of classified documents related to international communications among governments were stolen and posted on the Web—gave everyone access to valuable information related to global diplomacy. The scandal also posed an important question: May journalists and policy experts obtain information by illegal means? May they use this information in their professional activities? Declassified documents often reveal facts that governments want to conceal.

Of course, *some* secrecy is essential in diplomatic communications. But in a democratic state, the public still has the right to know if the government

Founder of the WikiLeaks website, Australian Julian Assange, at a press conference in London in 2010. The website posted tens of thousands of stolen classified documents from the correspondence between U.S. embassies and the U.S. government. This incident along with the 2013 case involving Edward Snowden were the biggest leaks of secret information in U.S. history.

made the best possible decision and did not misuse its power in the past. Further, the more information available for the public, the less room exists for rumors and conspiracy theories. When Lee Harvey Oswald assassinated President John Kennedy in November 1963, it turned out that the suspect had lived in the Soviet Union for a year and spent time in custody of the Soviet government. This could have led to rumors that the Soviets had a hand in the assassination—a politically dangerous proposition. Realizing the danger, the Soviet government quickly released a dossier on Oswald that suggested that he was a psychologically unstable loner and not a Soviet agent.

INTELLIGENCE

Leaders and diplomats rely on open sources, like newspapers and blogs, but also on intelligence sources. **Intelligence** is any information about the interests, intentions, capabilities, and actions of foreign countries, including government officials, political parties, the functioning of their economies, activities of NGOs, or the behavior of private individuals. Intelligence can be open and covert, electronic or human (in professional lingo, "elint" and "humint"). Today, approximately 80 percent of intelligence information comes from published and open sources such as blogs, press briefings, or newspaper articles. The 2013 scandal involving former US intelligence employee Edward Snowden not only revealed that governments had access to private communications of hundreds of millions of people but also raised important legal questions related to intelligence gathering in today's global world.

Not all this information or intelligence influences decision-making by state governments. First, to do so, the materials should have particular relevance for security and foreign policy. Information about a new plant being built in Iran might be irrelevant to foreign governments unless it is a nuclear plant. Second, the information needs to come from a reliable source or checked against other

CASE IN POINT > *Facts and Lies*

Sometimes governments or individuals spread deliberate lies and fabricate documents. By creating "fake" facts and news, political forces hope to manipulate public opinion, gather sympathy and support, justify their actions, or receive political and material gains. Consider the Katyn massacre.

In April 1940, Soviet authorities ordered the execution of more than 22,000 Polish officers after the Soviet Army had occupied a portion of Polish territory. The Nazis discovered the mass graves in 1943 and began to use them as a propaganda tool in hopes of splitting the anti-Nazi coalition of the Soviet Union, Great Britain, and the United States. Stalin's government resorted to denial, accusing the Nazis of committing the murders. The Western allies of the Soviet Union, willing to keep strategic relations with Moscow, accepted the Soviet government's version and downplayed reports of an international medical commission suggesting that the murders were committed by the Soviet secret police (Zaslavsky, 2004). During the Nuremberg trials in 1945 and 1946, the Katyn massacre was, with connivance of Western powers, ascribed to the Nazi regime. Only in 2010 did the Russian government openly acknowledge the murders, calling the tragedy a "military crime."

CRITICAL THINKING

We learn from history that politicians have often lied to their people about significant international developments. Have the incentives and opportunities to lie changed in today's world? Can you think of important factors that may reduce a leader's incentive to mislead the domestic and international community? Consider, among other things, the technological changes of the past ten years as well as the growing influence of NGOs.

---

sources. There are professional intelligence organizations gathering, verifying, and interpreting intelligence. Third, to become intelligence, the information needs to be trusted and accepted by political leaders, who often believe they are better judges of international relations than intelligence officials. For instance, Joseph Stalin ignored numerous signals from Soviet intelligence about Nazi Germany's surprise attack on the Soviet Union on June 22, 1941.

Another big problem is the multiplicity of intelligence signals, none of which are conclusive enough alone. In the United States, United Kingdom, Russia, and China, several intelligence services report to different government agencies. They may be in competition and not well coordinated. In retrospect, many intelligence failures are, in reality, the failures of the leadership to recognize foreign threats (Goodman, 2008). For instance, the U.S. government overlooked the impending attacks on the World Trade Center and the Pentagon in 2001 despite intelligence signals that indicated a possible criminal use of civilian aircrafts by foreign nationals.

SURVEYS

In **surveys**, groups of people answer questions on topics such as foreign policy. In the United States, presidential approval ratings are important indicators of popular support for U.S. foreign policy. Although public opinion does not set foreign policy directly, it does constrain it. Presidents and other decision makers are unlikely to go against overwhelming public opinion. To avoid an electoral defeat, a democratic government has to generate public support for its foreign actions and international programs (Shiraev and Sobel, 2006).

Two types of surveys are most valuable for the study of international relations: *opinion polls* and *expert surveys*. Opinion polls gather information, usually on a national sample, about attitudes related to other countries, international events, or their own country's foreign policy. Expert surveys reflect professional opinions about a country, a country's foreign policy, or an international problem. For example, NGO Freedom House in Washington, DC, publishes annual reports on the degree of democratic freedoms in most countries. Based on experts' evaluations, *The Freedom in the World* survey provides an annual evaluation of the state of global freedom. These ratings determine whether a country is later classified as *Free*, *Partly Free*, or *Not Free*. Transparency International (TI) is another NGO that uses surveys. To create its Corruption Perceptions Index, TI compiles surveys that ask international entrepreneurs and business analysts to express their perceptions of how corrupt a country is (see Table 1-1).

Focus groups are another survey method used intensively in foreign-policy planning, conflict resolution, or academic research. A typical **focus group** contains from seven to ten experts who discuss a particular situation and express their opinion about issues raised by the group's moderators. They are given the opportunity to analyze issues in an informal atmosphere, relatively unconstrained by their government, military rank, or academic position.

EXPERIMENTAL METHODS

The study of international relations can also rely—surprising as it may sound—on experiments. In **experiments** (often called *laboratory experiments* or *simulations*), scholars put participants in controlled conditions as in a game. By varying these conditions, the researchers can examine behavior and learn about stereotypes, perceptions, and habits (Kydd, 2005). Certainly nobody stages a small war to find out how countries would behave under extreme circumstances. Yet scholars have reconstructed "real-life" situations for decades.

One early contribution of experimental methods related to group decision-making, such as within a government team or the president's cabinet. It was shown, for instance, that when people make decisions in groups, they

TABLE 1-1 Corruption Perceptions Index, 2012 (Updated January 21, 2013) Selected Ranks and Countries

Rank	Country
Top 5 (least corrupt)	Denmark, Finland, New Zealand, Sweden, Singapore
20–25	Chile, Uruguay, Bahamas, France, St. Lucia
50–55	Rwanda, Georgia, Seychelles, Bahrain, Czech Republic
Bottom 5 (most corrupt)	Myanmar, Sudan, Afghanistan, North Korea, Somalia

The lower the rank of a country, the less corrupt the country is perceived to be. The United States is ranked 19 on the list.

DEBATE > THE CORRUPTION PERCEPTIONS INDEX

This index has become valuable in international business and political decisions. Private companies and governments often consider it in their decisions about international investments, loans, and agreements. We shouldn't forget, however, that this index has its biases. It is based mainly on experts' perceptions, which can be influenced by a score of factors possibly unrelated to corruption. A traveling diplomat may give a country a low score partly because luggage was mishandled at a local airport, for example, or a businessperson making a substantial profit in another country may overlook serious corruption.

WHAT'S YOUR VIEW?

What other subjective factors might influence perceptions of other countries?

 Go online to see the most recent Corruption Perceptions Index.

often become less critical to proposals initiated by the leader. This phenomenon is *groupthink*—the tendency of groups to make rushed or illogical decisions because of a false sense of unity and support for the leader (Janis and Mann, 1977).

Most experiments study conflict analysis and resolution. Participants play different roles and represent conflicting sides, such as Israeli and Palestinian authorities or the leaders of Iran, Syria, and the United States.

Analyzing Information

Facts, even the most comprehensive and accurate ones, have to be summarized and explained. Theory is a powerful tool in the studies of international relations. Theory allows analysts and decision makers to transform a formless heap of numbers and files into a logical construction. Theories can then be applied to evaluate specific situations and decision-making.

THE IMPORTANCE OF THEORY AND ITS APPLICATIONS

Knowledge of international affairs takes more than observation. *Analysis* is the breaking of something complex into smaller parts to understand their essential features and relations. This is difficult enough, but even more is needed. If politicians and diplomats did only analysis, they would remain hopelessly confused by the multitude of facts and events. Which are more important than others? Which deserve immediate action—and what kind? To answer these and other questions, decision makers have to look at the facts in light of broader ideas about how international relations works. The ancient Greeks called this knowledge "from above" **theory** (θεωρία). Theorizing about international relations requires both strong empirical knowledge and a measure of imagination.

Many foreign-policy debates ultimately rest on competing theoretical visions. The dominant theories in the last half a century were realism and liberalism. Most recently, a theory of constructivism began to win support among those who study international relations. There are other alternative theoretical approaches, including Marxism, postcolonial studies, and feminism (Walt, 2005a). Different theories present different rules for the analysis of international relations. It is becoming increasingly common these days to take into consideration several theoretical perspectives. In Chapters 2 and 3 we consider main theories describing international relations, their commonalities, and their differences.

Critical Thinking in International Relations

Critical thinking is an active and systematic strategy for understanding international relations on the basis of sound reasoning and evidence (Levy, 2009). It is not simply criticizing, disapproving, and passing skeptical judgments on your government or international developments. It is a set of skills that you can master. It is a process of inquiry, based on the important virtues of *curiosity*, *doubt*, and *intellectual honesty*. Curiosity helps you "dig below the surface," to distinguish facts from opinions. Doubt keeps us from being satisfied with overly simple explanations. And intellectual honesty helps in recognizing and addressing bias in our own opinions.

DISTINGUISHING FACTS FROM OPINIONS

Scientific knowledge is the systematic observation, measurement, and evaluation of facts. This knowledge is rooted in procedures designed to provide reliable and verifiable evidence. The study of international relations is not a "hard science." The behavior of states, NGOs, and international organizations is difficult to describe in terms of mathematical formulas and controlled experiments. We still, however, can learn to separate facts from opinions. Facts are verifiable events and developments. Opinions are speculations or intuitions about how and why such developments may have taken place.

One of the most dramatic episodes in international relations was the Cuban Missile Crisis in 1962. The U.S. representative to the United Nations, Adlai Stevenson, presented photographs of Soviet nuclear missiles in Cuba taken by an American spy plane. Stevenson presented facts: The Soviet missiles had been placed on the island a few weeks earlier. Years later, in 2003, U.S. Secretary of State Colin Powell similarly sought to persuade a skeptical United Nations to authorize the American invasion of Iraq. He presented pictures of Iraqi facilities that allegedly produced WMD. However, these facilities have not been found, and most experts today are certain that the U.S. administration did not have evidence of factories producing nuclear weapons in Iraq. At best, it acted on convictions and lacked the facts.

Distinguishing facts and opinions is complicated. Some facts are deliberately hidden or distorted by state authorities or interest groups. Other facts are in dispute. For example, Armenia and Turkey for many years now remain in disagreement on the nature and scale of the mass death of Armenians at the hands of Turks in 1915. The Armenian position is that the Turkish state orchestrated the killings and that 1.5 million died. Turkey insists that the deaths were war casualties and the numbers were much smaller. The disagreements about the facts caused many years of tensions between Armenia and Turkey (Akçam, 2007).

Anyone seeking information on the Internet must be especially cautious: Many seemingly reliable sites are full of speculations and statements presented

One of the slides that U.S. Secretary of State Colin Powell displayed during his presentation to the UN Security Council in New York in 2003. U.S. authorities mistakenly believed these Iraqi facilities were associated with biological or chemical weapons.

as "facts." In reality, they are just unverified opinions. Even more often, facts are presented in a selective, one-sided way. People tend to embrace the facts that they like and events they approve of but ignore information that appears to challenge their views. A passionate supporter of democracy may argue in a blog that democracy always brings stability and peace. However, this person could easily overlook facts showing that a transition to democracy, especially in the countries with a history of ethnic and religious hostility, could contribute to even greater violence. Several powerful cases in point are Iraq, Afghanistan, Libya, and Egypt, and we will look at each of them in the course of this book.

Our desire to be objective is often constrained by the limits of language. Because people use language to communicate, they frequently "frame" facts, or put them into a convenient scheme. Most articles we read are framed so that contradictory and confusing information becomes simple. Often facts that challenge the article's view are omitted. Framing in the mass media works with remarkable effectiveness despite an often partial and imbalanced selection of facts (Graber, 2005; Ward, 1999).

We also attach convenient verbal labels to the subjects we discuss. Labels such as *hawks, warmongers, aggressors, victims, doves, defeatists, hardliners,* and *softies,* to name just a few, frequently appear in the media. How accurately do these describe specific behaviors and particular events? International relations provides many examples showing that decision makers, like most people, often assume things when it is convenient to do so.

Separating facts from opinions should help you navigate the sea of information related to world events. It can start with looking for new and more reliable sources of facts. Whenever possible, try to establish as many facts as possible related to the issue you are studying. Check your sources for their reliability. Some supposed facts may also be more plausible on the surface than others. If there is a disagreement about the facts, try to find out why the differences exist. What are the interests and motivations behind these differences? The more facts you obtain, the more accurate your analysis will be.

LOOKING FOR MULTIPLE CAUSES

Virtually any international event has many underlying reasons or causes. As critical thinkers studying international relations, we need to consider a wide range of possible influences and factors, all of which could be involved to varying degrees in the shaping of international events.

Look, as an example, at the global decline in fertility rates—the average number of children a woman has. Why is this decline taking place? Is it just a reflection of increasing living standards in countries like India? Or are women in countries like Turkey gaining more power within the family to decide how many children they have? Why does China still restrict the number of children a family may have? An answer should look for the many factors influencing fertility rates, including cultural practices, economic development, education, and government policies. (We will return to this topic in Chapters 6 and 9.)

As another example of multiple causes, many Americans tend to explain the collapse of Communism in Eastern Europe and the Soviet Union by Ronald Reagan's unrelenting military and economic pressure. Although this pressure was real, the Soviet Union's demise was caused by several intertwining factors, including disillusionment with Communist ideology, a growing economic and financial crisis, and the disastrous domestic policies of Soviet leadership. (See Figure 1.4.)

BEING AWARE OF BIAS

We have to keep in mind that our opinions, as well as the opinions of people around us, may be inaccurate. Every interpretation of the facts is made from someone's point of view. And people tend to avoid information that challenges their assumptions and gravitate to information that supports their views (Graber, 2005). Nobel Prize–winning studies show that people tend to bring emotional biases to simple logical procedures (Kahneman and Tversky, 1972).

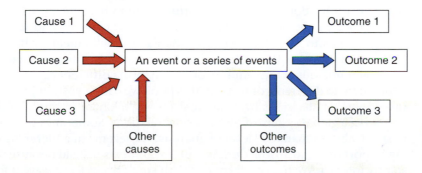

FIGURE 1-4 Multiple causes and outcomes of events.

When it comes to international relations, it is easy to support leaders we like and to oppose the policies of those we dislike. Our personal attachments, interests, preferences, and values have a tremendous impact on the facts we gather and judgments we make about international events. Ask your professor which periodical she or he reads the most. Opinion polls show that people's party affiliation is correlated with their choice of certain news sources (Pew Research Center, 2010). A professor who likes *The New York Times* more than any other publication is likely to have a more liberal view of politics than one who prefers *The Wall Street Journal and* does not like to read other papers. A professor who enjoys reading *The Economist* is likely to emphasize the benefits of capitalism and free trade. Another professor, one who subscribes to the British newspaper *The Guardian* but does not like *The Economist*, is likely to have a more critical view of the benefits of market-based international economic policies. Would you agree with these assumptions?

Bias is often caused by different experiences and life circumstances. Personal emotions can deepen misunderstandings and disagreements, by causing us to refuse to learn new facts and accept new information. **Parochialism**, a worldview limited to the small piece of land on which we live, necessarily narrows the experiences we can have. It is a powerful roadblock in the study and practice of international relations.

An emphasis on critical thinking will help you, as a student of international relations. You will learn to retrieve verifiable knowledge from apparently endless fountains of information, from media reports to statistical data banks. You will also learn to be an informed skeptic and decision maker.

CHECK YOUR KNOWLEDGE

▶ What is the Freedom of Information Act (FOIA)?
▶ Explain the method of content analysis.
▶ Briefly describe the three rules of critical thinking described in the chapter.

How Do We Apply It?

Theory alone is not enough: It must be applied and tested. In each later chapter, we will look at how we study the major issues in international relations, from war and terrorism to the environment and human rights. We want you to gain confidence as you learn to connect theory to practice. That way, you can think critically about the past and future—and to become an informed decision maker. Of course, we will also discover how complex and tricky it is to apply theories to infinitely rich realities. Each development—whether it is a declaration of war or the signing of a peace treaty—has its own chain of decisions by numerous actors. And theories may bring different conclusions as we apply them to different contexts. In this book we consistently apply theories to three contexts: decisions by individual actors, behavior of states, and the dynamics of a global system of international relations. Sometimes scholars prefer to speak about separated "level of analysis." Levels mean a hierarchy of growing importance and abstraction. We turn to contexts instead because they constantly interact. We treat each context with equal respect and leave it for you to decide when one is more important and relevant than the other or whether all of them are inseparable. Now let's consider each briefly in turn.

The Individual Context

Focusing on the role of political leaders and studying their decisions is a rewarding tool for the study of international relations. Each decision maker is a unique individual with a personal history, preferences, fears, prejudices, and idiosyncrasies. Some are indecisive. Others can be impatient and reckless. Still others come to the office with an agenda that they are reluctant to change despite the objections of their advisers (Logevall, 1999; Beschloss, 2007).

In January 1950, thirty-eight-year-old Kim Il Sung, the ambitious and nationalistic communist leader of North Korea, successfully lobbied Joseph Stalin into supporting his attack on South Korea. The Soviet and American military had divided Korea in 1945 during joint military actions against Japan. Such a division was seen as a matter of military and political convenience. Kim, with Stalin's help, decided to change this situation. Newly declassified sources from Soviet archives reveal that Stalin's decision to support Kim triggered the Korean War. At the same time, the road to war cannot be imagined without Kim's energetic and, as it turned out, misguided promises to win in a few weeks. Contrary to the expectations of Stalin and Kim, the United States immediately declared war on North Korea and obtained a U.N. resolution in support of U.S.-led international military action. For the Korean Communists, the war looked completely lost; but in October 1950 the leader of the Chinese Communist Party, Mao Zedong, decided under pressure from Stalin, but also acting on his own convictions, to help Kim Il Sung. Mao sent hundreds of thousands of troops to Korea, bringing the United States and China to the brink of a larger war. Fortunately, the U.S. Administration did not declare war on China and refrained from using nuclear weapons in the Korean conflict.

Leaders rarely make decisions single-handedly. Usually, decisions are the outcome of complex domestic struggles, bargaining, coalition building, and compromises. Let's turn next, then, to the state context.

The State Context

As an old expression has it, foreign policy begins at home. Domestic political, economic, and social factors all play a significant role (Putnam, 1988). Domestic issues influence the daily interactions of governments, NGOs, and international institutions. In democracies, policies are more transparent than in authoritarian states. People in democratic countries, NGOs, and media have more influence on foreign-policy decisions. However, they may also dislike when their leaders focus mostly on foreign policy and neglect domestic issues.

In July 1945, British Prime Minister Churchill came to an international conference in Berlin to negotiate with Stalin and President Truman. However, he had to leave the conference in just a few days because his Conservative party had lost elections to the rival Labor party. The leader who had led the country successfully through World War II could not get enough votes to keep his political power because of a range of domestic problems. Conversely, international developments can influence domestic ratings of political leaders. During most military campaigns abroad—especially if they are short and successful—the approval ratings of U.S. presidents go up. However, if casualties continue to mount among American troops, national surveys show that public support declines little by little, and the rating of the president goes down accordingly (Holsti, 2004). Often in this book, we will see how foreign-policy actions are designed, in part, for domestic purposes—to satisfy the voter.

Powerful domestic lobbies also play an important role in foreign policy. In the United States, lobbies represent lawyers, unionized workers, farmers, oil companies, and many other groups. There are also lobbies pushing for certain policies related to specific countries. Mass media—including newspapers, television, radio, and the Web—are also influential promoters or opponents of foreign policies. In some nondemocratic countries, powerful ethnic clans and religious authorities can play a vital role in foreign relations as well. In Iran today, an assortment of religious authorities (called ayatollahs) and government bureaucrats make calls on most foreign affairs issues. In China, the president, vice-president, and foreign minister are officially responsible for foreign policy. In reality, all important decisions regarding foreign policy and security are made by the Politburo Standing Committee of the Communist Party of China—a group of five to nine people, usually all men.

Important domestic factors affect international business and trade. Many of these factors are rooted in cultural and social norms. In China, international businesses often rely on *guanxi*, or "connections," and they have done so since the country opened its doors to foreign entrepreneurs in the 1980s. It is commonly understood that one should meet, based on the recommendations of Chinese counterparts, with selected government officials, receive the necessary permissions from local authorities, and make informal contacts with others to ensure that agreements or contracts are actually followed through. Although corruption should not be tolerated, many insist, the importance of local connections must be acknowledged and taken into consideration in politics as well

Ayatollah Ahmad Jannati, leader of the Guardian Council, delivers a prayer sermon at the Tehran University campus in 2011. This Council consists of the highest-ranking religious and political authorities in Iran; it runs Iran's foreign policy together with the Supreme Leader.

as business. Others reply that *guanxi* is simply corruption disguised as cultural norms. Which view would you support? Could both be accurate?

The Global Context

Individual decisions by state leaders and domestic political factors influence foreign policy and international relations. But it takes a global context to understand how international relations really work.

Two opposing tendencies are present in today's international developments. **Globalization** refers to the growing irrelevance of state borders, the importance of international exchanges of good and ideas, and increased openness to innovation. It is a major shift in politics, communications, trade, and the economy at large. Cellular phones designed in Finland and manufactured in China now ring in African towns and villages. Millions of people have jobs and bring home a stable income because factories create products for sale in other countries. Communications, travel, and international commerce have eliminated many political, legal, ideological, and cultural barriers. Optimists believe that the world is abandoning old prejudices. It is becoming more dynamic, flexible, and tolerant than ever before (Bhagwati, 2004).

There is, however, resistance. **Antiglobalization** is a complex international, political, and cultural movement that sees globalization as aggravating old problems and creating new ones. One of the most obvious problems is the growing contrast between wealthy and poor regions—often labeled the global North and South. Advocates of antiglobalization offer a variety of responses, ranging from a more active role for the state in economic affairs to religious fundamentalism. Some believe that resisting globalization is the only way to oppose powerful international monopolies and corrupt governments. Others are afraid of losing their jobs to other countries, where pay is far lower. The global market may sound appealing, but not in the homes of the unemployed (Held, 2007).

Studying international relations requires understanding the interaction of multiple factors, players, conditions, and contexts. Although events may appear chaotic, they can nonetheless be understood. Armed with the facts about what we study, the theories we use, and the contexts, we can recognize trends and avoid biased judgments. You will find exactly that as a consistent framework in each chapter. (See Figure 1.5.)

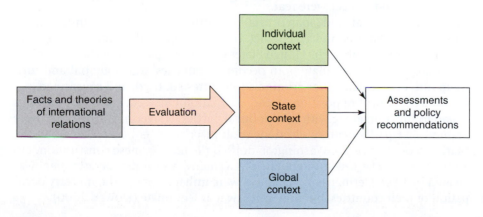

FIGURE 1-5 Analysis of international relations in three contexts.

Past, Present, and Future: Can Democracy Be Exported?

During a class discussion, we asked, "Can democracy be exported from one country to another?" Several students immediately said no. The United States, they reasoned, was trying to use military force to build democratic states in Afghanistan and Iraq. Washington committed significant human and material resources to achieve this goal. However, the students continued, this foreign policy experiment failed. They mentioned the casualties, the continuing political instability, and the violence that these countries have to face as a result of foreign occupation.

Other students disagreed. They turned to the examples of Japan and Germany more than sixty years ago. The governments of these two countries—both military dictatorships and both sworn enemies of the United States—had lost World War II, and the occupying powers established new political systems. Eventually, after years of transition, Japan and Germany became prosperous democracies and Washington's allies. In fact, a military occupation resulted in a peaceful democratic transition. "Democracy can be exported," the students concluded.

Whose arguments were more compelling? The discussion led to new questions as well:

- Why was democracy successful in Germany and Japan, and why is it failing in Afghanistan and Iraq?
- What is the difference between the international situation and conditions in Germany and Japan in the 1940s and in Afghanistan and Iraq today?
- How can foreign policy of the United States favor or hinder the "export of democracy"?

To address these questions, we decided to review some basic facts from the past and then critically compare them with more recent developments. Our assessments and predictions will help us in making more informed judgment about democracy, military conflicts, international conditions, and the future of foreign policy.

Japan lost more than three million people in the war and almost a quarter of its economy. Germany lost more than eight million people. In both countries, people were devastated by years of war. The threats of unemployment, lawlessness, and hunger were real.

In 1945, German and Japan officially capitulated. In May, the United States, Great Britain, France, and the Soviet Union occupied the entire territory of Germany. In September, the United States occupied Japan. From the beginning, the strategy was to eliminate both occupied countries' war potential and turn them into democracies. War criminals were arrested, tried, and prosecuted. No organized political opposition to the occupation emerged. New labor unions began to function along with new political parties. Universal voting rights were granted and parliamentary elections took place. Courts began to adjudicate. Market economies grew. Washington drafted the first Japanese constitution, enacted in 1947. The Federal Republic of Germany, a new democratic state, was created in 1949. Germans and Japanese were unhappy about the military occupation of their countries, but they still saw it as legitimate (Dower, 2000).

Unlike Germany and Japan, Iraq and Afghanistan did not fight in a major war against the United States and its allies (as we will see further in Chapter 7). Neither country signed a capitulation agreement. Most people in Iraq and Afghanistan saw the U.S military presence as illegitimate. It was commonly perceived as part of a Western strategy directed at Islamic countries. Almost immediately, too, an organized armed opposition to foreign occupation emerged.

Also in contrast to Japan and Germany in the 1940s, Iraq and Afghanistan are culturally diverse communities with multiple ethnic, tribal, and religious groups. In Japan and Germany, too, the foreign occupational force successfully imposed its authority in provinces. In Iraq, and particularly Afghanistan, local warlords, not the central government, established their power in many places (Crawford and Miscik, 2010).

What, in summary, were the differences between the occupations of Germany and Japan, on one hand, and the occupations of Iraq and Afghanistan on the other? What were the differences in the U.S.'s policies in these cases?

LEGACY OF ETHNIC AND RELIGIOUS RIVALRY

A country's composition and a history of rivalry among ethnic and religious groups have a serious impact on the central government's ability to establish authority and to govern. Where such rivalry is absent or insignificant, democratic reforms may succeed, as in Japan and Germany. In places ridden by conflict, democracy begins to look more like anarchy.

HISTORY OF MODERN INSTITUTIONS AND DEMOCRATIC GOVERNANCE

In the twentieth century, before the war, both Germany and Japan had experience with modern bureaucratic and civil institutions and (in Germany's case)

A small store advertises its wedding video services in the old city of Kabul, Afghanistan, in 2013. Despite years of occupation and international efforts, economic recovery in Afghanistan is slow, and democratic institutions are extremely weak.

a constitutional democracy. Afghanistan and Iraq had very little experience with modern institutions, not to mention democratic governance.

GEOGRAPHY AND TERRITORY

Political reforms require an authority (either foreign or domestic) that can manage a country. Good roads and efficient communications make a country better connected and manageable. In Germany and Japan, the occupational forces effectively controlled the territory. It was more difficult in Iraq, and Afghanistan, because these countries are a combination of mountains and deserts, one of the most difficult terrains on the Earth.

ECONOMIC DEVELOPMENT

Before the occupation, Germany already was the most industrialized country in Europe, with advanced education and science. Japan held the same distinction in Asia. Both countries had educated professional classes. The United States helped German and Japanese exports and pulled these countries' economies into the U.S.-led international trade system. Iraq and especially Afghanistan didn't have advanced economies and sizable professional classes. Iraqi oil can stimulate this country's economy. Afghanistan, however, does not have easily available natural resources.

POLITICAL MOBILIZATION DURING OCCUPATION

In Germany and Japan, there were no significant forces capable of or willing to organize an armed resistance against the occupying powers. In fact, political groups, which collaborated with the occupation authorities, mobilized people to accept change and to build democratic institutions. In Afghanistan and Iraq, opposition to the occupation—despite infighting—worked to dismantle democratic reforms.

LEGITIMACY OF OCCUPATION

Any foreign occupation may be viewed as illegitimate. A long occupation further erodes the legitimacy of local authorities. In Germany and Japan, the United States was using the perceived threat of the Soviet Union to prolong the occupation. In Iraq and Afghanistan, there was no such a significant foreign threat. The population in these countries commonly viewed the democratic governments in Baghdad and Kabul as "American puppets."

INTERNATIONAL SUPPORT

Both occupation and institution building require lasting domestic and international support. In the 1940s, the vast majority of Americans, according to Gallup polls, supported the war and occupation of Japan and Germany. They gave their troops full support at home. American allies, such as Great Britain, France, and South Korea, welcomed for their own reasons the presence of the American forces in Germany and Japan. In contrast, the engagements in Afghanistan and particularly Iraq divided the nation. And the occupations of Iraq and Afghanistan created divisions among U.S. allies and caused significant criticism globally. (See Table 1-2.)

   We have briefly compared the conditions in four countries and linked them to the ability to conduct democratic reforms while under military occupation.

TABLE 1-2 Building Democracy Under Occupation: The Cases of Four Countries

Developments	Japan	Germany	Afghanistan	Iraq
Declaration of War by the United States	Declared	Declared	Not	Not
Military Occupation	By the United States	By the United States and allies	By the United States and allies	By the United States and allies
Ethnic Composition of the Occupied Countries	Relatively homogeneous	Relatively homogeneous	Ethnically and religiously diverse	Ethnically and religiously diverse
Infrastructure of the Occupied Territory	Relatively developed	Developed	Almost absent; difficult to administer	Underdeveloped; difficult to administer
Perception of Foreign Occupation	Perceived as a result of their own military defeat	Perceived as a result of their own military defeat	Perceived as a foreign aggression and invasion	Perceived as a foreign aggression and invasion
Experience with Democracy	Modest experience before the 1930s	Experience before 1933	Almost absent	Almost absent
Economic Factors	Developed economy	Developed economy	Underdeveloped economy	Underdeveloped economy
Accountability of New Officials	High	High	Low	Low
Political Mobilization Against the Occupation	None	None	Significant and persistent	Significant and persistent
Foreign Support of the Occupation	Strong	Strong	Mixed	Mixed

As you can see, we have found ourselves drawing on history, political science, economics, sociology, and other disciplines as well. You may add your own assessments and bring new facts. You may even disagree with some points we have presented. What's your view?

CONCLUSION

It is possible to live in peace, Gandhi believed. But that possibility is not yet a reality. We need to find the inner logic in the kaleidoscope of decisions, mistakes, and success stories in today's tightly interconnected world. Do we need theory to understand international relations? Which theoretical visions are most helpful today, and in which situations? How can we apply those views to solve real-life problems and to build peace? We invite you to join us in considering such questions across time, borders, and disciplines. You will not be just a passive reader, we hope, but an active explorer. The better you understand the world today, the better you will be able to navigate it in the future.

CHAPTER SUMMARY

- International relations (IR) studies the many interactions among states as well as the activities of nonstate organizations.
- IR includes international politics, or the study of how states protect their interests. International political economy, the study of the complex interactions of economics and politics, is another important topic. International law studies formal rules and regulations concerning interactions among states, institutions, and organizations involved in IR.
- State sovereignty is a central concept in the study of IR. A state is a governed entity with a settled population occupying a permanent area. Sovereignty generally refers to the independent authority over a territory.
- State governments conduct foreign policy—actions involving official decisions and communications, public and secret, with other state governments, nongovernmental organizations (NGOs), corporations, and international institutions. Diplomacy, in general terms, is the practice of managing IR by means of negotiations.
- A growing set of nongovernmental actors plays an increasingly important role in foreign policy of many countries. Besides sovereign states and NGOs, the third major player on the field of IR is international organizations.
- Understanding IR will provide you with analytical tools and confidence in explaining and addressing the most significant problems facing the world today and tomorrow. Among these problems are the possibility of nuclear devastation, regional and global instability, environmental problems, poverty, and violations of human rights. The study of IR does not focus exclusively on threats and problems. Two of the reasons we study this subject are to give an informed opinion and to build policies that will help the world to become a stable, healthy, and prosperous place.
- Part of the study of IR is informational: It gathers and describes facts, events, and developments. A second part is interpretive: It analyzes facts and explains why events take place based on a theory.
- It is important to study facts of IR within at least three contexts. The first is individual decisions or contexts. Next, almost every step taken by a state or an NGO can be viewed from the standpoint of state policies. Finally, facts and theories can be viewed in the context of global developments.

KEY TERMS

Analysis 24
Antiglobalization 31
Content analysis 20
Critical thinking 25
Experiment 24
Eyewitness accounts 19
Focus group 23
Foreign policy 9
Globalization 31
Intelligence 21

Intergovernmental
  organizations (IGOs) 10
Internal affairs 8
International law 3
International political
  economy 3
International politics 3
International relations 2
Nation 8
Nongovernment organizations
  (NGOs) 11

Nuclear proliferation 14
Parochialism 28
Separatism 9
Sovereignty 8
State government 9
Survey 22
Theory 24
Weapons of mass destruction
  (WMD) 14

1. What do we study, and why?

KEY CONCEPTS
- Security
- International political economy
- International law
- Sovereignty, nations, and states

KEY ACTORS
- State governments
- IGOs as associations of several states
- NGOs as public or private interest groups

GLOBAL ISSUES
- Instability, violence, and war
- Nuclear proliferation
- Environmental problems
- Poverty
- Human rights violations
- Economic challenges

2. How do we study it?

GATHERING INFORMATION
- Open sources such as reports, speeches, and statements
- Intelligence
- Surveys
- Experiments

ANALYZING INFORMATION
- Theories present different rules for the analysis of international relations
- Theories must be applied, connected to practice
- Facts can be considered within three contexts: individual, state, and global
- Opinions are not necessarily facts
- Most events have multiple causes
- Bias may distort information

3. How do we apply it?

THE INDIVIDUAL CONTEXT
Focuses on the role of political leaders and their decisions

THE STATE CONTEXT
Focuses on the role of domestic political, economic, and social factors

THE GLOBAL CONTEXT
- Globalization: The growing irrelevance of state borders, the growing importance of international exchanges of goods and ideas, and increased openness to innovation
- Antiglobalization

Critical Thinking

- Why do domestic politics matter in foreign policy decision-making?
- Can a state not be sovereign? When might this happen?
- What explains the increased role of NGOs today?
- Why are experimental methods useful in IR? What are some limitations?
- When and how can government intelligence information be biased?

CHAPTER

2

CHAPTER OUTLINE

The Berlin Wall, built in 1961
by East Germany with Soviet
assistance, became a dramatic
symbol of communism. The
Wall fell in 1989, a ripple effect
of Mikhail Gorbachev's "new
thinking." This spectacular event
demonstrates the importance of
ideas in changing international
relations.

Realism and Liberalism

IN 1987–90, THE SOVIET UNION, UNDER THE LEADERSHIP OF MIKHAIL GORBACHEV, DRAMATICALLY CHANGED ITS INTERNATIONAL BEHAVIOR. PREVIOUSLY, THIS COUNTRY ACTED AS a military superpower and the United States' rival, zealously protecting its domination in Eastern Europe and its motley collection of allies around the world. Suddenly, the Soviet Union initiated policies that, one by one, led to the end of the Cold War and the beginning of cooperation with the United States on a number of vital international issues. Gorbachev argued that to achieve global security and peace, world leaders should change their thinking. First, they must reject the arms race and the use of force in foreign policy. Second, they must put aside ideological differences in the name of nonviolence and cooperation. And third, they must build a new international community. As he said a year later, from the podium at the General Assembly of the United Nations, states must "search for a consensus of all mankind." The Soviet leader, to everyone's surprise, acted on his words. He refused to use violence in Eastern Europe, where Communism collapsed in 1989, and he agreed to the reunification of Germany and its membership in NATO.

Decades have passed since then. The Soviet Union is no longer on the map. Yet has the world embraced those universal principles of cooperation that Gorbachev described so passionately? Just watch today's headlines and you can easily say that we are very far from a cooperative, nonviolent world. So was Gorbachev idealistic and naïve? Why didn't the world embrace his vision of peace? And if the Soviet Union was able to alter its confrontational behavior so dramatically, can we expect that other countries may do the same?

Understanding any country's behavior is a challenge. It takes much more than casual observation of international politics. For starters, one should begin with *analysis*—that is, the breaking of something complex into smaller parts to understand their essential features and relations. This is difficult enough, but even more than analysis is needed. There are simply too many facts, events, and dissimilar opinions about them. Which are more important than others? Which deserve immediate action—and what kind? To answer these and other questions, decision makers have to look at the facts in light of broader patterns of how international relations works. We need to not only think but *theorize* about international relations. Doing so requires both strong empirical knowledge and a measure of imagination.

Learning Objectives

After reading this chapter, you should be able to:

▶ describe the key principles of realism and liberalism and explain how these principles evolved over time;
▶ discuss the concept of power in international relations;
▶ explain the meaning of states' interests, balance of power, and polarity;
▶ explain why and how liberalism dismisses the principles of power politics;
▶ distinguish different approaches and traditions within realism and liberalism;
▶ interpret realpolitik as a key application of realism; and
▶ critically apply realism and liberalism within three contexts of international relations: individual decisions, specific policies of states, and global developments.

What Do We Study?

Debates about international relations ultimately rest on competing theoretical approaches. Different theories present different rules for the analysis of international relations and provide different explanations. For instance, some experts believe that Gorbachev was mistaken in his rhetoric and policies of

1987–1990: Violence has always been part of human civilization and the use of force in international relations is inevitable. The same skeptics maintain that an international community of equals is simply unrealistic because stronger states will always dominate the weaker ones. Others argue that it is extremely difficult—but not impossible—to reach a consensus about *how* to build a peaceful and prosperous world.

It is becoming increasingly common in the studies of international relations to consider several theoretical perspectives together. They are compared, then applied and tested. We will try to implement this method in the following chapters. We want you to gain confidence as you learn all these theories, compare them, and connect them to practice. That way, you can think critically about the past and future—and to become an informed decision maker. You will discover how complex and tricky it is to apply theories to infinitely rich realities of today's world. Each development—whether it is a declaration of war or the signing of a peace treaty—has its own chain of decisions by numerous actors.

Let's now consider the two most significant approaches to international relations: realism and liberalism.

Realism: Main Principles

Realism is an approach to international relations that focuses on state power, security, and interests. According to realism, only "states" (sovereign countries) can be players in international relations. They defend their interests, protect their resources, create alliances, react to outside threats, and impose their will on others (Walt, 1987). Their ability to do so is called **power**. Across history, state interests change and expand, and power takes on different forms: military, economic, political, and other.

POWER

Power in international relations is the ability of a state to defend itself, guard its interests, and impose its will on other states. But what gives a state this ability? Is it simply weapons or something less tangible, like fear? The earliest embodiments of power were sharpened stones and fire, but also totems and symbols. Since ancient history, military force, economic-financial wealth, as well as religion, were important forms of power.

In the twentieth century, power was calculated: The numbers included men and women in reserve, tons of steel produced, battleships, submarines, tanks, aircrafts, and the stockpiles of nuclear warheads and missiles, as well as quality of railroads and access to seaports. The economic competition between the capitalist and Communist systems brought forth the importance of **gross domestic product** (GDP), or the value of all goods and services produced within the borders of a state. During the Cold War, as we saw in Chapter 1, the West demonstrated statistically its growing strength in economic and financial power.

Some aspects of power cannot be calculated. Ideology can be as important as religion. For instance, during the Cold War the American ideology of freedom and capitalism proved often to be more attractive than Communist ideology. This added to the power of the West over the Soviet Union and its allies (Jarausch, 2008). We will learn more about these forms of power later in this chapter.

ANARCHY AND POWER DISTRIBUTION

According to realists, states try to build order in the situation of **anarchy.** Anarchy does not mean chaos and confusion. It is the lack of any executive power above individual states capable of regulating their behavior. Anarchy remains a basic condition of international affairs, no matter how many international agreements are signed and rules sanctioned. No order can last forever. Great powers rise and fall. There are **status quo states** that seek to keep what they already possess. There are also **revisionist states** seeking to expand their power and to change (or revise) an existing international order (Schweller, 1997). Living with anarchy does not mean that politicians and diplomats should not reach agreements, strive for peace, and create international rules. This means, according to realists, that the real choice is between imperfect international relations and something much worse (Jackson, 2005).

Hans Morgenthau ([1948] 2006), the scholar who first formulated principles of realism, argued that because of anarchy, states usually rely on their own power, and each state tries to maximize its power, acting sometimes as aggressive and greedy individuals. Political conflict is the essence of international relations mainly because it is rooted in human nature (Rynning and Ringsmose, 2008). States, however, cannot be equal, because their powers are not equal. Countries differ in size, geographical position, and economic and military strength. There are great powers, smaller powers, and the rest. Great powers have more choices than weaker ones. Their economic and political interests extend around the world. They can offer protection to weaker ones in exchange for political and economic concessions. Weaker states may accept this protection or seek other options at their own risk. Their interests are limited and mostly local (Donnelly, 2009).

International relations therefore depends on power distribution. When a state has enough power to impose its will on its neighbors, this situation is called **hegemony.** Various empires in the past, from ancient Rome to Great Britain in the nineteenth century, enjoyed such power. Power distribution, however, can change relatively fast, sometimes during one or two decades. The reasons include other states' resistance, the erosion of political will among political leaders, the end of imperial ideology, and the exhaustion of economic resources—the conditions together known as **imperial overreach.** The United Kingdom, France, Germany, and the former Soviet Union experienced this process during the past century: They either had to scale down or collapsed completely.

INTERNATIONAL ORDER AND BALANCING

International order emerges out of anarchy because states check and balance each other according to the existing distribution of power. As states gain or lose power, they alter the international order. According to the realist approach, the design of such international order is determined by power distribution

The Congress of Berlin, by Anton von Werner. This 1878 meeting led by German Chancellor Otto Von Bismarck marked the peak of an international system based on a balance of power among several of the most influential European states.

among states. We will study three designs, according to power distribution: *unipolar, bipolar,* and *multipolar.*

In the nineteenth century the international order was **multipolar**. A few European great powers, including France, Great Britain, and Russia, dominated the world with exception of the Western hemisphere, where the rising power of the United States was a decisive factor. Great Britain was the most powerful state financially until the end of the nineteenth century, when the United States and Germany surpassed Great Britain as industrial powers and centers of education and scientific-technological innovation.

During the first forty years of the twentieth century, the world remained largely multipolar. But the defeat of Germany and Japan in World War II and the decline of Britain and France in the 1940s transformed the old multipolar order into a new **bipolar** order, dominated by the United States and the Soviet Union. The **Cold War** emerged. This was the period of tensions and competition between the two international blocs: the one created and dominated by the Soviet Union and the other comprised of the countries led by the United States. During the 1970s and 1980s, the emergence of other regional centers of power (an integrated Western Europe, Japan, and the oil-producing countries of the Middle East) had begun to erode this bipolarity. The Nonaligned Movement, which included a number of countries (such as India, Yugoslavia, and Egypt) not belonging to any major power bloc, gained influence by exploiting the struggle between the two superpowers (Willetts, 1983).

When the Soviet Union collapsed in 1991, the international order of the 1990s became **unipolar**, because no single state or a coalition of states could seriously challenge the military might of the United States. The United States appeared to be the world's hegemonic power. The Nonaligned Movement withered. The European Union (EU) emerged in 1992 but did not become a powerful political player. However, unipolarity in the twenty-first century was

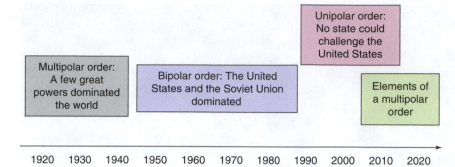

FIGURE 2-1 Power distribution in the world order of the 20th and 21st centuries.

seriously challenged when American forces became embroiled in Iraq and Afghanistan. Economic and financial problems further weakened America's power. In the past several years, signs appear of a possible return to a multipolar order. Among the causes of such a change is economic ascendancy of a number of countries (Zakaria, 2008; Hiro, 2010). Brazil, Russia, India, and above all China became regional powers. Together these four countries account for nearly 30 percent of the world's land, and are home to almost 45 percent of the world's population (Borah, 2011). These countries pursue their own interests and do not accept the predominance of the United States. (See Figure 2.1.)

International relations involves *balancing of power*—states' constant search for the best position within the international order. States use violent and non-violent means to keep or change the balance of power—or to prevent other states from doing the same. The ultimate violent policy is **war**. Nonviolent policies include building alliances, increasing economic and military strength, and engaging in diplomacy. These policies are known as **realpolitik** (a term borrowed from German). It is based on realist assumptions that states have no principles, only interests—and this makes them balance each other. Prussian statesman Otto von Bismarck used realpolitik to unify Germany in the 1860s while isolating its enemies one by one. (See Figure 2.2.)

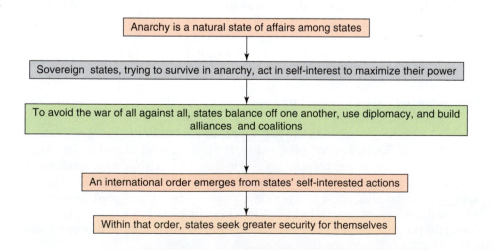

FIGURE 2-2 The logic of realism.

NEOREALISM

In the 1960s, political scientist Kenneth Waltz concluded that one single factor can explain international relations. This factor, he wrote, is a "structure" of international relations that results from power distribution. If the world is divided between the United States and the Soviet Union, then all other states will have to adapt to this *bipolar* structure. Their behavior would have been different if the world had a *multipolar* structure. States do not seek more power for power's sake; they rather seek more security within the established "structure" of the international order (or system). And this explains that an international order can acquire some stability, and wars can be checked (Waltz, 2001).

These conclusions became the foundation of **neorealism**, also called *structural realism*. Unlike earlier realist analysts, neorealists believe that human nature, aggressiveness, and greed has nothing to do with the nature of international relations. Also, the nature of political leadership and domestic politics are secondary to the "structure" of international relations. Sovereign states—seeking security—adapt to the international system, and leaders and domestic politics just interpret and implement the need for such adaptation.

Structural realists were poorly prepared to explain the sudden change of Soviet policies under Mikhail Gorbachev, followed by a rapid reduction of international tensions and the end of the Cold War in the late 1980s. Facing new international realities and the surprising end of the global rivalry, some supporters of realism began to question its assumptions and pay closer attention to the role of leaders and the nature of domestic politics of states (Walt, 1998). Today, the majority of realists and neorealists still argue that states are engaged in power games and continue to treat other states as potential adversaries (Mearsheimer, 2003).

Soviet Premier Aleksei Kosygin (at microphone) and U.S. President Lyndon B. Johnson at a Summit in Glassboro (New Jersey), June 1967. During the Cold War, global power was mostly distributed between the two "poles"—the Soviet Union and the United States.

CHECK YOUR KNOWLEDGE

▶ What is anarchy in the context of international relations?
▶ Why can't states be equal according to realism?
▶ What is neorealism, and how is it different from realism?

DEBATE > CAN REALISM BE ETHICAL?

Debates about the role of the United States in the world flared up in the early 2000s. Should the US build a unipolar order or delegate power and authority to its allies? For instance, in *Ethical Realism*, Anatol Lieven and John Hulsman (2006) wrote that the United States cannot act alone in a global world: It would quickly exhaust its resources and fail. America should therefore continue to play a leadership role but voluntarily restrain its power: act more cautiously, pay greater respect to other states, and use the strengths of its allies. In a word, the United States should act as an ethical citizen among other citizens.

Critics of ethical realism maintain that power determines the international order, and most other states are incapable of making a difference (Joffe, 2009). This means that the United States is bound to be the leader for some time, whether other states want it or not. Moreover, as soon as the United States gives up its domination, the world will quickly fall into chaos.

WHAT'S YOUR VIEW?

Do you think, based on what you have read so far, that powerful countries can become less "selfish," thus making power politics more "ethical"?

 Read more about ethical realism on the companion website, www.oup.com/us/shiraev.

Liberalism: Main Principles

International liberalism (or simply **liberalism**) is an approach to international relations based on three principles. First, it rejects power politics and inevitable conflict among states as the result of anarchy. Liberalism questions explanations based on zero-sum outcomes of international relations: One country's gain does not necessarily mean another country's loss. Second, it emphasizes international cooperation and mutual benefits. And third, it sees international organizations and nonstate actors as shaping state preferences and policy choices. Liberalism is not only *descriptive* when it criticizes realism as a framework for analyzing international relations. It is also *prescriptive*: It suggests how the world can and should function (Betts, 2008, 119).

SOURCES OF LIBERALISM

Liberalism has several important sources. (See Figure 2.3.) Long before it developed as an approach alternative to realism, it emerged as a set of ideas rooted in the rich philosophical and political traditions, cultivated in Europe. First, liberalism was based on European *idealism* and *humanism*. From this strand come attempts to ban and limit wars and promote antiwar movements.

Second, *republicanism* assumed that representative state governments are capable of maintaining international stability through shared rules and norms of cooperation. German philosopher Immanuel Kant ([1795] 2003) wrote about "eternal peace"—a state of international relations that can be achieved

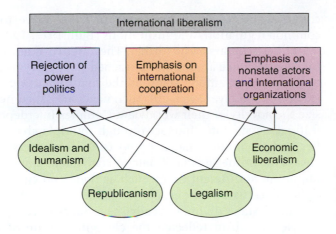

FIGURE 2-3 International liberalism: Sources and fundamental principles.

only through a consensus among free republics with representative forms of government. This strand was boosted in the nineteenth century by political democratization—a powerful movement that challenged the nobility's inherited privileges.

Third, *legalism* emphasized the possibility for the rule of law in international relations, thus limiting state sovereignty. Hugo Grotius (1583–1645), a Dutch diplomat and thinker, in *Mare Liberum* (1609; 2005) formulated one central principle called **freedom of the seas**: A state's sovereignty ends at the edge of its territorial waters. Although not every state accepted these principles at first, they eventually did, and these rules survived for centuries.

Finally, in the early twentieth century came *economic liberalism*. British writer Norman Angell, in *The Great Illusion* (1910), denied that states prosper largely through power games and territorial expansion. Wars, he wrote, disrupt economic order. The territorial gains achieved by war cannot compensate for much greater losses in business and international trade. Economic liberals maintained that states could mutually gain from interdependence, international trade, and cooperation.

LIBERALISM ON ANARCHY AND COOPERATION

In contrast to realism and neorealism that center on power balancing and "structure" of international order, liberal approach focuses on the capacity of international cooperation. Instead of one factor explaining world's affairs, liberals came up with numerous explanations. There are many liberal approaches, not just one. After the 1960s, when liberal ideas began to challenge realism in scholarly journals and in specific policies, diversity within liberalism grew.

More moderate liberals do not deny the presence of anarchy in international relations. At the same time, they believe that states cannot be compared to billiard balls that just take various configurations on the international field. In *The Anarchical Society*, Australian scholar Hedley Bull (1977) argued that sovereign states can develop a "civilized" international society, with shared rules and norms, that diminishes the effects of anarchy. Bull showed that countries, despite a frequent lack of trust, strive to develop and observe common regulations and institutions (Bull, 1977; 1983).

Other scholars went further. They argued that development of **complex interdependence** among states reached the point when anarchy was replaced by cooperation among states as the main feature of international relations (Keohane and Nye, 1989, 20). Such views are called **neoliberalism** to emphasize the novelty of their worldview. Complex interdependence has three main features. First, states interact through multiple channels including informal ties and economic, financial, and cultural contacts. Second, security is not always the prime agenda of state-to-state interactions. Different issues become important at different times, such as trade and currency regulations, human rights concerns, and the economic assistance of wealthy countries to poor ones. And third, states do not typically use military force against other countries.

Neoliberalism reflected the changing nature of international relations after 1945. The primacy of military power as a policy choice remained, but the importance of economic, environmental, and other forms of interdependence increased drastically—as well as the realization that states should cooperate to survive and prosper (Crane and Amawi, 1997).

LIBERAL INSTITUTIONALISM

The end of the Cold War established the dominance of liberal ideas in the studies of international relations. Realism and neorealism appeared to be the thing of the past. A prominent Harvard scholar wrote that the former anarchy of states, vying for supremacy, has been replaced by the "global community" (Iriye, 2002). Liberals began to attribute special roles to international organizations or institutions. In Chapter 1 we already discussed that international organizations can be **international governmental organizations (IGOs)**—when several states voluntarily delegate parts of their sovereignty to an international association. Also international organizations can be **nongovernmental (NGOs)**. There are global international organizations open to any country, like the United Nations.

Indian and Pakistani delegates meet in New Delhi, India, in 2012 to resolve a maritime boundary dispute.

There are regional organizations, like NATO, that include countries from a certain geographical area. In terms of their goals, IGOs can be security-related, economic, financial cultural, educational, and so on. We will examine the structure and functioning of several IGOs in the following chapters.

Liberal institutionalism argues that the existence, proliferation, and growing influence of the international organizations (or institutions) changed international order fundamentally. The web of these organizations create mutual obligations, provide more equal access to security information, and reduce uncertainty that countries face evaluating each other's policies (Keohane, 1989; Keohane and Martin, 1995). A number of authors began to focus on the prospects of **global governance**—the notion that means the management of an increasing number of global problems affecting many states in the spirit of cooperation and mutual benefit. This notion also implies that states become too interdependent to act alone and have to accept international norms, rules, and regulations, even at the expense of state sovereignty.

> ▶ Name three fundamental and interconnected principles of liberalism. Give examples.
> ▶ What is complex interdependence? Name three of its main features.

CHECK YOUR KNOWLEDGE

Experts have done much to corroborate or falsify (critically evaluate) theories of liberalism. Critical evaluations have focused on the persistence of war, appeals to the power of diplomacy, the assumption of "democratic peace," and what is called *soft power*.

LIBERALISM AND WARS

One of the most compelling arguments of the liberal approach to international relations is that war is no longer a primary threat to the international order. Not only can anarchy diminish, but also human beings can learn from experience. American political scientist John Mueller wrote in *Retreat from Doomsday: The Obsolescence of Major War* (1989) that Europe had learned from its experience of two world wars, overcome national rivalries, and constructed a peaceful community. Europeans, he argued, had outlived a centuries-old principle that military confrontation is the most appropriate way to solve international disputes. Warfare had become as outmoded as duels and slavery (Mueller, 1989).

At the same time, it would be wrong to argue that liberals completely exclude the use of military force as a feature of international relations. Most liberals today do not share the ideals of pacifism and complete disarmament. All scholarly approaches, including neoliberalism and institutional liberalism, accept the importance of state sovereignty, the desire of states to avoid anarchy, or the power of professional diplomacy (Sharp, 2009). Liberal internationalists often advocated war against other countries to pursue liberal goals (Doyle, 1986). (See Figure 2.4.)

LIBERAL DIPLOMACY

Diplomacy, which we began to discuss in Chapter 1, is the managing of international relations through negotiations. Sovereign states establish embassies

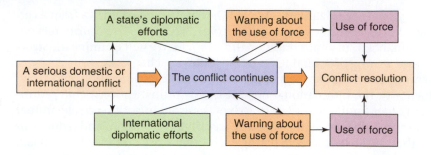

FIGURE 2-4 Supporters of the liberal tradition accept interventionist actions to solve some international crises.

DEBATE > WHEN SHOULD LIBERALS GO TO WAR?

Advisers to President Clinton supported air strikes against Yugoslavia in 1999. Similarly, President Obama and his advisers supported a military campaign against Libya in 2011. The disagreement between realists and liberal internationalists is about when and how this force should be used.

WHAT'S YOUR VIEW?

What are some liberal goals that justify, in your view, the use of military force of one country against other countries? What is the main difference between liberal internationalists and pacifists?

@ Go online to read Obama's statement on Libya, August 2011. Editorial: *Washington Post* liberal comment: "Obama Chose the Right Course on Libya," by David Ignatius.

---

in other states and keep channels of communication through them. Realists traditionally viewed diplomacy as a tool of realpolitik when each side tries to maximize its gains and minimize its losses. Supporters of liberalism see diplomatic practices differently, as a movement toward successful global cooperation and governance. Liberalism argues that diplomacy can be effective in these ways so long as state leaders act honestly, express goodwill, and aim for nonviolent solutions. A political leader who acts unilaterally often becomes unpredictable in the eyes of neighbors and even allies. Not knowing what to expect can be dangerous, especially in a case of military tensions. The most obvious way to dispel mistrust and build legitimacy is through direct consultation with the political leaders of other countries.

Liberals also view diplomacy as an arena for many more actors than realpolitik means. Not only great powers, but smaller states, the United Nations, and numerous NGOs are diplomatic actors. Liberals point out that small European countries, such as the Netherlands, played a crucial role in making human rights a basic principle for European diplomacy in the 1970s—while the United States and the Soviet Union still played realpolitik games. In 1975, the Conference on Security and Cooperation in Europe signed the Helsinki Final Act. This document bound the 25 states, that signed it, including the United States and the USSR, to respect and protect humanitarian and human rights, such as the right to receive information, exchange ideas, or unify families across the state borders. It was a triumph of the liberal internationalism (Thomas, 2001).

CASE IN POINT > *Diplomatic Efforts in an India-Pakistan Conflict*

In December 2001, in the wake of a terrorist attack on India's parliament by Pakistan-based militant groups, India and Pakistan amassed over a million troops on the Indo-Pakistani border. These countries had gone to war several times before, the last time in 1971. Now they threatened each other with nuclear missiles. The entire international community joined urgent efforts to avoid what appeared to be imminent violence. After weeks of relentless diplomatic talks, the standoff eased out, and reciprocal concessions began. Pakistan's leaders promised to stop cross-border infiltrations of civilian combatants into Indian-controlled Kashmir. India, in exchange, withdrew its navy from the North Arabian Sea and lifted the over-flight ban imposed on Pakistani commercial jets. India also agreed to upgrade diplomatic ties with Islamabad. Indo-Pakistani relations remain tense and difficult, but international diplomacy proved its efficacy in easing military threats.

CRITICAL THINKING

Why did diplomacy work in this particular conflict but fail in others, such as during the conflict between the United States and Iraq in 2003? Compare these two conflicts by paying attention to (1) the willingness of the involved governments to communicate with each other and (2) the ability of the international community to influence the conflicting sides. Can you think of other, more contemporary conflicts that lead to a peaceful resolution because of diplomatic efforts?

In sum, the liberal approach takes a very expansive view of the role of diplomacy in today's world. Once an instrument of power shrouded in secrecy, diplomacy is changing to become more open and includes a growing number of actors.

DEMOCRATIC PEACE

Many scholars have elaborated Immanuel Kant's thesis on "perpetual peace" among the republics. Michael Doyle, Bruce Russet, and James Lee Ray propose what is known as **democratic peace theory**. It suggests that although democratic states can go to war against non-democratic ones, democracies do not fight one another. Most twentieth-century wars took place between non-democratic countries or between democracies and authoritarian régimes. There is hardly a single case in which democratic countries governed by stable political institutions went to war against each other. Why? Democratic peace theory gives three reasons. (See Figure 2.5.)

First, the institutions of representative democracy tend to discourage going to war against other democracies. These institutions include parliaments, a free press, pluralist public organizations, and public opinion (Owen, 2005). Second, because of shared values and shared norms of behavior, democratic states regard each other as partners rather than enemies and develop a culture of compromise and negotiations. Because democracies are more open, they feel less threatened by one another (Maoz and Russett, 1993). Third, economic interdependence makes war unacceptable for economic reasons. Therefore, state leaders and business groups will regard military conflicts as ruinous because they damage a complex economic infrastructure (Oneal and Russett,

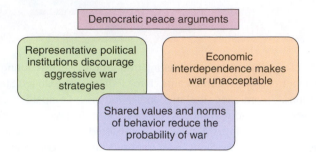

FIGURE 2-5 major arguments of the democratic peace theory.

1997). The Democratic Peace theory became very influential during the 1990s to early 2000s. Later we shall see how this concept affected practical policies.

SOFT POWER

In the 1980s, American political scientist Joseph S. Nye argued that besides power and security, states are also influenced by the examples set by other states, their governments, and their people. Traditionally, states are said to exert "hard power," or economic and military power. Nye suggested that states also possess **soft power**—the ability to influence other states by example. Examples of economic and social success can include ideas, values, and more broadly a way of life. Soft power does not rely on intimidation; it wins hearts and minds. It produces voluntary followers, not reluctant satellites (Nye, 2004).

If we associate soft power with democracy only, this will not be necessarily correct. During the early phases of the Cold War, the Soviet Union had soft power as well. Communist models were popular in Asia, Africa, and Latin America, especially in countries struggling for independence from European colonial rule. India, Indonesia, Afghanistan, Burma, Algeria, Egypt, Angola, and many other states turned to the Soviet model of state-driven industrialization and social egalitarianism (Westad, 2007).

Soft power is volatile and fluid; state actions or policies in one to two years can erase or reshape the achievements of decades (Gause, 2005; Mitzen, 2005). American soft power experienced surfs of increasing strength and ebbs of decline. The Vietnam War in the 1960–70s, the occupation of Iraq in 2003, and the crisis of the global financial system in 2008–2011 were all serious blows to American soft power. Still, in comparison to other countries, American predominance in this type of power survived.

Soft power, unlike hard power, is difficult to calculate. It operates more through *perceptions* than numbers—including the perceptions of state leaders, elites, and public opinion. More often than not, emulation, not competition, reduces the likelihood of war and promotes peace. When one country emulates another country, both are unlikely to engage in mutual hostilities. (See Figure 2.6.)

Soft power applies not only to states; IGOs and NGOs can serve as models, too. They demonstrate, as supporters of liberal internationalism hope, the advantages of liberal ideas over power politics. At the same time, it is incorrect to consider concepts of soft power as equivalent to liberalism, and hard power as only the element of realism. Joseph Nye was the first to argue for using them in combination.

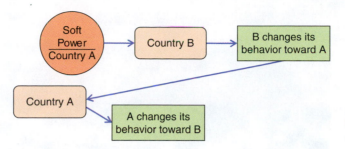

FIGURE 2-6 The effects of soft power.

▶ Why is war no longer a primary threat to the international order?
▶ Describe three major arguments of democratic peace theory. What examples can you suggest to support or counter these arguments?
▶ Give examples of soft power. In your view, does China possess soft power today? Explain your answer.

How Do We Think About It?

Two of the most influential approaches to understanding international relations, realism and liberalism, are not well-rounded, settled theories. To better understand these approaches, we need to critically examine how they analyze particular international situations and what actions they suggest to address them. Here we will describe the way realists and liberals think.

Examining Realpolitik

We now examine several principles of power politics (realpolitik) in various international situations. We also explore power shifts and situations in which some states are acting in violation of international rules. Finally, we turn to how states respond to threats to international stability.

RULES OF ENGAGEMENT

A state's geographical location, history, ideology, political regime, or economic conditions, as we have seen, affect its power politics. Realist and neorealist approaches outline several rules or principles that states must take into consideration when they are engaged in realpolitik. Consider just three such rules.

First, the chances to succeed are significantly higher when the state has a substantial power. A strong economy and massive armed forces diminish other countries' capacities to impose their will or retaliate. There is a relative and absolute advantage. The former is called hegemony, as you will remember. The United States established such superiority in the late 1990s (Mearsheimer, 2003). Overall, a successful realpolitik begins at home: The stronger the country is economically and politically, the more effective its foreign policy becomes.

Second, to survive in the anarchy of international relations, states must combine their military power with successful diplomacy. To keep most powerful states in check, Great Britain in the nineteenth century developed temporarily coalitions with other countries or went to war against its rivals before they

Vietnamese border guards watch the U.S. Seventh Fleet's USS *Blue Ridge* entering Tien Sa port in 2012. Vietnam and the United States held five days of "noncombatant" naval exchange activities, prompted by both countries' security concerns related to China.

acquired too much power. Diplomatic treaties do not necessarily prevent wars but ensure a better chance for victory in conflict (Fearon, 1998).

Third, a state should not constrain its freedom of action. Conducting foreign policy under moral considerations or out of solidarity or commitment may often hurt your own state's interests (Nau, 2002). For example, Washington's support of an independent Taiwan, on the grounds that this state is democratic and friendly toward the United States, can also be a strategic liability for Washington (Carpenter, 2006). This support may drag America into a conflict with China, which rejects Taiwan's sovereignty. Likewise, America cannot help, with military force, every popular uprising against oppressive governments in the Middle East and North Africa.

POWER SHIFTS

Rapid shifts of power create international instability and lead to war. They also cause counteractions that may affect any existing power balance. A common source of power shifts is a revisionist (or "predator") state acting belligerently in regard to other states, in systematic disregard for international rules. Two types of responses to instability are common. First, strong status quo states form alliances against an emerging threat. Second, weaker states make deals with revisionist states, bargaining for a place in a new world order that these states may eventually create by conquest and aggression.

Supporters of realpolitik believe that power politics, for the most part, tends to make the war less likely—and peace more stable. In reality, it is not always so. If a state perceives a weakness in an existing international order, it may challenge this order. With Hitler in control, Germany rapidly armed itself and began to act as a revisionist-predator state in Europe. In 1938, Germany annexed Austria; in 1939, it occupied Czechoslovakia; and later, in alliance with the Soviet Union, it attacked and dismembered Poland. In the Far East in 1931–40, Japan acted in the same fashion against China.

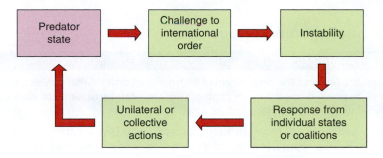

FIGURE 2-7 Power shifts, revisionist (predator) states, and international order.

Predator states by their actions may dramatically shift the balance of power in a region or even globally. These rapid power shifts, however, generate a backlash against revisionist states in the form of international coalitions and alliances. (See Figure 2.7.)

NEOREALIST STRATEGIES

Supporters of neorealism argue that military confrontations are potential but not inevitable outcomes of shifts in power. In support of this argument, neorealists directed attention to the structure of international relations. Two arguments are used.

First, it is beneficial for a state to stay away from violence and to demonstrate self-restraint. Neorealists Kenneth Waltz (2001), Stephen Van Evera (2001), and Jack Snyder (2005) have argued that state leaders consider war only as a last resort. They view wars as a tragic result of major shifts of power. This happened in 1914, when World War I broke out in Europe. In this case, they argue, great powers are drawn into conflict by uncertainty and fear. This group are *defensive realists*.

The second group, known as *offensive realists*, includes Randall Schweller (2008), Peter Liberman (2006), and John Mearsheimer (2003). They suggest that stronger states tend to maximize their power all the time and tolerate international institutions so long as they serve their interests. In contrast with defensive realists, this group argues that great powers tend to act ahead of serious threats to the international order. Moreover, acting decisively against revisionist states is the best way to respond. The failure of great Western powers to stop Hitler in the 1930s was a tragic mistake. Going to war against Germany earlier, rather than "appeasement" such as compromises and negotiations, would have been the correct policy (see **Table 2-1**).

NONMILITARY RESPONSES

Realists also discuss peaceful, nonmilitary means of power balancing in foreign affairs. Economic incentives, direct economic help, or sanctions are examples of nonmilitary responses. Such was the Marshall Plan (1947–1952), when the United States provided 13.5 billion dollars to the countries of Western Europe to recover after the Second World War. This plan removed the danger of a Communist takeover in those countries and helped to create the Western anti-Communist alliance (Hitchcock, 2008). The United States also provided

TABLE 2-1 Neorealist Arguments About War

Neorealist Views	Main Assumptions
Defensive Realism	Wars are result of the breakdown of international order. Great powers, on most occasions, seek to prevent open military conflicts. Yet they can be drawn into wars by the anarchic dynamic of international relations.
Offensive Realism	Wars and the use of force are more than accidents. They are tools that great powers use to build and protect international order so as to prevent revisionist states from destroying the existing hierarchy of power.

massive aid simultaneously to Israel and Egypt as an economic incentive to balance power and keep peace in the Middle East.

At the same time, states often use *economic sanctions* to punish other states that fail to cooperate, including limits on trade and financial operations. In recent history, the United States has applied economic sanctions against Iraq, Iran, Libya, Cuba, and North Korea. As we will see in Chapter 6, evidence for the impact of economic sanctions is ambiguous.

Diplomacy of coalitions and alliances, as we have already read, is a powerful nonmilitary response. An alliance created by skillful diplomats can be a great factor of security, in addition to superior armed forces. In the nineteenth century, Great Britain practiced it well: British diplomacy was admired by allies and was called "perfidious" by enemies.

Today's realists recognize that states have a wide range of foreign-policy options—including military and nonmilitary responses—to pursue their interests. Still, realism has difficulty explaining many international developments, as we see later in this chapter.

CHECK YOUR KNOWLEDGE
- ▶ What is a revisionist or predator state?
- ▶ Explain offensive and defensive realism.
- ▶ Explain the rules of engagement in realpolitik.

Examining Liberal Policies

To understand the logic of liberalism we turn to specific international circumstances and policies. Already in the nineteenth century, leaders of states and international organizations began to understand diplomacy as a strategy of mutual compromises. The primary goal was to impose "civilized" constraints on warfare. At international disarmament conferences in 1899 and 1907, many European states signed the Hague Conventions, which banned some lethal technologies in warfare and regulated the treatment of prisoners and civilians during wartime.

WILSONIANISM AND THE LEAGUE OF NATIONS

World War I (1914–18) took the lives of more than 16 million people, providing a frightening lesson to supporters of liberal ideas. During the war, most

CASE IN POINT > *The North Atlantic Treaty Organization (NATO)*

This case illustrates how states behave in a time of uncertainty and fear. The alliance emerged in 1949 at the urging of the Netherlands, Belgium, and Denmark. They feared the power of the Soviet Union and a possible resurgence of Germany after World War II. Losing trust in Britain or France, these small countries asked the United States to provide protection to Western Europe. The United States, worried that an unstable Europe might fall into the orbit of the rival Soviet Union, immediately accepted the offer.

For the next four decades, NATO solved several problems that European balance of power could not. The dangerous rivalry between Germany and France, which led to several wars, was over. After a few years of French objections, in 1955, West Germany became a full-time member of NATO (Zelikow and Rice, 1995). Above all, NATO helped the United States to become a European and then a global power. Although NATO claimed to be a defensive alliance, the huge military superiority of the United States allowed some strategists to entertain plans to "roll back" the Soviet sphere of influence in Eastern Europe. These plans had to be dropped when the Soviet Union had become a nuclear superpower. Although the nuclear issue remained a significant problem, a nuclear balance between NATO and the Soviet Union seemed achievable. From the realist view, such a balance should have brought stability, but mutual fears and mistrust continued.

NATO played a role in the peaceful end of the Cold War: Gorbachev, with support of Soviet security experts, agreed that the unified Germany should better be part of NATO rather than a source of instability. The rapid disintegration of the Soviet Union in 1991 left NATO without its original purpose. There was no longer a Soviet bloc or Soviet power to contain. Many experts believed that NATO had no future. Instead, many experts in the United States argued that NATO must remain an international institution to guarantee regional security and promote democratic peace in Central and Eastern Europe. In 1996–2009, twelve new countries joined NATO. In 1999, NATO bombed Yugoslavia to halt its militaristic actions. More than a dozen NATO states sent troops to fight in Afghanistan and helped the United States during its occupation of Iraq. In 2011, NATO launched a military campaign in Libya.

NATO's expansion, globalization of its actions, and the attempts to design new roles for the alliance led to serious debates between defensive and offensive realists (Sloan, 2010). The former argue that the expansion of the North Atlantic alliance was a mistake because NATO did not face any realistic threat. The new NATO members, they suggest, deliberately exaggerated external threats, particularly from Russia (Goldgeier, 1999). Followers of offensive realism disagreed with this assessment and proposed NATO's enlargement even further, to include Ukraine and Georgia. Yet even the most serious supporters of these actions had to backtrack when the prospect of such an enlargement produced tensions in the relationship with Russia and contributed to a Russian-Georgian war in 2008.

CRITICAL THINKING

Some realists argue that the alliance has outreached its boundaries and revealed its limitations. Do you think that U.S. plans to use NATO as an instrument for unipolar international order ran into serious problems? Does NATO have serious enemies today? On the other hand, new threats may arise. Should NATO exist just to protect its members from those threats? What should be NATO's policy toward a more assertive China and Russia?

countries' leaders acted like predators and wanted nothing less than a military victory. At the same time, at the end of the war urgent calls for international cooperation were now heard all over the world. U.S. President Woodrow Wilson, a former president of Princeton University, actively promoted cooperation among countries on the notion of free trade and equal respect. In 1917, with the United States entering the war, he began to tout a League of Nations—an international organization based on the principle of **collective security**—when an aggression against one, even a small country, would be a concern for all other countries. But such an organization would be only a first step: The major players must also change *internally*. Only the spread of liberal democracy could provide international stability, resolve conflicts, and reduce the likelihood of war. Wilson also hoped that one day European great powers would relinquish control over their colonies.

The League of Nations was formally established in 1919 at a peace conference in Paris. The League was the first global organization aimed at prevention, mediation, and peaceful resolution of interstate conflicts; support of the rights of ethnic minorities; disarmament; and economic cooperation. The League, however, soon met with many intractable problems. The U.S. Senate refused to support Wilson's internationalist policies, and the United States never joined the League. Also, the League failed to act on the principles of collective security because the great powers, Britain and France, were not ready to play the role of "global policemen." The League stood by impotently when various states violated the rights of ethnic minorities or committed aggressions against other states. Wilsonianism (Wilson's approach to international relations) was discredited above all in Germany, on which the punitive peace was imposed in 1919. Instead of being united, Europe became divided not only by the past war but also by new borders, visas, and protective trade tariffs. Finally, under the pressure of economic crises and nationalism, liberal democracy quickly failed in many European countries, giving way to authoritarian, militarist regimes (Shirer, 1990; Mazower, 2000).

Woodrow Wilson became the first American leader to promote the global ideology of liberal internationalism. He succeeded in creating the League of Nations but failed to win support for it in the United States. This photo shows Wilson on a speaking tour in St. Louis, Missouri, to promote the League in September 1919.

In the 1930s, Japan, Hitler's Germany, Mussolini's fascist Italy, and Stalin's Soviet Union brazenly defied the League. In August–September 1939, Hitler and Stalin attacked Poland and divided its territory between themselves. France and Britain declared war on Germany, the Second World War started, and the League became a political corpse. Many critics of the League, among them the British journalist and historian E. H. Carr ([1939] 1969), rejected the principles of liberal internationalism. They claimed that the future belongs to powerful states. Those who still believed in international cooperation watched in despair.

NEW BEGINNING FOR LIBERALISM

The news of liberalism's demise was premature. In 1941, the United States entered the Second World War under the reformed slogans of Wilsonianism: free trade, security cooperation, and equality among nations. President Franklin D. Roosevelt also entertained the idea that the United States, Great Britain, the Soviet Union, and China could play the role of regional "cops" as part of a new international organization, the United Nations. A council of the great powers would have special responsibilities to preserve peace. Roosevelt's successor as president, Harry S. Truman, was an ardent supporter of international liberalism.

Roosevelt revived the League under the name of the United Nations; this organization was founded in San Francisco in April 1945 (see Chapter 5). Permanent members of the UN Security Council included the United States, Great Britain, the Soviet Union, France, and China. (The idea of regional "cops" was quickly dropped because of growing Western mistrust of Stalin's Soviet Union.)

The economic strand of liberalism also flourished after World War II. In 1944 American and British politicians and economists launched the World Bank and IMF. (Attempts to create an International Trade Organization to promote free trade was not at first successful, as we will see in Chapter 6.) The later General Agreement on Tariffs and Trade (GATT) aimed to reduce or eliminate barriers to international trade. In 1947, the Marshall Plan, as we read, offered unprecedented financial help to a Europe devastated by war. From the 1950s through the 1980s, the World Bank, IMF, and GATT remained pillars of institutional liberalism. With substantial American assistance, Western European nations, including Germany, created institutions of cooperation that gradually evolved into the European Community, and, in the 1990s, the European Union.

You can learn more about the Marshall Plan from the Library of Congress website at www.loc.gov/exhibits/marshall/

During the Cold War it was becoming clear that foreign policy driven by mutual interests and common values could bring substantial benefits. In the 1950s and 1960s, free-market democracies enjoyed tremendous economic growth. The new realities of international organizations and European economic integration began to challenge the old realist agenda of power balance, deterrence, and containment.

LIBERAL UNILATERALISM AND MULTILATERALISM

Until the Second World War, the United States often practiced what the press and politicians called "isolationism." This did not mean, however, that

Washington wanted to remain completely detached from the rest of the world. Rather, it meant that U.S. statesmen wanted to keep a freedom of choice in the world dominated by other great powers, which practiced, as many believed, cynical realpolitik. In other words, the United States in the 1920s–1930s practiced **unilateralism**. Understandable as a reaction against complexities and problems in international relations, such liberal approaches did not help to preserve peace and contributed to favorable conditions for predator states, such as Japan and Germany.

Since the Second World War and during the Cold War, the United States adopted the approach of liberal **multilateralism**. This approach means that one state that abides by liberal principles seeks cooperation with other states that are ready to accept similar principles, in the name of common security and for solving international conflicts. This approach helped the United States to sustain a strong NATO and remain an effective leader of the Western bloc against the Soviet bloc. The international organizations can play, if not always, an important role in legitimizing the multilateral liberal policies. During the Gulf War of 1990–91, the United Nations passed a resolution that denounced the occupation of Kuwait by Iraqi leader Saddam Hussein. This gave international legitimacy to the United States to create a multinational coalition and then liberate Kuwait.

In contrast, in 2003, the United States occupied Iraq without the resolution of the United Nations and against the will of American allies, such as France and Germany. Critics of this occupation argued that this was an American return to liberal unilateralism, which threatened to split the Western alliance and complicated the task of conflict resolutions in the Middle East. We will return to unilateralism and multilateralism in Chapter 4. See **Table 2-2**.

Comparing Realism and Liberalism

What are the main points of comparison between the realist and liberal approaches? Table 2-3 summarizes these comparisons from three angles.

First, realism thinks about sovereign states, and liberalism relies more on international institutions. Many realist thinkers have gradually acknowledged the strength of IGOs and NGOs but believe that no international institution can change states' tendency to balance each other (Mearsheimer, 1994). For the liberal thinker, states continue to be major actors, but they become less

TABLE 2-2   Unilateralism and Multilateralism in the Context of the Liberal View of International Relations

Multilateralism. We as a country must cooperate with other countries in finding solutions to international challenges. We should act collectively and seek compromises. We also use military force for a liberal cause that other countries support.

Unilateralism. We act on the belief that the world is not ready for liberal principles, and other great powers practice cynical realpolitik. Therefore, we prefer to act alone in defense of liberal principles.

TABLE 2-3 Liberal and Realist Views of International Relations Compared

Issues	The Liberal Tradition	The Realist Tradition
International Actors	States are important but not the only actors in international affairs. International institutions and nonstate actors gain greater importance.	Sovereign states are the principal actors in international relations, yet the role of IGOs and NGOs can be acknowledged.
International Order	Security and stability are achieved through absolute gains by all participants of international order; through interdependence; and by good will, mutual trust, and compromise.	Order and stability are achieved through relative gains and by the power balancing among states and by mutual fear of a major war; this does not completely exclude compromises and cooperation.
Means of International Relations	Military force is used to restrain the aggressor and only after international diplomacy fails.	Military force or threat to use force are the most efficient means of power balancing.

significant with the growth of international institutions and nongovernment organizations.

Second, according to the realist views, a gain in power by one state is often a "zero-sum" game and represents an essential threat to other states. Therefore, states should watch each other's *relative* gains. Neorealists believe that states tend to maximize their security but not necessarily power; this necessitates compromises and cooperation (Schweller, 1997). Liberal institutionalism focuses on *absolute* gains in security, achieved through compromise and cooperation of states in building an international order. International organizations, open markets, and diplomacy should help to avoid a "zero-sum" game and maximize interests of all countries involved.

And third, realists believe that war cannot be eliminated and avoided because military force or the threats to use them are the most effective means of power balancing. Liberalism accepts the use of force for liberal goals but does not regard an interstate conflict as a necessary element of international order.

Both traditions, despite significant differences and disagreements between their followers, may seek and establish common ground related to international conflict, cooperation, and international organizations. On the following pages, you will see how realist and liberal principles are applied in specific international contexts.

▶ What were the main weaknesses of the League of Nations?
▶ Explain unilateralism and multilateralism from the liberal view.
▶ What are some similarities between realism and liberalism?

CHECK YOUR KNOWLEDGE

How Do We Apply It?

Applying Realism: Critical Evaluations

How successful was realism in interpreting international relations? What are the strengths and weaknesses of this approach? As we saw in Chapter 1, we need to examine the issue in three levels: the individual context, the state context, and the global context.

THE INDIVIDUAL CONTEXT

Hans Morgenthau ([1948] 2006), the classic theorist of realism, wrote about the role of morality, intuition, and emotion in the actions of state leaders, but the next generation of realists became less interested in the impact of individuals on power politics. To most of them, the course of international relations is shaped not so much by the personal choices of leaders but rather by the international structure. Leaders of states adapt to this structure and cannot act otherwise. Neorealists use the rational model to explain the actions of leaders and states alike.

This logic of realism, however, fails to explain the appearance of predator states and sudden threats to international order. If realists are correct, it did not matter that Hitler became chancellor of Germany in 1933. Germany, according to their logic, would have acted as a revisionist state anyway because it was not satisfied with its place in the international order. Many historians and political scientists, however, reach different conclusions. Without Hitler's aggressive ideas and without the Nazi Party, Germany would not have amassed formidable military power so quickly and could not have conquered most of Europe (Tetlock et al., 2006).

We have already seen that the lack of attention to the individual context left neorealists unprepared for the peaceful end of the Cold War. In response, defenders of neorealism argue that Gorbachev was an exception that proves the rule. The Soviet leader reacted to waning Soviet power by trying to keep the power balance by novel means, including disarmament and diplomacy. He made too many mistakes, however, and as a result, the Soviet Union disintegrated and Gorbachev himself lost power. Still, the end of the Cold War obliged policy-oriented realists to take a closer look at individual leaders. Following the work of Alexander George (1969), they began to accumulate case studies that take into account the individual choices of state leaders (Goldgeier and Tetlock, 2001).

One test of realist theories comes with the death of a state leader. Can the

Adolf Hitler before members of the German Reichstag in Berlin in September 1939, announcing that Germany was at war with Poland. Without Hitler's aggressive ideas and without the Nazi Party, Germany would not have amassed formidable military power so quickly and could not have started World War II.

DEBATE > INDIVIDUAL LEADERS AND THEIR FOREIGN POLICY

Does an assassination or the death of a country's leader change its foreign policy and international relations? As we see in Table 2-4, death may indeed signal a dramatic change. Yet in other cases there was no change, and the state continued with the same policies.

WHAT'S YOUR VIEW?

As a critical thinker (see again Chapter 1), to draw an educated conclu-sion about the impact of political assassination on policy you have to examine as much evidence as you can gather. Would other assassina-tions not listed in the table tell a dif-ferent story?

Moreover, a leader's death is just one event among many do-mestic and international factors that affect state policies. Most probably, a combination of these multiple factors sways foreign policy from its course or keeps it in place. Which specific factors would you consider?

@ Using the Web you can put together a more comprehensive database of state leaders' deaths and subsequent foreign policies. Follow the format as in Table 2-4. Study these cases and make your own conclusions.

---

loss of an individual produce important shifts in foreign policy? Some facts provide supportive evidence. When Franklin D. Roosevelt died in April 1945, and Harry Truman became a president, the United States began to act with less restraint toward the Soviet Union. The death of Egyptian President Gamal Abdel Nasser in 1970 brought to power Anwar Sadat, who abandoned the radi-cal politics of his predecessor, restored Egypt's diplomatic relations with Israel, and brought Egypt closer to the United States.

THE STATE CONTEXT

While insisting on the importance of economic and military policies, realists in the past were often reluctant to consider other domestic political factors. Realists generally believed that states, democratic or not, tend to disregard ideological and political differences with other states if it suits their security interests. For years, despite its consistent claim of support for freedom and democracy, the United States supported a wide range of dictatorships and non-democratic regimes in Latin America, Africa, and Asia.

Robert Putnam (1988) argues that foreign policy is conducted on at least two levels: the domestic and the international. At home, domestic groups pursue their interests by pressuring the government to adopt favorable poli-cies. Politicians respond to those groups' pressures. At the international level, governments play a balancing act between domestic interest groups and foreign-policy goals. Leaders of sovereign states have to act simultaneously on both levels, like a game played on two chessboards. That is why this model is called **two-level game theory.**

Domestic lobbies and social movements play a significant role in foreign policy of democratic states. Interest groups could be representatives of the mili-tary, corporations seeking defense contracts, the national security elite, for-eign-policy experts, or lobbying groups (Wittkopf & McCormick, 2004). In peacetime, and in the absence of immediate foreign threats, democratic states

TABLE 2-4 Foreign Policy Consequences of a Leader's Death

Leader's Death	Consequences for Foreign Policy and Power Balance
Joseph Stalin, Soviet Leader Date: 03/05/1953	Stalin's death led to the crises in Eastern Europe and later produced the Sino-Soviet rivalry; these events resulted in a perceived dramatic shift in power between East and West.
John Kennedy, President of the United States. Date: 11/22/1963	There were no significant changes in U.S. foreign policy; no changes in the power balance between the United States and the Soviet Union took place. Kennedy's successor, Lyndon Johnson, continued and escalated the Vietnam War started by Kennedy.
Gamal Abdel Nasser, President of Egypt Date: 09/28/1970	Under President Sadat, Nasser's successor, an important policy shift followed; he signed a peace treaty between Egypt and Israel and brought Egypt closer to the United States.
Anwar Sadat, President of Egypt Date: 10/6/1981	Sadat was assassinated for his reconciliatory polices with Israel. There was no significant change in Egypt's foreign policy. Egypt under Sadat's successor, President Mubarak, relied on the United States and kept peace with Israel.
Indira Gandhi, Prime Minister of India Date: 10/31/1984	Gandhi was assassinated by her Sikh bodyguards. Her son Rajiv succeeded her. He continued the foreign course of nonalignment but was leaning toward the Soviet Union.
Yitzhak Rabin, Prime Minister of Israel Date: 11/04/1995	Rabin was assassinated by a Jewish fundamentalist who attempted to torpedo the peace negotiations with the Palestinians. Israel, however, continued peace talks; they failed later for different reasons.
Lech Kaczyński, President of Poland Date: 04/10/2010	After Kaczyński died in a plane crash in Russia, his successor Donald Tusk abandoned harsh anti-German and anti-Russian rhetoric. Poland remains firmly tied to NATO.
Muammar Qaddafi, President of Libya Date: 10/20/2011	Antigovernment fighters killed Qaddafi. Libyan insurgency received substantial Western military aid. The future of a new Libya remains uncertain.
Kim Jong-il, Supreme Leader of North Korea Date: 12/17/2011	After the sudden death of Kim Jong-il, his young son Kim Jong-un succeeded him. The North Korean regime shows no immediate signs of change in domestic and foreign policy.

find it more difficult to conduct power politics. Any initiative in international relations requires **bureaucratic bargaining**—compromises with bureaucracies and lobbies, which often pursue different agendas (Marrar, 2008). A ruling political party, for example, may make concessions to the opposition party on domestic policy in exchange for support on foreign policy—a process known as **log rolling** (Laver, 1979, 1997). During the early stages of the Cold War, many U.S. congressmen and senators supported the containment of Communist threats, but only if new military bases would go to their constituents. These bases created jobs, brought additional revenues, and satisfied many voters.

Defensive realists acknowledge the importance of domestic political factors. Historically, governments initiate military conflicts under pressure from domestic political forces, which often do not foresee the negative international repercussions of their actions (Van Evera, 2001). For decades, Israeli and Palestinian politicians have failed to reach a permanent peace treaty or to agree on the creation of Palestine as an independent state. And one of the most significant reasons was domestic politics. After the Oslo Accords of 1993 and 1995, the United States and the world community pushed both sides to the negotiating table. In Israel, however, supporters of the political right, especially settlers in the occupied territories, resisted the very idea of Palestinian sovereignty. In 1995, a Jewish settler assassinated Israeli Prime Minister Yitzhak Rabin as retribution for his conciliatory polices toward the Palestinians.

In sum, domestic political factors play a serious role in foreign policy and international relations, and supporters of realism increasingly take it into account.

THE GLOBAL CONTEXT

The realist view of international relations had its greatest influence during the Cold War. Supporters of realpolitik then brought up the entire experience of world history, from ancient Greece to European nation-states, to argue that preponderant power and containment of the Soviet Union was the best strategy to pursue. Yet now the Cold War is long over. How well does the realist view of international relations explain the complexity of today's world?

Neorealists today remain skeptical regarding liberal claims of "global community" and "global governance" based on cooperation values. Instead, realists generally remain convinced that countries will pay attention to their security and are unlikely to maintain peaceful and mutually profitable co-operation without a consolidating force to keep global and regional developments in check (Betts, 2011). Neorealists also argue that the end of a bipolar world could bring more rather than less instability, particularly on a regional level. Some regional balances are likely to show clear signs of strain. Most recent developments validate realist concerns. For instance, the runaway growth of China's regional power in the twenty-first century may generate tensions in Sino-Japanese, Sino-Indian, and Sino-American relations. Japan and India, China's old-time regional rivals oppose any rapid and forceful shifts in the balance of power in China's favor. India has moved to balance China off by strengthening its ties with America. Russia for the last ten years regarded China as a useful balance against the superior American power. In turn, China began to fend off the growing challenges to its power in the region by building closer ties with Russia and Pakistan (Pant, 2011).

As neorealists believe, power politics is not obsolete, and the time for power balancing has not passed. The traditional problem of domination in the international system did not disappear. The debate continues among neorealists how the United States can play a dominant role in world affairs (Booth & Wheeler, 2007). At the same time, most neorealists recently became advocates of nuclear disarmament. They particularly favor the elimination of small, tactical types of nuclear weapons. They point out that proliferation of such weapons as nukes is extremely dangerous, especially if it involves failing states and terrorist groups.

CHECK YOUR KNOWLEDGE

▶ Explain log rolling as a feature of bureaucratic bargaining.
▶ Why do neorealists remain skeptical regarding liberal claims of "global community"?
▶ Why do neorealists favor nuclear disarmament?

Applying Liberalism: Critical Evaluations

How well have liberal ideas stood the test of reality? We will now examine liberal assumptions in light of decisions by individual leaders, state policies, and the global context.

THE INDIVIDUAL CONTEXT

The liberal approach, like the realist one, is based on the rational model. In an attention-grabbing piece published in *Foreign Affairs*, biologist Robert Sapolsky argued using biological and anthropological evidence that humans are not naturally aggressive. Human choices are the product of rational calculation and social context. Rational choices by state leaders should therefore help avoid violence (Sapolsky, 2006).

If people are by their nature inclined to peace, why do counties so often engage in conflicts and wars? One answer is the weaknesses and strengths of individual state leaders as they struggle with domestic politics and domestic groups of interests. Weak political leaders, as liberals argue, often yield to domestic pressures and choose war. In July 1914, German Kaiser Wilhelm II and Russian Czar Nicholas II became hostages of their own plans for war, and military mobilization became their only option. Both empires suffered defeat and collapse. In the 1930s another weak leader, Emperor Hirohito, succumbed to pressures from Japanese generals and admirals who saw a historic opportunity to build an empire that would dominate the Far East. The Japanese army first occupied Manchuria, then invaded southern China, and at last the Japanese navy attacked the United States and Great Britain in the Pacific. After four more years of barbaric war, the Japanese Empire surrendered.

German Chancellor Willy Brandt kneels before the monument to the Jews killed by the Nazis during the uprising in the Warsaw Ghetto in Poland. Brandt fought against the Nazis during World War II. Democratic and liberal Germany spent considerable resources to atone for the war crimes of the Third Reich and to build better relations with its eastern neighbors.

The implementation of liberal principles in international relations requires political strength and courage. President Woodrow Wilson failed to convince the opposition at home when he pushed for U.S. participation in the League of Nations. Franklin Roosevelt was more strong and skillful and succeeded in establishing the United Nations and other pillars of institutional liberalism. In West Germany in the 1970s (when Germany was divided into West and East), Chancellor Willy Brandt (1913–1992) pushed for engagement and collaboration with European Communist states, believing that cooperation would work better than conflict. The peaceful end of the Cold War vindicated him and his choices.

In sum, supporters of liberalism believe that it takes courage and wisdom to make rational decisions in the spirit of cooperation and engagement. Liberal principles remain only wishes unless they pass the test of domestic politics.

THE STATE CONTEXT

Domestic politics strongly influence foreign policy. Political outcomes in turn depend on the type of government, the nature of policy institutions, the frequency of elections, and the design and ownership of the media. All these affect state leaders' international priorities.

Consider again democratic peace theory, introduced earlier in this chapter. It assumes that democratic states are unlikely to engage in war against one another (Christison, 2002; Jervis, 2002). However, Jack Snyder and Edward Mansfield looked at countries that are not fully democratic but only *in transition* to democracy. These countries might actually be *more* prone to war compared to stable but authoritarian regimes. Why? Democracy allows political

CASE IN POINT > *U.S. Public Opinion and the Use of Force Abroad*

Despite substantial reservations in principle to the use of force abroad, most Americans support short-term military action with limited casualties. From the 1990s to 2003, engagements in Kuwait, Kosovo, Afghanistan, and Iraq all had substantial public support—at least at the beginning (see Table 2-6). Conversely, with declining public support, military interventions have been scaled back in Korea, Vietnam, and more recently in Iraq. No open military interventions have begun when public support was weak, as in Angola and Ethiopia.

During the crisis in Darfur (Sudan), despite most Americans' support for some military engagement, there was no direct U.S. military action in that region. According to the 2007 poll by CNN/ORC, most Americans supported their country's military involvement to stop the massive loss of life in the Darfur conflict. Yet the Bush administration ruled out military action there.

CRITICAL THINKING

If you were president then, what reasons would you give for your noninvolvement? Consider other conflicts the United States was involved in at that time, the schedule of presidential elections in the United States, and the nature of the conflict in Darfur. What is the situation in Darfur today? Why do you think both Republican and Democratic contenders for Presidency in the 2012 elections did not insist on sending U.S. troops to Syria to stop a civil war there?

groups to compete openly. If democratic institutions are immature and unstable, some of these groups may use nationalist, populist, and demagogic slogans and agendas to devastating effect (Mansfield and Snyder, 1995; Snyder, 2000). In the Middle East and Central Asia, efforts to replace autocracies with democratic institutions can generate instability and war (Gause, 2005). In Pakistan's history, some periods of democratic rule were followed by long periods of military dictatorship. It is unclear, however, which governments of Pakistan—authoritarian or democratic—were less confrontational against India.

Democratic peace theory has other limitations. War often finds support of public opinion in democratic countries (Chan, 1997). Perhaps democracies in the recent past have had other reasons for not going to war against each other (Layne, 1994). For instance, the Soviet Union provided a common enemy, and the United States was the overwhelmingly strongest democratic state, discouraging the United Kingdom and France to challenge it. Therefore, it was an easy choice for the Western powers to form the U.S.-led military and political bloc against the Soviet Union. This allowed them to resolve their differences peacefully.

Consider now another issue—public support for foreign policy. Realists give public opinion a limited role: Realpolitik is not supposed to be bound by public opinion. On the contrary, the strong liberal internationalist policy may depend on public support (Kagan, 2004a). The U.S. policy of containment, with its strong liberal multilateral component, worked as long as it enjoyed wide public backing and agreement between the Republican and the Democratic parties (Nacos et al., 2000). Since the war in Vietnam, the White House could not always enjoy such support and agreement. After the end of the Cold War, the Clinton administration briefly tried to engage American troops in Africa, but quickly withdrew from Somalia in October 1993 after guerillas downed

TABLE 2-5 The Impact of Public Opinion on Foreign Policy

The impact of public opinion on foreign policy is likely to increase if:

1. A national election is scheduled in the near future and opposition is strong: Incumbent officials need public support for reelection.
2. Support or opposition to a certain foreign–policy-related issue is overwhelming and consistent: Officials may argue that they have a "mandate."
3. Majority opinion agrees with decision makers: Officials are likely to use polls as justification for their action or inaction.

The impact of public opinion on foreign policy is likely to weaken if:

1. No national election is scheduled in the near future and the political opposition is relatively weak.
2. Support or opposition is weak or inconsistent: Officials may argue that the public is uncertain or divided.
3. Majority opinion disagrees with decision makers: Officials are likely to ignore or downplay the polls.

Sources: Rosenau, 1961; Holsti, 1992; Sobel and Shiraev, 2003; Yankelovich, 2005.

TABLE 2-6 Public Opinion and U.S. Use of Force Abroad

Event	Polls	General Approval (Percent)	General Disapproval (Percent)	Outcome
The war against Japan 1941	December 1941; NORC, Personal, 1,283	82	12	War
The Korean War 1950	December 1950; NORC, Personal, 1,252	55	36	War
The Korean War 1953	June 1953; NORC, Personal, 1,285	38	51	End of the war
The Vietnam War 1967	August 1967; Gallup, 1,525	60	32	War
The Vietnam War 1972	June 1972; Gallup, 1,535	35	64	End of the war
Military involvement in Angola, 1976	January 1976; Yankelovich, Skelly, & White, 951	21	59	No ground troops
Military actions in Ethiopia, 1978	April 1978; Harris, 1,529	13	71	No ground troops
Military intervention in Grenada, 1983	October 1983; ABS/WP, 1,505	71	22	Occupation
Invasion and arrest of president of Panama, 1990	January 1990; HTRC, 1,510	72	18	Invasion
Military involvement in Rwanda in 1994	June 1994; CBS, 978	28	61	Non-involvement
Air strikes against Yugoslavia, 1999 (U.S. and NATO)	April 1999; CBS, 878	59	29	Strikes
Military actions against terrorist groups in Afghanistan, 2001	October 2001; Gallup, 2,042	89	5	War
Military actions against Iraq, Spring 2003	Various polls, spring 2003	60–70	20–25	War
Participation in an international military action in Darfur 2007	CNN/ORC poll, October 2007	61	32	No U.S. direct military action
Military Actions against Libya, Spring 2011	Gallup, March 27, 2011	47	37	Strikes

Abbreviations: NORC: NATIONAL OPINION RESEARCH CENTER; HTRC: Hart-Teeter Research Companies.

Source: Shiraev and Sobel, 2006.

two Black Hawk helicopters and images of a dead U.S. soldier appeared in the media. Clinton feared that losing American lives in liberal interventions might easily cost him reelection in 1996.

In summary, although public opinion does not necessarily direct foreign policy, it can constrain it. (See Tables 2-5 and 2-6.)

Leaders can shape public opinion to an extent only. The **policy climate** is the prevailing sentiment among policy makers and other influential individuals. It includes beliefs about what the government, international organizations, and nongovernment groups should do on the international level—particularly faced with international conflict or security threats. Opinion leaders air their views in public debates, speeches, policy statements, televised interviews, printed publications, and the Internet (Sobel, 2001; Page and Shapiro, 1988). The principles of liberal internationalism may prevail within a favorable policy climate. Effective policies of liberal internationalism depend on maturity of government, public opinion, and the policy climate.

THE GLOBAL CONTEXT

Globalization, or the growing interdependence of countries and their economies, brings not only opportunities, but also new challenges for liberal approaches to international relations. Economic liberalism must find better answers to how to face a growing threat of instability of global financial markets: A financial panic among banks and their patrons may lead to a flight of capital from one or many states—this results in disappearance of billions of dollars, the end of investments, the unfinished constructions, and massive unemployment. Only big countries or countries with great financial resources can resist volatility of financial markets. Among them are the United States, the European Union, China, Germany, and a few others.

An antiglobalization activist protests against the construction of a Walmart megastore in Mejicanos, El Salvador, in 2012.

Institutional liberals supported NATO and EU enlargement in the 1990s. They continued their support when both institutions experienced difficulties in the past several years. Still, they have to prove that global governance would work, say in the absence of the American leadership. After all, until the U.S. intervention, the European Union could not stop a genocidal war in Yugoslavia in the 1990s. And what would NATO do with a regime such as the Taliban if it comes back to power in Afghanistan?

Optimists remain undaunted. From their point of view, the world's interdependence diminishes the ability of powerful states to act unilaterally, which reduces the chance of military conflict. Globalization stands for interconnectedness and, therefore, for multiple interests. The complexity of and urgency of global problems may also support liberal ideas. International projects in the twenty-first century increasingly require the shared economic and financial resources of many states. Even the United States, the biggest economic and military power today, cannot police the world. The role of international and nongovernment organizations will increase simply because there are no alternatives.

As we have seen, democratic peace theory still has to be tested on a global scale. In today's world, states that try to borrow from Western democracy often fail in the face of corrupt bureaucracies; inertia; fierce opposition; and political, ethnic, and religious violence. Russia, Ukraine, Colombia, Pakistan, and many other countries have all had difficulty building democratic institutions. Sadly, weak democratic states may have to resort to violence internally and externally. Does this mean that illiberal non-democratic regimes, such as in Singapore and China, are better partners for international relations than Pakistan where democracy is weak? Does it mean that the democratizing Egypt is a less reliable partner for regional stability than the Egypt of military dictatorship?

The next decades may provide some answers. Robert Keohane, at Princeton University, believes that most important remedies to domestic conflicts and violence are land reform, environmental cleanup, better education, and health care. These policies can best promote stability and prosperity. The military will still have a role to play. However, international organizations, economic support, and international cooperation can strengthen civilian public sectors and address ethnic and social problems (Keohane, 2005). Although very few would probably argue against better education and health care, a key challenge is to find sufficient resources to accomplish these ambitious projects.

Some ideas of liberal internationalism may sound quite revolutionary. Gidon Gottlieb in 1994 offered an idea of "states plus nations": Ethnic groups should receive the special legal and political status of a nation. A world of traditional states, in his view, would evolve into a system of many nations, not necessarily with physical borders. Citizenship in a nation could be granted to people living in separate states, such as people of Chinese descent in Europe, Asia, and America. They would still pay taxes and serve in the military where they live. However, nationality would be matter of cultural heritage, not the "motherland," and territorial conflicts would decrease. Massive migrations in the twenty-first century should put Gottlieb's proposal to the test.

@ Look up these abbreviations: G-3, G-5, G-7, G-8, G-10, G-20, and G-77. What do they represent, and what functions do they serve? How many still exist today? Are there any new groups with similar aims?

CHECK YOUR KNOWLEDGE

▶ Leaders applying principles of liberalism in foreign policy frequently face strong domestic opposition. Why?

▶ How do public opinion and the policy climate affect foreign policy?

Past, Present, and Future: The European Union

The EU seems to represent the greatest triumph of liberal institutionalism. But it is not a good time to celebrate. The financial crisis that began in 2008 revealed major problems in the EU design, which lacked functionality under economic strain. The acute financial problems in Greece, Italy, Ireland, and Portugal sharpened the discussion of the future of the European Union. There is a powerful argument that a single European currency makes any effective responses to economic or financial crises more difficult to implement. The future of the European Union depends on collective action to resolve these financial and economic problems. In 2010–12, member states created the European Financial Stability Facility to preserve financial stability of the union and agreed on serious financial measures to avoid a deep crisis. They obliged the governments of Greece, Spain, and Italy to take serious austerity measures to reduce their national debt. The search for coordinated policies continues. (We return to the international economy in Chapter 6.)

Let's compare the arguments of liberal institutionalism and its critics:

• **Integration or protectionism?** The European Union was created to defend four economic freedoms: the free flow of capital, labor, products, and services. Supporters of early unification argued that integration in one functional area

The debates about the direction of EU policies have energized many, including musicians. In Estonia in 2013, musicians rehearse a new operetta titled "Nostra Culpa" (Latin for "Our Fault"), inspired by a social media feud between Estonian President Toomas Hendrik Ilves and Nobel Prize-winning American economist Paul Krugman over austerity policies.

would almost necessarily lead to integration in others (Haas, 1958). European states managed to combine economic growth with generous support of social programs. Governments invested heavily in education, health care, employment, and the environment. Europe seemed to be a continent characterized by long-lasting peace and stability. To many, the liberal ideas have shown their effectiveness.

Critics today point out instead that the crisis is pushing European states back to protectionism. History shows that sovereign states tend to protect their own economies against cheap foreign products, services, and labor. Today, Greece, Italy, and Spain suffer very high unemployment among their young populations, and free labor migration in the EU contributes. An influx of young workers from Eastern Europe—particularly Poland, from the Middle East, Africa, and other parts of the world—has led to growing opposition to immigration. Freedom of labor movement created strong resistance from the labor unions in France and Italy. Recently a number of European countries began to cut their spending on education and other social programs. Critics also argue that Germany, the most successful economy of the EU, became like a "dictator" promoting free-market rules and neglecting unemployment and social protection.

- **Euro-bureaucracy or national decision-making?** Liberal supporters of the Union insist that the progressive decline of sovereignty of European states was a good thing. It makes rivalries and wars in Europe impossible. There is no way back, liberals argue—only forward—to a more efficient Europe, capable of dealing with financial and social problems of all its member states. The Union, supporters suggest, should further expand the mechanisms of "collective rule" in Brussels: work on criminal law, taxation, and standards in social policy—including unemployment benefits, pension plans, funding for education, and a few more issues. The Union should also have a central office in charge of EU foreign affairs and a small but viable military force.

Critics disagree. They believe that further erosion of state sovereignty is harmful because it transfers sovereignty to bureaucrats in the central government and further away from voters. Local authorities and communities can no longer decide what is right for *them*. Critics in particular focus on the sprawling Euro-bureaucracy. There are too many offices, institutions, rules, and regulations in Brussels. Still other critics think that new institutions are actually useless because they cannot substitute for sovereign states. Take, for example, the EU office of foreign affairs. Will it have real power to make decisions or become a new expensive institution? Many argue that all attempts to create a European military are impractical.

Opponents also predict that if the financial crisis continues or reemerges, Europe would be essentially split between successful states, such as Germany, and the states in debt, mostly in the southern part of the continent. They say that future battles in Europe will be about nationalist ideas and national identity.

- **Is the European "project" in decline, or is it in transition?**

Some observers warned that populist, nationalist regimes would take over in much of Europe and thus weaken democracy (Zizek, 2009). They may also

@ For more information about the European Union, opinion polls of EU countries, and Pew Global Surveys, visit the companion website at www.oup.com/us/shiraev.

weaken the transnational sense of belonging to Europe rather than to specific territories and countries. *Eurobarometer,* a regular series of surveys in the EU countries, show a steady decline in popular support for membership in the Union. Nationalist politicians argue that European states should take back their sovereignty to deal with unemployment and boost social programs.

Liberals stick to their principles. They are confident that the European project will be successful. It has survived difficulties in the past. Liberals also argue that a common "European identity" is widely shared by young and successful professional classes, and it is crucial for the future of the European project. The debates continue. Please join them.

CONCLUSION

Even a brief description of rival approaches to international relations reveals that none of them provide all answers for all cases. During the Cold War the realist view was predominant. Power and the reactions of states to international anarchy were seen as vital to explaining the world's security. Ruling elites, watching the changing balance of power, saw realism as the only way to keep international order intact. The lessons of World War II backed realist arguments. If great powers had acted earlier to stop Nazism and Fascism, the argument goes, 70 million people would not have perished.

Yet even while the Cold War lasted, realism failed to take too many new factors and developments into account. The peaceful and sudden collapse of the Soviet Union left realists with a complex and often puzzling world. The United States was now the only great power and yet failed to create a stable international order. It is not even clear if the United States can remain the world's leader for long. What kind of realist policies will the future see?

Twenty years ago, the baton of leadership passed to the liberal approaches. In the liberal tradition, state preferences, not state power, should define international relations. Countries, like humans, are capable of self-restraint and cooperation. Long-term moral purposes and values are more important in international relations than power-driven calculations. War and conflicts can be contained through diplomacy, economic interdependence, cultural exchanges, and transnational institutions. Contrary to realpolitik, supporters of the liberal tradition emphasize the growing importance of NGOs and IGOs in forming foreign policy. Yet most recently the optimistic judgments of liberals, based on the rational model, ran into unexpected challenges. The trends toward economic integration, free trade, and financial integration reduced the state willingness to fight each other. Yet, the same trends laid foundations for global financial shocks that took the states and the international institutions by surprise. If liberal norms and institutions are to become the core of the international order, what should we do with the problem of international terrorism? And would the European Union, the most successful case of liberal internationalism, be able to act rationally and coherently?

It is unlikely that the field of international relations will be dominated by only two approaches. In the following chapter we turn to a variety of approaches that in many ways challenge realism and liberalism. The study of international relations appears to be an "orchestra" with a growing number of players and instruments. Each and every person adds to the complexity of the music, each new approach or theory can add to our understanding of the world's complexity. But what makes different instruments produce great music instead of a noisy cacophony? Like a musician learning musical theory to understand music, a student of international relations should master all these approaches.

CHAPTER SUMMARY

- Realism is a school of international relations that focuses on security and state interests.
- States are main actors in international relations. International relations in the context of realism appear as a constant balancing of power in which states try to make sure that others do not become significantly stronger, thus violating an established balance of power. States try to avoid anarchy—the absence of any authority above the states, the agency that can control the states from above. The emphasis on international structure is a hallmark of so-called neorealism.
- States constantly gain or lose power, affecting the international order. According to the realist approach, the design of the international order is determined by the distribution of power among states. We study three types of power distribution: unipolar, bipolar, and multipolar.
- Great powers emerge by spreading their influence far beyond their borders to establish an international order favorable to their interests. They do it above all with the help of superior military power. But other forms of power, especially diplomacy and the ability to achieve balance, can be crucial. Actions based on considerations of power are often labeled power politics or realpolitik. A state's geographic location, history, ideology, political regime, or economic conditions can affect its power politics.
- Liberalism is based on three interconnected principles: (1) the rejection of power politics as the source and outcome of international relations, (2) an emphasis on international cooperation and mutual benefits, and (3) the importance of international organizations and nonstate actors in shaping state preferences and policy. The premises of liberalism include the power of diplomacy, democratic peace theory, and "soft power." Liberalism promotes the idea that states can solve problems by acting together. To achieve this outcome, states need effective cooperation that cannot be achieved without international institutions.
- In an ideal world, say supporters of liberalism, an increasing number of leaders will find the courage and wisdom to conduct policies in the spirit of cooperation and engagement. Cooperation, in turn, will reduce confrontation. However, liberal principles must be tested in action.

KEY TERMS

Anarchy 42
Bipolar order 43
Bureaucratic bargaining 64
Cold War (1946–1989) 43
Complex Interdependence 48
Democratic peace theory 51
Diplomacy 49
Global governance 49
Gross domestic product
  (GDP) 41

Hegemony 42
Imperial overreach 42
Intergovernmental
  organization (IGO) 48
International order 42
Liberal institutionalism 49
Liberalism 46
Log rolling 64
Multilateralism 60
Multipolar order 43

Neoliberalism 48
Power 41
Realism 41
Realpolitik 44
Revisionist (predator) state 42
Soft power 52
Status quo state 42
Two-level game theory 63
Unipolar order 43

Visual Review REALISM AND LIBERALISM

1. What do we study?

CHARACTERISTICS OF REALISM

- States are the main actors in international relations
- States focus on power, security, and national interests
- States try to avoid anarchy
- Neorealism emphasizes power structure and order

CHARACTERISTICS OF LIBERALISM

- Rejection of zero-sum power politics, emphasis on international cooperation, and emphasis on international organizations and nonstate actors
- Neoliberalism: State interests are realized in the context of interdependence among states
- Liberal Institutionalism: International order cannot be achieved without international institutions

2. How do we think about it?

LESSONS OF REALPOLITIK

- States need a strong economy, the military, efficient diplomacy, and few international commitments
- Rapid power shifts threaten stability
- Wars are likely yet avoidable

EXAMINING LIBERAL POLICIES

- Peace and disarmament conferences
- Wilsonianism and the League of Nations
- The Marshall Plan
- The United Nations
- Multilateralism

COMPARING REALISM AND LIBERALISM

- Both views can be compared in terms of international actors, order, and the means of international relations
- Despite many differences, neoliberalism and neorealism share common views on a range of issues

3. How do we apply it?

THE INDIVIDUAL CONTEXT

- Individual factors may play a role in power politics, but realists tend to overlook them
- Liberals show that the choices of political leaders affect outcomes of war and peace

THE STATE CONTEXT

- States' foreign policy is formed on two levels: the domestic and the international
- Domestic forces affect foreign policies of democratic and non-democratic states

THE GLOBAL CONTEXT

- Realists argue in favor of a consolidating force to keep global developments in check
- Liberals argue that mutual interests in the era of globalizations should affect choices and political outcomes in international politics

Critical Thinking

- How did principles of realism evolve over time? What are the similarities and differences between realism and neorealism?
- Why is realpolitik considered a key application of realism?
- Why do realists associate bipolarity with international stability?
- How does realism explain individual foreign policy decisions, specific foreign policies of states, and particular global developments? Give examples.
- How does liberalism argue against the principles of power politics?
- What are the differences among the various approaches and traditions within liberalism? Give examples.
- How does liberalism explain individual foreign-policy decisions, specific foreign policies of states, and particular global developments? Give examples.

CHAPTER

3

Local residents gather outside the house where Al-Qaeda leader Osama bin Laden was caught and killed in May 2011, in Abbottabad, Pakistan. Ten years earlier, the Taliban government in Afghanistan refused to turn Bin Laden over to the United States. This decision contributed to a long war.

Alternative Views

I don't carry any early childhood trauma around with me, if that's what you're hinting at. The story of the bicycles—and there were three of them which were stolen from me—I've dealt with it well.
—GERMAN CHANCELLOR ANGELA MERKEL, ON WHETHER HER CHILDHOOD EXPERIENCES AFFECT HER POLICIES

AFTER SEPTEMBER 11, 2001, THE TALIBAN—AN ISLAMIC MOVEMENT THEN IN POWER IN AFGHANISTAN—REFUSED TO GIVE AWAY OSAMA BIN LADEN, THE MASTERMIND OF that day's devastating attacks. In response, the United States and its allies threatened war. Had the Taliban leaders used strategic calculations and acted as realists, they would have realized that they could not possibly withstand the U.S. military. The balance of power was simply not on their side. Yet the Taliban rulers chose neither course. Rather, against enormous odds, they chose resistance.

In 2003, President Saddam Hussein of Iraq refused to cooperate with the United Nations, which accused Iraq of hiding weapons of mass destruction. Why did he continue to resist when, in fact, he did not have such weapons? Had he forgotten how in 1990, massive U.S.-led force defeated the Iraqi army and threw it out of Kuwait? Instead, he remained defiant and witnessed the fall of his regime.

As you can see, the Taliban leaders and the Iraqi dictator chose neither realpolitik nor cooperation with the international community. What motivated their decisions? Neither realism nor liberalism can answer this question. This chapter will explore alternative approaches that go beyond realism and liberalism in explaining international cooperation, conflicts, and wars. We will explore how identities, perceptions, social norms, conflicting economic interests, gender and race, and psychological factors shape the behavior of leaders and states.

Learning
Objectives

After reading this chapter, you should be able to:

▶ describe the shortcomings of realism and liberalism and the necessity of other interpretations of world politics;

▶ explain alternative views to international relations, including constructivism, conflict theories, feminism, identity formation, and political psychology;

▶ give examples of how perceptions, conflicts, inequality, social norms, gender, race, political culture, nationalism, and psychological factors shape international relations; and

▶ apply the knowledge to interpret international behavior of leaders, states, and international organizations

What Do We Study?

Realism assumes that states act to protect their interests and maximize power in their reaction to international anarchy. Liberalism emphasizes cooperation through mutual interests, international trade, and international and nongovernment organizations. Yet neither necessarily explains *how* states define their interests and *why* nongovernment organizations choose *cooperation*. Both realists and liberals argue that states and organizations tend to make rational choices. But in reality many decisions are made by individuals based on ideology, greed, honor, deep-seated beliefs, and misperceptions. This chapter presents approaches to international relations that try to address these issues:

- *Constructivism*, a fresh and influential approach, argues that states develop their interests and notions of security according to diverse social norms and historic experiences.
- *Conflict theories* focus instead on inequality as a defining factor in international relations. For example, it may be economic inequality, explored by Marxist theories, or it may be race and gender inequality, explored by postcolonial and feminist theories.
- Another approach, close to constructivism, focuses on *identities*, or the ways people and institutions perceive themselves and others.
- Finally, *political psychology* focuses on decision makers and how they react to international change, opportunities, and crises according to their experiences, emotions, biases, and misperceptions.

How Do We Think About It?

If you saw two little boys fighting, whose side would you take? You may choose not to get involved, of course, assuming that breaking up a fight is not your business. But as a responsible adult, you may intervene. But why? Which boy would you help first? Your decision, obviously, depends on many circumstances. So do the decisions and actions of states and organizations.

The Constructivist View

Canada and Cuba are neighbors of the United States. Yet one is an American partner and friend, and another was for many years an adversary. Obviously, the Cuban and the United States' governments viewed the entire international order differently (Reus-Smit, 2009). Advocates of the **constructivist** view (or **constructivism**) believe that states' actions and policies are based on how leaders, bureaucracies, and societies interpret or *construct* the information available to them. Constructivism posits that *power, anarchy,* and *security* are not just abstract categories. Rather, they have different meanings for different states (Wendt, 1992). A serious threat for one state may not be an issue for another. Like individuals, societies can exaggerate external threats or overlook them (Buzan and Hansen, 2009). As when you step in to break up a fight, countries act based on their ideas of what is fair or unfair in international relations. If two countries agree on what is fair, they are more prone to cooperate.

States, of course, pursue their vital interests. Realists, as you will remember, assume that these interests always push states to react to anarchy by building up their power. Liberals insist, on the contrary, that interests in peaceful trade push states to cooperate. Constructivists raise a critical question: *Where do state interests come from?* Who defines which interests are to be respected as vital, legitimate, and essential—and which can be disregarded? To answer, constructivists emphasize the importance of social norms, perceptions, and rules in defining state interests (Wendt, 1999; Checkel, 1998). (See Figure 3.1.) They argue that state leaders learn from past errors and accomplishments (Hudson, 1999; Hemmer, 1999).

Be careful, however! Constructivism does not say that beliefs, perceptions, and lessons just spring from the imagination. Rather, they are *collective* perceptions, shared by powerful societal groups. A good example of such perception is a question, constantly discussed in the United States: "What is our country's mission?"

SOCIALLY CONSTRUCTED MEANINGS

Socially constructed meanings have governed political decisions from ancient times. In the 5th century BC, Thucydides (2003) described how fear and honor, in addition to self-interest, provoked Greek cities to go to war. Constructivists would agree with much of what Thucydides wrote. Fear, of course, is a major factor in realism as well, for instance, fear of international anarchy. Yet the realist approach does not explain why a state's military power evokes intense fear of neighbors in one situation but not in another. For instance, Russia today has

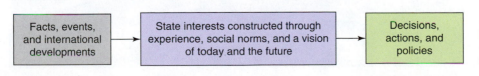

FIGURE 3-1 The constructivist approach to international relations.

a much greater nuclear arsenal than the Soviet Union's during the 1950s. Yet the United States no longer fears that Russia would attack them, as they had feared the Soviet Union would.

Fear can shape international interactions and state interests for a long time. The sudden Japanese attack against the United States in 1941 transformed American foreign policy for decades. After Pearl Harbor, Washington sought to maintain a position of absolute military superiority and often acted preemptively if it perceived a security threat from abroad. The September 11, 2001, attacks seemed to validate old fears of foreign attacks on American soil. Did Washington overreact as a result?

From the viewpoint of constructivism, Thucydides' "honor" is also a social category that shapes international behavior. It is a state's search for respect, international credibility, prestige, and reputation. "Honor" can also take a pervert expression. Saddam Hussein in 2003 challenged the United Nations and the United States because he was afraid that concessions would reveal his weakness. Hussein also wanted to maintain his image in the Arab world of an uncompromising fighter against Western powers (Primakov, 2009). As Thucydides might have argued, Hussein's defiance was a matter of fear and a perverted sense of honor.

THREE TYPES OF INTERNATIONAL ENVIRONMENTS

Perceptions of how states should act—if these perceptions are shared by other states—translate into actions and shape a particular international environment:

Pearl Harbor under attack, December 7, 1941. This event shaped American perceptions of national security for decades after.

- States may consider, for example, the international environment as a gigantic battlefield. Here individual states compete as enemies for power and resources, using all means necessary to win (Wendt, 1992). This view of competing states recalls the violent and anarchic society described by Thomas Hobbes (1588–1679), the English philosopher, and is called the *Hobbesian model.*
- Other states may perceive their environment differently. To them, states are not necessarily enemies. Instead, they interact as reasonable opponents: They observe the rules of the game and try to compromise with one another to balance their interests. This view is the *Lockean model* and has its roots in philosophy of John Locke (1632–1704), an Englishman.
- Finally, some states may see the world as driven by fundamental norms of ethics, based on recognition of the rights of others and a genuine desire to preserve international peace. This is the *Kantian model,* named after Immanuel Kant (1724–1804), the German philosopher. (See Table 3-1.)

↳ states = enemies

– reasonable opponents.

→ perserve peace.

At pivotal moments in history, especially at the end of major wars, dominant states and their leaders have to decide on the principles of a new postwar international environment. For instance, U.S., British, and Soviet leaders met in Yalta in 1945, a few months before the end of World War II. British prime minister Churchill clearly preferred the Lockean model. He wanted to maintain a strong British Empire and was prepared to divide a postwar world divided into spheres of influence. In his view, power balancing would contain any rivalry.

President Roosevelt gravitated instead toward a Kantian world, with lasting institutional foundations for postwar peace and partnership. He hoped that a new global intergovernmental organization, supported by American wealth

TABLE 3-1 Key Assumptions by Type of International Environment

Type of Environment	Key Assumptions
Hobbesian (after Thomas Hobbes)	• States are enemies and rivals • They are engaged in power politics • This politics is about zero-sum outcomes • Self-interest and security are states' prime interests
Lockean (after John Locke)	• States are competitors • Force and compromises are used in combination • Mutual restraint is a norm of behavior • International treaties build security
Kantian (after Immanuel Kant)	• States are partners • Cooperation is the main mechanism of international relations • Nonviolence is a norm of behavior • Collective security is the ultimate goal of all states

Sources: Wendt, 1992; 1999.

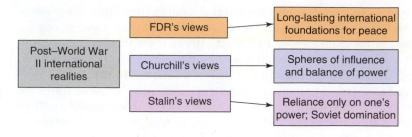

FIGURE 3-2 Three leaders, three world-views. A post-Yalta world from the constructivist perspective.

and goodwill, would consolidate the world. Soviet leader Stalin, however, tended to see a Hobbesian environment. He never believed in a lasting cooperation between the Communist Soviet Union and the capitalist powers; he wanted to expand Soviet territory and to build a security "buffer zone" between his country and the West. The three leaders could not agree on a common vision of the postwar world. As a result, fears grew, and the global confrontation known as the Cold War began (Plokhy, 2010). (See Figure 3.2.)

HISTORY LESSONS

States draw different lessons from international relations and may have very different understandings of what constitutes a fair game. Returning to the start of this chapter, why did Canada and Cuba choose different policies toward the United States? Canada, a former British colony, was for a long time in confrontation with the United States yet achieved an equal relationship with Washington on the basis of common values and mutual trade. Cuba, a former Spanish colony, fell under the United States' economic domination and was run by U.S.-backed dictators until 1959. Fidel Castro and a group of young revolutionaries, when they came to power, rejected Washington's domination and allied with the distant Soviet Union. In 1962, in the worst crisis of the Cold War, Soviet missiles targeted American cities from the Cuban territory (see the end of this chapter).

For constructivists, history lessons shape international environment. If diplomacy does not bring justice to the suffering, or if the world leaves an aggressor unpunished, then a Hobbesian environment is likely to emerge. In contrast, if states interact peacefully and support international institutions for a long time, then a Kantian environment is possible (Wendt, 1992).

CHECK YOUR KNOWLEDGE

▶ In which ways can fear affect behavior of states?
▶ Describe three environments in international relations.
▶ Explain key differences between the historical experiences of Canada and Cuba.

Conflict Theories

Conflict theories emphasize economic, social, and political inequality as a prime source of contradictions and international tensions. These theories highlight the role of social classes, ruling elites, males, and other dominant groups in shaping foreign policy and global affairs. Dominant groups or states impose their will on less powerful groups or states, create an unequal order to serve their interests, and so generate conflicts, violence, and wars. Only liberation from this order and the end of inequality can reduce tensions both domestically and internationally.

MARXISM AND LENINISM

Marxism has been one of the most influential schools of thought. Karl Marx (1818–1883) regarded human history as driven by the struggle between social classes—the *haves* and *have-nots*. Marxism views a state as an instrument of the dominant classes or groups, such as aristocracy or capitalists, to oppress and exploit other classes, such as peasants or workers. The state conducts its foreign policy according to the interests of the ruling classes. These interests are the maximization of power and wealth at the expense of other social classes. Marxism understands international relations as a struggle between states' ruling elites over territories, people, and resources. Only a revolution of industrial workers, the *proletariat*, can save humanity from the eternal cycle of oppression and injustice, by establishing **Communism**—a classless political and social order of equals free from oppressive governments (Marx and Engels, [1848] 2011).

Vladimir Lenin (1870–1924) adapted Marxism to explain the developments in the early twentieth century. According to Lenin, capitalism concentrates wealth in the hands of the few banks and industrial corporations. This, in turn, produces unbridled **imperialism**, a global struggle for territories and resources. According to Lenin, sovereign states participating in this struggle are just obedient "executive committees" of powerful corporations and banks expressing the interests of super-wealthy elites. In search of new markets and resources, Lenin argued, just a handful of capitalist countries of Europe and North America colonized Africa and Asia in the nineteenth century and kept Latin America in a state of dependency. Lenin called for a world revolution as the only way to save humanity from imperialism and war (Lenin, [1916] 1996).

Throughout the twentieth century, Communist revolutionaries justified violence as long as it was aimed against capitalism or the revolutionaries' opponents. Communist states included the Soviet Union, the People's Republic of China, parts of Eastern and Central Europe, Vietnam, Cuba, and North Korea. Marxism-Leninism promotes a theory of *distributive justice*, according to which the contemporary world's distribution of resources is fundamentally unfair. Marxism-Leninism rejects liberal values, political democracy, pluralism, and individualism in the same way it rejects the free-market economy. Capitalism here is viewed as a source of exploitation and inequality. Political democracy is ridiculed as a façade to deceive the oppressed and the poor, to divide them, and to rule over them (Ziegler, 1981). (See Figure 3.3.)

After World War II many Communist parties in Western Europe distanced themselves from Leninist views. They turned instead to social-democratic models in which all social classes can share wealth and power. Lenin's theory

FIGURE 3-3 Marxist view of Communist and capitalist countries' foreign policy.

of imperialism, however, remained particularly popular among the champions of antielitism, decolonization, and national liberation. Critics of Western domination in postcolonial Africa, Asia, and Latin America (called the global "South") often turned to Marxism-Leninism to criticize the developed capitalist countries of the global "North." Embracing the same assumptions, **postcolonial studies** embraced the conflict approach to international relations.

DEPENDENCY AND WORLD-SYSTEMS THEORY

In the 1960s and 1970s, some Western thinkers turned to **neo-Marxism** to argue that world capitalism should not be destroyed but rather reformed through science and smart policies. In Asia, Africa, and Latin America neo-Marxist scholars were reacting against *liberal modernization*, which advised states to follow the American market-based model of economic and social development. An Argentinean scholar, Raul Prebisch (1901–1986), argued that the structures of international relations—and trade in particular—make it impossible for countries to grow out of poverty. The free market keeps poor states

Activists of Sri Lanka's Marxist political party, People's Liberation Front, push carts with portraits of Communist leaders (from left) Karl Marx, Friedrich Engels, Vladimir Lenin, and Rohana Wijeweera (a local Marxist leader) during a street march in 2012. Communist parties have lost most of their influence, but Communist ideas still find popular support.

dependent on rich states while supplying the latter with cheap labor and raw materials. Only by building its own industries and "substituting" for foreign goods by producing its own can a state emerge from dependency. These views became the foundation of **dependency theory**.

An American sociologist Immanuel Wallerstein (b. 1930), formulated a related view known as *world-systems theory*. He used a Marxist concept, *hegemony*, which claims that a few industrial countries have an advantage in world affairs, whereas other states are kept behind (Wallerstein, 1979). World-systems theory divides the world into a **core**, consisting of the developed states that exercise their hegemonic power, and the **periphery**, including former colonies and underdeveloped and chronically poor states. The core states, located mainly in North America and Western Europe, impose free-market rules on the poor states to keep the periphery in permanent poverty and dependence (Gereffi and Korzeniewicz, 1993).

The interests of the core and the periphery are in conflict. The core states share an interest in maintaining the established economic order while eliminating challenges from the periphery. The Soviet Union and China in the twentieth century challenged the capitalist core. Yet the Soviets and Chinese never could reshape the world economic, financial, and trade systems. In the end, China and the Soviet Union (shortly before its collapse) decided to become part of a world system dominated by the United States, Western Europe, and Japan (Goldfrank, 2000).

The financial global crisis that started in 2008 brought these theories fresh attention. They became a major stimulus for radicals from the *antiglobalist movement*, but also for development studies and the discussions of how the global North can assist the global South (Wallerstein, 2004; Arrighi, 1994; Arrighi and Lu Zhang, 2011). We will return to these studies and discussions in Chapter 6.

Marxist-Leninist views also influenced the postcolonial studies. This approach sees the very language of international relations as shaped by European imperialism and racism (Said, 1994; Spivak, 1999). Advocates of postcolonial studies argue that the West retained its dominance over the rest of the world by means of cultural and informational hegemony: Western scholars and journalists defined the West as a norm, and depicted every attempt to overthrow Western domination as counterproductive and irrational (Said, 1979 Fanon, 2005). They claim that the Cold War was mainly waged in Africa, Latin America, and Asia, preventing their development and causing suffering of non-Western peoples (Chakrabarty, 2007; Westad, 2007).

▶ What are the key points of Lenin's theory of imperialism? Do you see some of these points as valid today?

▶ What is export substitution?

▶ What is distributive justice? Give an example.

▶ Explain the core and the periphery in Wallerstein's arguments.

CHECK YOUR KNOWLEDGE

THE POLITICS OF GENDER

Other conflict approaches focus not on social classes and wealth, but on social divisions such as gender and race. Again, social and political injustice are seen as a source of conflict in international relations.

Feminism is the view that women do not have equal rights and opportunities with men, and global changes are needed to achieve social justice. Feminist scholars have produced a wealth of work linking gender inequality to international relations. They argue that existing approaches reflect gender bias in a male-dominated world (Hirschman, 2010).

First, feminists say, men created legal and cultural rules, government institutions, and policies that systematically discriminate against women and satisfy men's needs. Global studies show that women not long ago filled fewer than 20 percent of parliamentary seats worldwide—and fewer than 15 percent of ministerial-level positions (Hunt, 2007). Outside Western countries, women seldom play a significant role in policy-making in defense, security, or diplomacy. The task is therefore to give women institutional support to represent their interests in the policy-making process globally (Waylen, 2010). (See Figures 3.4 and 3.5.)

Second, feminists say, defense and security policies reflect a masculine culture that accepts war and violence rather than consensus and peace (Cohn, 1987). For centuries women's views of politics were not taken into consideration. And in fact studies show that women tend to differ from men in their leadership style and understanding of security (Ayman and Korabik, 2010). If women occupied more positions of power and if feminine qualities and attitudes rather than masculine ones were more valued, many feminists conclude, we all would live in a more peaceful world (Hunt, 2007). Postcolonial feminists may even criticize Western feminists to give due credit to nonwhite, non-Western women.

Third, there is a strong correlation between violence against women and violence in foreign policy. Countries that tolerate aggression against women are more prone to use force abroad as well (Patterson, 2006). Conversely, domestic gender inequality influences a state's choices between violence and cooperation, peace and war, even in democracies (Caprioli and Boyer, 2001). In sum, feminist scholars argue, women should have the freedom and

FIGURE 3-4 Women in single and lower house of parliament, percentage of total selected countries. *Source: Inter-Parliamentary Union, 2012.*

Sweden	Netherlands	Britain	China	Italy	U.S.	Russia	India	Brazil
45	40	22	21	21	17	14	11	9

FIGURE 3-5 Women on Corporate Boards, percentage of total selected countries. *Source: Beck, 2011.*

Norway	Sweden	France	Britain	Germany	U.S.	Spain	China	Brazil	India	Russia
35	25	20	16	16	16	11	9	7	5	5

opportunities to make their own choices in everyday life and politics alike (Snyder-Hall, 2010).

Researchers and advocates of feminism have directed attention to serious international issues—including modern sex slavery, the trafficking of women and children across borders, rape and other forms of sexual violence, the protection of women and children during war, and AIDS (Buzan and Hansen, 2009, 212).

RACE AND ETHNIC CONFLICT

Theories of **racial and ethnic prejudice** maintain that world politics remains rooted in the superiority of some racial, national, cultural, or ethnic groups over others. Racial and ethnic prejudice affect international relations in at least two ways. First, political leaders interpret the world in racial or cultural terms; and second, dominant states primarily pursue the interests of white majorities.

We have already mentioned that postcolonial studies focus on how racism shapes international relations. Indeed, during the nineteenth and most of the twentieth century, theories of racial superiority, such as social Darwinism, justified European domination, slavery, and colonialism. Later anthropological and cultural studies rejected these ideas, emphasizing multiculturalism and equality. Yet new theories have also appeared, claiming inevitable differences between ethnic and cultural groups. Samuel Huntington (1993) and other scholars argue that the major conflicts in world politics are not between states but rather between "civilizations" unified by cultural or spiritual values. Iran and Iraq are rivals, in this view, not only because of their competition for oil but rather because of a deep-seated animosity between Persian and Arab civilizations. Similarly, Western Europe has treated Russia with great suspicion, not just because of its policies but because Europe views it as an alien, unpredictable, and dangerous civilization (Huntington, 1993; Neumann, 1996).

Postcolonial studies, too, may point to sources of racial and ethnic conflict. In this view, Western powers have long represented a white culture of colonialism and racism. This leads to double standard in their foreign policy. For example, the major powers took almost no action to stop the conflicts involving black Africans in Biafra in the 1960s and in Rwanda in 1994. Western powers may continue to doubt Africa's capability of self-governance (Gates, 1998).

> ▶ How does masculine culture relate to security in the feminist view?
> ▶ Explain the main focus of postcolonial studies.

CHECK YOUR KNOWLEDGE

Identity Factors

The power of battleships and the size of economic investments can make a difference in global affairs. However, a foreign country's military and economic power is often not enough to affect values, beliefs, and affiliations. In different

A boy holds his stepsister in Nyamata, Rwanda, in 2004, ten years after the civil war that left him orphaned. The world's most powerful countries were late to respond to the extreme violence that took the lives of hundreds of thousands of Rwandan people.

parts of the world, people tend to resist foreign influences simply because they are foreign. People tend to defend their way of life and their identity. **Identity** refers to how people see themselves as members of national, ethnic, religious, gender, or political groups. Common identity comes from history, culture, and language—and can generate passions in state-to-state relations that economic self-interest cannot. Nationalist and religious passions can be particularly destabilizing and even dangerous. During the war in Vietnam, American leaders spoke of winning "hearts and minds"—and this is often more difficult than winning a military conflict. Successful foreign policy is impossible without attractive cultural symbols—"soft power" that we discussed in Chapter 2.

POLITICAL CULTURE

Culture is a set of values and symbols shared by a large group of people, expressed in behavior and communicated from one generation to the next (Shiraev and Levy, 2013). **Political culture** is the attitude of a community or country toward political authority and politics in general. Political culture is not a consensus on political issues; people still tend to disagree on almost everything. Rather, it is a dominant perception concerning the rights and obligations of citizens—and the rules of political participation.

We can identify at least three types of political culture (Almond and Verba, 1963). In traditional or *parochial* political culture, citizens are only remotely

TABLE 3-2 Types of Political Culture

Parochial	People are only remotely aware of the government; they do not form a political community
Authoritarian	People obey the government, act like subjects, and have little impact on its policies
Participatory or Democratic	People act like citizens, have the right to influence politics, elect their leaders, organize associations, and express their opposition
Mixed or Hybrid	Elements of other two or three types of political cultures coexist

aware of the presence of central government. Most of them make local decisions regardless of state policies. In *authoritarian* political culture, people obey the government in most areas of their life. They have little opportunity for feedback, dissent, or voluntary participation in politics. In *participatory* or democratic culture, the government may remain powerful, but citizens have the right to influence politics, elect their leaders, organize associations, and express their opposition—and they have the habit of doing just that. Also, mixed types of political cultures may exist, especially when countries undergo political transition (Levitsky and Way, 2010).

In the United States or France, the elements of participatory democracy are strong, whereas the elements of parochial or authoritarian culture are insignificant. In contrast, in Afghanistan or Iraq, parochial culture has dominated for centuries, and participatory culture had little opportunity to develop. Countries like Russia or Pakistan show elements of all three political cultures, but authoritarian culture still prevails. (See Table 3-2.)

▶ What is identity? How can your identity affect your views of specific international events?
▶ Explain *parochial*, *authoritarian*, and *participatory* political cultures.

CHECK YOUR KNOWLEDGE

In democratic countries, like the United States, Canada, and the United Kingdom, participatory political culture is part of people's identity. The citizens there tend to view their countries as democracies. Furthermore, the governments of these countries base their policies toward one another on shared identities, thus rejecting confrontation and war (see arguments about democratic peace in Chapter 2).

Political cultures do not change overnight. They are acquired and transformed during an individual life span. In history, it was important for political authorities to control education and information in their countries. Authoritarian states employ the means of *communication* to spread information

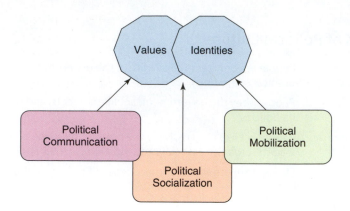

FIGURE 3-6 How values and identities related to politics are formed.

that may be politically useful; they use censorship to limit access to information that they think can hurt them. Authoritarian states also can mobilize masses against other states, to distract them from domestic problems, using the slogans of violence and hatred (Fukuyama, 2011).

Until recently, ruling elites in authoritarian countries almost had a monopoly on information. This allowed them to control the process of political mobilization. In the twenty-first century, the Internet, cellular phones, Facebook, and Twitter have eroded technological barriers and geographic distance. The revolts in Tunisia, Egypt, and Syria are examples of how modern means of communication can destabilize authoritarian states. These realities have caused authorities in China and elsewhere to censor their communication networks and limit the free flow of information. (See Figure 3.6.)

IDENTITIES AND CIVILIZATIONS

Identities are certainly broader than political cultures. Let's turn to a familiar example of Canada and Cuba. Can identity factors help us to understand the difference between their relations with the United States? Probably yes. Canada and the United States share common identity roots as parts of the British Empire influenced by Anglo-Saxon traditions. Cuba had different identity roots founded in the Spanish Empire, Catholicism, and the Caribbean culture. Do you think these factors perhaps did play the role when the Castro government launched its anti-American policies and convinced its people about the threat of imperialism coming from the north?

Samuel Huntington (1993) argued that cultural factors and identities became more important today than political and economic interests in international affairs. He believed that several countries can share common identities and form a "civilization" rooted in centuries of collective experiences and practices. Liberal-democratic political culture, Huntington argued, is a product of the Western civilization based on the classical legacy of Greece and Rome; Catholicism and Protestantism; European language; a separation between religion and state; the rule of law, social pluralism, civil society, traditions of representative rule; and individualism. Other civilizations are based on different values and experiences associated with Islam, Buddhism, Hinduism, Eastern

Orthodox, and other religions. Whereas in Western Christian countries politics became separated from religion, in Islamic countries a unity of religion and politics is often emphasized. Huntington believed that non-Western civilizations would resist the expansion of democracy and Western political culture. Like tectonic plates in geology, civilizations will have friction along their fault lines.

NATIONALISM AND OTHER POLITICAL ATTITUDES

Identity-related attitudes affect politics especially when people express solidarity with social groups to which they belong against "others." There are at least four kinds of such attitudes—nationalism, tribalism, xenophobia, and fundamentalism. They have a direct impact on diplomacy and global affairs.

Nationalism has many definitions, but generally it is an individual and collective form of identity with a country or a nation. Members of an ethnic group—Arabs, Russians, or Chinese—may never see one another, and yet they view themselves as a unified group, particularly when threatened (Anderson, 2006). Nationalism is often the belief that an ethnic group has the right to form an independent state. Nationalism can serve simultaneously as a consolidating and a dividing force (Muller, 2008). Before 1948, Jews and Arabs in Palestine lived together in Palestine under the British administration. When the British withdrew, the Jews in Palestine formed an independent state of Israel supported by the Soviet Union, the United States, and several Western countries. The neighboring Arab leaders went to war against Israel and lost. This led to the flight of the Palestinian Arabs from their lands and the formation of two sharply distinct groups, Israeli Jews and Palestinian Arabs, that remain in conflict for years (Fromkin, 2009). More recently, the collapse of Yugoslavia led to the emergence of several independent nations.

National identity can be a peaceful and respectful kind of group solidarity, which we usually call patriotism. Many other forms of nationalism, however, use violent or radical means to achieve their goals and separate "us" from "them" (Theiss-Morse, 2009). One such form of nationalist hatred is *chauvinism*, a belief in national superiority. Even more radical is neo-Nazism, a dangerous combination of anti-Semitism, militarism, and racism. National identity is a very powerful factor of political mobilization during conflicts and wars. People often put aside their political differences to stand shoulder-to-shoulder as citizens against another state. Political parties mend their differences to defend their country under a foreign threat. In its virulent, active form nationalism can be an effective substitute for a participatory political culture especially in non-democratic states. During World War II many Germans followed Hitler to the end. Despite their serious disapproval of the authoritarian leader Slobodan Milošević, the Serbian political opposition moved to his side during NATO's bombing campaign against Serbia in 1999.

Nationalism is not necessarily a universal form of identity. In the Arab Middle East, in Afghanistan, and some parts of Africa, **tribalism** is widespread—an attitude based on strong loyalty to tightly knit, usually small, ethnic and religious groups. These groups usually function on the basis of ancient traditions preceding the formation of modern states. Tribalism appears in

DEBATE > WHO ARE PATRIOTS AND NATIONALISTS?

The labels "nationalist" and "patriot" are often confusing. Just what does it mean to be a Korean, Mexican, or American patriot? In public discourse, as research shows, to be a "patriot" has always been more suitable than to be a "nationalist" (Kosterman and Feshbach, 1989). "Patriotic" behavior is sometimes associated with agreeing with a majority. Moreover, the terms *nationalist*, *patriot*, *patriotic*, or *unpatriotic* are often deliberately misused to boost one's popularity and scorn political opponents.

WHAT'S YOUR VIEW?

Do you think it is patriotic to support your country's leaders unconditionally and at all times? Why or why not? When do you think it can be patriotic to criticize your country's policies and its leaders? Give an example of an unpatriotic statement or behavior.

@ You can easily search for the media's interpretation of "unpatriotic" acts or statements—for example, "Fox Accuses Google of Being Unpatriotic" by Chris Matyszczyk (June 2012). See the companion website.

the form of political loyalties to *clans* that bond by marriage and kinship—meaning biological, cultural, or historical descent.

Both nationalism and tribalism may be associated with **xenophobia**, which is fear and hatred of foreign countries and foreigners. In Afghanistan as well as some regions in Central Asia, the resentment against any foreign presence has a long history (Hopkirk, 2004). Xenophobia exists in democracies as well, as a fear of immigrants. A 2011 study found that in the European Union, many believe that immigrants "are taking employment opportunities from the local population" (Eurobarometer, 2011).

Under the watchful eye of mounted British police officers, members of the English Defense League march on the Tower Bridge in London in 2011. The English Defense League insists it is a peaceful organization opposing Islamist extremism, but its past actions have often resulted in violence.

Fundamentalism is another form of identity rooted in religious beliefs. Fundamentalists advocate a return to the past—often an imagined past, before modern influences came to undermine traditional values. To them, openness, globalization, and democracy threaten local cultures and their status. *Private* fundamentalism can be found among devout believers in Islam, Christianity, Judaism, and other religions. It has little impact on international politics. *Political* fundamentalism, in contrast, advocates its vision alone of how government should function and which foreign policy it should conduct (Husain, 2005). Many Christian fundamentalists in the United States have long argued that the U.S. government should unconditionally support Israel and its policies in the Middle East because Israel is the place for the "second coming" of Jesus Christ (S. Spector, 2008). The Islamic revolution in Iran in 1978–1979 led to the victory of political fundamentalism and had enormous influence on the whole Middle East. According to the Iranian Constitution, all laws "must be based on Islamic criteria" (Article 4). The Iranian government began to consider the United States as "the Great Satan," the enemy of the entire Islamic *ummah* (community).

> ▶ How does nationalism influence international relations? Can this influence be positive?
> ▶ Define xenophobia and suggest several examples of it.
> ▶ Explain the meaning of political fundamentalism.

CHECK YOUR KNOWLEDGE

Political Psychology

Every time the United States elects a new president, political strategists around the world start guessing. Will there be a new policy direction in Washington? After all, human beings make decisions and conduct policies on behalf of states. And these individuals may be vindictive or forgiving, rely on ideology or on intuition, and turn to advisers or act alone. **Political psychology** studies the interactions between political and psychological factors in individual and group behavior.

Political psychologists use the behavioral and cognitive sciences to gather information about world leaders and analyze their policies (Houghton, 2008). Some of their data comes from experimental studies. Most, however, comes from politicians themselves—their statements, interviews, press conferences, speeches, memoirs, and policy-making.

RATIONAL DECISION-MAKING

According to the **rational model**, political leaders try to maximize the positive outcomes and minimize the negative consequences of their decisions. In other words, they act, for the most part, rationally. Before imposing sanctions against a foreign state or going to war, for example, a president might follow these steps (Hindmoor, 2006; Baldoni, 2004):

- Understand the problem.
- Set goals to address this problem.
- Articulate and explain these goals through public statements, interviews, and diplomatic channels.
- Seek resources to implement these goals.
- Make a decision and monitor its implementation.
- Detect and evaluate threats and obstacles.
- Study the outcomes of the decision.
- Finally, adapt the decision to changing circumstances.

Mutual trust based on interpersonal contacts becomes crucial, so that state leaders will act openly and sincerely (Cholett and Goldgeier, 2002), try to narrow their differences, and arrive at a mutually acceptable solution. This process involves concessions, goodwill gestures, proposals, retractions, and compromises (Barner-Barry and Rosenwein, 1985). In the difficult 1990 negotiations over the reunification of Germany, for example, decision makers were able to find reasonable compromises. The Soviet leader Mikhail Gorbachev agreed to withdraw troops from East Germany in exchange for West German financial assistance to the Soviet Union and pledges not to expand NATO eastward beyond Germany (Sarotte, 2009).

Approaches based on rational models also maintain that if we, as observers, had full access to information, we could explain international relations as a bargaining process. The problem, however, is that political leaders are guided not only by pragmatic calculations. They may have personal attitudes, aspirations, and ambitions that affect their policies as well.

BIASED DECISION-MAKING

Decisions in international relations are too ambiguous and complex to explain by rational models alone (Hart, 1991). Human thinking is not completely rational even when people believe they act logically (Steinbruner, 1974; Cutler, 1981). **Prospect theory** (for which one of its authors, Daniel Kahneman, won the Nobel Prize in 2002) states that people, even when acting in a seemingly rational way, consistently miscalculate their chances of success and failure (Kahneman and Tversky, 1979). Emotions and misperceptions affect how politicians evaluate the international situation (Larson, 1985; 1997).

What kind of biases occur and why? In **consistency bias**, new information is more likely to be accepted if it accords with an individual's existing opinions. Similarly, in **resistance bias**, people tend to stick to their decisions even when new evidence challenges their assumptions (Levy, 2009; Heider, 1959). Finally, **accessibility bias** occurs when people pick not the best option but one that is easily available and easily understood.

What do these biases mean for international relations? Biases tend to steer politicians to hawkish, violent choices more often than to nonviolent, reconciliatory strategies (Kahneman and Renshon, 2007). They often exaggerate the evil intentions of their adversaries and underestimate peaceful initiatives. Leaders also tend to be uncritical of their own actions and reluctant to compromise. Former president George W. Bush might have displayed consistency and resistance bias when the United States started two wars, in Afghanistan in 2001 and Iraq in 2003. Bush's initial self-confidence led him to reject views critical of his foreign policy (Woodward, 2007; Renshon, 2009).

GROUP PRESSURE

Another source of bias in foreign-policy decisions is **group pressure**: The presence of other people, such as Cabinet members, alters individual decisions, an

French President Francois Hollande speaks with his Argentine counterpart, Cristina Fernandez, during the G20 summit in Los Cabos, Mexico, in 2012. Meanwhile, Russian President Vladimir Putin meets with U.S. President Barack Obama. Can body language reveal how these leaders get along?

Visit the companion website to examine Murray's work.

example of *group inhibition*. Conversely, other people can encourage decision makers to act carelessly and recklessly, an example of *group facilitation*. People frequently care about competition with other people, not about confronting the problems in front of them (Deutsch and Krauss, 1962). Experiments on obedience to authority (Milgram, 1963), repeated in many countries, show that individuals tend to make unethical decisions if they feel protected by an authority figure. The perpetrators feel less responsibility for their actions when they are "only following orders."

POLITICAL SOCIALIZATION

Can we understand foreign-policy decisions better by studying how decision-making develops? **Political socialization** examines how individuals acquire their political knowledge and beliefs (Sears et al., 2003). Classic psychological studies in this field include Henry Murray on Hitler's abnormal personality (1943) and Erik Erikson on the nonviolence of India's most honored leader, Mahatma Gandhi (1969). These studies point to a combination of psychological factors, both rational and irrational—from wisdom and moral values to anger, jealousy, and insecurity.

TABLE 3-3 Political Psychology: U.S. Presidents and Their Formative Years

President	Politics as a Way to Address Personal Issues
Richard Nixon	Lonely and anxious as a child, Nixon shunned people and used politics to compensate for personal insecurities. As president, he avoided the media and preferred closed-door deals, which led to success in some of his realpolitik designs but also to the Watergate scandal at home.
Jimmy Carter	From his youth, Carter was committed to do "right" and to avoid violence. These attitudes motivated him to put human rights at the center of his foreign policy. His idealism led to successes but also serious mistakes in foreign policy.
Ronald Reagan	Raised in a lower-class family, Reagan made his way up using his persistence, hard work, and excellent communication skills. He acquired strong conservative beliefs later in life.
Bill Clinton	Growing up as an orphan, the future president developed a profound ambition to distinguish himself. He was often brilliant in domestic politics and cautious in foreign policy, but reckless in his personal life.
George W. Bush	Raised in a secure upper-class environment, in a powerful family, Bush grew up with severe personal problems. He overcame alcoholism by turning to religion and work. He developed a sense of self-righteousness, which led him to seek limited feedback from others. As president, he saw the *War on Terror* as a global struggle between good and evil.
Barack Obama	As a biracial child growing up in such distinct social environments as Hawaii and Indonesia, he developed a respect for the world's diversity. His mother's death from cancer made him determined to reform American medicine and to make it more accessible. Brought up by white grandparents, Obama became an overachiever and learned to navigate the American political system successfully, often preferring compromise to confrontation.

Sources: Reeves (2001); Post (2005b); Glad (2009); Renshon (2004; 2011); Takiff (2010).

Unfortunately, these factors are difficult to measure. Contemporary studies in political socialization have therefore turned to more verifiable facts (Jost and Sidanius, 2004). These studies conclude that political leaders tend to form many of their beliefs in childhood or adolescence. Some biographical evidence suggests that entire careers are shaped by the desire for recognition, love, power, and redemption (Volkan and Itzkowitz, 1984; Renshon, 2011). Of course, this intriguing suggestion requires future critical discussion. (See Table 3-3.)

As you can see, there are parallels between political psychology and constructivism, in that both describe how political leaders construct and interpret information. Political psychologists, however, attempt to look inside the human mind through empirical research and experiments.

▶ Why don't rational models explain international behavior in full?

▶ What are consistency, resistance, and accessibility biases? Suggest examples.

▶ What do political socialization studies add to our understanding of international politics?

CHECK YOUR KNOWLEDGE

How Do We Apply It?

How well do constructivist, conflict, feminist, and political psychology approaches hold up in practice? To judge, we have to apply them critically to actual cases and contexts in international relations.

The Individual Context

Constructivist views, with their emphasis on social meanings, and political psychology share a concern for how state leaders make decisions. Rich empirical data show the importance of individual character, thinking, and emotion in shaping political choices (Sears et al., 2003). What do these studies reveal?

VISIONARIES AND FANATICS

Mikhail Gorbachev, the last leader of the Soviet Union, changed international relations fundamentally in 1988 with the idea of a *common European home* from Vancouver to Vladivostok. In this vision, the United States, Canada, other NATO countries, and a reformed Soviet Union share similar values, including universal peace. Gorbachev called for nuclear disarmament and the renunciation of the use of force in international relations (Rey, 2004). At the time, many realists dismissed Gorbachev's vision as unworkable, but his ideas were a catalyst for the peaceful overthrow of Communism in Eastern and Central Europe.

Gorbachev's visionary ideas were supported by his values and identity. First, he became convinced that the West was no longer an enemy. Second, Gorbachev turned to the West not only because of growing Soviet economic difficulties but also because he began to believe in Western economic and social models. Culturally, Gorbachev was a *Westernizer,* in sharp contrast with previous leaders in Moscow (Rey, 2004; Zubok, 2007). A shift in values and perceptions, as constructivists would argue, has changed Soviet foreign policy.

Adolf Hitler was another leader who challenged the entire international system. His beliefs and values in the 1930s and 1940s were xenophobic, anti-Semitic, and antielitist. He envisioned Germany's global domination and was fanatically obsessed with the "racial purity" and the removal, and even physical elimination, of Jews. He hoped to restore an Aryan culture of obedience and pride based on its mythic roots. Many Germans, disillusioned with liberal democracy and hoping that a strong state would solve their problems, followed him (Kershaw, 2000). If Gorbachev was a visionary of a transnational community based on Western values, Hitler was a fanatic of a dangerous myth promoting war, racism, and anti-Semitism. Both cases suggest that, at certain points in history, a single person's cultural values and identity can change the course of history.

RATIONAL AND BIASED CHOICES

We have already discussed that leaders may make biased decisions caused by emotions, misperceptions, and erroneous expectations. State leaders frequently face uncertainty, deadlines, and pressure from supporters or opponents of a specific policy. They may not always search for the best decision but instead settle on the first acceptable or convenient alternative. They may be stubborn—afraid of appearing weak or unwilling to lose credibility. As Jerrold Post, a former CIA analyst, wrote in a memorandum to Congress in 1990 describing Saddam Hussein, "Saddam's worldview is narrow and distorted, and he has scant experience out of the Arab world" (Post, 1990). Saddam presented himself as the only Arab leader to champion the Palestinian cause and was not afraid of U.S. support for Israel. He appealed to Arab masses across the Middle East and accepted international pressure against his regime as part of the struggle that every great leader should endure. If need be, he was prepared to go down heroically. Negotiations or surrender did not fit his self-image of a great revolutionary leader.

ANALOGIES AND INDIVIDUALS

Decisions can also be biased by a reliance on **analogy**. Comparing new situations to familiar ones can provide quick answers. As we have seen, analogies in policy-making may reflect both rationality and bias (Jervis, 1976; Cholett and Goldgeier, 2008). After World War I, most European statesmen feared that any international crisis would lead to war. Constrained by this frightening analogy, British and French leaders signed a deal with Hitler in Munich in 1938, allowing him to dismember Czechoslovakia. In time their action became the basis of an analogy, too. After World War II, Western leaders pointed to "the Munich analogy" to argue why it was necessary to stop Communism wherever it existed. President Lyndon Johnson and his advisers evoked the Munich analogy in sending U.S. troops to defend South Vietnam. Anything less would be "appeasement" (Khong, 1992).

The Munich analogy was used again in 1991, when Iraq occupied Kuwait. President George H. W. Bush compared Saddam to Hitler to justify a U.S.

invasion. Negotiations with the Iraqi dictatorship, he believed, would endanger regional and world peace.

IRRATIONAL DECISION-MAKING

Some leaders obviously have irrational motives. Illness or individual pathology can diminish an individual's ability to reason. So can personal crises or extreme circumstances. Alexander George pioneered the study of leadership under stress. He found that a leader's psychological problems can fatally disrupt strategic decision-making (George, 1969). Soviet leader Leonid Brezhnev's addiction to medication, for example, may have contributed to the fateful decision to send Soviet troops to Afghanistan in December 1979 (Zubok, 2007).

Many states lack legal mechanisms for replacing a sick or unstable leader. Authoritarian regimes often conceal the sickness of leaders because of fear of domestic instability. Cuban authorities did not reveal Fidel Castro's declining health until he passed authority to his brother Raul in 2007. North Korea similarly refused to discuss the health of its leader, Kim Jong-il, in 2011. Even in a more transparent democratic society, a leader's emotional outbursts or illness may affect foreign policy, although the risk is less significant.

The rise of terrorism also points to the importance of studying irrationality in decision-making. We return to this discussion in Chapter 7.

EARLY AND LATE SOCIALIZATION

The evidence about early socialization of political leaders remains inconclusive. Did Castro's early beliefs about Cuba–U.S. relations shape his revolutionary policy? Did Gorbachev's early experience of war make him adverse to the use of violence when he became the Soviet leader? How did Obama's childhood

North Koreans pay tribute in 2012 to the statues of late leaders Kim Il Sung (left) and Kim Jong il in Pyongyang, North Korea. In authoritarian countries, leaders' personal lives remain a state secret even after they die.

affect his effectiveness and strength as a leader during his presidency? Did the stolen bicycles—the opening quote in this chapter is referring to them— affect German Chancellor Merkel's political choices? We can only speculate about the answers. Although early life events surely affect decisions, we have little reliable and verifiable evidence connecting a leader's formative experiences with specific actions (Post, 2008; Kowert, 1996). Political preferences of Castro, Gorbachev, Merkel, and Obama may be better explained by many other factors that shaped their identities later in their lives. Biographical and psychological studies of political leaders, military commanders, and diplomats provide important information. Unfortunately, this information is also incomplete, selective, and sometimes misleading.

CONFLICT THEORIES TESTED

Conflict theories focus on classes, groups, and social structures. Marxists argued for a long time that once oppressive social classes are defeated, equality and justice can win. Yet in Cuba, the Castro revolutionary regime after 1959 became even more oppressive, relying on the arrest and execution of opponents. Iran after 1979 demonstrates that one-man dictatorship was replaced by dictatorship of a group of Ayatollahs and religious authorities, even more repressive and corrupt. If Marxists paid more attention to individual factors, they would have admitted that their Marxist social utopia was always brushed aside by people competing for power and money.

What about the feminist idea that women would do better than men if they occupied positions of power? Women in power have not always engaged in peaceful policies. They often cannot eradicate corruption either. U.S. secretaries of state Madeleine Albright in the 1990s and Condoleezza Rice and Hillary Clinton in 2001–2013 did not steer foreign policy decisively on the path of peace. Albright and Rice had to justify military campaigns in Kosovo, Afghanistan, and Iraq. Clinton did not challenge Barack Obama's military actions in Libya and constant use of unmanned planes to kill militants in Pakistan and Afghanistan.

CASE IN POINT > *Obama's Missing Father*

What role did Barack Obama's absent father, a one-time herdsman from Kenya, play in the development of the forty-fourth president of the United States? When Obama became senator in 2005, he was highly critical of humanitarian violations in Africa, particularly in Darfur (Sudan) and Zimbabwe. When Obama became president, people in Kenya danced in joy, and many African leaders hoped that he would make conflict-ridden Africa a greater priority in foreign policy. They assumed that the son of an African immigrant should do great things for the land of his fraternal ancestors (D'Souza, 2010). However, despite some impressive rhetoric, U.S. policy toward Africa has not changed significantly during his presidency.

CRITICAL THINKING

Do you believe that Obama's personal background has much or little to do with his foreign policies as president? Provide arguments to support your opinion.

Feminist scholars may argue back to these examples: to succeed, a woman must adapt to a political and cultural environment created by men. Women, they may argue, compared to male leaders, do possess a more conciliatory approach to foreign policy (Schein, 2002). Yet they may not have the resources to reduce corruption and violence. They also have to work in a predominantly male atmosphere.

> ▶ Whom do we call visionaries in international relations?
> ▶ Explain the Munich analogy. Turn to contemporary examples to illustrate.
> ▶ Describe how socialization studies explain decision-making in international relations.

CHECK YOUR KNOWLEDGE

The State Context

Alternative views can enrich our understanding of how state politics and institutions affect a country's international behavior. Most national leaders face a host of factors and political forces that constrain their freedom of action and influence international policies. (See Table 3-4.)

BUREAUCRACY AND COGNITIVE MAPS

In most countries, decision-making is a result of **bureaucratic bargaining**. Political groups and institutions fight for their interests and make compromises. We looked at "log rolling" from the realist perspective in Chapter 2. The constructivist approach suggests many more ways through which bureaucracy

TABLE 3-4 Critical Evaluation of Prominent Women in Power

Name, Country	Position and Years in Power	Examples of Corruption or Forceful Responses
Golda Meir, Israel	Prime Minster: 1969–74	Led Israel in the 1973 war against Arab states (the Yom Kippur War).
Indira Gandhi, India	Prime Minister: 1966–77; 1980–84	Led India in the 1971 war against Pakistan. Frequently used tough measures to deal with domestic and international issues.
Isabel Peron, Argentina	President: 1974–76	Accused of corruption and the disappearances and assassinations of opposition leaders.
Margaret Thatcher, United Kingdom	Prime Minister: 1979–90	In 1982, initiated a tough military response against Argentina's military in the Falkland Islands. Believed nuclear weapons help to keep peace.
Benazir Bhutto, Pakistan	Prime Minister: 1988–90; 1993–96	Charged with corruption while in office and was a key figure in Pakistan's nuclear program.

can bias foreign policy. During the Cold War, for example, the *domino theory* became common wisdom in the United States: The loss of a single country to Communism in Asia or Latin America would trigger a chain reaction, and soon all neighboring countries would fall into Communist hands. After the end of the Cold War, democratic peace theory (Chapter 2) became nearly as influential in Washington.

Constructivism also helps in understanding of how cognitive factors shape international behavior in authoritarian states. In the 1950s, the American analysts hoped to predict how the political beliefs of members of the Soviet Politburo translate into foreign policy. **Cognitive maps**, or diagrams of information processing and decision-making, were used (often unsuccessfully) to predict Soviet decisions. As we saw at the beginning of this chapter, the Taliban in Afghanistan is a political movement based on revolutionary Islamist ideology (Husain, 2005). The core of the Taliban's cognitive map is spiritual solidarity with Muslims fighting for a caliphate, a regional religious commonwealth. It was therefore inconceivable for the Taliban leadership to cede to U.S. pressure to hand over another Muslim, Osama bin Laden, after the attacks of September 11, 2001. In those circumstances, the Taliban leaders chose war. (See Figure 3.7.)

ACCESS TO INFORMATION AND STATESMANSHIP

State leaders have an important edge over many rank-and-file officials, citizens, and the media—exclusive access to human and electronic intelligence. This advantage does not, however, always guarantee the most effective foreign policy. In many countries, intelligence experts avoid making policy suggestions because they are not supposed to influence decision-making. But political leaders often put pressure on intelligence efforts. Sometimes experts fail to resist the erroneous perceptions of policy makers, who may have already decided on a course of action. Joseph Stalin and Saddam Hussein forced their advisers to tell them what they wanted to hear. The Bush administration, critics say, pressed the CIA to report that Iraq was on the verge of producing nuclear arms (Goodman, 2008). The Obama administration officials in 2012, according to critics, were reluctant to call the assassination of the U.S. ambassador in Libya a terrorist act to avoid possible political fallout. Yet sometimes the realities on the ground change a country's foreign policy. France invaded Mali in 2013 despite president Hollande's earlier objections to interventionism. This policy change was caused by a rapidly deteriorating situation in this African country where Islamic fundamentalist fighters were about to take power by force.

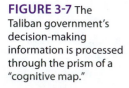

FIGURE 3-7 The Taliban government's decision-making information is processed through the prism of a "cognitive map."

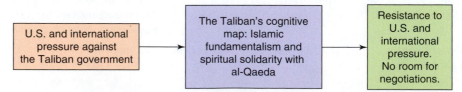

U.S. and international pressure against the Taliban government → The Taliban's cognitive map: Islamic fundamentalism and spiritual solidarity with al-Qaeda → Resistance to U.S. and international pressure. No room for negotiations.

The fast-growing volume and complexity of information is a serious challenge to any decision maker. Also, sometimes too much information can make decision-making difficult—just as too little information can (Nye, 2002). How can a leader transform information into a clear and accurate policy? Each U.S. president begins his workday by reading a document called the President's Daily Brief (PDB), a procedure created during the Cold War. Reducing complex and voluminous evaluations to a short PDB provides much-needed certainty and simplicity. However, it also risks losing regional and local contexts, along with crucial detail.

 Did the U.S. President's Daily Brief trigger war in Iraq? Visit the companion website for links.

TWO-LEVEL GAMES

Robert Putnam (Putnam, 1988) offers an aid to testing constructivist assumptions. As we saw in Chapter 2, his **two-level games** model suggests that leaders make foreign policy with one eye on international factors (the first level) and another eye on domestic developments (the second level). State leaders operate on both levels. Domestic forces affecting policy decisions include legislative institutions, lobbying groups, political opposition, the media, and often the military. The impact of these institutions depends on the state's constitution and democratic traditions. Democratic leaders have to think about reelection even in the midst of an international crisis. Most famously, Winston Churchill and George H. W. Bush led their countries in military victories in Germany and Iraq, but lost elections, in 1945 and 1992, respectively.

The conflict between Israel and the Arab states provides an incredibly complex example of a two-level game. Israel cannot make too many concessions to the Palestinians without antagonizing a big part of the electorate. Among the Palestinians, the groups and leaders that support negotiations with Israel often face domestic criticism as well. At the same time, supporters of a tough approach on both sides risk losing broad popular support (Mahler, 2004). Like Alice in Lewis Carroll's *Alice in Wonderland*, state leaders and diplomats have to run twice as fast to stay in the same place. Those who try to bring peace and stability to the Holy Land usually lag behind rapid developments on both sides of the divide.

THE DEMOCRATIC-AUTHORITARIAN CONTINUUM

In democracies, the decision-making process is relatively open to inquiry, scrutiny, criticism, and free discussion. In most democratic countries, parliamentary factions, the media, nongovernmental groups, and public opinion all play a role in the decision-making process. Political opposition and concerned groups can draw attention to a range of foreign-policy issues and can serve as a restraining force on many governmental decisions, especially those related to foreign aid or the use of military force abroad (Sobel, 2001; Nacos et al., 2000). Leaders of democratic states should therefore tend to seek broad political support for their decisions.

In authoritarian regimes, decisions are made in relative secrecy. The authoritarian leader secures support among a small inner circle of reliable supporters and imposes these decisions on the rest of the political elites. Individual leaders should therefore play a more significant role in foreign policy than in democratic political contexts. (See Table 3-5.)

Polish Parliament members protest their country's participation in an international intellectual property rights agreement in 2012. They are holding up Guy Fawkes masks, suggesting their opposition to what they believe would be the limiting of Internet freedom.

In reality, the differences are less clear. Officials in democratic countries too may shield valuable information from public scrutiny (Goodman, 2008). Since the 1940s, U.S. decision-making is disseminated to a narrow circle of people on a "need-to-know" basis. Strategic plans remain classified for decades, and foreign-policy errors are rarely subject to independent investigation. The United States used secret diplomacy and covert operations against the Communist powers for years. Similar strategies are pursued today against international terrorist organizations.

TABLE 3-5 Decision-Making in Authoritarian And Democratic Contexts

	Authoritarian Context	Democratic Context
Political Environment	Decision-making is made in political isolation and is not seriously scrutinized and influenced by other political forces.	Group decision-making is scrutinized and critically appraised by the media, political opposition, and public opinion.
Type of Political Support	The authoritarian leader secures support from a small inner circle of reliable supporters, secret police, and the military. The leader imposes decisions on the rest of the political elites.	Democratic leaders tend to seek broad political support for their decisions from government, the media, political parties, and public opinion.
Situational Factors	An individual leader's choices play a crucial role in decision-making.	Policy mistakes by an individual leader are likely to be prevented or corrected by other political actors, including individuals and institutions.

COLLECTIVE EXPERIENCES

After military defeat in 1945, both German and Japanese societies had to reinvent their identities. The collective experience of war, death, and suffering helped in defeating prewar nationalism, xenophobia, and chauvinism. Both societies adopted liberal values and peaceful policies. These values, as we have seen, guide the foreign policies of Germany and Japan today.

Collective experiences may also become obstacles to national reintegration. Although Germany has been a single state since 1990, citizens from former Communist East Germany continued for some years to harbor resentment toward fellow citizens and politicians from western parts. People in North and South Korea are still sharply divided by ideology and politics. Residents of Taiwan, although they may share similar language with their counterparts in China, have a vastly different collective experience and attitudes than those who live in the People's Republic of China.

Collective experiences of the very same events naturally differ from country to country. Europe in the twentieth century lost tens of millions of lives in wars and suffered massive devastation. For the United States, despite heavy casualties, these conflicts were for the most part foreign wars, and the country emerged in 1945 as the strongest and wealthiest in the world. As a result, many Europeans take a much more cautious attitude at the use of military force than Americans do (Costigliola, 2000). This could have contributed to divisions within NATO after the United States invaded Iraq. (See Table 3-6.)

In time, collective experiences may change. Germany occupied Ukraine and the Russian lands twice in the twentieth century, causing massive destruction and the deaths of millions of people. Yet, in 2011, 84 percent of Russians had a positive view of Germany. More than 38 percent of Russians believe the United States is their country's main enemy (Levada Center, 2013). Most Vietnamese these days do not consider the United States an enemy. Direct U.S.

TABLE 3-6 Collective Experiences in Foreign Policy: A Comparative Case

Country	Collective Experience and Foreign Policy
United States	The Great Depression shaped the identity of millions of Americans and helped the U.S. government in abandoning isolationism during and after World War II.
Soviet Union	Memories of the Nazi invasion in 1941 and the Great Patriotic War against Germany provided massive popular support for the Soviet regime. Soviet leaders and the majority of people believed that they had the right to occupy Eastern Europe after World War II and to defend themselves against Western imperialism.
Cuba	U.S. attempts to overthrow Castro's government in the early 1960s rallied millions of Cubans to its support. Their collective memories were shaped by images of heroic struggle against America.
North Vietnam	First China, then France, and then Japan colonized Vietnam. The Communists exploited this experience to conquer power in the 1950s and later to direct anticolonial sentiment against the United States.

investment in Vietnam has reached $16 billion and is increasing, and more than thirteen thousand Vietnamese exchange students attend U.S. colleges (Gang, 2011). Conversely, after the American occupation of Iraq and Afghanistan, more people in Muslim countries began to view America as hostile (Pew, 2010).

CHECK YOUR KNOWLEDGE

▶ Which factors shape a state's identity? How do you describe the identity of your country?
▶ What are cognitive maps? How do they affect decision-making?
▶ What are the two levels in Robert Putnam's theory? Can foreign policy affect domestic policy?

The Global Context

INTERNATIONAL FACTORS AND STATE INTERESTS

Earlier we saw that domestic social attitudes and political processes define and shape state identities, interests, and foreign policy. Global developments can do it, too. International structures, laws, norms of behavior, organizations, and institutions—all these can change international behavior (Finnemore, 1996). For example, in the past, states were concerned with accumulating wealth, viewing it as a "zero-sum game"—a game with clear winners and losers. However, by the end of the twentieth century, poverty was seen as bad for global stability and for the well-being of wealthy states as well as poor ones. Global poverty became a global challenge, just like environmental problems.

Not only changing structures, but also shifting values may encourage states to see their interests differently. After the end of the Cold War in the early 1990s, the United States seemed the only superpower left, with military capabilities superior to all other states combined. Yet the post–Cold War world devalued the use of military power and valued humanitarian agendas, such as policies to relieve poverty, protect the environment, and fight infectious diseases. The United Nations received from an increasing number of states more authority to make global decisions.

It was difficult for the United States to adapt to this new world. Relations between the Clinton administration and the United Nations in the 1990s grew difficult, and Washington was often reluctant to commit its armed forces under UN command. After the terrorist acts of September 11, 2001, Washington tried to reassert its role as unchallenged leader. Yet the war in Iraq quickly showed the limits of American power and raised concerns about unilateral actions. As a result, Washington in more recent years began to turn to the United Nations and other international and transnational organizations to regain international legitimacy and leadership (Cholett and Goldgeier, 2008).

HYBRID POLITICAL CULTURES

Globalization involves social, cultural, and ideological changes as well as political and economic ones. In response, some elites have turned to *hybrid* political cultures, based on elements of authoritarian and traditional culture, and many authoritarian states practice some form of democracy (Krauthammer, 2008). In the 1990s, Singapore's leader, Lee Kuan Yew, spoke eloquently about "Asian values." By advocating a form of capitalism based on Confucian values and strong authoritarian power, he sought to compete more effectively with the West (Mahbubani, 2002). Russian leaders proposed what they called *sovereign democracy* to defend authoritarian forms of governance combined with some democratic principles (Shiraev, 2013). In fact, after the Cold War, authoritarian countries had to switch to **competitive authoritarianism**—a strategy for preserving legitimacy and power (Levitsky and Way, 2010). Under competitive authoritarianism, elections are regularly held, but a single leader or party dominates. The government uses police, courts, and tax agencies to harass the opposition, control the media, abuse state resources, and manipulate electoral results.

Economic liberalization does not necessarily cause democratization. Germany, Japan, and South Korea abandoned authoritarianism and turned to democracy in the twentieth century—but the lessons of these success stories may not apply universally. Today Venezuela, Kenya, China, and Russia all combine free-market economies with authoritarian policies. Many countries in fact use nationalism to argue against democracy on Western terms.

"Export" of democracy to other countries usually fails when there are no local conditions and actors to support it (McFaul, 2009). Still, supporters of democracy should not become discouraged. Democracy has many faces and

During a protest rally in Moscow, Russia, in 2013, people carry posters of Russian President Vladimir Putin reading "March Against the Scum and Shame" and a banner reading "Dissolution of the State Duma." Thousands of people protested against Russia's new law banning Americans from adopting Russian children.

can adapt to many local conditions. And the outcome may not resemble the American, Canadian, or French models.

DO CULTURES CLASH?

Samuel Huntington believed that "civilizations" based on different religious, cultural, and political foundations are less likely to cooperate. He warned, as you remember, that future conflicts would happen, not between nation-states divided by interests, but between civilizations divided by values (Huntington, 1993). Huntington, for example, expected a serious clash—between the West on one hand and the Muslim and Confucian (or Chinese) civilizations on the other.

Critics of this proposition find it far too pessimistic. China ("Confucian civilization" in Huntington's typology) does not want to clash with anyone; its leadership speaks instead of peace and economic cooperation. Even in the Middle East, where al-Qaeda may have hoped to mobilize Muslims in a global war against the West, that moment has probably passed (Cronin, 2010). Optimists say that the decline of al-Qaeda's appeal and the revolutions in Tunisia and Egypt prove that a "clash of civilizations" is bogus. Pessimists point to the strength of Islamist parties in Egypt, the killing of the United States' Ambassador in Libya in 2012, and the continuing clashes in Syria, Yemen, Somalia, and Sudan. They predict that Islamic fundamentalism, despite its several setbacks, and anti-Western attitudes will flourish. We will return to this subject again in the concluding chapter.

GENDER AND SOCIAL CONFLICT PERSPECTIVES

More countries now promote women to positions of power. France, for example, requires large companies to raise the proportion of female directors to 40 percent by 2020. In Spain, public and large private companies by law must reach that same goal by 2015. Norway introduced a similar requirement more than a decade ago (Beck, 2011). Although few women are yet heads of state, more and more women, particularly young professionals from Western societies, are involved in nongovernment organizations. In fact, they do much better in general in NGOs than men. Why? Some political psychologists say that women adapt better to intercultural communication, display greater tolerance, and work better in groups. Because many NGOs are engaged in humanitarian and educational work, women may also have greater experience. More and more, educated and well-trained women successfully manage grassroots networking, humanitarian aid, and fund-raising. This influx of women in NGOs may, in turn, signal monumental changes to come in the whole of international relations (Hunt, 2007).

The financial crises in the first decades of the twenty-first century have renewed arguments of world-systems theories that the capitalist "core" serves the interests of a few wealthy states. The United States has allocated hundreds of billions of dollars since 2009 to support delinquent banks and insurance companies. At the same time, the old core, dominated by Washington, may be giving way to a new core centered in Asia. In China, the state has retained a firm grip on finances, accumulated multibillion-dollar reserves of Western currency, begun new economic transformations, and achieved impressive growth (Arrighi, 2010). We will return to these views in Chapter 6.

Past, Present, and Future: The Cuban Missile Crisis

The Cuban Missile Crisis was one of the most dramatic events of the twentieth century. It also could have been one of the most tragic, because the world came very close to a nuclear war. Which lessons of the Cuban Missile Crisis could be used in today's international relations? Can we apply the alternative approaches we have just considered?

In 1962 the Soviet leadership decided to place a number of nuclear missiles on Cuban territory. The missiles, if launched, could have reached most major cities in America. The Soviets moved the missiles surreptitiously and lied to the world community about their actions. U.S. President John F. Kennedy issued an ultimatum to the Soviet premier Nikita Khrushchev, demanding a stop to the missiles' deployment. Kennedy ordered a naval blockade of Cuba to prevent the Soviet vessels carrying the missiles from entering the area. (He called it a "quarantine" to avoid appearing to have gone to war.) Khrushchev promised retaliation. The world was on the brink of a major confrontation between Moscow and Washington: A nuclear war seemed inevitable. Fortunately, both leaders found a way to resolve the conflict. How did they do this, and what led to the conflict?

In *Essence of Decision* (1971), Graham Allison argued that bureaucratic politics provides the best explanation of the decision-making process during the Cuban Missile Crisis. For years, Allison's book remained a standard text for applying rational models of decision-making to crisis management in international relations. In a 1999 edition, based on new access to Soviet, Cuban, and American archives (Allison and Zelikow, 1999). The authors organize their discussion around three simple questions:

- Why did the Soviet Union decide to place offensive missiles in Cuba?
- Why did the United States respond to the missile deployment with a blockade?
- Why did the Soviet Union withdraw the missiles?

(See Figure 3.8.)

During the crisis, President Kennedy did his best to act rationally. He created a small group of advisers and key members of the administration, called ExComm, whose goal was the removal of Soviet missiles from Cuba. At the beginning, Kennedy withdrew from the discussions, thus reducing psychological pressure on his advisers. This cautious action allowed ExComm to debate the pros and cons of various options and come up with three choices:

- An immediate air strike against Cuba to destroy the Soviet missiles
- A naval blockade of Cuba
- A strong diplomatic protest

(See Map 3.1.)

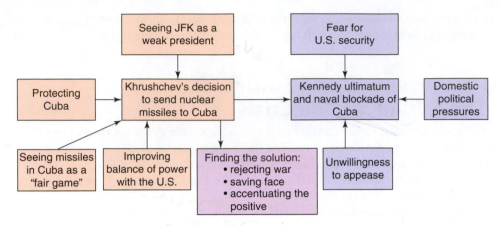

FIGURE 3-8 Perceptions and motivations of Khrushchev and Kennedy in the Cuban Missile Crisis.

What if we step aside from the rational model and look at the Cuban Missile Crisis through a constructivist lens? Several important details stand out. One year earlier, the United States had trained Cuban nationals to invade Cuba, and the CIA made plans to assassinate Castro. Most U.S. policy makers failed to understand that their provocative actions might have triggered Khrushchev's fears about a possible full-scale U.S. invasion of the island. For the Soviet leader, who boasted of the inevitability of a global Communist victory, a successful U.S. invasion of Cuba and the defeat of Castro would have been an unacceptable blow to his prestige and to the position of the Soviet Union in the world. Policy makers in Washington failed to understand how revolutionary prestige, as a factor "constructed" in Moscow and rooted in Soviet ideology and policies, could have driven Khrushchev. Intelligence in Washington also failed to detect the transfer of forty thousand Soviet troops and missiles to Cuba because such a daring action did not match the Soviet

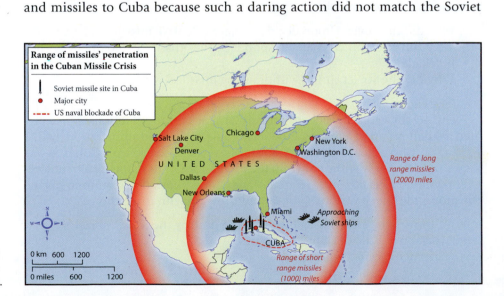

MAP 3-1 MT Range of missiles' penetration in the Cuban Missile Crisis.

On October 16, 1962, President John F. Kennedy announced to the American people that the United States established a "quarantine" of Cuba after he had discovered Soviet missiles there. The president promised that his country would deliver "a full retaliatory response upon the Soviet Union" if the Soviets attacked the United States.

cognitive maps. In accordance with consistency and resistance bias, this behavior was seen as highly unlikely.

To a conflict theorist, both Kennedy's and Khrushchev's decisions were ineffably human—and, as feminists would be probably quick to add, also male. They stepped back from the abyss but only after they had brought the world to the brink of a war. And what if Castro, instead of Khrushchev, had been the main decision maker on the Communist side? What if he had control over nuclear weapons? Castro was arguably more revolutionary minded than Khrushchev, and he was prepared to sacrifice Cuba on the altar of the world revolution. Postcolonial studies might describe him as reacting to the white male Western world. Fortunately, Khrushchev in this case proved more realist than revolutionary.

Political psychology too can help us analyze the Kremlin's actions. The rational model assumes that Khrushchev, like Kennedy, would have acted logically in weighing cost-benefit options. The Soviet leader might have wanted, for example, to improve the strategic position of the Soviet Union with respect to the United States. Yet this interpretation is incomplete. It fails to reflect Khrushchev's personal insecurities caused by his policy failures. He was unable to force Western powers out of West Berlin from 1958 to 1961. Chinese Communists criticized him for ideological mistakes, and his reform of the Soviet economy failed to produce the expected results. Khrushchev was therefore desperate to gamble to succeed in Cuba. He considered himself a clever decision maker, and his prestige depended on the outcome of his missile adventure (Blight, Allyn, and Welch, 1993; Taubman, 2004).

*Castro wanted to sacrifice Cuba.

New evidence from archives also reveals that Soviet leaders relied on erroneous assumptions about America's decision-making. Several individual factors influenced Khrushchev's behavior before and during the crisis. He evaluated Kennedy in a biased way, and he saw the president from the vantage point of his own life, shaped in the trenches of World War II. For Khrushchev, Kennedy was a spoiled "rich kid" from New England, a toy in the hands of hard-liners, and a pushover when it comes to international affairs.

Kennedy and his advisers also knew very little about the top leadership and decision-making in the Soviet Union. Washington received contradictory messages from Khrushchev: some of them quite belligerent and cocky, some more conciliatory. Kennedy was lucky to have an adviser, Llewellyn (Tommy) Thompson, who had just served as the U.S. ambassador in Moscow. Thompson met Khrushchev many times and interpreted his decisions not just in accord with the rational model but with knowledge of Khrushchev as a person. In the end, Thompson was convinced that Khrushchev was bluffing and recommended that Kennedy suggest a way for Khrushchev to save face—the secret trade of Soviet missiles in Cuba for U.S. missiles in Turkey. Thompson was right. As it turned out, Khrushchev never contemplated using the nuclear weapons and tried to reduce the chances of accidental miscalculation. He even ordered his commanders to keep the nuclear warheads in storage facilities.

This analysis of decision-making during a crisis becomes even more complicated when we apply the two-level game model to understand it. We know today that Khrushchev was facing increasing criticisms from opponents for his domestic-policy mistakes. He also had to fight criticism from the leadership of Communist China, which insisted that the Soviets were too cozy with capitalist countries. Kennedy, for his part, also faced critics who called him a weak president. Both felt hotheads breathing down their necks. General Curtis LeMay urged Kennedy to launch a surprise and massive aerial attack against Cuba to take all the Soviet missiles out. Khrushchev had to face Castro, who at a critical moment urged a preemptive missile attack against the United States (Fursenko and Naftali, 1997).

These perceptions and misperceptions pushed both sides to the abyss of confrontation in October 1962. Khrushchev, in a message to Kennedy, wrote that the United States and the Soviet Union were pulling at opposite ends of a rope and only made the knot tighter. Robert S. McNamara (1916–2009), secretary of defense in the Kennedy administration, concluded in retrospect that the world was lucky to have survived.

As veterans of World War II, Kennedy and Khrushchev shared a crucial formative experience. For all their differences as individuals, in the domestic pressures they faced, and in their ideologies and biases, the U.S. and Soviet leaders shared a common fear—the fear of unleashing a world war with nuclear weapons. This fear overcame powerful analogies. Kennedy rejected the Munich analogy that dictated he not "appease" the Soviets. Instead, Kennedy looked to 1914, when lack of negotiations brought great European powers to a world war. The last thing Khrushchev wanted was to provoke the United States, as the Japanese did at Pearl Harbor in 1941, into a full-scale war. For Khrushchev, nuclear weapons in Cuba were just a means of deterring U.S. aggression against Cuba.

The main lesson of the Cuban Missile Crisis is that rational decision-making is very difficult under extreme stress, with a fluid situation and time constraints. In such conditions, politicians may turn to their emotions and biases. Another lesson is the need to avoid a dangerous chain reaction of decisions that could drive opponents to make dangerous decisions.

We cannot guarantee that a dangerous crisis of similar proportion will never occur again. How will world leaders react if China attempts to attack Taiwan; Iran sends direct threats against Israel; or India and Pakistan, both nuclear powers, plunge into war over Kashmir? Will they have the time to assess the situation soberly, brush off the arguments of their most hawkish advisers, and find a solution short of war?

CONCLUSION

International relations are influenced by a great number of factors, and theories going beyond realism and liberalism can help explain them. Constructivism does not necessarily challenge mainstream theories of international relations. Rather, it provides valuable information about how and why states develop policies and interests. Conflict theories claim, often accurately, that state interests are defined by ruling elites trying to secure power. Identities, formed by history, religion, and culture, can affect foreign policy of states in many ways. And political psychology provides important information about how personal experiences, group influence, and other individual factors affect global affairs.

Some formative factors, group interests, identities, and perceptions in international relations are more important than others, and some circumstances are simply insignificant: but which ones? Only the careful study of international relations can provide answers.

CHAPTER SUMMARY

- Advocates of the constructivist view believe that state actions and policies are based on how leaders, bureaucracies, and societies interpret, or *construct*, the information available to them. Constructivist views argue that socially constructed meanings govern political decisions.
- Perceptions of how states should act—if they are shared by other states and for some time—translate into actions and shape the international environment.
- Conflict theories emphasize economic, social, and political inequality as a source of contradictions and tensions among social groups. Applied to international relations, conflict theories highlight the role of social classes, ruling elites, and other dominant groups in shaping foreign policy and global affairs.
- Marxism views a state as the instrument of dominant groups, such as the aristocracy or capitalists, to oppress and exploit others, such as peasants and workers. The state conducts policy, including foreign policy, according to the interests of the ruling classes.
- Dependency and world-systems theories argue that the structures of international relations—and trade in particular—make it impossible for underdeveloped countries to grow out of poverty. The free market was designed to keep them in a state of dependency. Poor states thus become permanent suppliers of cheap raw materials to a few economically advanced countries.

- Feminism argues that women do not have equal rights and opportunities with men, and changes are needed to achieve gender equality and social justice. Male norms and attitudes help undermine stability and peace

- Theories of racial and ethnic prejudice maintain that world politics is rooted in a belief in the superiority of one racial, national, cultural, or ethnic group over others.

- Political culture and identity are shaped by collective experience, religion and other factors. Political cultures can be traditional, authoritarian, participatory, or mixed. States with similar political cultures are more likely to cooperate, particularly if their identities are not in conflict.

- Identities are formed in part by the attitudes toward the other—another country, ethnic group, etc. They are several powerful forms of identity that reject the other—nationalism, tribalism, xenophobia, and fundamentalism. They can seriously complicate diplomacy and global affairs, or generate conflicts and wars.

- Political psychology studies the interactions between political and psychological factors in individual and group behavior. Political socialization examines how individuals acquire their political knowledge and beliefs. Most political psychologists maintain that political decisions are rational. However, leaders may have irrational motives or a diminished ability to reason.

- Biographical and psychological studies of political leaders, military commanders, and diplomats provide important information, but their relevance to decision-making is often unclear.

- In most countries, decision-making is a result of bureaucratic bargaining. Political groups express their interests, accept political trade-offs, and make compromises. Important differences exist between decision-making in authoritarian and democratic regimes.

- Global developments influence how states define their national interest. International structure, international laws, norms of behavior, international organizations and institutions—all these affect state preferences, interests, and foreign policy.

KEY TERMS

Accessibility bias 97
Analogy 100
Bureaucratic bargaining 103
Cognitive maps 104
Communism 85
Competitive
  authoritarianism 109
Conflict theories 84
Consistency bias 97
Constructivist view (or
  constructivism) 81

Core 87
Culture 90
Dependency theory 87
Feminist theories 88
Fundamentalism 95
Group pressure 97
Identity 90
Imperialism (Lenin's
  theory of) 85
Marxism 85
Nationalism 93

Periphery 87
Political culture 90
Political psychology 95
Political socialization 98
Postcolonial studies 86
Rational model 95
Resistance bias 97
Tribalism 93
Two-level games 105
Xenophobia 94

Visual Review ALTERNATIVE THEORIES

1. What do we study?

SHORTCOMINGS OF LIBERALISM AND REALISM
- How do international actors define their interests?
- Why do they choose one policy over another?

CHOOSING ALTERNATIVE VIEWS
- Constructivism emphasizes social norms and historic experiences of countries
- Conflict theories pay attention to different forms of inequality
- Identity theories turn to values and attitudes
- Political psychology focuses on political behavior and experiences

2. How do we think about it?

SOCIAL CONSTRUCTION
- State interests are constructed through interpretation, or *construction*, of facts
- Countries draw different lessons from history

INEQUALITY
- Marxism
- Dependency and world-systems theories
- Feminism
- Theories of prejudice

IDENTITY FACTORS
- Political culture and identity are shaped by collective experience, religion, ethnicity, and other group and individual experiences
- Nationalism, tribalism, xenophobia, and fundamentalism complicate global affairs

POLITICAL PSYCHOLOGY
- Policy decisions are not necessarily rational
- Individual and group actors affect foreign policy

3. How do we apply it?

THE INDIVIDUAL CONTEXT
Leaders' choices can be rational or biased, affected by both immediate and life experiences

THE STATE CONTEXT
Domestic bureaucracy, political competition, democratic contexts, and access to information affect foreign-policy decisions

THE GLOBAL CONTEXT
Global developments affect state interests and policies, which in turn affect the world

Critical Thinking
- What are the key shortcomings of realism and liberalism in understanding international relations?
- Compare and contrast constructivism and political psychology.
- Why are history lessons important for constructivists?
- Why have dependency and Marxist theories gained in popularity again in recent years?
- Give examples of "two-level games" in foreign policy.

CHAPTER 4

CHAPTER OUTLINE

Memorial lanterns float in Hiroshima, Japan, August 6, 2011, marking the anniversary of the U.S. atomic bombing. For millions of Americans, the attacks on Hiroshima and Nagasaki, provoked by Japanese aggression, helped in ending the war. Scholars disagree sharply over the moral and political consequences of this bombing for international relations.

International Security

Eternal vigilance is the price of liberty.
—DEMOSTHENES (384–322 BC)

ON DECEMBER 7, 1941, A FLEET OF AIRCRAFT CARRIERS OF THE EMPIRE OF JAPAN COMMANDED BY ADMIRAL ISOROKU YAMAMOTO SUDDENLY ATTACKED THE U.S. Naval base at Pearl Harbor, Hawaii. Japanese forces also attacked Guam, Wake Island, the Philippines, British Malaya, Hong Kong, Burma, and the Dutch East Indies. In response, America immediately declared war on Japan. After four years, culminating in the atomic bombing of the Japanese cities of Hiroshima and Nagasaki, Japan surrendered.

For centuries, leaders believed that security of their country was linked directly to military power and its effective use in time of war. However, Japan's defeat in World War II suggests other lessons. Its military elites drew the country into an unwinnable conflict. The use of force did not provide security for Japan. On the contrary, Japan lost the war, at a cost of well over 3 million lives. Under occupation by the United States, Japan adopted a provision in its new Constitution stating that its people would forever renounce war as a sovereign right and the threat or use of force as a means of settling international disputes. The Constitution also required Japan not to have military forces on land, at sea, or in the air (Koseki, 1998). For more than sixty years now, the United States has guaranteed military protection to Japan, a security shield that Japan has willingly accepted.

How do countries define and build their security strategies? Why do these strategies often lead to wars? Is global security achievable, and by what means? In this chapter we will examine security challenges and policies in today's world.

Learning Objectives

After reading this chapter, you should be able to:

▶ define national and international security;
▶ discuss security from realist, liberal, constructivist, and alternative perspectives;
▶ explain variation in security policies;
▶ apply major views of security to realities of international relations at each level of analysis; and
▶ evaluate the effectiveness of particular security policies.

What Do We Study?

States act to protect their own sovereignty and territorial integrity from domestic and foreign threats. Some act alone, relying on their economic might and armed forces. But most seek help from foreign states and international organizations and prefer negotiations and compromise to avoid military conflict. Security policies of the twenty-first century are supported by gigantic bureaucratic and military machines, influenced by political parties and lobbying groups. In the United States alone in 2010, more than 850,000 people had top-secret security clearances (Priest and Arkin, 2010b). This number is increasing. To understand better the complexity of national and international security, we begin, as usual, by defining key terms.

Security

National security has traditionally been understood as the protection of a state's sovereignty, territorial integrity, and interests. Maintaining the armed forces, obtaining and modernizing weapons, keeping aircraft and battleships, training specialists, and developing mass-mobilization plans are essential for national security (Sarkesian et al., 2007). National security used to be treated as distinct from domestic security, which is commonly associated with fighting criminal activities and is handled by the police. However, the growth of home-land security bureaucracy in the age of terrorism has created a third element between national and domestic aspects of security. Many factors define security priorities of a state. Geographic location and protected borders were crucial in the past—the protection by the seas provided security advantages to Great Britain and the United States. Today, the strength and health of domestic economy is more important.

International security refers to mutual security issues involving more than one state. Security is *bilateral* when it involves two states and *multilateral* when it involves more than two states. NATO is the best known multilateral security organization, formed more than half a century ago. In Shanghai, China, in 1996, Kazakhstan, China, Kyrgyzstan, Russia, and Tajikistan signed the Treaty on Deepening Military Trust in Border Regions and later agreed to reduce their military forces in those areas. This security organization came to be called the Shanghai Cooperation Organization or *Shanghai Six* after Uzbekistan joined the treaty. Internationalization of security is natural in the era of globalization. Table 4-1 provides a sample of international security pacts.

Studying conflict and war is also essential for our understanding of national and international security. A **conflict** is any antagonism between states, IGO, or nongovernment organizations. Conflict typically reflects the inability of a state or an international organization to achieve its goals because of the resistance or unwillingness of other actors. Conflicts remain nonviolent if conflicting sides use no force to resolve them.

Violent conflicts involve the use of force. Their ultimate form is **war**, an organized violent confrontation between states or other social and political entities, such as ethnic or religious groups. Victory is achieved by superior force and not by negotiations or legal rulings. Only after hostilities end in an armistice do negotiations resume. If war ends in surrender, one side is forced to accept conditions imposed by the victors. Scholars of international relations agree that states try to avoid wars, yet there are always exceptions.

In our times, threats to international security increasingly emerge involving **failing states** and **nonstate actors**. Failing states are those in which governments are incapable of exercising their major functions, defending borders, or making key decisions. Somalia, Chad, Sudan, Niger, and several other countries may be considered failing. A failing state is marked by lawlessness, extreme violence and civil wars, and massive suffering of the population. (Fund for Peace regularly posts the Failed State Index at www.fundforpeace.org/global.)

South Korea historically relies on multilateral security. NATO Secretary-General Anders Fogh Rasmussen, second from right, receives a briefing from a U.S. officer during his visit to South Korea in 2013.

TABLE 4-1 Examples of International Security Pacts

International Security Pact	Major Goals
The Treaty of Friendship, Cooperation and Mutual Assistance (Warsaw Pact): created in 1955.	Organized by the Soviet Union, this organization involved Communist states in Eastern Europe. Major goal: to keep Soviet military presence in Central Europe against NATO.
OAS: The Organization of American States. Formally created in the late 1940s.	Initiated by the United States, it includes the countries of North, Central, and South Americas. Major goals: security of the American continents, common action on the part of those states in the event of aggression.
ASEAN: The Association of Southeast Asian Nations. Created in 1967.	Includes countries located in Southeast Asia: Indonesia, Malaysia, the Philippines, Singapore, Thailand, Brunei, Myanmar, Cambodia, Laos, and Vietnam. Major goals: to contain Communism and have mutual protection.
CENTO: Central Treaty Organization. Created in 1955. Dissolved: 1979.	Included Iran, Iraq, Pakistan, Turkey, and the United Kingdom. Major goal: containment of the Soviet Union.
The Shanghai Cooperation Organization. Created in 1996.	Includes Kazakhstan, China, Kyrgyzstan, Russia, Tajikistan, and Uzbekistan. Major goals: keeping separatism in check, confronting terrorism, and balancing U.S. power in the region.

To protect their strategic interests, and to reduce or eliminate domestic and international threats, states develop security policies. These policies affect a broad range of international issues and, ultimately, the behavior of other states and international organizations. Security policies are born out of continuous debates among political elites, security officials, military experts, and the media. These debates focus on the nature of war and its types, causes, and consequences, as well as classification of strategies and the possibility of preventing war and conflict resolution.

Types of War

On September 1, 1939, German troops crossed the Polish border and advanced into the territory of a sovereign state. This is an example of an *offensive* war. For Poland, though, it was a *defensive* war. Labeling a war defensive or offensive is important for several reasons. One of them is international legitimacy, which affects other states' reaction to the war. Defensive wars evoke sympathy and support, whereas offensive actions typically lead to criticism, condemnation, or forceful resistance. Governments therefore seek to camouflage offensive actions as defensive (Levy, 1984).

The intentions and policies leading to wars, however, are not always simple. Some states start *preventive wars* to protect themselves if they believe that other states might threaten them in the future. Some believe that the U.S. war against Iraq in 2003 was preventive. There are also, *preemptive wars* that are launched to destroy the potential threat of an enemy when an attack by the adversary is imminent (Beres, 2008). In 1967, Israel launched a surprise air attack against Egypt, Syria, and Jordan. The Israeli government was convinced that those Arab states were mobilizing to attack Israel. The United States and most Western countries agreed with Israel, but Arab states and the Soviet Union called Israel the aggressor. These classifications remain controversial, a subject to which we will return later.

In terms of their scope and consequences, wars can be *local*, *regional*, and *global*. Local wars typically involve two states, but a massive armed conflict within a country, such as a civil war, need not engage other neighboring states. Local conflicts, especially in today's world, are likely to draw in other countries in close geographic proximity. That makes clear distinctions between a local and regional war difficult to draw.

Some local or regional conflicts grow into global wars, or *world wars*, with global consequences. World War I was triggered by the declaration of war on Serbia by the Empire of Austria-Hungary in 1914. Germany's attack on Poland in 1939 launched the Second World War. These wars brought a massive change in the global international order, as many old states collapsed and new ones were created.

Wars, conflicts, as well as security threats in general, can be *symmetrical* and *asymmetrical*. A classic example of a symmetrical security conflict was the United States' long confrontation with the Soviet Union. In a symmetrical conflict, an attack by one state is likely to cause a comparable response from the other. During the last two centuries states prepared their armed forces to fight in open, symmetrical conflicts. An asymmetrical conflict does not involve regular armies but rather small groups of rebels who try to avoid open fighting (Fearon and Laitin, 2003). **Guerrilla warfare** (often called irregular, unconventional warfare) involves irregular combat units that typically hide in difficult terrain (forest, mountains) and are usually not distinct from civilian population (Boot, 2009). Guerilla wars create significant security problems for states because they require special military strategies. The United States failed to win a guerilla war in Vietnam (1964–75) and the Soviet military had to withdraw from Afghanistan after a long war with local guerrillas (1979–88).

International terrorism has become the most significant asymmetrical threat to national and international security. Networks of committed fighters operate surreptitiously outside international and national institutions. To deal with their threats, special policies are necessary. The impact of terrorism on international security and on international relations will be considered at length in Chapter 7.

In the past, states commonly pursued territorial conquests and engaged in *predatory wars* for treasures, raw materials, trade routes, territories, and human beings as a potential workforce. Colonial expansion in the nineteenth and twentieth centuries—conducted by European powers such as France, Great Britain, Belgium, Italy, and Russia in Africa and Eurasia—is an example. Iraq occupied Kuwait in 1990 to gain possession of its vast oil resources and infrastructure. Other wars, called *retaliatory wars*, are waged by a state to weaken or punish another. China attacked Vietnam in 1979 to punish Hanoi for occupation of Cambodia and removal of the Communist regime there.

The difference among offensive, retaliatory, and preventive wars is often unclear. A smoke and dust cloud from an explosion rises into the sky after a NATO airstrike in Tripoli, Libya, in June 2011.

 **Predatory Wars and Responses to Them.** Learn more about Operation Desert Storm in video from the companion website. See how the world responded to a predatory war waged by the Iraqi government in 1990.

There are also *ethnic* and *religious wars* caused by conflicts between various groups struggling for their rights, territories, and independence (Soeters, 2005).

Our brief classification of wars need not be complete. Many types overlap, and you can add your own. For example, a war can be offensive, local, and preventive at the same time.

A central task for the state is to avoid war, and, if that is impossible, to protect itself from its worst consequences, from defeat and destruction. What security strategies can serve this purpose? We look next at types of security strategy and policy.

Security Policies

Prominent Prussian military thinker Karl von Clausewitz (1780–1831) wrote that "war is a continuation of policy by other means." He meant that states should put wars under their control and make them instruments in achieving their policy goals. In Europe in the nineteenth and early twentieth century many tried to combine rationality and morality to develop an international system of rules and regulations for warfare and ban the use of certain arms (we will turn to the concept of "just war" in Chapter 5). During World War I (1914–18) and World War II (1939–1945), however, states turned to the "total war" strategy to achieve victory for one side and unconditional surrender for the other. The concept of "total war" is generally rejected today. Moreover, states, IGOs, and NGOs continue to develop policies to limit weapons of mass destruction (WMD)—nuclear, chemical, and biological. In 1968 the leading nuclear powers signed the Non-Proliferation Treaty (NPT) with the goal to stop the dissemination of nuclear weapons. In 1975 the Biological Weapons

Convention banned development and possession of these weapons of mass destruction. A similar convention for chemical weapons entered in force in 1997. During the last decades, however, *conventional weapons* and smart technologies to deliver them have been drastically upgraded so that they, too, can bring destruction on a large scale.

States' failure to choose the right strategy may have serious consequences. The United States during the Cold War often responded asymmetrically to the Soviet security threat, that is, tried to achieve the position of absolute superiority using its wealth and economic growth. The Soviet Union, although its economy was much smaller, attempted to respond symmetrically, that is, achieve power parity with Washington in terms of the number of nuclear weapons (Gaddis, 2006; Zubok, 2007). The variety of state responses to foreign threats only begins with symmetry–asymmetry. (See Table 4-2.)

Security policies can also be based on **unilateralism** and **multilateralism**. In unilateral policy, a state relies primarily on its own resources (Kane, 2006). All great powers in the past practiced unilateralism; a recent example is the United States in 2003 occupying Iraq. In contrast, states adopting a multilateral policy coordinate their efforts with other states or international organizations. When Saudi Arabia faced a significant threat from Iraq, which had already occupied neighboring Kuwait in 1990, it joined in multilateral military action against the Iraqi government and allowed foreign troops, including the United States, to establish temporary military bases on the Saudi territory.

Isolationism is a policy of noninvolvement in international alliances. It does not mean that an isolationist power always stays away from international conflicts; rather, it means that this power prefers to remain free to act as it wishes. Isolationism largely governed U.S. policy until World War I and remains a strong current in public opinion today: more than 40 percent of Americans say that their country should "mind its own business" internationally (Pew, 2010). Similarly, some states choose nonalliance with any military bloc or coalition. (See Figure 4.1.)

Interventionism is a policy of interference in other states' affairs and conflicts without regard for their consent. During the eighteenth and nineteenth centuries, European great powers including Britain, France, Russia, and then Germany intervened around the world, expanding their colonial empires. From 1898 until 1917, the United States, although "isolationist" toward Europe,

TABLE 4-2 Types of War and Strategies

Intentions and Policies	Offensive, Defensive, Preventive, Preemptive, Symmetrical, Asymmetrical
Purposes	Predatory, Retaliatory, Political
Strategies	Conventional, Nonconventional, With Weapons of Mass Destruction; Symmetrical and Asymmetrical
Scope and Consequences	Local, Regional, Global

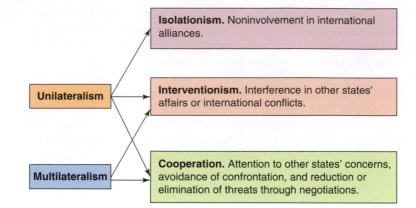

FIGURE 4-1 Basic security policies. *Sources: Wittkopf, 1990; Sobel, 2001; Hinckley, 1992.*

intervened unilaterally in Central America (O'Brien & Clesse, 2002). After 1895, Japan became the first modern Asian power to act in the same way in China and the Pacific. As you saw at the start of this chapter, Japan's interventionism was a cause of its war with the United States.

Other states prefer a policy of **cooperation** (Newman et al., 2006). Unable to defend its strategic positions in the Mediterranean and the Middle East against the Soviet Union, Britain preferred in 1947 to act as an ally of the

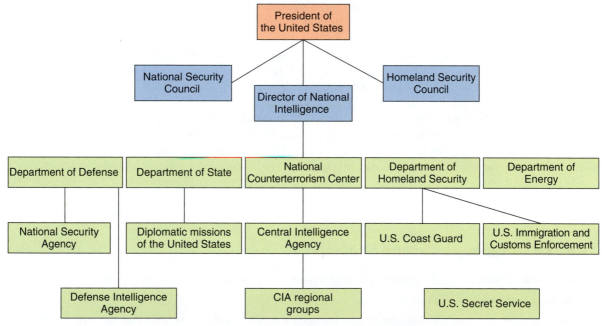

FIGURE 4-2 Major U.S. actors and agencies involved in national security.
Source: Security policies of the twenty-first century are supported by gigantic bureaucratic and military machines, influenced by political parties and lobbying groups. In the United States alone in 2011, more than 850,000 people had top-secret security clearances.

United States. For another example, the small democratic state of Finland in the 1950s chose to cooperate with its neighbor, the Soviet Union. From Finland's viewpoint, it was a reasonable bargain, while the Soviet Union saw it as a way to declare its peaceful intentions toward other European states.

Most security policies involve a complex combination of foreign, defense, and domestic policies. In most countries, the head of state (president or prime minister) directs security policies with the help of a complex bureaucracy. In Washington, the National Security Council (NSC) is part of the Executive Office of the President of the United States. Presidents also direct the activities of other government departments, organizations, and agencies dealing with national security. (See Figure 4.2.)

▶ Explain the difference between predatory and retaliatory wars.
▶ Can a country's isolationist policy be interventionist at the same time?

CHECK YOUR KNOWLEDGE

How Do We Study It?

Realism

According to realism, security is the main and exclusive responsibility of states. They always try to maximize their power and tend to act according to their interests in assessing threats and their own defensive capabilities. The core element of every state's security, according to realism, is power and the ability to use it.

REALIST PRINCIPLES OF SECURITY

How do states provide for their security? First, geography is frequently the subject of security concerns and policies. Oceans, rivers, and mountains can act as natural security barriers. Japan, the United Kingdom, and the United States for many years thought of the seas as protection from foreign intrusions; whereas Belgium, Poland, China, and Russia were more vulnerable. States are frequently involved in conflicts over international trade routes—such as the Strait of Gibraltar between Europe and Africa, the Suez Canal in Egypt between Africa and Asia, and the Dardanelles in Turkey between Europe and Asia.

Security, according to realism, also depends on the quantity and quality of the armed forces and their mobility. The centerpiece of British security policy from the seventeenth through the twentieth century was the Royal Navy. The acquisition of nuclear weapons in 1945 gave the United States absolute military superiority—until the Soviet Union tested its atomic weapon in 1949. Countries that pursue nuclear weapons today, including North Korea and Iran, think of them as a security guarantee. The concept of *revolution in military affairs* became a prevalent outlook on the future of war. It is based on the debates about the rapidly changing role of modern technology in warfare and security (Adamsky, 2010; Table 4-3).

TABLE 4-3 Examples of Realist Arguments Related to Security

Elements of Power	Example
Quantity of weaponry and military forces: numbers matter	The central goal of British security policy from the seventeenth through the twentieth century was ensuring that the Royal Navy was larger and more advanced than the largest navies of the other great powers.
Quality of weaponry: ability to destroy matters	Development of fast-moving motorized military units and new military tactics helped Nazi Germany achieve quick victories the first three years of World War II. The "drone" technology gives superiority to the United States today compared to other countries.
Presence of armed forces abroad	During the Cold War the Soviet Union and the United States kept their armies in Central Europe. The United States continues to keep its armed forces around the world.

Smaller states have less room for diplomacy acting alone when they lack economic and military clout (Waltz, 2001). They often try to receive security guarantees from more powerful states and organizations. Poland, Hungary, and the Czech Republic joined NATO in 1999 for a host of reasons—but above all fear of Russia (Goldgeier, 1999). In the twenty-first century, Vietnam and the Philippines rely increasingly on the United States to secure their interests in the South China Sea. The United States and its European allies consider Saudi Arabia a stabilizing factor in an extremely unstable region and assist it militarily (Friedrich, 2011).

International security is a dynamic process. The changing behavior of individual states affects the stability of the entire international system. After 2010, political instability in Libya, Egypt, Syria, Mali, and several other countries jeopardized the security of the entire North Africa, Middle East, and sub-Saharan Africa. In other regions, military programs in North Korea, Iran, and Venezuela destabilize regional and world security by disrupting the established balance of power.

THE SECURITY DILEMMA

Often, countries generate instability unintentionally, as they make the difficult choices between unilateral security and cooperation. One state, for example, may decide to improve its security by strengthening its defensive capabilities. But this makes a neighboring state see its security as diminished, and it may retaliate in kind. This dynamic is the security dilemma, and it can result in an arms race.

The security dilemma helps in understanding why a disruption of the power balance or a change in the structure of the international system increases international tensions (Booth and Wheeler, 2007). During the Cold War, for example, the United States built up its naval and air bases nearest the Soviet Union to contain the spread of Communism to Europe and Asia. On its side, the Soviet Union maintained a huge army in Central Europe. Moscow was ready to invade Western Europe in the event of an attack. Western countries, scared by the Soviet buildup, asked the United States to deploy nuclear missiles on their territory. The international system was bipolar at that time, which made this arms race very difficult to stop. This dangerous competition contributed to spiraling tensions and the Cuban Missile Crisis, as we saw in Chapter 3.

NUCLEAR DETERRENCE

The security dilemma helps explain the policy of nuclear **deterrence**—maintaining nuclear weapons with the intention not to use them but to deter others from nuclear attack. In the 1960s, top politicians in the United States began to realize that the use of nuclear weapons would be a calamity of global proportions. They also understood that attempts to achieve superiority in nuclear weapons did not guarantee security. The United States therefore adopted a security strategy of **mutual assured destruction (MAD)**: If both countries had enough nuclear weapons to destroy the other even *after* a surprise nuclear attack, this would serve as deterrence. Some critics of this approach urged instead an unlimited arms race, including the construction of an antimissile defense. Other critics believed that nuclear weapons should be abolished altogether.

MAD could not stop the arms race, and so Washington and Moscow began to negotiate rules for arms control. Yet new nuclear weaponry and the two-pole structure of international relations quickly revived the security dilemma until 1987, when Mikhail Gorbachev and Ronald Reagan put a halt to the vicious circle (Leffler, 2007).

THE DOMINO THEORY

One practical application of realist principles to security was the *domino theory*. In this theory, the international system resembles a row of dominos standing

@ Learn more about MAD (Mutual Assured Destruction) on the companion website. See the competition between offensive and defensive security strategies, both promising to bring peace.

Robert McNamara remained Defense Secretary during the Kennedy and Johnson administrations and masterminded American military escalation in Vietnam. He believed that "a loss" of South Vietnam to the Communists would cripple American credibility and security globally. Washington, however, refused to send troops into Communist North Vietnam for fear of a nuclear war with China and the USSR.

on end. If a single domino falls, so will the rest. In the 1950s, President Dwight Eisenhower and other U.S. policy makers argued that Communist takeover in even a small country could initiate the "domino effect" (Boot, 2007).

One of the most compelling reasons for U.S. involvement in the Vietnam War in the 1960s was fear of a domino-like fall of anti-Communist governments throughout Southeast Asia if the United States kept out of Vietnam (McNamara, 1996).

SECURITY REGIMES

One way to avoid the domino effect is through multilateralism. In a **security regime**, a powerful country or several countries provide protection to other states in exchange for their cooperation (Jervis, 1982). NATO emerged in 1949 as a security regime in which the United States provided a nuclear "umbrella" protecting Western Europe from the Soviet Union. Less formally, the United States in the past decades became the security regime guarantor for Saudi Arabia, Kuwait, and the United Arab Emirates (the wealthiest Arab states), against Iraq, and later against Iran (Fouskas, 2003). In case of a nonproliferation regime for WMD, five permanent members of the UN Security Council usually act in concert because this security regime serves their interests.

CHECK YOUR KNOWLEDGE

▶ Explain the security dilemma.
▶ Apply the domino theory to explain the U.S. intervention in Iraq in 2003.

Liberalism

Supporters of international liberalism recognize the primary role of states in security policies but also point to the increasing role of international organizations and nonstate actors. They believe that the power of states and security regimes is no longer the only key to peace in today's world.

LIBERAL PRINCIPLES OF SECURITY

In the liberal view, neither economic nor military power alone can bring lasting security, and military threats are seldom the best choice of action. Instead, the desire for mutually acceptable outcomes and the complexity of international problems give countries the incentive to cooperate (Bull, 1977; 1988; Ikenberry, 2011a).

Realists assume that states have few choices; they either increase their power or align with some states against the others (Herrmann & Lebow, 2004). Supporters of the liberal view maintain that states have other options, such as negotiated settlements to avoid war and the creation of new institutions and norms of international cooperation (Fearon, 1995). These experts believe the world was lucky to survive the Cold War, with its dangerous security dilemma and nuclear deterrence strategies. In the logic of MAD, as we have seen, a miscalculation by one side could easily have led to a devastating nuclear war.

According to the liberal view, security policies in democratic societies should be part of the democratic process: they should be transparent and accountable whenever possible. The decision-making process should be more open to discussion, especially in the vital areas such as military actions overseas or international agreements. Policy makers should take into account nongovernment organizations, the media, and grassroots organizations. In other words, not only a small group of security professionals, but also representative institutions and nongovernment organizations should influence strategic security decisions affecting the lives of millions (Stoddard, 2006).

Liberals may accept war in pursuit of liberal goals of a secure world. **Liberal interventionism** means that a coalition of states and IGOs can act preventively against a predator state when international security is at stake. Of course, this intervention is possible only after all diplomatic and nonviolent means are exhausted. In 1990, the United Nations denounced the occupation of Kuwait by Iraq. A multinational coalition then liberated Kuwait in 1991.

INTERNATIONAL ORGANIZATIONS AND THE SECURITY COMMUNITY

The sheer complexity of economic, political, and environmental issues today makes it difficult for individual states to make security decisions on behalf of others. By governing collectively, international organizations can reduce the risk of mistakes. In 1918 and 1919, U.S. President Woodrow Wilson's Fourteen Points already called for **collective security**, an arrangement in which security of one country becomes the concern of all who provide a collective response to threats. Collective security was supposed to replace a shaky balance of power in Europe (Adler and Barnett, 1998). These principles inspired many leaders in Western Europe after World War II and Soviet leader Mikhail Gorbachev from 1988 to 1991.

International organizations are not designed to please everyone or to avoid conflict at all cost. They can still impose sanctions and authorize the use of force. However, they offer greater legitimacy for their decisions because they are collective. Recently, regional international organizations have begun to play a more active role in conflict prevention, peacekeeping, humanitarian assistance, and postwar reconstruction (Tavares, 2009). We will return to this topic in Chapter 9.

An alternative to the security regime is the **security community**—based not on force, fear, and secret agreements, but on mutual interests, voluntary cooperation, and open discussion. The idea of a security community rests in part on the sharing of rational and moral anticipations and dispositions of self-restraint in using force (Adler, 2008). Security communities emerged relatively recently as governments, political leaders, and other influential groups agreed on joint action and nonviolent conduct to maintain security and avoid war (Deutsch et al., 1957). The United States, Canada, and Mexico, for instance, may be a good example of a security community in North America.

Constructivism

In the constructivist view, countries act according to historical experience, identities, perceptions, and social norms. Canada, for example, has no concerns about U.S. military superiority because the two countries remain at peace and have not intervened into each other's affairs for at least a century. In contrast, countries such as Latvia, Estonia, and Lithuania harbor security fears toward Russia because the Soviet Union annexed and incorporated them by force from 1940 until 1991.

PERCEPTIONS, IDENTITIES, AND ATTITUDES

A **security policy** is often based on perceptions (or misperceptions) of other states, such as their *propensity to use force*. For example, North Korea's development of nuclear weapons alarms South Korea and Japan because it has acted belligerently in the past. Other countries may see the United States as a friend, a distant partner, an isolationist, an outcast, or an enemy. For instance, in 1979, the religious rulers of Iran labeled the United States the Great Satan. A group of radical students seized the American embassy in Tehran and took American diplomats hostage. Hostility between the two states continues to this day.

An even more important factor in security policies is a state's international *identity*—the perceived role it plays in a regional or global community. The Soviet Union's identity was linked to international Communism and the defeat of capitalism, and for this reason Soviet security strategies remained unilateralist and interventionist on the global scale. The United States views itself as a beacon of freedom and democracy: this caused it sometimes to intervene unilaterally, but more fundamentally to build cooperation with other democratic states and allies. Security identities can be shaped by painful memories: China's identity is linked to the suffering in the past at the hands of colonizing powers including Japan, which occupied parts of China in 1931–45. And Japan changed its identity after 1945 from imperialist and aggressive to peacefully democratic and cooperative.

Iranian students climb over the wall of the U.S. embassy in Tehran during the Iranian Revolution, November 4, 1979. The students went on to hold 52 of the embassy staff as hostages for 444 days. The U.S.–Iranian conflict continues to shape American security policies in the Middle East and Central Asia.

Historical memories, perceptions, and identities can form lasting *attitudes* of states toward other states—ranging from mutually friendly to hostile. Hostilities can feed on each other, but only if states let that happen—especially in the absence of mutual agreements (B. Cronin, 1999). If countries learn to overcome the record of mutual resentment, they eliminate a very source of security dilemma. After World War II, France and Germany, two countries with a long history of mutual violence and mistrust, began to engage in economic and political integration that led to a united European market (see Chapter 2). Neither country now regards the other as a threat. Different developments occurred between the Soviet Union and the United States during the Cold War, and also between India and Pakistan after their creation in 1947. For decades, each country saw the other as hostile, and their security policies reflected these attitudes.

A crucial feature of a country's security policies is its definition of security. Some countries may define their security only in military terms, while others consider economic and environmental security as well (Buzan and Hansen, 2009). Along with history and the international environment, a security definition may also be rooted in social norms. Most of today's affluent, democratic societies reduce the role of military force in their security policies.

MILITARISM AND PACIFISM

Militarism puts a premium on the use of military force in response to most foreign threats. This attitude to international security glorifies war, conquest, domination, and weapons. **Pacifism**, in contrast, is a principled opposition to war and the belief that international disputes should be settled by nonviolent means. This social attitude glorifies restraint, mutual concessions, respect, and peace (Zinn, 2002). In the United States, militarism and pacifism reflect the never-ending argument between *hawks*, who support tough measures, and *doves*, who reject violence in foreign policy.

Public attitudes shift constantly between militarism and pacifism. As the result of the heavy U.S. casualties during the war in Vietnam, domestic political dissent and protests grew in the United States in the late 1960s and early 1970s. Yet militarism did not lose its public appeal and capacity to set policy (Hanson, 2001). Today, the elites of most democratic countries include both hawks and doves. For example, in Israel the generally hawkish politicians of the Likud party must contend with the more dovish Labor party leaders. These attitudes evolve and may change with new threats on the horizon.

Conflict Theories

According to other views, states maintain international security to protect key interests of the dominant social groups. Marxism and feminism have long criticized international security policies, claiming that they are state centric, dominated by special interests, and gender biased.

MARXISM

In the Marxist view, security policies reflect the interests of the ruling economic and political elites. To protect their wealth and power, these elites wage

---

DEBATE > WHY HAS OBAMA ENGAGED IN SEVERAL ARMED CONFLICTS?

Few state leaders support war as the only security option, whereas even the most passionate advocates of peace often see preparations for war as vital security measures. Domestic critics of President Obama before he took office often charged him of being dovish. Indeed, Obama was very critical of Washington's military engagements overseas and moved to reduce nuclear weapons (Parker, 2010). But Obama did not withdraw immediately from Iraq and even increased U.S. military presence in Afghanistan in 2010. Moreover, in 2011, he intensified missile strikes against suspected terrorists in several counties and ordered military operations against the Qaddafi regime in Libya.

WHAT'S YOUR VIEW?

Does Obama's attitude toward armed conflicts seem reasonable and consistent to you? Do you think he succeeded in finding a good balance between seeking peace and relying on military force?

 Book review: "In Bob Woodward's 'Obama's Wars,' Neil Sheehan sees parallels to Vietnam." Find more on the companion website.

---

war, create international organizations, sign international treaties, and pursue their own interventionist or isolationist strategies. Marxists compare international security to an old colonial system of domination.

In the Soviet Union, Marxist-Leninist ideology reinforced Soviet imperialist policies (Shlapentokh et al., 2008). Soviet ruling groups felt insecure as long as the country was surrounded by non-Communist states. After winning World War II, the Soviet Union expanded its ideological vision of security by creating a security belt of Communist regimes; and after the 1950s, it began to help radical anti-Western regimes around the world (Zubok, 2007). It also imposed tight security controls within its borders: The Soviet population was not supposed to know that living standards in Western countries were much higher.

Contemporary Marxist views on security go beyond the security policies of Communist states of yesterday and today. Today's Marxists claim that international politics reflects above all the interests of wealthy, well-organized groups. These interests are supported by the corporate media and global financial institutions; they are embedded in countries' educational systems.

Marxists often avoid the state-centered analysis of security and shift the discussion toward global aspects of security. Marxists challenge neoliberalism and the entire capitalist world order for generating an increasing economic disparity and insecurity of the vast majority of people. Unemployment, consistent financial troubles, and the erosion of the middle class are viewed as the most significant security problems of today (Davis, 2011).

FEMINISM

Traditionally, feminism argued that in negotiation, diplomacy, or decision-making, women could add an important element of trust in international relations, something that men failed to achieve. The key problem was that few women were allowed to help shape military and security policy (True, 2009). The past two decades have brought significant changes in the way some countries expanded the role of women in national security areas. Women began to occupy top government positions not only in Western liberal democracies but also in others. Argentina, India, Costa Rica, Kyrgyzstan, Liberia, and Kosovo among others have elected women as their heads of state. At the same time, feminist views of security cannot be reduced to the issue of how many women serve in government offices. Rather, many feminists also seek to reframe the way we all understand security, not unlike Marxism.

Feminist challenges to traditional views, norms, and values of security emerged in the 1960s on the campuses of North American and West European universities. Feminists first criticized the state monopoly on security issues. They were particularly wary of realism because it defined national and international security in terms of state sovereignty and domination—two key values associated with masculinity. During the 1980s and later, feminists argued that the male-dominated narrative of force and war should be replaced with other narratives including individual safety, interdependence, agreement, and shared power (Reardon, 1985; Enloe, 2000 and 2007; Wibben, 2011). When the Cold War ended, feminists shifted the discussion from *national* security to *global* security, focusing on the problems of violence, gender and racial discrimination, and environmental degradation. Feminists also argued that the understanding of security as the absence of war is incomplete. There should be *positive peace*—with guarantees of basic social and economic rights to all (Hirschman, 2010; Tickner, 1992).

No discussion of security today can be complete without "gendering," or analyzing from the feminist perspective, every major element of traditional approaches and issues (Sjoberg, 2009).

Cecilia Chacon swears in as Bolivia's Minister of Defense at the government palace in La Paz, Bolivia, in 2011. Chacon is the first woman to be defense minister in Bolivia's history.

▶ Describe the differences between security regimes and security communities.

▶ How can a state's identity affect its security policies?

▶ What is the propensity to use force?

CHECK YOUR KNOWLEDGE

How Do We Apply It?

The U.S. Constitution gives the president authority in the areas of national security and international relations. Yet evaluating security risks and seeking adequate responses must take place at several levels, only beginning with individual leaders. These different contexts help in understanding the complexity of defining and building international security.

The Individual Context

During the Cold War, the U.S. President accumulated extraordinary power to decide on the issues of national security. The U.S. Congress even granted the White House a discretion to start wars, for instance in Vietnam, without congressional authorization. As a result, almost every U.S. President since 1945 has significantly altered national security strategy (Gaddis, 1982). The trend continued after the end of the Cold War, when President Clinton conducted a major reevaluation of global threats. Whereas President George W. Bush brought his own vision of security threats, focusing on international terrorism and the rogue regimes of Iraq and Afghanistan, President Barack Obama moved to more traditional realist strategies. In other countries with strong executive power, such as France and Russia, new leaders introduce new security agendas. In Russia, for instance, former President Boris Yeltsin (1992–1999) pursued a strategy of security cooperation with the United States and NATO. His successor Vladimir Putin views policies of Washington and NATO as a security threat to Russia.

LEADERS AND ADVISERS

Waging a war is often the individual choice of a political leader and close associates, but only within limits. In democracies, there are constitutional limits on power. Political opposition, public opinion, and the media limit the choices too. In non-democracies, leaders' choices to wage war seem unrestrained. Yet their lives and safety are often under threat if they leave office (Goemans et al., 2009). They may therefore choose war simply to secure political power. Statistical analysis suggests that non-democratic leaders indeed have a higher propensity to wage war because of political insecurity (Debs and Goemans, 2010).

Moreover, decision makers seldom act alone on security issues. They depend on analysts and advisers who may have their own theories about how the country should evaluate and respond to security threats. The policy of containment, formulated by George Kennan in 1946–47 (see Chapter 2), was especially influential. Kennan, a State Department official, believed that Communism would eventually collapse under the weight of its contradictions. In contrast, Paul Nitze, another U.S. security official, believed that the

---

DEBATE > ARE VETERANS MORE LIKELY THAN NON-VETERANS TO SUPPORT THE USE OF FORCE?

A detailed study of the U.S. foreign policy elite between 1816 and 1992 found that politicians with a military background were less likely to support the use of force than non-veteran leaders (Gelpi and Feaver, 2002). In fact, the more military experience policy makers possessed, and the greater the percentage of veterans serving in government, the less likely a military response. Once a military response was underway, however, veterans were more supportive of greater use of force for a longer period. In contrast, non-veterans tended to become less supportive of the use of force as a conflict continued.

WHAT'S YOUR VIEW?

Why do you think veterans are less inclined toward the use of force? And why do you think veterans are more supportive of wars once a military response is under way? What are the reasons and motivations behind such a pattern? Ask the students who have served in the military (and especially those who served in Iraq or Afghanistan) to share their views.

 Article: "Prudence, War and Civil-Military Relations," by LTG James M. Dubik, U.S. Army retired. Article: "Success Matters: Casualty Sensitivity and the War in Iraq," by Christopher Gelpi, Peter D. Feaver, and Jason Reifler.

United States needed significant peacetime rearmament to fight the Soviet threat (Thompson, 2009). The competition between these two views lasted for many years.

PEACE PSYCHOLOGY

To some political psychologists international security is achievable through education and good will. They develop **peace psychology,** which tries to understand the ideological and psychological causes of war and find practical applications of their findings (MacNair, 2003). Their goal is to develop educational programs to reduce the threat of violence. Certainly, more often than not, political leaders read intelligence reports through the prism of preconceived beliefs. Yet leaders and ordinary people, they believe, can look beyond old images of "the enemy" and find possibilities for dialogue. Peace psychology made important contributions to U.S.–Soviet relations during the Cold War and the relaxation of international tensions in the 1980s (Greening, 1986). They organized face-to-face meetings between officials, students, teachers, and other professionals in the United States and the Soviet Union to promote trust. At the end of this chapter, we will see how both institutional and psychological factors brought about the end of the Cold War.

Should women in high offices be psychologically prone to peaceful conflict resolution? As we noted in Chapter 2, with so few women in charge of foreign policy, it is difficult to know how much women in high offices would make a difference. But in the past Golda Meir in Israel, Indira Gandhi in India, and Margaret Thatcher in the UK were more prone to use force than some of the male politicians that surrounded them. In the United States, Madeline Albright, Condoleezza Rice, and Hillary Clinton acted very tough as secretary of states.

Visitors view an exhibition of artwork by Japanese and Chinese cartoonists in Nanjing, China, in 2013. The event opened half a year later than originally planned after a wave of anti-Japan riots in China sparked by a territorial dispute. Peace psychologists believe that leaders and ordinary people must look beyond old images of "the enemy" and find possibilities for dialogue.

CASE IN POINT > *GRIT and the Spiral of Insecurity*

During the Cold War, advocates of nuclear disarmament argued for an exit from the cycle of mutual insecurity. Frustrated by the superpowers' inability to guarantee international security, they believed that real policy change could begin with small, incremental steps. Such goodwill gestures would include student exchanges, trade deals, and joint projects and interviews. An American psychologist, Charles Osgood, developed the **graduated** **reciprocation in tension-reduction** (GRIT) model in the 1960s, and Soviet leader Mikhail Gorbachev relied on it during 1987 to 1989 when he transformed the security doctrine of the Soviet Union. The result was the end of the Cold War.

CRITICAL THINKING

If GRIT was so successful, why don't countries use it to settle other bilateral conflicts? As you can attest now, there should be particular and favorable conditions for the strategies like GRIT to work. Which conditions should there be, in your view? Think about individual qualities of countries' leaders, political contexts in their states, and the international situation in general. Do these conditions exist, for example, in the Israeli-Palestinian conflict? Would you use GRIT to ease tensions in Afghanistan? If not, why? If yes, how?

CHECK YOUR KNOWLEDGE

▶ What does peace psychology study?
▶ Explain graduated reciprocation in tension-reduction.

The State Context

As realists insist, a country with massive military power has more security options than a weaker state. However, military strength alone is not a guarantor of security. A country also needs trustworthy allies, domestic political stability, and national unity. During the American Revolution, the Americans' alliance with France compensated in part for their military weaknesses. French political disunity in the late 1930s allowed Hitler to crush France and its allies quickly in 1940. These examples show the importance of domestic factors in foreign and security policy (Walt, 1991).

PUBLIC OPINION

In democratic countries, national security is the subject of public debate, and political pressures exert considerable influence (Nacos et al., 2000). Yet during the time of international tensions or when a war appears immanent, public tends to "rally around the flag." Experts call it *rage militaire*—euphoric expectations of a confrontation and a quick victory. Knowing that effect, some political leaders may engage in a *diversionary war*, to distract domestic public opinion from pressuring problems at home. Ideally, this war should distract from a domestic problem and strengthen the government's position in power (Sobek, 2008). Yet usually the military fervor does not last long. After the Vietnam War the public in the United States no longer supported long war and military commitments overseas, and developed very low tolerance for casualties (Shiraev and Sobel, 2006). (See Table 4-4.)

There are cycles in public opinion, related to generational experience. Before World War II, Americans were largely isolationists. Most believed that their country's security does not depend on the situation in Europe or elsewhere. After World War II, American public opinion tended to be more interventionist. Consensus in support of interventionist policies lasted until the middle of Vietnam War, roughly 1968, when Americans became divided.

IDEOLOGY

In today's democratic societies, according to opinion polls and electoral results, people on the left are more likely to oppose military confrontations, in accord with liberal views of international relations. Those on the right are more likely to be nationalistic and pro-military, in accord with the realist perspective. These views are reflected in popular perceptions of the major political parties. In the United States, Democrats are often seen as "soft" and Republicans as "hawkish." Studies show that conservative presidents' foreign policy tended to be hawkish (Dueck, 2010). In Germany, Christian Democrats (a conservative party) are frequently viewed as too tough in dealing with international threats and Social Democrats (a liberal party) as too weak (Shiraev and Sobel, 2006).

These perceptions are not always accurate. Conservative governments, which are generally reluctant to raise taxes to subsidize the military, frequently choose diplomacy, coalition building, and bargaining with adversarial states (Narizny, 2003). Liberals recently became more supportive of the use of military force against governments perceived to be capable of atrocities against their own people. The constructivist perspective offers another explanation for why liberals do not necessarily express soft attitudes and conservatives hawkish ones. People tend to respond to national security threats according to

TABLE 4-4 Confrontations, Hostilities, and Public Support

Period, Country	Descriptions of Public Reaction
Britain, mid-1850s	Fear of Russia was rampant among decision makers and the educated public, who viewed Russia as a danger to British colonies. The two countries fought between 1853 and 1856.
China, 1965–69	The Chinese Communist Party launched a massive propaganda campaign, blaming the Soviet Union for selling out Socialist values. The campaign fueled a wave of anti-Soviet sentiment in China and led to bloody skirmishes on the Sino-Soviet border in 1969.
Russia, 1999	NATO military strikes against Serbia, a country viewed as friendly to Russia, led to anti-American outbursts and the Russian government's abandonment of its pro-Western course in foreign policy. After 1999, Russia began to regard NATO as an adversary.
China, 2005	Nationalistic sentiment and attempts by the Japanese government to downplay the atrocities committed during World War II led to the eruption of anti-Japanese demonstrations in all major cities in China.

their *self-perceptions*. Conservatives may feel more comfortable in the foreign-policy arena because they already support a forceful defense and therefore do need to use force all the time (Reeves, 2001). Liberals, who may feel less secure about their ability to mount a military response, may overreact.

LOBBYING AND SECURITY BUREAUCRACY

Lobbying is activity by individuals, groups, and corporations to influence public officials in support of legislation or policies. Its methods include mail campaigns, mobilizing voters, funding political campaigns, and op-ed pieces in the media. Advocates of conflict theories argue that lobbying helps the ruling classes determine foreign and security policy. During the twentieth century, however, lobbies represented different approaches toward securities. Some business groups pushed for American economic and military expansion. During the Cold War, Quakers and other groups promoted negotiations with Soviet leaders to prevent nuclear war, while ethnic Americans from Eastern Europe and Catholic organizations were anti-Soviet and supported federal spending to maintain U.S. military superiority. A powerful pro-Israeli lobby emerged between 1967 and 1973 and used strategic security goals to justify U.S. support for Israel (Mearsheimer and Walt, 2007).

During the Cold War, government security bureaucracy and industrial corporations shared their common interest in the perpetuation of the arms race and confrontation with the Soviet Union. In 1960, President Dwight Eisenhower spoke of the "military-industrial complex" that had come to dominate his country's security policies (Eisenhower, 1960). After the terrorist attacks of 2001, a new powerful bureaucracy emerged. Homeland security now combines domestic and national security tasks. The impact of homeland security bureaucracy on foreign policy decision-making is yet to be seen, but it clearly represents a powerful new factor in security policies.

Lockheed Martin Executives guide then-Defense Secretary Robert Gates, center, through the F-35 Lightning II assembly line at Lockheed Martin Aeronautics Company in Fort Worth, Texas, in 2009. A prime target for painful spending cutbacks, the plane also had a daunting constituency: some 130,000 jobs in 47 states and Puerto Rico and plenty of support in Congress.

The Global Context

With the increasing interconnectedness of economies and policies, more and more events and factors have implications for national and international security. The essence of international relations becomes not just about state and regional politics, but about energy resources as well.

GEOPOLITICS

For centuries, sovereign states struggled for territorial and geographic advantage. Many of them used **geopolitics**—the theory and practice of using geography and territorial gains to achieve political power or seek security. Geographical position gave some countries clear advantages in security matters, while others remained vulnerable. New research in history suggests that geopolitics played a crucial role in the rise and fall of the great world powers (Morris, 2010). In Afghanistan, the country's vast and rough terrain and underdeveloped infrastructure pose significant challenges for military operations to achieve stability in this country. At the same time, an unstable Afghanistan is a source of regional and global insecurity.

A significant change took place after the end of the Cold War. Irregular wars (conflicts involving guerillas, instead of regular military) proliferated in the second half of the twentieth century. In the 1990s, wars had shifted away from Asia and Latin America and toward Eurasia, the Middle East, and sub-Saharan Africa. This shift was caused, in addition to some domestic political and economic factors, by a massive dissolution of states and political regimes in these regions following the end of the Cold War (Kalyvas and Balcellis, 2010, 423).

International terrorism altered the face of irregular warfare. It does not respect geographical boundaries. Individuals and groups who do not represent sovereign states can easily threaten global security, as demonstrated by terrorist acts in the United States in 2001, Spain in 2004, and Great Britain in 2005. (We will discuss terrorism in Chapter 7.) Small nuclear weapons can now be delivered to cities in a suitcase, and nuclear proliferation is now an acute security issue. Because a *dirty bomb* (one that combines radioactive material with conventional explosives) does not need sophisticated means of delivery, the spread of nuclear materials could have global consequences. Countries have few options other than cooperation on security and law enforcement. The gathering and sharing of intelligence has become crucial. International organizations over the last decade play a greater role in global security.

REGIONAL SECURITY

Territorial integrity and sovereignty remain important issues affecting global security. A country's breakup or the interference of neighboring countries can create regional instability—especially in multiethnic zones with weak governments. India, for example, supported the partition of neighboring Pakistan and the creation of the independent country of Bangladesh in 1971; Pakistan quickly retaliated. And attempts to suppress political movements aiming at breaking up a state are likely to cause international reactions, as in the former Yugoslavia. These days, ethnic violence in the world's poorest regions, such as West Africa, may become the most significant threats to global security in the next decades.

@ Learn more about the Central America Regional Security Initiative from the companion website. What is the U.S. role in this program? If you were president, what would you change in this program to make it more efficient?

Some multilateral steps toward regional security have already been taken, such as the Central America Regional Security Initiative (CARSI, 2010). This collective effort of governments, law-enforcement agencies, and NGOs aims to prevent the spread of illicit drugs, the violence associated with them, and transnational threats. The initiative attempts to reduce the flow of narcotics, arms, weapons, and bulk cash generated by drug sales and to confront gangs and criminal organizations. If efforts like this succeed, they will demonstrate the importance of international organizations and coordinated policies.

ENERGY, RESOURCES, AND SECURITY

In the twentieth century, the struggle for access to oil contributed to international conflicts. During periods of robust economic growth, when the demand for fuel is high, any disruption in the production of oil has serious consequences. The Arab oil embargo against the West in the 1970s contributed to a serious, widespread recession (Bryce, 2009). For the United States, dependence on foreign oil is not only an economic problem but a security challenge as well. Energy self-sufficiency is likely to be a major strategic goal of future administrations. In terms of new strategic relations in the twenty-first century, new political alliances are likely to emerge. Former ideological and political allies may turn away from their former partners and gravitate toward energy-rich nations, thus weakening strategic security regimes. Germany, for example, may turn to oil-producing Russia at the expense of NATO and the United States (Guérot, 2010). New emerging energy alliances could easily be perceived as threats to other states' security.

Energy independence does not guarantee security for the United States, however. The twenty-first century has marked the rapid economic growth of China, India, and Brazil—so-called emerging economies. They too need an uninterrupted supply of oil and natural gas, at the lowest possible price, and they are likely to make substantial investments in their militaries to protect it. China's economic growth could contribute to global tension in other ways as well: Its

Protecting energy supply lines will likely remain a serious international security issue. The proposed Enbridge Northern Gateway Project will pipe oil from Canada to the United States to be shipped overseas by oil tankers. This 2012 photo shows the proposed termination point for the pipeline in British Columbia, Canada.

massive exports could undermine other countries' economies and key manufacturing industries, weakening their job markets (Peerenboom, 2008). The competing principles of realpolitik and cooperation will be tested once again.

CHECK YOUR
KNOWLEDGE

▶ What are the relative roles of public opinion and lobbies?
▶ Explain geopolitics.
▶ What is the "military-industrial complex"?
▶ What is the Central America Regional Security Initiative?
▶ How has the global economy become a global security issue?

Past, Present, and Future: Ending the Cold War

Why did the Cold War, a global conflict that had lasted for decades, end so suddenly and without significant violence? In the early 1980s, the future of global security appeared bleak. The most common assumption among professional analysts and politicians was that the next decade would be the most dangerous period since World War II. This expectation was driven in part by the logic of the security dilemma: The U.S. military buildup under President Ronald Reagan was believed to lead to a Soviet buildup, and more tension (Gray, 1982). Yet in 1987 and 1988 the fear and insecurity faded away. President Ronald Reagan and the new Soviet leader Mikhail Gorbachev established mutual trust. In the Intermediate Range Nuclear Forces (INF) treaty of 1987, they agreed to destroy missiles of intermediate and shorter range (from 500 to 5,000 kilometers). And in 1989–90, Soviet troops began to pull out of Eastern Europe.

The peaceful transformation of the security landscape and the entire international system in 1988–91 took most experts by surprise. *Triumphalists*, mostly conservatives in the United States, were quick to claim a U.S. victory, an expected result of the military buildup and constant pressure against the Soviet Union. By creating a military deadlock for the USSR in Afghanistan, supporting Solidarity (an anti-Communist, anti-Soviet movement) in Poland, building advanced military systems, encouraging Saudi Arabia to reduce oil prices (the main source of Soviet finances), and taking a belligerent stand in the war of ideas, the United States undercut the Soviet Union's power bases, undermined its self-confidence, and forced it to surrender in the Cold War.

Declassified documents and interviews made clear that the triumphalist thesis is simplistic. Soviet archives reveal that the key to a security transformation was Gorbachev's desire for domestic reforms and his refusal to see the world through the prism of the security dilemma. The Soviet leader acted from the position of growing weakness: Soviet economy and finances were in disarray. But he also wanted to build an international community in Europe and Asia that would include NATO countries. The Soviet leader spearheaded a new image of a just, secure world and a path to achieve it—what he called the "new thinking." Liberals in the West proclaimed Gorbachev their champion. They acknowledged that he shared many ideas with the neoliberal domestic and transnational intellectual communities (English, 2000; Evangelista, 1999). Among them was

Robert Osgood's GRIT model. By applying these ideas to international relations, Gorbachev succeeded in breaking the deadlock of the security dilemma. Many all over Europe and the world applauded the Soviet leader when he declared at the United Nations in 1988 that international security is "one and indivisible" and rejected the use of force in international relations.

One can even reassess the role of U.S. president Ronald Reagan in the light of liberal theories. Although the Reagan administration initially did not trust Gorbachev's intentions, Reagan recognized that the Soviet threat was disappearing and seized the opportunity to build a new framework of agreements and cooperation with the Soviet Union. The emerging mutual trust between Reagan and Gorbachev helped to break the cycle of insecurity. They proceeded despite the resistance of powerful national forces, including the most belligerent members of the military on both sides and government officials with hostile attitudes about the other country. (Chernyaev, 2000; Leffler, 2007).

Realists and neorealists too began to search for more sophisticated explanations of the end of the Cold War. They argued that the Soviet Union's uncertain role in the new structures of international relations and its weakening stand in the global balance of power affected the behavior of the Soviet leaders. A younger generation of Soviet leaders, including Gorbachev and foreign minister Eduard Shevardnadze, realized that the Soviet Union had to avoid a new round of arms race that it could not win. Because the USSR could not prevail over the West, it decided to join the West (Wohlforth, 2003). Gorbachev's new perception of common security emerged as an alternative to confrontational policies seen as dangerous, expensive, and counterproductive (Herrmann and Lebow, 2004).

Constructivist assessments help explain the evolving ideas on security by the Soviet and U.S. political leadership. Gorbachev, unlike the older generation of Soviet leaders, no longer identified himself with a Soviet military superpower. In contrast, he viewed nuclear weapons as ensuring Soviet security against external threats. Nor was he obsessed with memories of World War II that had left Soviet elites deeply insecure when it came to the West. Gorbachev's personal aversion to the use of force and his preference for nonmilitary means to respond to security challenges were almost pacifist.

Liberals, neorealists, and constructivists agree that a peaceful resolution like this one does not come about exclusively from military pressure. It takes rethinking national security, after traditional approaches end in crisis or deadlock. The colossal military power of the Soviet Union was undermined by a corrosion of ideology and political will (Lévesque, 1997, 252). Influential Soviet elites became convinced that Western models based on political freedoms, private entrepreneurship, and consumerism had more to offer. Had the Soviets and Americans had different political leaders, most probably the Cold War would have continued. Yet not just the Kremlin, but ordinary people had begun to think differently. They were no longer prepared to shed blood for a cause they did not believe in and an empire they did not benefit from. In the end, ideas and values transformed international security.

Advocates of alternative approaches to international relations draw different lessons from the peaceful end of the Cold War. Marxists argue that the Soviet Union was never a truly Socialist country (Shlapentokh et al., 2008). Gorbachev and Soviet elites simply shifted from one mode of domination and

President Ronald Reagan and Soviet General Secretary Mikhail Gorbachev meet in 1986.

insecurity to another neoliberal model based on global capitalist exploitation, inequality, and again, insecurity. Feminist critics argue that the narrative of the end of the Cold War should not revolve around the actions and thoughts of just a few male leaders, such as Gorbachev, Reagan, and Bush. Moreover, the global outcomes of 1989 were not nearly as revolutionary: Instead of building peace and cooperation, Western statesmen preserved and expanded NATO, perpetuating the same old security agenda (Sarotte, 2009).

Drawing lessons from the end of the Cold War is not easy. It stands as a unique case—the meltdown of a major power. Yet it has generated rich and valuable discussions that reopen and reassess the tenets of national and international security.

CONCLUSION

For centuries, states' security policies were secret. Monarchs and prime ministers defined national interest as political sovereignty and territorial integrity. As soon as national interest was protected, the state could pursue other interests through foreign policy. This view of security is generally supported by realists, who identify the goal of security policies as a favorable international balance of power.

Supporters of international liberalism believe that realist considerations lead to actions that undermine national and international security. Rather than relying on force, they seek a greater role for international and nongovernment organizations. Public opinion is important, too, but only if it can be expressed freely. Western Europe has shown the world that democratic states can build a stable peace based on security communities.

Why do some state leaders choose military actions while others seek peaceful solutions? In part, these attitudes are socially constructed. We have seen in the opening case how Japan's political leaders changed their views of their country's vital interests and security policies. Values, fears, and misconceptions guide policy makers through the maze of international and domestic politics and a constantly changing world.

International security may seem like a gigantic chess game. It takes knowledge, skill, and intelligence to understand all the moves. It takes a heart, however, to recognize that behind all these pieces are human beings.

CHAPTER SUMMARY

- National security is the protection of a state's sovereignty, territorial integrity, and vital interests. International security refers to mutual security issues involving more than one state.
- Conflict is antagonism between states and international or nongovernment organizations. Its ultimate form is war, including offensive, defensive, and preventive war.
- The two most common types of security strategy are unilateralism and multilateralism. A state can also choose isolationism, interventionism, or cooperation.
- According to realism, states try to maximize their power and win a better place in the international system. The security dilemma explains why the disruption of a balance of power increases international tensions. In the domino effect, a change of government in one state produces a chain reaction in others. In a security regime, a powerful country provides protection to other states in exchange for their cooperation.
- In the liberal view, neither economic nor military power alone can bring lasting security. The desire for mutually acceptable outcomes gives countries an incentive to cooperate through international institutions and the security community.
- In the constructivist view, states act according to their identities, ideologies, and social norms.
- Marxists argue that security policies reflect the interests of the ruling economic and political elites.
- Feminists see traditional world politics as an emphasis on domination and power—values associated with masculinity.
- Leaders perceive international security according to their experience, ideology, and individual perceptions. Although presidents and their close advisers have considerable power to shape security policies, domestic opinions and political pressures exert considerable influence, especially in democracies.
- Domestic politics help or constrain discussion of security policies. Lobbies and interest groups influence public officials in support of policies and legislation.
- In the past, a country's geographic location has been crucial to its security, but economic interdependence and new military technologies devalued the territorial factor. Failed states, nuclear proliferation, and threats to energy resources and supplies remain serious challenges to global security.

KEY TERMS

collective security 131
conflict 121
cooperation 126
domino theory 129
failing states 121
geopolitics 141
graduated reciprocation in tension-reduction (GRIT) 138
guerrilla warfare 123
international security 120

interventionism 125
liberal interventionism 131
isolationism 121
lobbying 140
militarism 133
multilateralism 125
mutual assured destruction (MAD) 129
national security 120
nuclear deterrence 129

pacifism 133
peace psychology 137
preemptive war 124
preventive war 122
security community 131
security dilemma 128
security policy 132
security regime 130
unilateralism 125
war 120

Visual Review INTERNATIONAL SECURITY

1. What do we study?

KEY CONCEPTS

- **National security:** protection of a state's sovereignty, territorial integrity, and interests
- **International security:** bilateral or multilateral
- **Conflict:** antagonism between states or international organizations
- **War:** organized violent confrontation

TYPES OF WAR

- **Intentions and policies:** offensive, defensive, preemptive, preventive
- **Scope and consequences:** local, regional, global
- **Strategies:** conventional, non-conventional, weapon types
- **Purposes:** predatory, retaliatory, political, ethnic, religious

SECURITY POLICIES

How many states are involved in the policy?

- unilateral
- multilateral

How do states address foreign threats?

- isolationism
- interventionism
- cooperation

2. How do we study it?

REALISM

- Security depends on the quantity and quality of armed forces and their mobility
- States try to maximize their power
- Security dilemma: A state's attempt to improve its security creates insecurity in other states

LIBERALISM

- Neither economic nor military power alone can bring lasting security
- States almost always have options for negotiation
- Collective security: the security of one state is the concern of all

CONSTRUCTIVISM

- States act according to experience, ideologies, perceptions, and social norms
- Militarism: glorifies war, conquest, domination
- Pacifism: principled opposition to war; disputes should be settled nonviolently

ALTERNATIVE AND CONFLICT THEORIES

- Security policies reflect and protect the key interests of the dominant social groups
- Marxism: critical of political and economic elitism
- Feminism: critical of exclusion of women from policy-making

3. How do we apply it?

INDIVIDUAL LEVEL

- **Leaders and advisers**
- **Psychology**

STATE LEVEL

- **Public opinion**
- **Ideology**
- **Lobbying**

GLOBAL LEVEL

- **Geopolitics**
- **Regional security**
- **Global energy and resources**

Critical Thinking

- Compare and contrast the realist, liberal, constructivist, and alternative perspectives on security.
- Explain two applications of security policies at each of the following levels: individual decisions, government politics, and global developments.
- Give an example of a security policy you consider effective and one you consider ineffective. Explain your choices.

CHAPTER

5

A Palestinian protester throws stones at an Israel border police officer during a protest against Israel's separation barrier in the West Bank, 2013.

International Law

Insofar as international law is observed, it provides us with stability and order and with a means of predicting the behavior of those with whom we have reciprocal legal obligations.
—J. WILLIAM FULBRIGHT (1905–1995)

IN JULY 2001, THE GOVERNMENT OF ISRAEL BEGAN TO BUILD A SECURITY BARRIER SEPARATING ISRAEL FROM THE PALESTINIAN TERRITORIES. THE WALL, WHICH IS ABOUT 450 MILES (720 km) long, is in fact a 160- to 330-feet-wide (50–100 m) engineering project. It consists of a fence with electronic sensors, a ditch up to 13 feet (4 m) deep, a two-lane asphalt patrol road (the "trace strip") built parallel to the fence with sand smoothed to detect footprints, and barbed wire. No longer could people cross the fenced area through a checkpoint without a permit issued by Israeli authorities.

The Palestinian government has long considered this construction project illegal and repeatedly asked the Israeli government to stop it. The General Assembly of the United Nations decided to investigate in 2003, and the UN International Court of Justice decided by a majority vote that the wall was illegal. The court obliged Israel to cease construction without delay and to repeal all laws associated with it. Israel was also under an obligation to make reparation for all damage caused by construction. Other countries were advised not to give assistance to Israel in advancing the project, and the UN Security Council was asked to consider further action.

What happened next? Israel did not halt construction of the fence and completed most of it. The government submitted a written statement justifying the fence as a security measure against terrorist attacks. Legal scholars in Israel wrote that a sovereign state might construct a temporary security barrier in an occupied territory. The Israeli Supreme Court ruled that the fence was legal. Still, it ordered some changes in the barrier route to accommodate Palestinians. A new route would return some 140 acres (approx. .5 square km) to the Palestinians.

Which side's legal arguments appear stronger in your view? Should the governments of sovereign states always obey the decisions of international organizations including courts? Do international organizations have the responsibility to protect the rights of individuals? How do you coordinate international law with the interests of independent states? These questions have critical significance in today's global world; yet there is no consensus. This chapter deals with the principles and consequences of international law and its role in international relations. (**Sources:** *International Court of Justice 2004. Israel High Court Ruling, 2005.*)

Learning Objectives

After reading this chapter, you should be able to:

▶ explain the principles, sources, and evolution of international law;
▶ realize the opportunities as well as the limitations of international law;
▶ recognize the principal differences among various views and approaches to international law; and
▶ apply key principles of international law to individual decisions, particular policies of states, and global developments.

What Do We Study?

In general terms, a *law* is a rule either prescribed or recognized as binding. **International law** is a set of principles, rules, and agreements that regulate the behavior of states and other international actors. In theory, states and international organizations should agree on a set of general rules and then enforce them properly. In reality, it is a daunting mission.

Law, the Role of IGOs, and International Relations

There is no formal document or code to set forth worldwide legal principles. Nor is there a global constitution, global supreme court, or worldwide law-enforcement agency. In reality, international legal regulations are effective only as long as key international actors recognize and follow them rather than ignore or reject them. As we have seen already, Israel rejected international law when it refused to halt construction of a security barrier. Is it really necessary, then, or even practical, to have international law? The answer is *yes*, absolutely. At least three reasons explain why.

A need for a secure international environment. Sovereign states, organizations, businesses, and ordinary people need a secure environment rather than law-lessness (Bull, 1977). States and international organizations set rules and establish sanctions against violations of such rules. Take piracy, for example. A significant increase of piracy near Somalia and the Horn of Africa in the twenty-first century created a collective international response to uphold and enforce international anti-piracy laws (Boot, 2009).

A need for conflict resolution. Internationally observed rules help countries to resolve border issues and property rights so that agreements are kept without violence (Linklater, 2009). In the 1990s, Yemen and Eritrea disputed over control of the Hanish Islands in the Red Sea. Violence was about to erupt. In 1998, the Permanent Court of Arbitration, one ofthe oldest institutions for dispute resolution, determined that the archipelago belonged to Yemen. Eritrea accepted this legal decision, and violence was avoided.

A need to coordinate domestic laws in a global world. States have different constitutional, administrative, criminal, contract, family, and property laws. Numerous disagreements naturally emerge, especially in an era of global trade and travel (Keohane, 2005). Think of divorce and custody disputes, trademark violations, traffic accidents, financial obligations, and compensations for faulty products or services. International law should also be applied to fight transnational organized crime including extortion, drug and human trafficking, kidnapping, and money laundering.

 On the companion website, you can examine several cases showing the interaction between countries' legal systems.

Principles and Sources of International Law

International law establishes legal principles—or general rules of law application—for two, several, or even all countries (Kahler and Lake, 2003).

A masked Somali pirate near a Taiwanese fishing vessel that washed up on shore after the pirates were paid a ransom and released the crew in 2012. The heyday of Somali piracy may be over because most countries consider piracy as a threat to the laws of the seas.

MAP 5-1 Previously disputed Hanish Islands belong to Yemen now thanks to international arbitration.

When is a foreign diplomat subject to arrest for breaking U.S. law? Must a diplomat pay taxes? Can countries declare a diplomat unacceptable or unwelcome? Visit the companion website to learn about *diplomatic immunity* and *persona non grata.*

For example, international law applies only within its **jurisdiction,** which defines how far it can reach. Anti-piracy laws have universal jurisdiction because they apply everywhere. Other laws are more specific. The European Union, for example, restricts certain food products imported to its countries (Rankin, 2010). Switzerland, a nonmember, is free to use its own food regulations.

To become subject to international law, a state must be *sovereign*, which means that its government should be lawful and exercise supreme authority within its territory (see Chapter 1). International organizations are subject to international law too. They, as well as sovereign states, are engaged in *diplomacy*— the managing of international relations by means of negotiations. Rules of *diplomatic protocol* are based on centuries of tradition and prescribe how these activities between states and organizations should be performed.

Where do the legal principles and rules regulating international relations come from? As we see next, the **sources of international law** include treaties, customs, general principles, and the actions of courts and other international organizations. (See Table 5-1.)

International treaties (also called *agreements, charters, pacts, covenants,* and *conventions*) are formal, written commitments between international actors, and they often suggest sanctions if those commitments are violated or ignored. A state or organization usually can cancel, or *abrogate,* a treaty—especially if the treaty has term limits. In 2002, soon after the terrorist acts of September 11, 2001, the United States abrogated the Anti-Ballistic Missile Treaty, concluded with the Soviet Union in 1972, so that Washington could build an antimissile defense. Generally, however, countries do not walk out of treaties. By their

TABLE 5-1 Sources of International Law

International Treaties	Formal, written commitments between international actors. An example: In 2005, the United States approved the *Central American Free Trade Agreement* upholding free trade among the United States, Costa Rica, El Salvador, Guatemala, Honduras, Nicaragua, and the Dominican Republic.
International Customary Law	Derives from the past practices of sovereign states. An example: Diplomatic representatives and members of their families are free from criminal persecution and civil liability in countries where they work and live unless their governments revoke such "immunity."
General Principles of Law	Widely accepted principles of morality and common sense. Examples: An international agreement is supposed to be kept; a sovereign state has the right to control the use of resources within its territory; a sovereign state has the right either to recognize or not to recognize another country.
Resolutions of International Organizations or Judgments by International Courts	Examples: Resolutions of the United Nations, the International Court of Justice, NATO, or the European Union.

lasting nature, these documents help protect the international community from sudden changes.

International **customary law** derives from the past practices of sovereign states. International actors simply come to see these "customary actions" as normal and expected under particular circumstances. For example, every sovereign state with access to the sea is expected to claim jurisdiction over its territorial waters, which extend 12 nautical miles or 22 kilometers—originally, the distance of a cannon shot fired from the shore. States are expected not to deploy weapons in earth orbit (Gangale, 2009).

A third source is **general principles of law**, which are common, cross-cultural principles of morality and common sense. Legal decisions, for instance, should be passed based on *equity*—the need to be balanced and impartial. States have the right of self-defense, but their actions should be proportional to the aggression. If states, organizations, and businesses damage the environment of other states, they should compensate. In 2010, oil company British Petroleum immediately offered compensation to people and organizations for the damages caused by a massive oil leak in the Gulf of Mexico that lasted more than one hundred days.

The judgments of international organizations along with works by legal scholars and political analysts are another source of international law. In 1980, following Israel's decision to make Jerusalem its capital, the UN Security Council issued Resolution 478, declaring the Israeli law a violation of international law. In part because of this resolution, most foreign embassies in Israel remain in Tel Aviv.

Most contemporary international agreements, treaties, and rules derive from a rich legal history. We are turning to that history now.

CHECK YOUR KNOWLEDGE

▶ Explain three arguments in support of international law. Come up with your own example to justify the importance of international law.

▶ Explain the jurisdiction principle. Give an example related to your own country.

▶ Name four sources of international law. Would you consider "an eye for an eye" principle as part of customary law?

Development of International Law

The Treaty of Westphalia established an early foundation of international law in 1648, as you will remember from Chapter 1. The acquisition of new lands also required justification. During the period of colonial expansion, European rulers often used the legal term *terra nullius*, or land belonging to no one, to claim lands such as Australia as their lawful possessions (Lindkvist, 2007). Much later, this term was applied to Antarctica, the moon, outer planets, and the deep seabed—but now to prevent claims of sovereignty.

LAWS OF THE SEA

The Laws of the Sea are among the oldest in international law. States involved in overseas commerce had to deal with competition, the safety of shipments, and financial disputes. They needed the freedom to travel by sea and to trade with other countries, and rules became a necessity, to minimize preventable

Frenchmen meet Australian aboriginals in this drawing, done between 1818 and 1820. European great powers often used the legal term *terra nullius*, or land belonging to no one, to colonize lands where aboriginals lived.

losses. These laws are based on compromises, agreements, practical needs, and legal scholarship. Hugo Grotius (1583–1645), a Dutch diplomat and thinker, in *Mare Liberum* (1609) formulated one central principle, **freedom of the seas**: A state's sovereignty ends at the edge of its territorial waters. Although not every state accepted these principles at first, they eventually did, and these rules survived for centuries. Today, outside of territorial waters of other states, countries and individuals have the right to navigate, conduct scientific research, use aircraft, and even lay cable or pipelines. In the second half of the twentieth century, many new agreements were reached to regulate international navigation and sea borders. New agreements also regulate exploration of the ocean surface, its seabed, and protect its flora and fauna. After the 1970s countries began to claim legal rights over the exploration and use of marine resources within their *exclusive economic zone* (EEZ), which stretches to 200 nautical miles (370 km) from the country's coast.

 On the companion website, you can read classic laws of the sea and learn what they mean. Notice how detailed and specific some of those rules are. Most of these rules continue to regulate the international behavior of states and organizations.

LAWS OF WAR

In the eighteenth and nineteenth centuries, a consensus emerged among ruling elites on the need to regulate war and to minimize its increasingly deadly consequences. Influenced by the philosophy of "just war," in 1899 Czar Nicholas II of Russia and Queen Wilhelmina of the Netherlands assembled an unprecedented international conference in The Hague (in the Netherlands). The First Hague Conference involved representatives from twenty-six states, including high-level delegations from the United States and Japan. The Second Hague Conference was called in 1907 with forty-four states present.

The participating countries agreed that war must be the last resort in settling international disputes, and the right to declare it should be limited. Limits must also be put on the use of violence during war. Poisoned gases, for example, were banned because they caused great suffering to soldiers and civilians. The documents also recognized the rights of prisoners of war and outlawed using the enemy's flag and military uniform for deception. Pillaging, bombarding towns not defended by the military, punishing civilians, and refusing to care for wounded enemy soldiers were all deemed illegal. (See Figure 5.1.)

The Hague Conference outlined the **laws of war**—common principles that states should follow in case of an armed conflict. For example, a state should declare whether it initiates hostilities against another state with a *declaration*

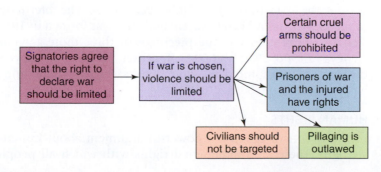

FIGURE 5-1 Major decisions of the Second Hague Conference (1907).

of war. A state at war has *belligerent rights*, such as the right to visit and search merchant ships, seize cargo of the enemy, or attack and destroy military forces and equipment of the enemy. States at war also expect to have their soldiers and officers treated in accordance with the decisions of the Hague Conference, regardless of who started the conflict or who has moral right to use violence. A suspension of hostilities was called **armistice**. A country's formal surrender should stop all military actions, but the victors could impose the conditions of peace, as happened later with the end of World War I in 1918 and World War II in 1945.

It was acknowledged that a state could choose **neutrality** by rejecting any formal military or political alliance. Several states today have proclaimed neutrality, including Costa Rica, Finland, Sweden, and Switzerland. They are obliged to use all means to ensure that their territory is not used by other countries to stage aggression or to engage in hostile actions, such as spying.

The Hague Conferences seemed to signal a new era in international relations. Yet for all its declarations, the Conferences brought only few practical results. For one thing, talks reached an impasse over the issue of appointment of international judges. Every delegation wanted to see a representative of its state appointed, and bigger states wanted a bigger share of votes. Worse, many legislatures back home, mostly for domestic political reasons, failed to ratify the Hague resolutions or attached serious amendments, making the resolutions ineffective.

HUMANITARIAN ISSUES

Declaring limits on the use of war was nevertheless an important step in the development of international law. Many politicians and thinkers were increasingly concerned about the fate of ordinary people in wars—both combatants and civilians (Abrams, 1957). Who can protect them from excessive violence and harm? There was a growing agreement that all human beings regardless of their nationality or creed have basic rights that international law must protect.

In 1863, Jean Henri Dunant (1828–1910) founded the International Committee of the Red Cross (ICRC), to help wounded soldiers on the battlefield regardless of their nationality or alliance. The Red Cross was instrumental in the first Geneva Convention for the Amelioration of the Condition of the Wounded in Armed Forces in the Field, signed in August 1864 by fourteen states, on the humane treatment of captured and wounded soldiers. Dunant became the first winner of the Nobel Peace Prize. The International Federation of the Red Cross and Red Crescent Societies was formed in 1919, and the 1864 Geneva Convention was the precursor of three more agreements signed in Geneva in 1906, 1929, and 1949. Together, the Geneva Conventions legalized the rights of the captured and wounded, as well as civilians and other noncombatants (Borch and Solis, 2010).

HUMAN RIGHTS

In the twentieth century, a powerful argument about **human rights** gained strength. These are fundamental rights with which all people are endowed regardless of their race, nationality, sex, ethnicity, religion, or social status. The United Nations became a major vehicle for producing and promoting international legal norms on human rights. In 1948, the UN General Assembly adopted the Universal Declaration of Human Rights. The Covenant on Civil and Political Rights and the Covenant on Economic, Social, and Cultural Rights, adopted in 1966, came into force in 1976. A year earlier, the Conference on Security and Cooperation in Europe, including the United States and the Soviet Union, signed the Helsinki Final Act. This document bound the twenty-five states that signed it to respect and protect humanitarian and human rights, such as the right to receive information, exchange ideas, or unify families across the state borders. It was a triumph of liberal internationalism (D. Thomas, 2001).

The concept of human rights tied international law to natural law: All humans, by their nature, are entitled to some basic rights regardless of nationality. Why, then, can't states create a system to encourage the observance of human rights globally? The Carter Administration (1977–81), supported by nongovernment groups and legal scholars, made human rights a key goal of its foreign policy. International law, it argued, should allow interference with the affairs of states found responsible for massive and systematic human-rights violations.

The evolution of attitudes toward human rights is a remarkable success of international law. The fourth Geneva Convention of 1949 and the Genocide Convention of 1948 have become widely recognized treaties. The 1948 Convention defined **genocide** as the deliberate extermination or prosecution of national, racial, ethnic, and religious groups, whether in war or in peacetime. This term "genocide" was coined in 1944 by a Polish lawyer of Jewish descent, Raphael Lemkin. These and other humanitarian agreements aim at limiting suffering and death during military conflicts. They protect prisoners of war and civilian noncombatants against indiscriminate violence against them. These laws also assume that states, even nondemocratic ones, must respond today to the international community if authorities engage in arbitrary arrests for political reasons, systematic torture, rape, or the deliberate killing or injury of civilians. These deliberate offences became known as *crimes against humanity*.

@ On the companion website, you can find the Geneva Convention for the Amelioration of the Condition of the Wounded in Armies in the Field and other international treaties on the fate of combatants and civilians. What did these agreements suggest about their enforcement?

EARLY LEGAL INTERNATIONAL INSTITUTIONS

The Hague conferences established the Permanent Court of Arbitration (known as the Hague Tribunal) to make binding decisions on disputes between cooperating states. The idea of international arbitration was very popular in the United States as well in the early twentieth century, and President Theodore Roosevelt asked the Court to settle a dispute with Mexico. The Permanent Court of Arbitration remains the oldest legal institution for international dispute resolution.

In the nineteenth and the early twentieth century, other international organizations were established to promote cooperation in technology, communication, and law enforcement. Among them were the International Telegraph Union (founded in 1865), the International Telecommunication Union, and the Universal Postal Union (formed in 1874). The countries joining

An Interpol employee looks at fingerprints at the agency's headquarters in Lyon, France, in 2012. About 190 countries have joined Interpol to coordinate efforts in monitoring criminal activities and database assistance. Interpol, however, has no jurisdiction to act as world police.

Look up the most recent activities of the Universal Postal Union, the International Telecommunication Union, and Interpol. Are they useful and practical? Do countries need these organizations, or can they coordinate their legal efforts independently?

the Universal Postal Union pledged to cooperate in setting prices and standards for delivering mail, both domestic and international. The International Criminal Police Commission, founded in 1923 in Austria following consultations with law enforcement professionals from several countries, was not a global police force. Nonetheless, *Interpol* (as the organization is called today) has eased cross-border police cooperation to prevent and combat international crime. Both the Universal Postal Union and the International Telecommunication Union are today UN agencies, and Interpol has become one of the largest international organizations.

FROM THE LEAGUE OF NATIONS TO THE UNITED NATIONS

The League of Nations officially came into existence in January 1920. This was the first global organization, as you will remember from Chapter 2, born out of practical calculations and idealist thinking. The League's structure included the Council (its top executive body, with both permanent and nonpermanent members), the Assembly (which included all representatives), and the Secretariat (playing supporting and administrative functions). Autonomous but closely connected to the League were the Permanent Court of International Justice and the International Labour Organization. The League also operated several committees and commissions on health, refugees, slavery, and other issues (Henig, 2010). The League had some success in taking care of refugees fleeing wars and revolutions, settling some international disputes, and fighting slavery. Unfortunately, the League's inability to stop several aggressive wars in Africa, Europe, and the Pacific undermined its authority; and during World War II the League of Nations was replaced by the United Nations.

The term *United Nations* was coined by U.S. president Franklin D. Roosevelt. On January 1, 1942, representatives of twenty-six states signed the Declaration of the United Nations and pledged to continue fighting together against Nazi Germany, fascist Italy, and imperial Japan (S. Schlesinger, 2003). In 1945, representatives of fifty countries met in San Francisco to draw up the UN Charter, signed on June 26, and the United Nations officially came into existence on October 24. Membership was open to all states that accepted the charter. The first session of the General Assembly of the United Nations convened in March 1946 in London, with representatives of fifty-one states. In 1952 the UN moved to its new headquarters in New York City.

From the start, the UN Charter and decisions of the United Nations, its agencies, and affiliated international organizations became an important source of international law. The United Nations does not have legislative power to enact binding rules of international law. It cannot force countries to change their domestic laws. However, its recommendations have been crucial to the development of international principles of human rights and their defense. The United Nations created the International Court of Justice (ICJ), located in The Hague, to resolve legal disagreements submitted by states. Its role is "to settle legal disputes submitted to it by States and to give advisory opinions on legal questions deferred to it by authorized United Nations organs and specialized agencies."

 On the companion website, read more about the ICJ, composed of fifteen judges elected to nine-year terms by the United Nations General Assembly and the Security Council.

> ▶ Explain the *freedom of the seas* principle of international relations.
> ▶ Do the *laws of war* ban wars?
> ▶ Why did the League of Nations fail?

CHECK YOUR KNOWLEDGE

How Do We Study It?

The Realist View of International Law

The realist approach to international law makes several interconnected assumptions. First, sovereign states by definition have no higher authority over them—not even international law. Second, international law can regulate relations among states, but it should not undermine a sovereign country's core interests, including security. Finally, without proper enforcement, international law is simply ineffective (Morgenthau, 2006). Because the task of enforcement cannot be granted to a global organization, individual countries and their coalitions should remain the guarantors of global security. (See Figure 5.2.)

The realist approach does not advocate lawlessness. The anarchical nature of today's global international system, realists argue, makes international law important, but also difficult to implement. To be effective, realists argue, international law should be considered in each of the contexts we have mentioned: state sovereignty, state interest, and means of enforcement.

FIGURE 5-2 The realist view of international law.

SOVEREIGNTY

Imagine for a moment that the United Nations passes a resolution outlawing the death penalty in all countries, once and for all. Does this mean that sovereign states recognizing capital punishment must now follow this new international law? Realists dismiss this possibility, because the UN has no power to enforce such a resolution. Each state is bound only by those rules of international law to which it has consented (Vattel, 2001). Thus Israel could accept or reject the ICJ's decision about its security barrier, discussed at the start of this chapter, because it is a sovereign state. Moral objections to Israel's policies are a separate issue.

In cases of aggression, realists continue, the victim state does not have an obligation to consult with international law about how to respond. It has the right to defend itself and to seek help from others. Nor does a state have an obligation to defend other states in the absence of a defense agreement. The United States must defend Japan against aggression because of an agreement signed between these two countries. But no international law can compel the United States or China to send their armed forces to defend one another.

STATE INTEREST

The goal of the 1997 Kyoto climate change conference was to commit governments to reduce greenhouse gas emissions. Although the United States signed

---

CASE IN POINT > *Norway's Moral Objection*

Do moral issues matter in the implementation of international law? Back in 2009, Norway's ministry of finance sold its holdings from one of the companies participating in the construction of the Israeli security barrier. The officials explained this decision by saying that government investments abroad should meet ethical guidelines. "We do not wish to fund companies that so directly contribute to violations of international humanitarian law," said the Norwegian finance minister (Haaretz Service, 2010).

CRITICAL THINKING

Do you believe the government of Norway made the right decision even though it didn't affect the construction of the wall? Or do you think it was a futile symbolic act because, as realists posit, international law without proper enforcement remains largely ineffective?

this agreement, it has not been submitted to the Senate for *ratification*, or approval, because of strong domestic political opposition.

Governments typically reject any international law that may undermine their interests or impose undesirable legal, financial, or other obligations. Realists believe that states have the right to choose their own policies toward international organizations, including the United Nations. The main provisions of certain international laws are ambiguous exactly because they leave room for states to interpret them in the way they want, to avoid conflict with opposition at home or from other states (Morgenthau, 1978). Governments, as a rule, condemn violations of international law highly selectively. When such violations do not affect a country's national interest, these breaches are routinely ignored. After the attacks of 9/11, the United States removed sanctions on Pakistan and India that had been imposed earlier against their developing nuclear weapons. Washington needed help from Pakistan, but the sanctions were removed from both countries to avoid objections from India (Sathasivam, 2005).

LAW ENFORCEMENT

International law can be enforced under certain conditions. For instance, decisions of international organizations could also be enforced by **international mandate**, or legal permission to administer a territory or enforce international law. In the 1920s, France and Great Britain, the two most powerful members of the League of Nations at that time, established such mandates to rule on a vast area of the former Ottoman Empire. The territories where now you find Iraq, Palestine, Israel, and Jordan were entrusted to Great Britain. France took control of Lebanon and Syria. Under the assumption that the people of those territories were not ready to govern themselves, the French and British governments declared the legal right to "administrative advice and assistance." This system of mandates survived World War II, but by now almost all mandated territories have become sovereign states.

The Liberal View of International Law

The liberal tradition challenges realpolitik and pays more attention to the advantages and opportunities provided by international law. It makes three main arguments, and we'll look at each in turn. First, states, like individuals, are capable of managing their relations based on shared principles. Second, international institutions can play a bigger legal role in international affairs by applying the principles of extraterritoriality and supranationalism. Last but not least, a state's claims of a legal right to wage war should be limited, as well as a state's sovereignty to commit atrocities against its people. (See Figure 5.3.)

REASON AND SHARED PRINCIPLES

International law, liberalism argues, is not an artificial creation of lawyers and politicians. It addresses our common and compatible needs that cement the fabric of international relations.

Interdependence, mutual consent, and legal obligations are the products of common reason backed by common law (Gruber, 2000). For instance, the laws that regulate our lives do not rely on coercion alone. Most people observe

DEBATE > WHY CAN'T WE OUTLAW WAR?

Could the United Nations pass an international law to ban wars altogether? Realists use history to argue that such a law would be ineffective unless it is enforced. A 1928 international agreement known as the Pact of Paris (or Briand–Kellogg Pact) was signed by fifteen nations, including Canada, France, Germany, Great Britain, India, Japan, South Africa, and the United States. The agreement stated that war should be abolished forever as a means of resolving international conflicts. Yet it remained empty without proper enforcement.

Right after the Pact of Paris was signed, the U.S. Senate ratified the treaty. However, the lawmakers made it clear that the United States would not be compelled to use force against countries that violate the treaty. In other words, Washington promised not to punish future aggressors, and so aggressive wars could continue. And they did. In the 1930s, the world community did not stop aggression by Japan against China, Italy against Ethiopia, or the Soviet Union against Finland (Oppenheim, 2008). The League of Nations could not stop hostilities between Paraguay and Bolivia. International law enforcement became, under the critical eye of realists, a serious problem of international law.

WHAT'S YOUR VIEW?

And yet, let's assume that next year most countries of the United Nations, including the United States, agree to legally ban wars between states altogether. Based on what you have read, suggest several conditions under which this law would be effective. Which country or organization could be capable of creating and maintaining such conditions, and how?

@ The Office of the Historian of the U.S. Department of State provides information about earlier legal attempts to outlaw war.

The signing of the Briand–Kellogg pact in 1928, which renounced aggressive war and prohibited the use of war as an instrument of national policy except in matters of self-defense. Despite their support of the pact, German, Italian, and Soviet leaders started aggressive wars in the next decade.

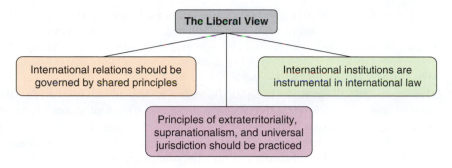

FIGURE 5-3 The liberal view of international law.

domestic criminal laws not only because they are afraid of jails or expect retribution from their neighbors. They accept the law mostly out of a sense of social duty, shared rules, and moral principles. True, some citizens commit illegal acts and, if caught and convicted, pay penalties. Yet in general even laws that carry little threat of sanction for their violation are observed.

States and international organizations, for similar reasons, tend to observe international law. Like domestic common law, international customary law is supported by daily, habitual, and voluntary transactions. International finance, trade, and commerce all work because they are based on international rules without which the global economy could not function—especially given the growing complexity of global interdependence. International law thus becomes an increasingly practical alternative to local laws enforceable only within a limited territory.

EXTRATERRITORIALITY AND SUPRANATIONALISM

If sovereign states exercise supreme authority within their territories, what legal argument can be made in support of international law? The liberal view invokes the principle of **extraterritoriality**, or exemption from the jurisdiction of local law. In the past, some foreign residents living in certain areas were free from the jurisdiction of local courts. Merchants from Genoa and Venice who traveled to Istanbul, for example, were exempted by the Ottoman rulers from following the Sharia, or Islamic law. Similarly, many Americans lived in China under a combination of U.S., European, and local ordinances (Scully, 2001). Today, extraterritoriality applies to heads of states, diplomatic missions, and foreign military bases.

Supporters of the liberal view further argue that with the advancement of international organizations, ever-increasing travel, international commerce, and electronic communications as well make territoriality increasingly difficult to enforce. The sheer necessities of our daily interactions will encourage states and businesses to turn to extraterritoriality.

Liberal theorists understand that lack of enforcement is a major weakness of international law. Therefore, liberalism turns to **supranationalism**—the delegation of authority from sovereign states to international institutions or organizations. Supranationalism does not mean that states give up their sovereignty once and for all. They merely delegate some of their sovereignty to an international institution that assumes the role of a supranational power (Close, 2000). Such

Sudanese President Omar al-Bashir addresses Parliament in Khartoum in 2013. A number of politicians and military and intelligence officers remained in jail, accused of plotting to overthrow al-Bashir, who seized power in a military coup in Sudan in 1989. Al-Bashir has been legally charged for human rights violations committed in his country.

an institution can regulate international relations based on shared principles, which can be expanded or amended as needed. The European Union, for one, has a long history of such gradual changes and legal adjustments (Mak, 2008).

UNIVERSAL JURISDICTION

The arguments about human rights discussed earlier advanced the idea about international law allowing interference with the affairs of states engaged in massive and systematic human-rights violations. Liberalism advanced the concept of **universal jurisdiction**: Government officials and political leaders—even individuals with diplomatic immunity—who are perpetrators of heinous crimes against their own people should not escape justice when they leave their countries. Universal jurisdiction justifies their arrest and extradition. In the past, a similar concept, *hostes humani generis* ("enemies of the human race"), was applied to pirates, hijackers, or hostage takers operating outside any state's jurisdiction. In recent times, former Chilean dictator Augusto Pinochet, former head of Yugoslavia Slobodan Milošević, and the president of Sudan Omar al-Bashir have been legally charged for human rights violations they committed in their countries. We look in depth at their cases and others at the end of this chapter, and we return more broadly to humanitarian issues in Chapter 9.

THE LEGALITY OF WAR

Liberalism refers to the principles of "just war" as a means to limit violence in international affairs. What are these principles? First, only sovereign states may pursue their strategic goals by the means of war. Second, war is justified only when it is based on the principle of proportionality in the use of force. Third, even if two states are at war, they should respect humanitarian concerns for honesty and mercy (Lauterpacht, [1933] 2011) Liberalism also argues that wars can be significantly limited if sovereign states turned to the principles of international law to justify war. States may start wars in self-defense but they may not use aggression, to which international law gives special attention.

Aggression is an attack by a state aiming at retribution, territorial expansion, or conquest. In 1974 a UN special committee named seven offenses falling in this category. (See Figure 5.4.) However, if these actions are sanctioned by the United Nations, they are not considered aggression.

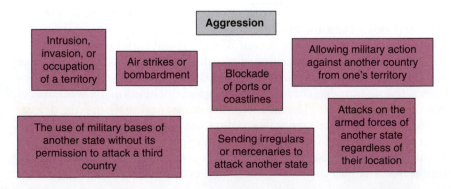

FIGURE 5-4 Aggression as defined by the United Nations.

Aggression

- Intrusion, invasion, or occupation of a territory
- Air strikes or bombardment
- Blockade of ports or coastlines
- Allowing military action against another country from one's territory
- The use of military bases of another state without its permission to attack a third country
- Sending irregulars or mercenaries to attack another state
- Attacks on the armed forces of another state regardless of their location

Supporters of the liberal tradition do not rule out war. States may use violence as their last resort or if they are under attack. Any use of force, in their opinion, is justified to restrain an aggressor or to stop systematic and deliberate violence especially against ethnic or religious groups. Compelling legal arguments, however, are needed to sanction military intervention. The Charter of the United Nations (Chapter VII) suggests conditions necessary for the use of military force, such as threats to peace, breach of the peace, or acts of aggression.

Constructivism and Other Views of International Law

Supporters of other approaches share some assumptions with the realist and liberal traditions. However, they pay most attention to specific factors and contexts to explain international law.

CONSTRUCTIVISM'S VIEW OF IDEOLOGY AND LAW

States have their own expectations and create their own norms when it comes to international law. Revolutionary governments or radical movements usually reject the existing norms; their key goal is to change the system, not to uphold it. The leaders of the French Revolution in the late eighteenth century denounced the Westphalian *balance of power* system and sought to liberate Europe from royal tyranny in the name of universal rights. After the Russian revolution in 1917, the Bolshevik government canceled unilaterally all international treaties that the Russian Empire had previously signed.

Ideology and values are another important factor; driven by them, states can reject, but also embrace international agreements and organizations. NATO, for example, as a defense organization, rested on more than a shared perception of the Soviet threat. Gradually, NATO members, different as they were, developed a common understanding of international law, based on respect for national sovereignty and respect for plurality of opinions. One can argue that this ideology cemented the alliance for many years (Schmidt, 2001). Advocates of NATO insist that today it has a greater goal than common defense: It supports a community of legal norms, based on common values.

Constructivists also argue that the common values of social improvement and the desire to eliminate hunger and diseases, and to stop genocide, could serve as a foundation for an efficient international legal system. The challenge is to agree on such goals and their implementation.

PERCEPTIONS OF INTERNATIONAL LAW

A key argument of constructivism is that international law is based on shared values and perceptions. Here constructivists turn to political psychology to interpret those factors (Reus-Smit, 2009). For example, the United Nations gives a general definition of aggression, but leaders may interpret aggression according to their own interests. They initiate hostile actions as an act of self-defense; in this way, they hope to avoid sanctions against them.

NATO's 1999 war in Kosovo illustrates the importance of perceptions in international law. Here a group of countries challenged the right of Serbia to retain the territories of the former Yugoslavia. In the eyes of Serbia, however,

NATO countries were attacking its sovereignty within its legitimate borders. The Serbian military sought to restore control over the province of Kosovo and to defeat the ethnically Albanian pro-independence armed forces. The Clinton administration and the governments of other NATO countries rejected Serbia's explanations. They accused Serbia of aggression against the Albanians, who were the ethnic majority in Kosovo, and demanded that the Serbian army stay out of this region. When the UN Security Council couldn't pass a resolution to approve international sanctions or military action, because of opposition from Russia and China, NATO bombed Serbia. To justify war, NATO claimed that Serbian officials had initiated a terror campaign against ethnic Albanians, and air strikes were the only option to stop genocide (Ramet, 2005). Serbia, Russia, and China disagreed. They claimed that accusations of human-rights violations should not allow international law to trample laws of sovereign states. In Russia's opinion, NATO created a dangerous precedent: Any states or groups of states now could justify their aggression by humanitarian reasons. To Serbia, in fact, human-rights violations in Kosovo took place precisely as a result of the NATO's strikes.

What was the most important outcome of this conflict? An independent state in Kosovo was created in 2008, protected by NATO troops. More than one hundred countries including the United States had recognized Kosovo by 2013. The 1999 events in the former Yugoslavia are just one dramatic example of different interpretations of and disputes over international law and universal jurisdiction. (Compare again the views of NATO, Russia, and Serbia.)

CONFLICT THEORIES

Conflict theories maintain that international law is, for the most part, a convenient instrument to serve the interests of powerful social groups. For Marxists, governments, corporations, banks, and even big international organizations create legal rules that benefit mostly the rich (Miéville, 2006). The entire international legal system is designed to maintain economic and political superiority of a few West European and North American states at the expense of the rest of the world. For example, with the exception of China, all permanent members of the UN Security Council are nuclear states of Europe and America. Although international humanitarian law made significant progress, powerful states and groups pay only selective attention to violations.

Theories of racial and ethnic prejudice make similar points but from a different perspective. Instead of pointing to class interests, they insist that, deliberately or not, international law is consistently used to promote the interests of the privileged countries of Europe, North America, and Japan. The big powers support international law so long as it does not threaten the status quo—and their superiority (Blanchard, 1996). These powers generally reject any attempt to give more power to countries in South and Southeast Asia, Africa, and Latin America. They are unwilling, for example, to reform the United Nations and other international organizations, and they often abuse the principle of universal jurisdiction to justify acts against less powerful states. As an illustration, in 1984 the International Court of Justice held the United States responsible for violation of international law by an armed rebellion against the Nicaraguan

DEBATE > FROM KOSOVO TO THE RUSSIAN-GEORGIAN WAR

In the summer of 2008, war broke out between the Russian federation and Georgia (a sovereign country and former republic of the Soviet Union). Georgia accused Russia of aggression. Russia, in turn, claimed that Georgian troops were the first to open fire against the Russian military, which protected peace in South Ossetia. This small region had seceded from the former Soviet Republic of Georgia after the Soviet Union collapsed and never recognized Georgian sovereignty. Russian authorities explicitly used the Kosovo case as a legal precedent to justify force; they claimed that they were protecting an endangered ethnic region from Georgia's armed forces. Almost immediately after the war broke out, Russian authorities announced that Moscow recognized South Ossetia and another secessionist region, Abkhazia, as independent from Georgia—again citing Kosovo's independence as a legal precedent. The United States and other NATO countries claim that the two cases are different and continue to recognize South Ossetia and Abkhazia as part of sovereign Georgia.

WHAT'S YOUR VIEW?

Russians compared the case of Kosovo with the case of Ossetia. Many Western observers disagreed. Compare NATO's challenge to Serbia with Russia's to Georgia. Which position do you find stronger from the international law perspective and why?

@ An article in the *Economist* presents the opinions from both sides but argues that the cases of Kosovo and Ossetia are dissimilar: "South Ossetia is Not Kosovo," August 28, 2008. See the companion website.

South Ossetian separatist fighters rest during the Russian-Georgian war of 2008. Russia supported ethnic separatists and defeated Georgia, which wanted to rout them. This war, caused by local dynamics, raised tensions in the relations between Russia and NATO.

government and by mining the country's harbors. Washington blocked the enforcement of this decision using its veto power in the UN Security Council (Schulte, 2005).

From the feminist perspective, gender relations are an integral part of international politics and international law (True, 2009). Historically, international law was based on an exclusively masculine perspective focusing on power, power balance, and ultimately war. Women's expectations and values were commonly excluded or their importance diminished in early legal agreements among states. Significant progress was made in the past century to promote legal foundations for gender equality, civil rights, and humanitarian issues. The law specifically protects women as victims of violence during ethnic and social conflicts. However, international law does not go far enough in protecting the rights of women globally. Segregation, sex exploitation, slavery, and systematic abuse continue. In many countries, women are routinely denied legal protection. Often these violations are explained by local authorities as cultural traditions, and the extraterritoriality principle of international law is ignored (Chappel, 2008). Feminist scholars underline the importance of extraterritoriality in support of *care ethics* in global relations, which focuses on the responsibility for all for the suffering of human beings and, to a lesser degree, for all issues related to state sovereignty and power.

CHECK YOUR KNOWLEDGE

▶ Explain the concept *hostes humani generis* ("enemies of the human race").
▶ Define extraterritoriality and supranationalism. Give examples.
▶ May the principle of universal jurisdiction be applied to you personally? Under what conditions?
▶ What were the most significant outcomes of the Kosovo conflict in relation to international law?

How Do We Apply It?

The Individual Context

It takes individual leaders to initiate, interpret, and uphold international law. They may see direct personal benefits from the application of international law to their countries' foreign policy. In the past, neither realism nor liberalism paid enough attention to the role of individuals. Constructivism provides important insights here.

POLITICAL AUTHORITY

The political authority exercised by leaders at home often shapes their attitudes about international law, treaties, and bilateral agreements. **Autocratic rulers**, who claim unlimited power, typically follow international and domestic law only when it suits them. They often refer to a sense of mission, religion, or ideology to justify their actions. Mobutu Sese Seko, the ruler of Zaire (today part of the Congo) from 1965 to 1997, declared that "democracy is not for Africa." He also rejected democratic principles of government at home, allowed his associates to violate business agreements with foreign companies, redistributed illegally the resources of foreign companies, and imprisoned opponents without a trial. His human rights record was dismal (Wrong, 2002).

An extreme form of autocratic ruler is a **tyrant—another word for a dictator**. Like Hitler and Stalin, tyrants are not constrained by laws, not even those they themselves impose. They use unlimited power to oppress the people of their own country or its foreign possessions (Wallechinsky, 2006). Saddam Hussein of Iraq and Kim Jong-il of North Korea can be also regarded as dictators for their brutal and illegal polices. These examples may suggest a major weakness of international law: Many autocratic rulers in the past simply ignored international agreements and global conventions, especially when it comes to human rights (Burt, 2010).

Democratic leaders, by contrast, tend to pursue their policies within the framework of domestic and international law. Their behavior thus provides support for democratic peace theory and the liberal approach to international relations. However, contemporary developments in many countries present a significant challenge to this view. Some authoritarian leaders, as we saw in Chapter 3, run for elections and allow limited civic freedoms in their countries. Other leaders make a travesty of elections and democratic procedures at home, creating a "hybrid" regime that combines democratic legitimacy with authoritarian practices. In their foreign policy, they are likely to take a cynical

Go online to find the current Democracy Index compiled by *The Economist*, listing the world's most authoritarian countries. Do some research to try to establish which countries on this list have friendly relations with the United States. Does Washington support most of them or only a few of them?

Dictator of Zaire Mobutu Sese Seko (1930–1997) routinely ignored international agreements on human rights. Dictators pose significant challenge to international law because frequently they simply disregard it.

view of international norms and treat international law arbitrarily, according to little more than immediate interests (Singh, 2010). Yet other leaders may use authoritarian means domestically but respect international law, as it happened in Egypt in 2013 when the military dismissed the country's elected president.

The State Context

Realists argue, most often correctly, that states treat international law in the context of domestic politics, policy, and security strategies. For example, South Africa, Israel, India, and Pakistan refused to sign a nonproliferation treaty that would have placed legal restrictions on their development of nuclear weapons. In another case, take Article 2(4) of the UN Charter, which tells all states to refrain from the use of force that violates the territorial integrity or political independence of another country. Two exceptions exist: the UN Security Council's authorization or self-defense. However, the last sixty years show that democratic governments do not necessarily follow Article 2, which prohibits violence, but turn instead to Article 1 of the UN Charter, which allows the prevention and removal of threats to the peace (Loyola, 2010). In other words, countries often choose legal uncertainties and contradictions to justify their policies including war.

INTERNATIONAL LAW AND THE UNITED STATES

The U.S. president or secretary of state may not enter into obligations to other nations that are binding on Congress. The constitutional powers of the legislature cannot be given away to other branches of the government, and Congress may or may not ratify a treaty. Ever since the Jay Treaty (named after Chief Justice John Jay) in 1795, a treaty requires a two-thirds vote in the U.S. Senate. The rules are a bit easier for trade deals; for them, *executive agreements* need only a majority vote in both houses of Congress. Sometimes, when opposition in the legislature is strong, the executive branch may not want to engage in a political battle. The Clinton administration, for instance, did not push for ratification of the 1997 Kyoto protocol to fight global gas emissions. But even after Congress ratifies a treaty, the legislature can render it ineffective by not allocating funds— or by attaching restrictions on how funds are to be used (Grimmett, 1999).

Presidents may also reconsider their position on international law under pressure from Congress or constituencies. In 1993, President Clinton pledged to link trade to China's policies toward human rights, in compliance with the U.S. Trade Act. However, Clinton turned away from his pledge as opposition grew, thanks to growing profits from trade and investments, as well as increasing consumer reliance on inexpensive goods manufactured in China.

Conflicts can also arise between U.S. and international law. For example, section 201 of the 1974 Trade Act states that the president may impose temporary trade barriers if an increase in imports would hurt domestic industry. Such actions may violate the rules of the World Trade Organization prohibiting trade barriers. However, because of powerful lobbies and the need to get the votes of people with manufacturing jobs, presidents from time to time impose trade barriers to help certain domestic industries. International law is pushed aside to pursue domestic goals.

At other times, conflict with U.S. law may mean that a treaty's ratification is postponed indefinitely (Moravcsik, 2001). Congress did not ratify the American Convention on Human Rights, signed by President Carter, because it challenged federal and state laws by placing serious restrictions on abortion rights and implementation of the death penalty. Even existing agreements may be reconsidered. For example, the Optional Protocol to the Vienna Convention on Consular Relations lets the International Court of Justice make the final decision when citizens have been illegally detained abroad. The United States initially backed the measure as a means to protect its own citizens overseas. It successfully sued Iran for taking fifty-two hostages from the embassy in Tehran in 1979. But the United States withdrew from the accord in 2005 after some countries that had abolished capital punishment successfully complained before the ICJ that their citizens were sentenced to death in the United States. The U.S. State Department argued that international law might interfere with domestic criminal law (Jordan, 2005).

Finally, some agreements are signed but later rejected for apparent irrelevance or ambiguity. The Convention on the Elimination of All Forms of Discrimination Against Women disallows all forms of exploitation of women and girls; it also guarantees equal access to education, employment, and health care. Why didn't the United States ratify this treaty? Both Republican and Democratic administrations argued that U.S. law already ensures gender equality, whereas women in other countries have little or no legal protection. Declarations without proper global enforcement, they declared, are useless (Kirkpatrick, 2002). (See Figure 5.5.)

@ On the companion website, learn more about international treaties signed by the United States but later delayed or not ratified by Congress. See how domestic politics and law affect international agreements.

The Global Context

For centuries, international law was instrumental in economic exchanges between states, organizations, and individuals. (We return to economic issues in the next chapter.) International agreements have settled territorial disputes and probably prevented many wars. The laws of war—especially those dealing with the humane treatment of civilians, captured or wounded soldiers, and nonmilitary personnel—have saved millions of lives. International agreements today protect travel, property, family rights, due process, and the well-being of many around the world.

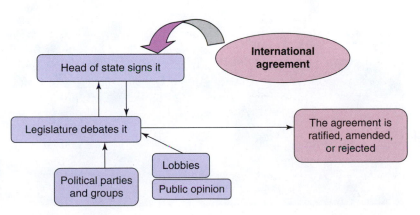

FIGURE 5-5 Domestic factors and international treaties. Many domestic factors affect international law. In most democratic countries, international agreements signed by executive leaders must be approved (ratified) by the legislation. Influenced by political, economic, and other interests, legislators may approve, amend, or reject treaties.

International law concerning genocide and war crimes continues to attract attention. The creation of the International Criminal Tribunal for former Yugoslavia (ICTY) in 1993 in The Hague was a remarkable event. The idea came from German foreign minister Klaus Kinkel, and Resolution 827 of the UN Security Council created the institution. The court has jurisdiction over certain crimes committed on the territory of Croatia, Bosnia, and Herzegovina, which were parts of the disintegrated Yugoslav state after 1991. The court hired its staff from many countries.

The ICTY served a model for the second similar tribunal—the International Criminal Tribunal for Rwanda (ICTR). It was created in 1994 by the UN Security Council (Resolution 955) to prosecute those responsible for the mass killings and violence in Rwanda during a civil war there. Because the continuing tensions in Rwanda make fair decisions based on domestic law almost impossible, it was imperative to apply international law under the watch of the ICTR.

Although critics complain about the high cost and bureaucratic inefficiency of international courts, these institutions were generally successful. They gave many victims an opportunity to seek justice. Most governments and millions of people around the world support the courts' work and consider them legitimate. Carla del Ponte, a former Swiss attorney general who served as prosecutor for ICTY and ICTR, became one of the most recognized and respected lawyers in the world.

@ On the companion website, read more about Carla del Ponte and her work.

The success of international law should not hide its failures and excesses. The League of Nations ended up as a failure. Wars and atrocities still take place. Many international laws protecting human rights remain little more than declarations

In The Hague in 1998, Bosnian Serbs accused of serious crimes sit behind their defense lawyers prior to a session at the International Criminal Tribunal for the former Yugoslavia. The court has jurisdiction over certain crimes committed on the territories of Croatia and Bosnia—parts of the pre-1991 Yugoslavia. Since 1994, the Court has indicted more than 160 and sentenced more than 65 persons.

in some countries. Other countries argue that human rights violations just give the West an excuse to intervene in domestic affairs of other sovereign states (as we will discuss in Chapter 9). Opponents of "big government" at home argue, too, that the world surely does not need a global government imposing legal restrictions on communications and business.

FROM NATIONALISM TO SUPRANATIONALISM

At the same time, the complexity of today's world requires a greater coordination among states and international organizations. Urgent environmental issues, global poverty, and natural disasters—as the events of the past decade have shown—demand responses from across the global community. So do the worldwide financial and economic crises of the past decade. The growing strength of emerging markets in Southeast Asia, China, India, Russia, and Brazil may pose new problems as well, involving economic competition, global migration, and overpopulation. State bureaucracies often remain corrupt and inefficient, which highlights the importance of NGOs and international organizations in a growing number of global issues. These and other trends will almost certainly require strengthening and expanding international law.

Supporters of supranationalism point to the success of the European Union and the **East African Community** (EAC). In 2000, Tanzania, Uganda, Burundi, Kenya, and Rwanda formed this economic and political union, with the goal of a common economic market, a single currency, and one unified federation by 2015. Although a similar plan collapsed back in the 1970s, steps thus far suggest that these countries can achieve their goal. Most important, the EAC example, if it is a success, will show that states can put aside religious, tribal, and political differences; accept binding legal rules; and move toward a common goal.

BACK TO REALITY

The concepts of supranationalism and universal jurisdiction find significant support. They also have been under criticism for some time. Who should implement international law? Critics have complained for some time that NGOs and IGOs, staffed by unelected officials, should not have the power to make legal decisions of global significance (Kissinger, 2001). Moreover, supporters of conflict theory including feminist scholars mention that many NGOs promote an agenda set mostly by the educated upper class from Western countries. Lack of accountability of unelected professionals is another problem, even if they act with the best of intentions (Wapner, 2002).

Universal jurisdiction, as you remember, assumes that individuals are legally responsible for certain illegal actions regardless of where they live. Critics of universal jurisdiction are skeptical that judicial procedures alone without proper debate will be effective in international politics. Of course, acts of genocide or other blatant human rights violations should not be left unpunished, but only when they are proven and carefully investigated. Otherwise, legal decisions may be motivated by politics or ideology. In other cases, some individuals and organizations may simply misinterpret international law because they are acting out of their own interests (Agier, 2010). Moreover, some legal decisions or initiatives can be simply impractical.

CASE IN POINT > *Rwanda and Belgium Law*

A 1993 Belgium law aimed at protecting civilians in time of war by relying on the principle of universal jurisdiction. Neither the accused nor the accuser needed to be Belgian citizens for a case to go forward. In addition, anyone could bring a criminal complaint, which a local magistrate was required to investigate to determine whether further action was warranted.

The law was first put to use after mass slaughter in Rwanda, a former Belgian colony. Eric Gillet, a prominent human rights lawyer, filed suit, accusing several Rwandans living in Belgium of horrible war crimes. Soon cases were filed against former Israeli prime minister Ariel Sharon, then-Iraqi President Saddam Hussein, the late Congolese ruler Laurent Kabila and his foreign minister, Rwandan president Paul Kagame, former Iranian president Ali Akbar Hashemi Rafsanjani, and several generals from Guatemala. Suits were also filed against international oil companies accused of connections with the military rulers of Burma, the Palestinian leader Yasser Arafat, Cuba's president Fidel Castro, and former U.S. President George H. W. Bush. Altogether, according to the Belgian Justice Ministry, more than thirty complaints were on file.

Things rapidly took an absurd turn. One British citizen arrived at the Belgian embassy claiming that the BBC, the British Broadcasting Company, was seeking to assassinate him. In an attempt to avoid a serious diplomatic crisis and stop frivolous suits, the Belgian government dismissed the law.

CRITICAL THINKING

What lessons can you draw from this case? Can you suggest any measures to prevent similar misuses of international legal rulings? Considering this case, would you have imposed high application fees for the plaintiffs to eliminate many frivolous lawsuits? For the same purpose, would you narrow down the definition of a war crime? Discuss these and other possibilities.

Realism provides a strong argument against supranationalism: to be effective, a law must be enforced. Unfortunately, in many cases, IGOs and NGOs rely instead on goodwill and legal norms. Take global nuclear policies. The Nonproliferation Treaty has slowed the spread of nuclear weapons, but the United Nations has not stopped North Korean and Iranian nuclear programs (Pelligrini, 2010).

Another argument against the expansion of international law comes from critics of globalization. They contend that any global law would primarily benefit wealthy countries. The gap between the rich and the poor will increase. Liberal democracy of the Western type will be forced on other countries, often against their will. Human rights can even be used as an excuse to wage aggressive wars (Bricmont, 2006).

CHECK YOUR KNOWLEDGE

▶ How do authoritarian leaders tend to regard international law?
▶ Article 2(4) of the UN Charter, which tells all states to refrain from the use of force, has two exceptions. What are they? Do you agree with them?
▶ What is the International Criminal Tribunal for the former Yugoslavia meant to deal with?
▶ Does international law apply similarly to wealthy and poor countries?

Past, Present, and Future: War Crimes, Genocide, and the Legacy of Nuremberg

Attempts to use international law to stop genocide and limit the deadly effects of war began more than one hundred years ago. These early efforts were ineffective and frustrating from the start. The most significant change took place at the end of World War II.

During World War II, Germany, Japan, and the Soviet Union imposed violence against civilians on a scale unprecedented in modern times. *The Holocaust* (in Hebrew, *Shoah*), or deliberate extermination of the Jews by the Nazi government, is one of the most profound cases of genocide in history. At the same time, the Japanese government massacred tens of thousands of civilians in China and was responsible for massive rapes and tortures in Nanking in 1937. Soviet authorities deported millions from the annexed territories in the Baltic region and Poland in 1939; they also deported large ethnic groups living in the Crimea and Caucasus in 1944. The German invasion of the Soviet Union that began in June 1941 quickly turned into a genocidal war, in which hundreds of thousands of Jews and Slavs were massacred. Small states in wartime Yugoslavia also practiced genocide against civilians. British and American carpet bombing of German and Japanese cities and the nuclear attacks on Hiroshima and Nagasaki in 1945 were clear violations of the Hague Conventions as well. The British-American massive bombing campaign aimed at causing unacceptable damage to Germany and Japan, to force unconditional surrender (Hitchcock, 2008).

After several meetings, the leaders of the United States, the USSR, and the United Kingdom agreed to hold the political and military leaders of Nazi Germany and imperial Japan responsible for crimes against humanity. But how could the government of a sovereign state be put on trial? The London Charter, announced by the Big Three on August 8, 1945, provided the legal arguments. It stated that the German government had lost its political authority, and the Allied states had the right to establish a special court to apply the laws of war against Germany. The court would have jurisdiction only over crimes that took place after the start of the war in 1939. Legally, the Charter followed up on the decisions of the 1907 Hague Conference. It became the grounds for the Nuremberg trials against Nazi criminals in 1946, with German political leaders charged on four counts:

- *Conspiracy to wage aggressive war*—a premeditated plan to commit war crimes.
- *Crimes against peace*—wars of aggression in violation of international law.
- *War crimes*—profound violations of the laws of war, including mistreatment of prisoners of war and slave labor.
- *Crimes against humanity*—actions in concentration camps and on occupied territories in Europe.

Judges were appointed, defense lawyers hired, and witnesses called. After testimonies and deliberations, the court handed death sentences to eleven top German officials. Two others were acquitted. The rest received long prison sentences.

The Nuremberg tribunals had a profound and lasting influence on international law. Similar trials were held in Japan, China, Australia, the Philippines,

Nazi leaders on trial in Nuremberg, Germany, in 1945. The Nuremberg Trials (1945–46), despite much criticism, had a profound and lasting influence on international law.

and other countries. For example, the International Military Tribunal for the Far East (also known as the Tokyo Trials) sentenced to death seven former top Japanese officials responsible for genocide and seventeen more to lengthy prison terms. In China thirteen separate trials were held. Over five hundred defendants were convicted and 149 executed. Gradually, expanded definitions of war crimes were accepted and agreements to implement them signed. The United Nations adopted the Convention on the Prevention and Punishment of the Crime of Genocide(General Assembly Resolution 260) in 1948. Based on these international precedents and documents, the term *genocide* entered international law to mean the deliberate extermination or prosecution by any government of national, racial, ethnic, and religious groups—whether in war or in peacetime.

Nuremberg had a lasting impact on international law. The trials initiated a series of developments to establish a permanent international criminal court. (It took almost half a century, though, before its statute was adopted.) The trials also served as a precedent for UN guidelines for determining war crimes. For example, if a country's laws do not impose a penalty for a war crime, this country's officials and even its head of state—if accused of committing war crimes—can be prosecuted under international law. So can ordinary citizens.

Advocates of liberalism and many influential nongovernment organizations have long demanded greater enforcement of international law, including the arrest and prosecution of state leaders who commit war crimes or similar acts. These demands gained momentum in the early 1990s, with support from many states and international organizations including the United Nations, and practical steps followed. The ICTY, created under auspices of the United Nations, during almost a decade of work, indicted 161 individuals and sentenced sixty-four. (Three died while serving their sentences.) In 1999, Slobodan Milošević, the former leader of Yugoslavia, was put on trial in The Hague by ICTY. Milošević was charged on sixty-six counts of genocide, crimes against humanity, and war crimes in Croatia, Bosnia and Herzegovina, and Kosovo between 1991 and 1999. The trial lasted four years, but Milošević died in jail in 2006.

The court also focused on atrocities committed by leaders of the paramilitary Bosnian Serbs in Bosnia—including those accused of killings, torture, and running concentration camps. After many years in hiding, the Bosnian Serb commanders Radovan Karadžić, Ratko Mladić, and Goran Hadžić were brought before the court. Their case may be investigated for years before judgment is passed. At the same time, the Tribunal on Rwanda (ICTR), now located in Arusha, Tanzania, finished fifty trials and convicted twenty-nine persons accused of war crimes and crimes against humanity. More trials are in progress.

The next important step was taken in 1998, when 120 countries adopted the Rome Statute, the legal basis for establishing the International Criminal Court, a permanent institution that "shall have the power to exercise its jurisdiction over persons for the most serious crimes of international concern." The ICC is located in The Hague in the Netherlands and is not part of the United Nations. The Rome Statute entered in force in 2002, and the ICC opened investigations in several countries. In 2009 it brought charges against the president of Sudan, Omar al-Bashir, for crimes against humanity, war crimes, and genocide. Whenever al-Bashir visited another country, he could be arrested and brought to The Hague for justice. In 2011 the Court brought charges against six officials from Kenya over their alleged involvement in the 2007–08 electoral violence in that country.

Some countries began to use diplomatic channels to bring their former leaders to justice. In 2009, the Special Criminal Court in Peru tried and sentenced former president Alberto Fujimori to twenty-five years in prison for grave human rights violations. This trial was the first time a democratically elected head of state has been extradited to his own country, tried for human rights violations, and convicted (Burt, 2009).

 Go online to find current cases at the International Criminal Court.

Critics of extraterritoriality and international trials, however, can base their arguments on the Nuremberg trials, too. Realists, of course, have been skeptical about the effectiveness of international law. Yet they supported the Nuremberg trials, because these were initiated and enforced by powerful states—the United States, the USSR, and the UK. Realists note, too, that it took NATO's massive military campaign against Yugoslavia, including the bombing of cities, to put former president Milošević on trial. And al-Bashir, even under indictment from the ICC, remained in his country.

Civil libertarians also have reservations about international tribunals. In democratic societies, an accused murderer or rapist is only a *suspect*, not a criminal, before conviction in a court of law. Will international tribunals maintain that standard of protection for the individual? Are they truly impartial? Will they be used instead to settle personal scores with the accused? International courts, critics fear, can easily become a stage for *victors' justice*—in which a victorious country applies different rules to judge its own actions and the defeated enemy. During the Nuremberg trials, the Soviet Union used falsified documents to accuse the Nazis of massacring twenty thousand Polish officers in the

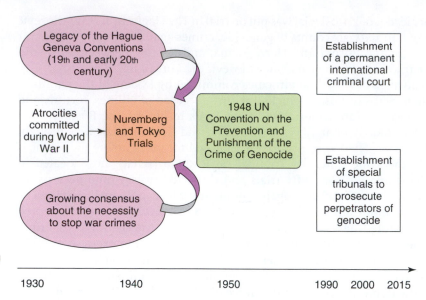

FIGURE 5-6 International law and the legacy of the Nuremberg Trials: A chronological snapshot.

Katyn Forest in Russia. This crime, as the Russian government acknowledged not long ago, was in fact committed on Stalin's order by the Soviet secret police (Sanford, 2009). The Soviets' own acts of genocide and mass deportations were not so much as mentioned during the Nuremberg trials. Moscow literally got away with murder because it was powerful and victorious.

For all its flaws and inconsistencies, however, the Nuremberg trials have played an important role in the development of international law. They have led to more than sixty years of international agreements. They serve as a model for future international trials as well, based on the principles of extraterritoriality and universal justice. The trials created a *legal precedent*—a ruling that international courts may develop in future prosecutions. Last but not least, Nuremberg gave hope that fundamental rights will be protected and justice will, eventually, be served. (See Figure 5.6.)

CONCLUSION

There is neither a universal world constitution nor written principles suggesting how states should act. No single judge or court is empowered to decide when a state violates international law. As we saw at the start of this chapter, Israel refused to accept the decision of an international court. Still, in many other cases states adhere to legal principles and to agreements with other states or international organizations. Everywhere, treaties are signed, trade agreements are made, and disputes are settled by legal means. Critics of international law stress its vagueness, inconsistency, and biases, along with the frequent objections of individual states. However, the rule of law has made substantial progress during the last century and a half. History shows that law prevails through agreement and not solely through coercion because it provides most citizens with a sense of security; brings them hope and stability; and makes the world a more open, free, and comfortable place to live. The world faces an even bigger challenge now: to make these rules work.

CHAPTER SUMMARY

- International law is a set of principles, rules, and regulations concerning international relations. Its sources include treaties, customary law, and the judgments of courts and international organizations.
- Increasing trade led states to outline rules related to travel and commerce. The Laws of the Sea are among the oldest examples of international law.
- By the nineteenth century the increasing destructiveness of war contributed to a growing consensus regarding the need to regulate war and to minimize its deadly consequences to both combatants and civilians. The laws of war are principles that states must follow in the event of an armed conflict.
- International organizations arose to promote cooperation in the fields of technology, communication, and law enforcement. The League of Nations came into existence in 1920, the United Nations in 1945, and the International Criminal Court in 2002.
- Realists believe that international law should not undermine a sovereign state's security and other interests. Without proper enforcement, they argue, international law is simply ineffective.
- Liberals believe that interdependence, mutual consent, and legal obligations can cement the fabric of international relations. Liberal principles include supranationalism, universal jurisdiction, and extraterritoriality. Wars, liberalism argues, could be significantly limited if states had to justify them according to international law.
- Constructivists believe that historical circumstances, socioeconomic differences, prejudices, and other factors determine perceptions of international law.
- In conflict theory, international law serves the interests of some countries and groups at the expense of others.
- Domestic politics often shape a leader's positions on international law and bilateral agreements. Sovereign states are more likely to join an international agreement if it has domestic political support and does not threaten a domestic political regime.
- Many who support a global legal system see it as a way to ensure stability, cooperation, and peace. Opponents see it as impractical or undemocratic.

KEY TERMS

Aggression 164
Autocratic rulers 168
Customary law 153
Democratic leaders 169
East African Community (EAC) 173
Extraterritoriality 163
Freedom of the seas 155

General principles of law 153
Genocide 157
Human rights 156
International law 150
International mandate 161
International treaties 152
Jurisdiction 152
Laws of war 155

Neutrality 156
Sources of international law 152
Supranationalism 163
Tyrant 169
Universal jurisdiction 164

Visual Review **INTERNATIONAL LAW**

1. What do we study?

KEY CONCEPTS, PRINCIPLES, AND SOURCES OF INTERNATIONAL LAW

- International law refers to principles, rules, and agreements that regulate the behavior of states and other international actors

- Territoriality and jurisdiction principles define how far laws can reach

- Sources of international law: treaties, customary law, general principles of law, and rulings by international organizations and courts

THE DEVELOPMENT OF INTERNATIONAL LAW

- The Treaty of Westphalia established an early foundation of international law in 1648

- The Laws of the Sea dealt with competition, the safety of shipments, and financial disputes

- The Laws of War dealt with common principles that states should follow in case of an armed conflict

- Early international legal institutions and organizations dealt with humanitarian issues and disputes among states

2. How do we study it?

REALISM

- International law should not undermine a sovereign state's key interests

- Without proper enforcement, international law is ineffective

LIBERALISM

- Interdependence, mutual consent, and legal obligations are necessary

- Evolving principles: supranationalism, universal jurisdiction, and extraterritoriality

CONSTRUCTIVISM

Historical and socioeconomic conditions, values, and identities determine perceptions of international law

OTHER THEORIES

- In conflict theory, international law serves the interests of a few at the expense of others

- In self-organization theory, justice administration and law enforcement require a "world state"

3. How do we apply it?

THE INDIVIDUAL CONTEXT

Leaders' choices strengthen or weaken international law

THE STATE CONTEXT

States treat international law in the context of domestic politics, policy, and security strategies

THE GLOBAL CONTEXT

Most states have a strong interest in developing and maintaining international legal norms

Critical Thinking

- What are the main limitations of international law?
- Compare and contrast the realist and liberal views of international law.
- Why did Nazi Germany and Imperial Japan withdraw from the League of Nations?
- Give arguments supporting and against universal jurisdiction.
- Suggest examples of extraterritoriality that you find useful and acceptable.

Rows of car engines at the Fiat Mirafiori plant undergo tests on an assembly line in Turin, Italy, in 1950. The Italian car industry benefited from new equipment provided by the United States under the Marshall Plan. This program launched the system of liberal institutions and interdependence that, as some argue, created the modern Western political and economic system.

International Political Economy

Practical men, who believe themselves to be quite exempt from any intellectual influence, are usually the slaves of some defunct economist.
—JOHN MAYNARD KEYNES

IN 1947, MANY EUROPEAN CITIES LAY IN RUINS AFTER WORLD WAR II. ECONOMIES BEGAN TO REVIVE BUT STILL STRUGGLED. UNEMPLOYMENT WAS RAMPANT. LACK OF FUEL, FOOD, and clothing was endemic. In France and Italy, the threat of Communist coups grew. Chaos and insecurity reigned from Poland to Greece.

In June of that year, the U.S. secretary of state, George Marshall, announced an assistance program to Europe that became known as the Marshall Plan. In 1948, Congress approved the first $5 billion in aid. By 1952 the United States had spent $13.5 billion in sixteen countries, an equivalent of about $120 billion today. It was a massive "stimulus" to stabilize finances and sustain economic growth.

Why did Washington provide this help? The ultimate goal of the Marshall Plan was to prevent Communism from spreading over Western Europe. The Marshall Plan was also good for the U.S. economy: Using American money, Europeans began to purchase American equipment, spare parts, technologies, and know-how. Hundreds of thousands of new jobs were created in America. The Plan helped to resurrect European liberal democracy, threatened by hunger, instability, and political radicalism. The plan pulled Western Europe into the U.S. financial and trade orbit, but also the political orbit, and initiated a host of institutions that shaped the modern West (Hitchcock, 2008).

The lessons of the Marshall Plan are relevant today. The global economic crisis that began in 2008 showed that governments still have a huge role to play in helping economies. Even the most dedicated supporters of market capitalism agree that regulations are necessary, especially in today's global economy. But how far must government regulations reach? China fifty years later combined private entrepreneurship with state controls, and it brought about remarkable achievements (See the Conclusion). Will this success continue?

In this chapter, we discuss the economic aspects of international relations. We consider the influence of economic interests on foreign policy agendas; the impact of states and their policies on international economy, finances, and trade; the opportunities and challenges of global economic interdependence; and the problem of wealth and poverty from a global perspective.

After reading this chapter, you should be able to:

▶ explain the major factors of international political economy;
▶ explain the principles of mercantilism, economic liberalism, constructivism, and conflict theories in the context of international economic policies;
▶ evaluate the impact of states on the international economy, finances, and trade as well as the challenges of global economic interdependence; and
▶ apply major economic views to realities of international relations within three contexts of analysis

Learning Objectives

What Do We Study?

International political economy (IPE) is the study of how politics and economics interact in an international context. Successful economic and financial policies guarantee material security of a country and contribute to international stability and peace. The failure of such policies could lead to a political and social crisis. Today, with the world so interdependent or "globalized," the financial or economic failure of just one state can have profound international consequences. Recent financial crises in the United States and European Union created uncertainty and tension in the entire international system.

How do state economic policies affect international relations? Which economic models are most successful in today's global economy and why? To answer these and other questions, political economists analyze such activities as production, consumption, finances, and trade.

The Major Factors of IPE

PRODUCTION AND CONSUMPTION

Economic **production** is the creation of goods and services with market value. For centuries, states accumulated resources and territories to enhance their power. States also controlled, funded, or regulated their productive capacities—from gold mines and oil wells to factories and trade companies. In the modern world, the power of states is measured in the size and growth of their **gross domestic product** (GDP), which is the monetary value of the goods and services produced at a given time. The GDP of the United States is now $16 trillion, China's is about $6 trillion, and South Korea's and Mexico's are around $1 trillion (World Bank, 2013).

In the twenty-first century more production is shifting from traditional economic powers—such as the United States, the United Kingdom, and Japan—toward emerging markets, or countries in the process of rapid economic growth, such as China, India, and Brazil. For the past couple of decades, mainly because of their lower wage costs, these countries have substantially increased their share of global manufacturing, reaching more than half the world's exports. Emerging markets also account for nearly half of global retail sales (Woodall, 2011).

A country's power is also inseparable from its scale of **consumption**, which is the selection, adoption, use, disposal, and recycling of goods and services. A country's consumption patterns affect its *imports,* or the products and services it purchases abroad. For example, the United States is the third largest crude oil producer in the world. However, through most of the 2000s, about 50 percent of its consumed oil (the United States is the biggest oil consumer in the world) comes from other countries, which creates dependency. This dependency on foreign oil is in sharp decline now, thanks to the innovative oil explorations on U.S. territory. In recent years, more attention has been paid to the byproducts of consumption—*waste* and *pollution*, which have become global problems. China still lags behind major developed countries in consumption, but its industries in the twenty-first century became major polluters (Economy, 2010b).

FINANCES

Historically a state's financial resources, or *finances*, consisted of gold reserves, stored in well-protected places (such as Fort Knox in the United States). The more gold a country had, the more power it was thought to possess. These days, finances most often mean the value of stocks and bonds traded on markets, and financial wealth is measured in paper notes or more complex indicators, tracked electronically and up to the minute.

For centuries, states sought to control and augment their finances. Financially wealthy states could pay for a large military force and lend money to other states in exchange for political favors and loyalty. Great Britain dominated the world financial system in the nineteenth and first half of the twentieth century, but it lost much of its wealth during World War II and dismantled its vast empire shortly after. The United States assumed the dominant financial role in the

A country's inability to manage its finances may result in a serious crisis. A protester carries a banner that reads "No to Imperialism—The only solution for Cyprus" during an anti-austerity rally in front of the Parliament in Athens in 2013. A few hundred people protested against austerity measures imposed on Cyprus by the EU.

1940s. Today it is still the wealthiest nation in the world by many standards, but over the last decade its expenses have surpassed revenues, and the U.S. dollar now depends on the financial backing of China and others. World finances are now so complicated that no state can manage and regulate them alone.

National **currencies**—such as dollars, Euros, pesos, and rubles—can be converted into other currencies at what is called an *exchange rate*. From 1945 until 1971 the value of the U.S. dollar was fixed to the price of gold (the so-called gold standard). Now, the dollar and other national currencies fluctuate vis-à-vis each other and gold; their exchange rate depends on many factors, including GDP growth, exports and imports, and political as well as economic events. The consequences of volatility of currency exchange rates may have significant impact on international trade and seriously affect all businesses and ordinary citizens. (See Table 6-1.)

TRADE

International trade is another volatile factor in international relations. Under most circumstances, states try to stimulate and expand their exports—goods and services that the country sells officially on the international market. And most states depend on their imports—goods and services that the country has to bring in from outside. The difference between the value of exports and imports is the **balance of trade.** It is positive when exports surpass imports and negative if a country buys more than it sells. Before the 1970s the United States had a positive balance of trade, but it has slipped into an ever-growing trade deficit, largely a result of goods imported from China and the import of oil from the Persian Gulf.

TABLE 6-1 Consequences of Shifting U.S. Currency Exchange Rates

Change in U.S. Currency	Consequences
More Expensive Than Previously	Good news for people who travel abroad because they can get more for their dollars. However, U.S. products will cost more abroad, and fewer products will be exported. This could easily cause a decrease in production and a loss of jobs in the United States. That's bad news for domestic manufacturers.
Less Expensive Than Previously	Bad news for tourists traveling abroad: They get less for their money. A weaker currency, however, means that U.S. exports can increase as they become less expensive and thus more competitive on the global market. That's good news for domestic manufacturers.

Why are trade deficits so important in international relations? For decades, trade imbalances created inequality in the distribution of wealth between wealthy and poor countries. African and most South American countries exported agricultural products and raw materials to developed countries at low prices, whereas the latter exported sophisticated products and services at high prices. As a result, poorer states owed substantial amounts of money to wealthy ones. Economic and political dependency became intertwined. In the past twenty years, the rapid growth of manufacturing in China, India, Brazil, and elsewhere has altered the global trade balance. Now consumers in Western

DEBATE > GLOBAL INTERDEPENDENCE AND LOCAL PRICES

Currency exchange affects almost all of us, immediately and directly. When we buy inexpensive goods with the label "made in China," we often save money—or so it seems. In reality, we pay another, hidden price—American jobs. Chinese goods are inexpensive because the cost of labor in China is cheap and because the Chinese state deliberately maintains a low exchange rate between its national currency, the Yuan, and two major currencies—the dollar and the Euro. As a result, factories in China manufacture goods that cost significantly less than if they were produced in, say, Boston or Paris (Meyerson, 2010). And Western firms increasingly move their production to China because it is cheaper to manufacture there. As a result, in the twenty-first century, the Western world is no longer the leading manufacturer. The United States alone has lost millions of industrial jobs over the past twenty years.

WHAT'S YOUR VIEW?

What are the consequences for the United States? What would you decide if you were president?

Consider two possibilities. Would you stop the continuing loss of manufacturing jobs to foreign countries while consumers pay a higher price for virtually everything? Or would you continue to adhere to liberal principles of minimal state regulation and see some jobs disappear? Could there be a third way? Suggest a "hybrid" strategy that would combine these two policy options.

Visit the companion website for a list of products made in the United States.

countries owe money to China where goods are manufactured. The ability of states to control the movements of goods and capital has declined sharply, especially in the era of the Internet. Many corporations move their production to China and other places with the large pool of cheap, educated, and disciplined labor. This affects manufacturing jobs in wealthy countries and worsens their financial problems.

Still, sovereign states have effective economic and financial policies at their disposal. **Protectionism** is the policy of restricting or discouraging imports and encouraging domestic production. One way is through **tariffs**—fees on imported goods, to make them more expensive. This gives domestic producers a chance to sell their goods, protects domestic workforce, and may reduce the negative trade balance. Presidents George W. Bush and Barack Obama both occasionally used tariffs. Another form of protectionism is direct subsidies to domestic industries, to keep jobs and make products more competitive abroad (Zahariadis, 2008).

Countries may also use **economic sanctions** against other states. These are the deliberate withdrawal, or threat of withdrawal, of customary trade and financial relations, to put pressure on a government to change its policies. The ultimate form of economic sanctions is an *embargo*, or the prohibition of trade. Iran has long been a target of embargoes imposed by the United States and the European Union to stop its development of nuclear weapons.

In the past, economic sanctions often preceded or followed a war. In the twentieth century, however, they began to play a role as an alternative to violence. They may be used in an attempt to restrain a belligerent government, punish aggression, contain a civil war, influence policies, or simply make a political statement (Hufbauer and Oegg, 2003).

Currently, American legislation allows economic and trade sanctions against countries that expropriate U.S. property, organize coups against elected governments, and support terrorism. Countries that violate human rights, harbor international war criminals, engage in nuclear proliferation, or fail to cooperate sufficiently with U.S. antinarcotics efforts may also become targets of economic sanctions. The Office of Foreign Assets Control of the U.S. Department of the Treasury administers and enforces economic and trade sanctions. Many of them are based on UN and other international mandates.

 Visit the companion website to learn more about international trade sanctions, their effectiveness, and their failures.

Economic policies are not always about bans and restrictions. States also use economic and monetary incentives to influence other countries. Loans and subsidies can help both sides achieve their economic and political goals. The Marshall Plan, described at the start of this chapter, is an outstanding example. As we will see in this chapter, trade agreements between states, international organizations, and nongovernmental institutions now play a greater role than ever in global economic affairs.

Economic policies of countries are related to economic theories and models as much as they are influenced by politics and other short-term factors. University-trained economists play a prominent role in countries' actions related to production, finances, and trade. To understand contemporary IPE we have to comprehend how these ideas and models occurred, developed, and applied. They also help explain the role of such intergovernmental organizations and agreements as the World Trade Organization, North American Free Trade Agreement (NAFTA), and the European Union in an era of globalization.

How Do We Study It?

We can take several different approaches to studying international political economy. Here, we will look at mercantilism (often linked with realism), economic liberalism, constructivism, and conflict theories. (See Figure 6.1.)

Mercantilism: An Economic Realism?

Mercantilism calls for the accumulation and protection of available resources in the name of the state. The seventeenth and eighteenth centuries were the apogee of mercantilism. This economic approach was widely accepted when absolute monarchies, such as France, followed mercantilist recipes to aggrandize power at the expense of their neighbors. Many countries, including the United States, later used mercantilism along with nationalist rhetoric (O'Brien and Clesse, 2002), and mercantilist arguments are making a comeback today.

PRINCIPLES OF MERCANTILISM

Mercantilists assume that, globally, wealth is limited and does not grow or shrink fast. To succeed, states should compete for territories, resources, and colonies. Their economic policies should therefore aim at accumulating natural resources and gold reserves, territorial expansion, establishing exclusive trade with colonies, and payments from defeated enemies.

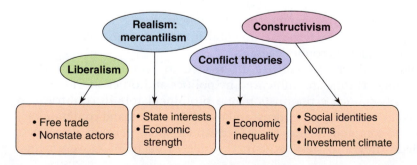

FIGURE 6-1 Major approaches of international political economy.

Mercantilist principles can be applied to the production, distribution, and consumption of resources and products (Ekelund and Hébert, 2007). First, states must make sure that most of the products and services they need are produced domestically and that natural resources—such as coal, gas, and oil—are primarily for domestic consumption. This encourages employment and limits other countries' opportunities to sell their products there. States should accumulate precious metals and stimulate overseas trade to ensure the flow of gold and silver into the state's treasury. These metals are important to stabilize finances, maintain armed forces, and fight wars.

Mercantilism says that imports of foreign goods should be limited, but in reality this principle is difficult to achieve. States should therefore maintain a positive balance of trade: They must sell more than they buy from foreign countries. Governments should also discourage foreign traders by establishing tariffs on imported goods, thus making them overly expensive. A foreign debt is a state's serious vulnerability.

Finally, it is necessary to support domestic manufacturers and merchants. Today, when international competition cannot be ignored, governments increase their subsidies for domestic producers. They keep the value of their currencies artificially low to make manufactured products cheaper and thus more competitive on international markets. (See Figure 6.2.)

MERCANTILISM AND REALISM

Mercantilism is often linked with realism, just as a country's economic strengths were commonly associated with its military capabilities (Thurow, 1992; Gilboy, 2004). Like realists, mercantilists argue that economic rivalry among states is only natural. In fact, it is a **zero-sum game**: Mutual benefits are seldom achievable, giving states two options—either win or lose (Harrison and Prestowitz, 1990). For example, many European states long considered the struggle for colonies as vital to their economies and national security. Later, the control of oil and gas resources and pipelines came to be as seen as a serious security issue.

The trade balance, too, can be seen in this way. China, for example, makes its trade surplus a top strategic priority. To limit foreign competition, China's government gave a local company UnionPay a near monopoly over the

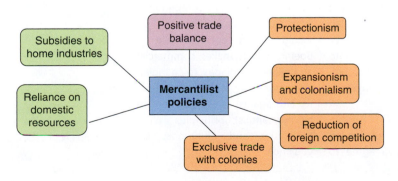

FIGURE 6-2
Mercantilism: A snapshot.

The first Reliance Fresh supermarket opened in Hyderabad, India, in 2006. India for years banned foreign supermarkets on its territory. These policies began to change several years ago.

handling of payments between merchants and banks. (We look more at China's success story at the end of this chapter.) India for many years banned foreign supermarkets on its territory that sell products more cheaply than their Indian competitors. Mercantilists also argue that protecting homegrown businesses is not just an economic but a patriotic issue—a matter of jobs and national pride. Wine producers in France, rice growers in Japan, and steel workers and fishermen in the United States all enjoyed government protection for many years (K. Anderson, 2005).

Opponents of mercantilism argue that subsidies and protectionism slow economies and harm trade and consumption. And the most consistent criticism of mercantilism comes from economic liberals—the supporters of free (or freer) trade.

Economic Liberalism

In the context of IPE, liberalism can be equaled with **economic liberalism**—the belief that only free production, trade, and consumption can produce the best economic results and lead to a peaceful, prosperous world. This is not a single theory but rather several approaches, all stemming from a few basic principles—including the importance of entrepreneurship, minimal state regulations, and the concept of the public good.

THE ROOTS AND PRINCIPLES OF ECONOMIC LIBERALISM

Adam Smith (1723–1790), the Scottish economist and philosopher, is a founder of economic liberalism. In *An Inquiry into the Nature and Causes of the Wealth of Nations* (1977), published in 1776, he opposed restrictions on international trade, arguing that commerce brings prosperity and peace among

---

DEBATE > NATIONAL PRIDE AND FOREIGN OWNERSHIP

In the United Kingdom, one of the most famous London soccer clubs, Chelsea, is currently owned by a Russian tycoon. Another Russian billionaire owns the Brooklyn Nets, an NBA team. The German auto giant Volkswagen, however, is sheltered by law from foreign buyers.

WHAT'S YOUR VIEW?

What is your opinion of foreign ownership? Would you agree to have the New York Yankees or the Boston Red Sox sold to a joint venture owned by a few entrepreneurs from Kazakhstan and Pakistan? Or would you accept the sale of Boeing, which makes commercial and military airplanes, to an Indian magnate? Compare the arguments for and against foreign ownership to mercantilist principles. What similarities and differences do you find?

@ Read the article "Foreign Ownership of American Sports Teams Is Here" by Darren Rovell on CNBC.com (September 2009).

nations. A noted follower, David Ricardo (1772–1823), believed that free trade is the best regulator of labor and natural resources. Another economic liberal, Friedrich List (1789–1846), suggested that commercial unions among states make trade flourish and enrich all participants (List, [1841] 2006).

Economic liberalism gradually replaced mercantilism as a dominant trend in economic policies in the second half of the nineteenth century. However, liberal economic ideas came under serious attack during the Great Depression and the rise of Communism, Fascism, and Social Democracy from the 1920s through the 1950s. Still, they retained significant strength. In *The Road to Serfdom* ([1944] 2007), the Austrian economist Friedrich von Hayek (1899–1992) asserted that only free competition among individual entrepreneurs creates the information and other conditions necessary for a successful production and consumption of goods. Hayek influenced American economist Milton Friedman (1912–2006), who in his *Capitalism and Freedom* (1962) also criticized state regulations. In the television series *Free to Choose* (1980), he contended that people's individual choices are better for economic development than state planning. Friedman, who taught at the University of Chicago, still argued that the state has a role to play: It should gradually increase the amount of money in circulation—an idea called *monetarism*. Economic liberalism also influenced British prime minister Margaret Thatcher, who pushed for fundamental economic reforms in the United Kingdom after 1979, and President Reagan. The deregulation of economic activities in the 1980s, combined with government control over the flow of money through changing interest rates, remained the dominant policy in the United States.

 On the companion website, read more about the bitter international commercial dispute between two manufacturing giants, Boeing and Airbus. Both argued that government support had led to unfair competition.

Jubilant crowds offer a cluster of hands for Britain's reelected Prime Minister, Margaret Thatcher, in 1983. Thatcher pushed for economic deregulation. Her policies drew both fierce resistance and enthusiastic support in the United Kingdom.

Free trade through international cooperation is the key goal of liberalism. An early argument in its defense comes from the principle (often called the law) of **comparative advantage**, which explains that it is beneficial for two countries to trade with each other instead of relying on their own domestic production. This law is attributed to Robert Torrens (1815), but David Ricardo made it famous two years later. Imagine England and the Ukraine making textiles and corn. In England, production of both takes less time than in the Ukraine, so it has an economic advantage over the Ukraine. Mercantilists would ask why, in this case, we need to import anything from the Ukraine.

Actually, the law suggests that both countries would benefit from mutual trade: If Britain would import corn from the Ukraine, it would save more labor time and resources to produce better textiles. In the same way, the Ukraine would gain from focusing on the production of corn while importing British textiles. In both countries, consumers would be better off because prices of both products would be lower.

In the same spirit, economic liberals argue that the benefits obtained from protecting domestic producers against foreign competitors are insignificant compared to the damage to the domestic economy as a whole: People have to pay much higher prices for domestic goods plus protected businesses have less incentive to develop, modernize, and be more competitive internationally. Economic liberals also argue that economic cooperation reduces the chance of war: Businesses are likely to lobby for cooperation and international law (Oneal and Russett, 1997; Rogowski, 1990.) This will induce states to choose cooperation. (See Figure 6.3.)

THE KEYNESIAN CHALLENGE

The principles of economic liberalism were challenged by John Maynard Keynes (pronounced *kānz*; 1883–1946), a British economist and a founder of **macroeconomics**, the study of the structure and performance of the entire economy. Not only did Keynes create an influential theory, he also could see it applied in economic policies of many countries. In *The General Theory of Employment, Interest and Money* ([1936] 1965), he argued that, contrary to the assumption of the efficiency of free markets, governments should regulate business and especially finances. According to **Keynesian economics**, national governments can ease the undesirable effects of economic recessions by spending more money than their revenues allow. By putting money into the economy, government can

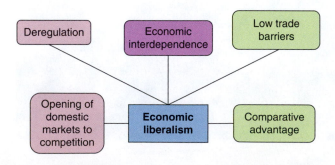

FIGURE 6-3 Economic liberalism: A snapshot.

fuel business transactions and purchases, stimulate production and consumption, lower unemployment, and create a prosperous middle class.

Following Keynes' ideas, states abandoned the gold standard and started to manipulate the supply of money through banking interest rates—a process known as **monetary policy**. For instance, the Federal Reserve, the central banking system in the United States, is responsible for maintaining the stability of the financial system. The Federal Reserve can determine the rise or fall of interest rates, thus making credit either more expensive or less, and so opening or closing the flow of capital into the economy. The government can also use government spending or taxes to influence the economy—an approach called **fiscal policy**. States can raise taxes and use this money to create jobs while at the same time fighting *inflation*, a rise in the prices. In the 1970s and 1980s, Keynesian principles came under heavy criticism from free-market advocates. But after the global economic crisis of 2008 through 2013, these principles deserved another look.

INTERNATIONAL ORGANIZATIONS

Economic liberalism, with Keynesian modifications, inspired the creation of international institutions to facilitate trade and provide financial stability worldwide. More efficient institutions, their supporters believed, would lead to a more prosperous and peaceful world (Ikenberry and Grieco, 2002; Keohane, 2005).

The Great Depression of the 1930s and World War II offered strong reasons to build international economic and financial institutions. Many believed that protectionism had slowed economic recovery and provoked nationalism. In 1944, representatives of the United States, the United Kingdom, the Soviet Union, France, and China met in Bretton Woods, New Hampshire, leading to the creation of the **International Monetary Fund** (IMF) and the **World Bank** (Peet, 2009). After the Soviet Union backed out of the Bretton Woods agreements in 1946, both institutions became the pillars of Western capitalism. Participating states agreed to contribute parts of their gold reserves to a global "pool" to maintain the balance of payments in international trade. The United States, the wealthiest contributor, played the leading role in the functioning of these institutions.

The IMF has grown from forty-five members in 1945 to more than 187 today. Its goals are to maintain stable exchanges between national currencies and to provide financial help to countries in trouble. The World Bank (more fully, the World Bank for Reconstruction of Development) involves almost all states (except for Cuba, North Korea, and a few others) and makes loans to developing countries for long-term projects. In both institutions the wealthiest donors have more authority. The IMF and World Bank provide financial help conditionally: Usually, the recipient of assistance must reform its finances according to these institutions' prescriptions. These prescriptions often draw criticism (Strand, 2013).

Other liberal international institutions created after the Bretton Woods agreements were the *General Agreement on Tariffs and Trade (GATT)*, signed in 1947 in Geneva, and the *International Trade Organization (ITO)*, created the next year in Havana. The members of GATT held periodic trade negotiations, gradually leading to reductions of tariffs. The ITO failed, however, because the U.S. Senate rejected its charter: Many American politicians feared that it would become a kind of global government. Only in 1995 was the project revived as the **World Trade Organization** (WTO), building on the success of GATT.

The WTO is the main international organization today designed to promote economic development and growth through the removal of tariffs and the opening of national markets to international trade. The WTO includes all major economies and assists its nearly 160 members in trade negotiations and agreements. It also helps enforce their agreements and resolve trade disputes (World Trade Organization, 2012). It does not act as a global government and does not negotiate on behalf of states but rather provides a framework for negotiations. The WTO insists that countries should adhere to the principles of nondiscrimination, reciprocity, and transparency in their trade policies (Hoekman and Kostecki, 2010). This means that countries should have equal access to foreign markets, imported products should be treated no less favorably than domestically produced goods, and no secret deals or domestic regulations should restrict free trade.

Supporters of the WTO hope that free trade will reduce poverty, improve standards of living, create employment, and provide new economic opportunities for billions (Narlikar, 2005). Critics disagree on at least three points. First, they believe that free trade benefits mostly rich countries of the global North while leaving underdeveloped countries of the South to produce raw materials and supply cheap labor (see more about it later in this chapter). Second, small countries can exercise less influence in the "rounds" of talks that produce new WTO rules. Finally, these rules harm small business: In free trade, critics maintain, only big multinational corporations can thrive. Critics also stress that the organization offered no new solutions to the global financial crisis that started in 2008 (Cottier and Elsig, 2011).

@ *Visit the companion website to learn more about the World Trade Organization and the World Bank.*

REGIONAL TRADE AGREEMENTS

Regional trade agreements are rules and mutual commitments based on international treaties that bind countries to pursue common economic and financial policies. They usually deal with tariffs and their reduction and elimination. They also deal with transportation, communications, intellectual property, environmental standards, investments, and trade policies. Today there are about 150 regional trade arrangements. One is the NAFTA, which went into effect in 1994. In it, the United States, Mexico, and Canada agreed to gradually eliminate most trade and investment barriers in dealing with one another. In 2011, twelve countries (the United States, Australia, Canada, Japan, Mexico, Brunei, Chile, Malaysia, New Zealand, Peru, Singapore, and Vietnam) expressed interest in forming the Trans-Pacific Partnership. Potentially, its possible members could together produce more than 40 percent of the world's GDP.

Why do countries need such agreements? They gain from lower prices. States also seek to secure access to each other's markets and products. Many less developed countries need economic security and pursue trade agreements with developed states. Wealthy countries seek cheaper products and services and expect new consumers' markets to grow (Whalley, 1997). The profiles of several of the most important regional organizations based on free trade are displayed in Table 6-2.

TABLE 6-2   Examples of Regional Trade Agreements

Regional Agreement	Main Features
European Union (EU)	The EU is the most ambitious project in economic and political integration, with the population of 500 million and GDP of $17 trillion. It has a common currency and central banking system (the Euro and the European Central Bank), and it has taken steps to develop a common foreign and security policy. (We examined the European Union in Chapter 2).
Southern Common Market (MERCOSUR)	Comprising Argentina, Paraguay, Uruguay, Brazil, and Venezuela (since 2006), the Southern Common Market represents a total population of 190 million people—all living in an area larger than the European continent. The organization promotes the movement of goods, people, and currency among these countries.
Asia-Pacific Economic Cooperation (APEC)	This group of twenty-one Pacific Rim countries, including the United States, meets regularly to purposely improve economic and political ties among member states. The group has working committees on a wide range of issues, from communications to fisheries.

▶ What is economic mercantilism? Which mercantilist policies benefit you personally?

▶ Explain the comparative advantage principle.

▶ How does Keynesian economics operate to stimulate growth and jobs?

▶ What is the main goal of key international trade organizations?

CHECK YOUR KNOWLEDGE

Constructivism

Material resources and economic policies, constructivism argues, are often seen through the prism of collective values and socially constructed priorities (Reus-Smit, 2009). The goals and structure of economic policies change from country to country depending on social, political, and cultural conditions in these countries (P. Evans, 1998). Ideologies and customs also influence economic policies. For instance, free trade may be viewed as a positive or negative development, depending on a country's role in the world market (Copeland, 1996).

Using constructivist ideas, one can see the Marshall Plan as not only an economic policy but also a way to promote beliefs in free markets and free trade—as opposed to mercantilism, not to mention Communism. The Marshall Plan fostered cooperation, mutual acceptance, and the willingness of European states to become "the United States of Europe."

A man fills a coin machine with Estonian coins to exchange them for euros, in Tallinn, Estonia, 2011. This Baltic state became the 17th European Union member to adopt the joint currency, the euro. Estonia's national purpose is "returning to Europe" and avoiding the Russian domination.

@ Go online to find out more about Transparency International and its annual surveys of the world's corruption.

NATIONAL PURPOSE

Just as individuals act according to their background, experience, and identity, states structure their economic policies according to how they see themselves and their role in the regional and world economies. Governments and business elites adopt a **national purpose**, and this purpose drives economic goals and policies of their countries. A vision of the country's future can bring its people together and affect their lives (Abdelal, 2001). When the Soviet Union imploded in 1991, some new post-Soviet countries—such as Estonia, Latvia, and Lithuania—turned rapidly away from Russia and did not seek economic cooperation with it. Belarus and Kazakhstan preferred cooperation: for decision-making elites there, it did not conflict with how they saw the future of their own countries.

Countries constantly redefine their national purpose. India, for example, beginning with its increasing economic rivalry with China in the 1990s, sought a stronger role in world affairs. It turned from longstanding protectionist policies to international cooperation and interdependence, allowed foreign investments, and promoted economic openness (Alamgir, 2008). According to constructivism, India's massive economic reforms were strongly influenced by its policy makers' perception of what India should be, especially in comparison with China.

ECONOMIC CLIMATE

States and the global community develop an **economic climate**, or set of values and practices that may or may not support official policies and visions of national purpose. According to economic liberalism, manufacturers, sellers, and consumers act in accord with the rules of supply and demand. In reality, constructivists say, scores of other factors affect their behavior.

For example, laws that protect the ownership of private property lead to a functioning free market unless a majority of the population follows them. An unfriendly business climate lacks both a legal foundation and trust.

A favorable economic climate means lower cost to business. International investors are likely to bring their money to a country in which they feel protected. In contrast, insecurity and corruption drive international investors away. Places perceived as corrupt, as a rule, lose international investors. Therefore, a country's foreign economic policies become inseparable from its domestic social policy and how it is perceived by others.

Conflict Theories

Conflict theories, as you know from Chapter 3, maintain that the world's economic structure unfairly benefits dominant social classes and groups, such as the wealthy, males, and whites. Such economic order, according to conflict theories, should be replaced by a new and fairer one through revolution or reforms.

MARXISM

Marxists argue that the world is dominated by a ruling class, which owns the major means of production, natural resources, and services. Throughout the twentieth century and after, the ruling class became increasingly global, as capital moved across borders and continents. Today, international corporations and banks, not the governments of sovereign states, are the true holders of global power because of their financial resources. States serve the interests of the ruling class of billionaires using diplomacy, international agreements, and international law to manage international relations, which in effect should lead to higher profits.

Supporters of Marxism argue that despite a wide range of democratic changes in the past century, the gap between a few rich countries and the rest of the world, between the global North and South, remains profound. Free-trade agreements are designed to enrich the international ruling class and give nothing to the middle class, workers, and peasants. But what do Marxists suggest? Their old recipes, urging violent revolutions to nationalizations of large banks and big corporations, lost their credibility after many attempts and failures in the past. The failure of the economies of the Soviet Union, Cuba, North Korea, and other Communist countries disenchanted many Marxist sympathizers. Today, Marxists cannot offer an alternative to global capitalism. They, however, support the antiglobalist movement that demands high taxes on the rich and rigorous social control over banks and corporations.

ECONOMIC DEPENDENCY

Dependency theory has its roots in the research of an Argentine economist, Raul Prebisch (1901–1986), and a German economist, Hans Singer (1910–2006). In their view, technology-driven developed nations, called the *core*, have been receiving more benefits from international trade than technology-deprived developing countries, called the *periphery*. Singer and Prebisch showed that core nations, but not periphery countries, benefit significantly from improvements in technology. Moreover, periphery countries cannot catch up with core nations under the conditions of free trade (Prebisch, 1989; Singer, 1999). The wealth of core countries was almost constantly increasing, whereas the wealth growth of the periphery was flat or decreased.

Dependency theory, like Marxism, explains in relatively simple terms the main causes of the world's economic and political problems. Poor nations provide natural resources and cheap labor for core nations; core countries are interested in continuing the state of dependency through various policies and initiatives involving trade, banking, and direct political control of the periphery. Local elites in poor nations benefit from the dependency and are not interested in changing the world's economic order.

Supporters of these views maintain that the discriminatory structure of the world's economy and trade is the main cause of global inequality and chronic poverty. They began to use the terms such as "global North and South" and "North–South divide" to direct attention to the failures of economic realism and liberalism. The poor, agricultural nations of the **South** (so-called although not all are in the Southern hemisphere) are totally dependent on the developed industrial **North**, both economically and politically. The latter is the core of the capitalist system, and the former remains on the periphery. These, as you will remember from Chapter 3, were main the points of world-systems theory (Wallerstein, 1979).

Supporters of dependency theory accept private property and acknowledge the importance of some elements of a free-market economy. Nevertheless, they believe that the rules governing markets should change and the world's economic order should be restructured (Scott, 2001). How to achieve these goals? First, developing countries have to use central state planning and mercantilism to build their own industries. This should help them in increasing their domestic production and easing their dependence on expensive imports, which is called *import substitution*. They will start benefitting from their own technical advancement. Next, wealthy nations must pay reparations for past colonialist policies, and multinational corporations should be heavily regulated and taxed. Prices for commodities should be guaranteed at the lowest level. Finally, developing countries must gain full access to world capital including massive subsidies. (See Table 6-3.)

Many economists in the Third World became influenced by dependency theory, and some of their recommendations produced visible results. The rise of Brazil's economic power in the last ten years can be credited to some of their prescriptions (Sweig, 2010).

CHECK YOUR KNOWLEDGE

▶ Explain the *core* and the *periphery*.
▶ What is economic climate?
▶ Which factors may affect an economic climate?

TABLE 6-3 Dependency Theory: Key Assumptions

What is the cause of dependency?	The world economic and financial structure is the cause of dependency and inequality among countries. The periphery countries have to import expensive technologies and goods, paying back in cheap raw materials.
Who benefits from this state of dependency?	The world financial and trade system is designed to benefit the core nations and local elites of the periphery, called the *comprador* class.
What are the solutions to this problem?	The countries of the periphery should reduce their dependence by creating their own industries (import substitution).
What else can be done?	The developed countries in the North should provide massive aid to the South. Centrally managed international economic policies should be established.

DEBATE > FAIR TRADE

Fair trade (known also as *trade justice*) initiatives suggest that developed countries should agree that developing nations can sell their products, primarily agricultural goods and resources, at assured prices. Manufacturers and distributors must not use child labor, slavery, an unsafe workplace, or other forms of abuse and discrimination. *TransFair USA*, a nonprofit organization, certifies and labels products manufactured under fair trade principles. Thanks to fair trade, certified coffee, tea, cocoa, fresh fruit, rice, and sugar are all available at tens of thousands of retail locations. Fair trade standards are set by a Germany-based umbrella group, *Fairtrade Labelling Organizations International* (FLO).

WHAT'S YOUR VIEW?

Would you support the application of fair trade principles to all food imports to the United States? Critics argue that you must then pay a higher price for food. Proponents of fair trade reply that in Norway and Germany, for example, higher food prices do not seem to devastate family budgets. Would a 10 percent price increase be acceptable, given *your* financial situation?

 Read more about fair trade on the companion website.

A model is dressed in fair-trade clothes while presenting "Slow Food" products in Stuttgart, Germany, 2013. The fair trade movement aims to support small farmers in developing countries by buying their products at a fixed price, thus cushioning them from fluctuations in global markets and affording them a better living. Slow Food promotes sustainable foods by local small businesses.

How Do We Apply It?

Few economists predicted the massive financial and economic crisis that peaked in 2008. As banks collapsed and property values plummeted, stock markets fell, and unemployment soared. Even fewer economists predicted how long the crisis would last. Signs of recovery appeared in 2010, when the economies of China, India, and Brazil showed some encouraging annual growth numbers, up to 10 percent. Still, many others were idling for years.

What are the international lessons of the crisis? Some were quick to blame the free market and unregulated capitalism. They urged a return to tight state regulations or even mercantilism, to stop states from running negative trade balance and deficits. Liberal economists fought back, defending free trade, but not its excesses. Politicians in many developing countries looked instead to dependency theory. They faced a difficult dilemma: Which economic path of development should they accept—one with more state regulations or less control? Should it be the free market so eagerly promoted by the West? Or should it be a Chinese model rooted in heavy state regulations but seemingly secured economic growth?

No single economic crisis, even the deep one that the world has witnessed, can prove success or failure for certain economic policies. Still, it is important to find out why states choose particular policies rather than others—and when these policies become effective. We must look at the individual, state, and global contexts and circumstances in which these policies developed.

The Individual Context

Many theories of international business and trade are tested on the level of **microeconomics**—the field of economics that considers the behavior of consumers, companies, and industries. Here individual decisions play a big role. Similarly, a choice of international economic policies may be rooted in the decisions of individual state leaders and the leaders of major international financial institutions. But how? Among the factors affecting decisions are leadership, ideology, and the economic climate.

POLITICAL LEADERSHIP

If policies were based only on ideology, a country's decisions would be predictable. A Communist leader promoting an isolationist foreign policy is likely to reject economic cooperation or trade with capitalist countries. And in fact Albania from the 1950s through the 1980s insisted on complete economic self-reliance; so has North Korea for more than sixty years. Their leaders assumed that a true Communist country is capable of building a prosperous economy alone. This policy, called **autarky**, has failed miserably: These states could barely provide the minimum resources for their populations.

Political leaders decide on economic policies based on a variety of ideas. (See Table 6-4.) They cannot afford isolation, but they still have to choose between multilateralism and unilateralism, cooperation and noncooperation with the international system. With the increasing price of oil and oil products in the mid-2000s, some oil-producing states began to act as unilateralists.

TABLE 6-4 National Leaders and Economic Policies

Name	Country	Years in Office	Economic Decisions
Kim Il-Sung (1912–94)	North Korea	1948–94	An authoritarian, Communist leader, he hoped to build a prosperous, independent state based on the ideology of *Juche* (spirit of self-reliance)—a blend of autarky, extreme centralization, and nationalism. Private property was prohibited and foreign trade was limited.
Fidel Castro (b. 1926)	Cuba	1959–2011	In his long tenure in government, Castro's economic policies were based on his belief in state planning and an inevitable confrontation with capitalism. Cuba, however, had to be subsidized heavily by the Soviet Union, and after the Soviet collapse, by Venezuela.
Mohammed Reza Pahlavi (1919–80)	Iran	1941–79	Pahlavi remained a reliable supporter of the United States, the free-market economy, and international trade. His reforms spawned massive corruption. He was expelled during the Islamic revolution.
Deng Xiaoping (1904–97)	People's Republic of China	Approximately 1981–92	After the economic and social disaster of the Cultural Revolution, Deng concluded that the Chinese economy could be restored only by a combination of state planning and market initiative. Deng's reforms set the foundations for the "economic miracle." With significant foreign investments, China became a leading economic power. It preserves, with few modifications, the old political system.
Margaret Thatcher (1925–2013)	United Kingdom	1979–90	Thatcher began to dismantle state regulation of the economy and weakened trade unions. She also resisted the UK's integration into the European Community, fearing that its regulations would reverse her reforms.
Lech Walesa (b. 1943)	Poland	1990–95	Walesa opposed Communist rule and led the independent trade union "Solidarity" against it. As president, he promoted free-market principles but hoped to avoid its excesses. He lost power in the midst of a Polish economic recession.
Robert Mugabe (b. 1924)	Zimbabwe	Since 1980	An authoritarian ruler, Mugabe advocated a blend of anticolonialism and nationalism. His economic policies were erratic and mostly mercantilist. Under his leadership, Zimbabwe remained one of the poorest countries in Africa.

(continued)

TABLE 6-4 National Leaders and Economic Policies (*continued*)

Name	Country	Years in Office	Economic Decisions
Hugo Chávez (1954–2013)	Venezuela	1999–2013	An exemplary Latin American populist, Chavez built his economic policies on a blend of Socialist ideas, anticolonial and anti-imperialist messages, and Bolivarianism (the unification of Latin America). A believer in dependence theory, he repeatedly tried to use his country's oil profits to finance anti-American policies.
Muammar Qaddafi (1942–2011)	Libya	1969–2011	Qaddafi's economic policy of "Islamic Socialism" established government controls of large industries but permitted small business. In practice, most national wealth, especially the oil revenues, went to him and his supporters. During his last years in power, Kaddafi improved relations with Western countries, hoping to benefit even more from high oil prices. He was overthrown by a popular insurrection supported by the West.

After 2006, the Iranian president, Mahmoud Ahmadinejad, openly pushed the development of Iran's nuclear program. He stated that Western countries would not dare to impose sanctions on his country because the West needed Iranian oil. Yet he miscalculated and the Iranian leadership understood that unilateralism could be risky.

MICROECONOMICS

Microeconomics can show how the behavior of individual consumers affects international markets and overall international stability. After the terrorist attacks of September 11, 2001, the world's stock markets fell drastically. Scores of investors decided to sell and put their money in what they perceived as a more secure investment, such as cash or gold. It was an instant emotional reaction to the crisis. Most people were not under direct threat but still felt insecure; acting on their instincts and impulses, they created a global financial disruption lasting for months. The same cycle repeated in the fall of 2008, when the stock market plummeted. In 2010 and 2011, rumors that Greece, a member of the European Union, might default on its national debt, thus threatening the Euro, created fears pushing people to buy state bonds and U.S. dollars. Usually, such "stampedes" are short-lived and help speculators to gamble on the fluctuations in value between currencies. The currency speculation, however, can destabilize the international financial system in the long run. Some European governments began to lobby for a tax on any exchange of foreign currency, to discourage currency speculation.

Even without speculators, financial markets can become volatile. News headlines, elections results, and statements made by leaders affect decisions by both individuals and companies. Millions of individual decisions, affected by mass reactions, produce greater financial volatility. Government officials generally comment as little as possible about economic problems, to avoid investors' panic.

CASE IN POINT > *Discoveries and Innovation*

Not only financial speculators and mass reactions affect international political economy; scientists and engineers do so as well. Discoveries, innovations, and other accomplishments may dramatically affect travel, trade, and the ways products and services are exchanged (Yergin and Stanislaw, 1998). The steam engine made possible rail and ship transportation—moving people and goods safer and faster across countries, continents, and oceans. In 1819, the American steamship *Savannah* crossed the Atlantic. It was the beginning of a new era of trade between the continents. It influenced global migration as well. In 1832, American inventor Samuel Morse developed a single-wire telegraph system; and after 1865, telegraph cables were laid across the floor of the Atlantic between the continents. The spread of these technologies powered a dramatic expansion of world trade.

CRITICAL THINKING

Not including the obvious example of the Internet, what are some other prominent innovations and discoveries of the past twenty years that, in your view, have had the most significant impact on trade and commerce? Which of today's innovations do you think would revolutionize markets in 2025?

A new Starbucks opens in Ostrava, Czech Republic, in 2012. This Seattle-based company has more than 20,000 coffee houses in nearly 60 countries. Starbucks is an example of a successful business method applied globally.

The State Context

State leaders are commonly seen as making reasonable decisions. However, most leaders represent business and financial interests, and make their economic decisions based on political obligations. In a democratic society, politics is often about promoting economic interests (Olson, 1971).

DOMESTIC POLITICS

Scores of domestic political factors affect a state's economic and financial policies, its international trade, and the country's overall international situation. In turn, economic factors influence politics. In the West today, some political groupings are likely to reject government economic regulations and to support market-oriented policies. Their political opponents are more likely to support state regulations and policies to protect the domestic labor force and various social groups against the perceived harms of the market.

It is difficult to promote deregulation and free-market policies in countries and regions devastated by poverty, violence, social neglect, and rampant corruption. These policies can produce more negative immediate effects than positive ones. It takes time to develop infrastructure, to find investors, to create jobs, and to develop a favorable business climate. Most governments do not have the luxury of time to experiment with free-market reforms. They need to show immediate and positive results. Therefore, many choose regulation.

In the United States, where labor costs are high, many manufacturing workers oppose open global competition. For two decades the U.S. economy has been steadily losing high-paid industrial jobs, as companies move their production facilities to countries where there are fewer regulations and labor is cheap—a practice called **outsourcing** (Bergsten, 2005). In response to complaints from labor and struggling middle class families, Presidents George Bush and Barack Obama issued protectionist measures to help the steel, tire, and automotive industries.

SURPLUS OR MANAGEABLE DEFICIT?

Domestic political and social factors affect the attitudes about *surplus-oriented* and *trade deficit-tolerant* economic policies. Surplus, as you will remember, was a core objective of traditional mercantilism. A trade deficit is generally acceptable in free-market economies. Consider several examples of how states deal with their deficit or surplus.

The role of state planning and surplus was crucial to the *Asian development model*, which originated in the 1950s out of cooperation between Japan's government and private businesses. Japan's Ministry of International Trade and Industry (MITI) identified potential overseas markets and then worked with private industries to assist them with their exports. The state also helped with market information, access to foreign technology, licensing, loans and subsidies, and, when necessary, state tariffs. This relationship between government and business helped Japan, after the economic devastation of World War II, turn into the economic powerhouse of Asia. During the 1960s, this model was adopted in Singapore, Hong Kong, Taiwan, and later Malaysia and South Korea, with remarkable results.

Years	1990	2000	2010	2012 (est.)
Developed countries	70	67	50	52
Emerging economies	30	33	50	48

FIGURE 6-4 Percentage share of world imports: Developed and emerging economies (1990–2012). *Source: Woodall, 2011.*

For years, East Asian economies were driven by policies to ensure a massive trade surplus. Political parties in these countries, despite a host of differences in their domestic platforms, maintained similar views about exports (which had to be stimulated) and imports (which had to be regulated). Yet the negative consequences of such policies eventually appeared—just as they did for the eighteenth-century's French mercantilism. The trade surplus pushed up labor wages and costs for services. As a result, Japan's exports became more expensive compared to exports from China and other countries. This contributed to Japan's recession in the 1990s and more than a decade of slow economic growth. The entire effectiveness of the Asian developmental model was in question.

In the twenty-first century, manufacturing boomed in countries with cheaper labor, and their share in world imports dramatically increased. (See Figure 6.4.) This pushed trade deficits to a new high in many developed countries, especially the United States.

What about models that allow trade deficits? American and Western European economies tend to tolerate deficits, after several decades of economic growth, mutually beneficial trade, and Keynesian regulatory policies. For many economists and investors, however, the U.S. negative trade balance is a dangerous development: It means that foreign countries have accumulated U.S. dollars. What if foreign holders no longer want to keep them? Will it be a serious problem? At least three possibilities have been proposed (Levey and Brown, 2005).

A pessimistic forecast suggests that at some point the dollar will drop sharply in value against other currencies. A global panic will cause the dollar to tank further and interest rates to skyrocket. The global economy will be dragged into a deeper crisis.

A less dramatic forecast predicts only a slow, moderate decline in the dollar. A short-term recession, combined with the cheaper dollar, will eventually reverse the negative trade balance: Americans will buy fewer expensive foreign products. Yet American products—including cars, software, and computers—will become more affordable in other countries.

In a more optimistic view, emerging economies will need to import advanced technologies, software, and equipment from developed countries to build new manufacturing facilities and improve their living standards. International investors and consumers will continue to invest, convinced that future technological innovations and successful business methods will help the United States to remain an economic leader.

Which view appears more realistic to you? We return to the debate over the role of trade at the end of this chapter.

The Global Context

Economic policies succeed and fail influenced by conflicts, recessions, and periods of prosperity. Increasingly, however, the choices are influenced not by domestic politics but by international and global developments. Battles over the direction and scope of economic policies in the era of globalization are likely to remain passionate. Advances in computer-based design and three-dimensional printing suggest the early signs of another industrial revolution (Marsh, 2012). Yet will it provide a stable economic growth for all countries?

WHICH ECONOMIC POLICY?

In times of peace and prosperity, the principles of economic liberalism gain strength. People begin to believe that "a rising tide lifts all boats"—an aphorism attributed to President Kennedy. The classic liberal approach often falls out of favor, however, during tough economic times. Reacting to the Great Depression and the ideological challenge from Communism, the Roosevelt, Truman, and Eisenhower administrations accepted Keynesian policies. This was a setback for free-market principles, but for some time it guaranteed capitalism's stability. Nevertheless, at least two problems were on the horizon.

Keynesian economics assumed that a well-educated elite could decide what is best for national and international economies. Yet the state often takes on an obligation to carry too many increasingly expensive welfare programs. (See Figure 6.5.) The second and larger problem was inflation and a decline in growth, as Keynesian support for full employment required state investments and higher taxes. The combination of high inflation and no growth in the late 1970s, called *stagflation*, led the Federal Reserve (the central banking system of

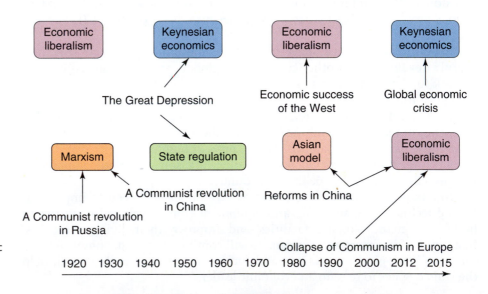

FIGURE 6-5 Economic theories and policies: A snapshot.

the United States) to sharply raise the interest rate to 11 and then even 20 percent. President Ronald Reagan combined some elements of Keynesianism with de-regulation of many industries, weakening of labor unions, and lowering taxes. These measures brought an unprecedented amount of foreign capital to the United States, curbed inflation, and boosted the economy for some time.

In the early 1990s economic liberalism reigned practically unopposed. Its principles have also been boosted by "democratic peace theory" (see Chapter 2): Economic liberals began to claim that the spread of free-market practices con-tributes to the spread of democracy—and ultimately lessens the probability of war among states (Gartzke, 2007). The IMF and World Bank began to stipulate that developing countries receiving their loans must implement such neoliberal economic policies as liberalization of trade, direct foreign investments, priva-tization of state enterprises, and deregulation of business.

Now take the case of corporate taxes. Should companies pay lower taxes, so that the growing market can lift the national and global economy? Or should companies pay higher taxes, with the government using the money to promote a healthy economy? Is there a "happy medium"? Would your answer differ for large and small businesses?

In the early 1990s, the failure of state-planned Communist economies pro-vided fresh arguments for supporters of government deregulation. Russia and other former Communist countries were adopting capitalism. China allowed elements of a free-market economy in a Communist society in which private property was prohibited for decades. Indian economic elites (which at times had looked with sympathy at the Soviet model of industrialization) also moved away from state economic planning and control. Indian economists concluded that even the most brilliant government bureaucrat could not consistently make great economic and business decisions (Bhagwati, 2004).

NORTH–SOUTH DIVIDE AND DEVELOPMENT

Dependency theory, as you remember, predicted that market capitalism and free trade would not reduce the gap between the South and North. Indeed, most countries of Africa and Latin America remained suppliers of cheap resources and services to the North. The *brain drain*, or the exodus of the most educated and skilled individuals from poor countries to developed countries, contin-ued. Some critics of liberalism claimed that deregulation of capital accounts in the 1980s–90s destabilized the global South even more: More individuals tended to keep their money in the banks of the North, and this created the "flight" of capital from the poorer countries. Also, global financial speculators ruined the currencies of Thailand and Argentina in 1998 (Stiglitz, 2002).

At the same time, developments of the last twenty to thirty years compli-cated North–South arguments. In Asia, Hong Kong, Singapore, Taiwan, and then China broke out of poverty and joined the countries of the North in wealth and development. By the 1990s, leaders of most developing countries gained greater access to global finance, markets, trade, and industrial production. Some states of the South, such as Brazil and India, began to integrate their economies into regional and global networks. This complicated the argument about North–South divide and the strategies of economic development.

A Pakistani laborer washes his clothes in a polluted stream on the outskirts of Islamabad, Pakistan, in 2013. The UN estimates that more than one in six people worldwide do not have access to 20–50 liters (5–13 gallons) of safe freshwater a day to ensure their basic needs for drinking, cooking, and cleaning. Some economists suggest that understanding individual-level decision-making may increase the effectiveness of economic aid and private entrepreneurship to reduce global poverty.

More than one billion people today in the global South still live on less than a dollar per day. Should the elimination or substantial reduction of poverty become a global policy? If yes, how it should be managed? There are at least three points of view regarding the fight against global poverty. Jeffrey Sachs (2005), an adviser to the UN from Columbia University, maintains that the solution lies in large direct investments. Poor countries cannot escape the "poverty trap" without substantial help from the North. In *The End of Poverty*, Sachs argues that poverty would be completely eliminated if the rich countries would pay around $200 billion for twenty years.

William Easterly (2001; 2006) of New York University and economist Dambisa Moyo (2010) represent another view. They believe that foreign direct help may destroy initiative, contribute to corruption, and creates a culture of dependency instead of private entrepreneurship. The poverty trap, Easterly and Moyo maintain, is avoidable only if the poor are given freedom and the right incentives.

Finally, economists Abhijit Banerjee and Ester Duflo (2011) turn to microeconomics. They maintain that both economic aid and private entrepreneurship may work only if we understand better how the poor make their financial and economic decisions. Help should be delivered, but the donors should know when and how it should be distributed and cases in which local initiatives and choices should be supported. An important key to success here is education and access to information. We will return to this subject again in Chapter 9.

GLOBAL INTERDEPENDENCE

Developments after the Cold War—and especially the growth of international cooperation and financial transactions—have led to a new economic and political interdependence (Doremus et al., 1998). Decisions on the national level can have a profound impact on others as well. A mortgage crisis in the United States in 2008 and a financial crisis in the European Union in 2010 and 2011 threatened the financial and economic stability of much of the world economy. Public debt, or the debt of a country's central government, surpassed many countries' GDPs. (See Figure 6.6.) These countries often need substantial international help to avoid a financial disaster. In the case of large economies like Italy or Japan, international institutions like the IMF are helpless. This chain of problems could easily result in disastrous financial and economic instability. A rising tide may lift all boats, but in stormy waters it becomes dangerous to be tied to a sinking ship.

On paper, the path to global economic prosperity may look easy. The United States should have an export-led expansion, and it should reduce import-based consumption. Europeans and Asians should slow their exports and buy more from the United States. The U.S. government should decrease its spending and increase interest rates. These steps will reduce consumer spending and encourage savings. However, instead of going down, U.S. government spending increased dramatically from 2001 to 2012. In the long run, this situation threatens the position of the dollar as the world's reserve currency and further destabilizes world finances. Meanwhile, the Chinese government is reluctant to permit their currency to rise against the dollar. These measures would make China's exports to the United States more expensive, and U.S. products would cost less in China. However, such policies are difficult to implement because of China's surplus-oriented and job-generating strategies. Instead, unlike the Euro, the Yuan is still pegged to the dollar.

Finally, Europe could reduce interest rates and regulations to promote investments. It could also trim social programs that weigh heavily on state budgets. However, lower interest rates would reduce the money supply to European banks. And cuts in social programs would require serious political sacrifices, which almost no political parties are willing to accept.

INTERNATIONAL INSTITUTIONS AND THE GLOBAL ECONOMY

Whereas many countries are unwilling to implement tough economic measures to combat global poverty, every economy is becoming increasingly interdependent. Does the world therefore need new institutions to take charge of the global economy and trade? Some suggest that we already have such a system, but an imperfect one.

Although the IMF, the World Bank, and the WTO are backed by the governments of the economically strongest states, they and other international institutions face strong criticism for the way they operate (Peet, 2009; Blustein,

Japan	212
Zimbabwe	209
Greece	167
Iceland	133
Lebanon	129
Ireland	128
Jamaica	125
Italy	121
Sudan	109

FIGURE 6-6 Public debt, percent of GDP, selected countries. *Source: The Economist, 2011, The World in 2012, 107.*

2009). Critics point to corporate bureaucracy and a lack of transparency. Some argue that these organizations act largely on behalf of a few wealthy state members (Stiglitz, 2002) and neglect the increasing importance in international trade of countries in Asia, Latin America, and Africa. Countries vote in global organizations based on their position in the world economy, an arrangement that evokes increasing criticism (Hoekman and Kostecki, 2010; Rapkin and Strand, 2006).

Loans are another focus of debates. Supporters of the IMF believe that loans help states of the South create independent economic and banking systems, develop efficient government institutions, build social infrastructure, and more. Critics argue, however, that the IMF dictates to sovereign states how they should run their banking systems and economies (N. Woods, 2007).

The classic assumptions of economic theories may need a fresh look today. Global trade means the erosion of state power and the increasing influence of nonstate institutions and even individuals, such as financial speculator George Soros, a famous philanthropist and sponsor of nongovernment organizations. Studies show that global corporations can make a profit and contribute to social policies at the same time (Hartman and Werhane, 2009). Yet governments may no longer protect their citizens economically, and corporations may choose to benefit their shareholders first before making responsible economic decisions (Madeley, 2009).

 Go online to read about George Soros's Open Society Foundations.

ECONOMIC GLOBALIZATION AND CONFLICT

How does economic globalization affect international conflicts? In the first decade of the 1900s, European economies were growing; countries placed fewer limits on imports, exports, immigration, and the exchange of products (Yergin and Stanislaw, 1998). Yet a global war broke out in 1914. Does this example mean that globalization cannot prevent another global conflict?

Concerns continue about the possibility of new international conflicts caused by economic fears. In the United States, some people wonder if China's growing economic power will lead to a conflict. Such fears are fed by historical analogies, but also by the logic of mercantilism. Yet, contrary to some predictions, the early twenty-first century shows that mutual trade creates interdependence and increases the chances for cooperation. And, as we have learned, mercantilism is often flawed. For instance, according to its logic, future wars are likely between countries that have vast oil and gas resources (such as Russia, Saudi Arabia, and the United States) and countries that consume these products but don't have them (such as Japan, China, or India). In this reasoning, oil and gas are strategic products that directly affect a nation's security. However, nothing says that such a scenario lies ahead these days.

CHECK YOUR KNOWLEDGE

▶ What is outsourcing?
▶ Explain the *Asian developmental model*. Why can't the United States apply this model domestically?
▶ What is the main argument of the book *The End of Poverty?*
▶ What are the differences between macroeconomics and microeconomics?

Past, Present, and Future: "The Beijing Miracle"

China's transformation from a country ravaged by Communist experiments into an economic and financial giant is a most dramatic story of recent times. During the century's first decade, China's economy grew by up to 9 percent each year, and its exports increased even faster. China is now the second-largest exporting country in the world, after quickly surpassing the United Kingdom and Germany. In 2010, it became the second largest economy in the world, outpacing Japan. China's contribution to global economic growth grew from 2.6 percent in 1981 to 9.7 percent in 2001 and may reach 27 percent in 2014. Even the global crisis that started in 2008 did not affect Chinese ascendancy, contrary to pessimistic expectations of many economists. If it continues this way, economists argue, China in twenty years may replace the United States as the vehicle of international economic development.

For students of international political economy, China's rise poses important questions. What were the domestic and international wellsprings of this success? Which economic theories and policies "worked" for China? What impact will China's rise have on international relations?

China's "economic miracle" is rooted in the 1978 reforms of the Communist leader Deng Xiaoping (1904–1997). He broke with Communist dogma by allowing small private property, retail trade, and profit making. More surprisingly, Deng's reforms showed that the Communist regime could shift from a state-directed economy that barred private property to a state-directed economy with private property—all without significant social disturbances. Chinese politicians and economies learned from the mistakes that contributed to the collapse of the Soviet Union. Unlike Mikhail Gorbachev, Deng did not combine economic liberalization with a shift from one-party rule to democracy. The Chinese leaders, like Gorbachev, wasted billions of dollars to keep afloat existing state-run industries. But in contrast to the Soviet leader, they also shepherded the emergence of a new economy, privately owned and run on market principles.

This economy from the start was focused on producing consumer goods for export. At first, China produced cheap, poor-quality clothing, toys, and other goods. During the 1990s, however, Chinese export became technologically advanced, using Japanese, German, and American know-how, for instance, to produce electronic goods and household durables. As a result of thirty years of uninterrupted economic growth, from three to four hundred million people, many of them peasants, have risen from poverty to the middle class.

China became the first big country in the global South to move rapidly to the position of an economic superpower,

Soviet leader Mikhail Gorbachev (L) shakes hands with Chinese senior leader Deng Xiaoping May 16, 1989, in Beijing. Both leaders inspired and managed dramatic economic reforms in their countries with dramatically different results.

avoiding many of the social and economic problems that plague other developing economies on the way up. China has not faced mass unemployment. It has not become dependent on foreign imports and loans. Instead, China has made the leading developed states, including the United States, dependent on *its* exports. Chinese leaders chose the export-oriented model of East Asian "tigers"—Taiwan, Singapore, and Hong-Kong—combining the advantages of cheap educated labor with foreign investments and technologies.

There were several domestic factors behind China's success. First, China had a strong authoritarian government, ruled by the Communist party. When in May 1989, on Tiananmen Square in Peking, thousands of students challenged the party leadership and demanded democracy, Deng cracked down. Thousands died, and the Communist leadership continued its economic reforms without democratization. Second, China had an almost unlimited supply of hard-working labor, mostly peasants. Moreover, unlike in most other poor countries, they were educated, thanks to a compulsory educational system modeled after the Soviet Union's in the 1950s. China today also has one of the largest pools of skilled professionals. Third, this workforce and their incomes remain under tight control of the party leadership, which maintains the *household registration system* in which people must obtain a government permit to establish residence. All employees in the city have to belong to *danwei* (the work unit) and receive their wages and benefits from it, including housing and medical coverage. Party leadership established a monopoly on large capital investments through a system of state-licensed banks—above all, the Bank of China. All peasants and city dwellers must deposit their wages to these banks. This means that the government still has significant power to regulate migration and the distribution of benefits. In this way, the Communist Party can prevent sharp social conflicts and direct a huge pool of Chinese labor (Gong, 2009), despite millions of illegal migrants from rural areas to cities.

Such arrangements would upset the vast majority in the United States, where they would quickly be branded as state socialism. In fact, the Chinese leadership calls its policies "Socialism with Chinese characteristics." Yet the party leadership was quick to realize that rigid methods of state control would fail, and it thus adopted a more sophisticated path to a "harmonious society." What economic methods and theories did China use?

Many of China's policies resemble mercantilism. Under mercantilism, strong states amassed wealth but also controlled the economy. At the same time, China's version of mercantilism worked well only because of its openness to a Western-built liberal international economic system. If other countries had practiced mercantilism just like China has done, Chinese export-oriented growth would have been impossible. (See Figure 6.7.)

Several international factors helped China. First, the United States after 1971 stopped treating China as a Communist enemy. In fact, after 1979 it began to treat China as a strategic partner in the Cold War against the Soviet Union. As a result of its improved relations with the West, China successfully negotiated the return of Hong Kong, a prosperous British colony, to Chinese jurisdiction in 1997.

Second, China's alliance with the United States allowed ethnic Chinese from Taiwan, Hong Kong, and Singapore to invest in the Chinese economy. This

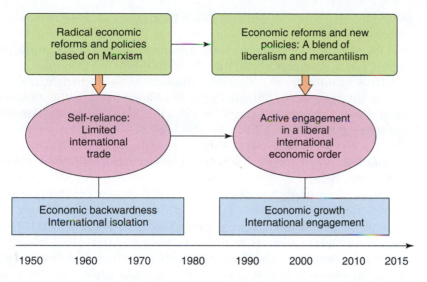

FIGURE 6-7 China's economic policies and international trade: A chronological snapshot.

policy brought massive foreign investments to China's export-driven economy—not only from other states, but from individuals and companies as well.

Third, the United States opened American markets to Chinese goods, and in 1994 President Clinton abolished all restrictions on Chinese exports. The United States made no systematic attempt to prevent outsourcing of American high-tech industries to China. Other Western states practiced outsourcing as well, in competition with the United States.

What, then, can be the impact of China's growth on international relations? From a realist point of view, China sooner or later will use its economic and financial power to achieve political goals. Chinese leaders now realize that fulfilling their domestic needs demands a more activist global strategy (Economy, 210a). It could continue to rely on the global free-trade system while practicing mercantilist goals. China became a member of the World Trade Organization in 2001, but it often looks at international trade as a one-way street. Instead of importing Apple's iPods, Ford trucks, and Heineken, it seeks to create competitive Chinese models (Aaronson, 2010). As a popular German journal stated, "China is seeking to engage with the West, but on its own terms" (*Der Spiegel*, August 27, 2010). The biggest worry is China's dogged reluctance to allow the Yuan to fluctuate in relation to the U.S. dollar and other currencies. This, economists argue, helps China steal millions of jobs from countries with high-paid labor (Krugman, 2009).

From a realist perspective, China may also challenge Western security. The Bank of China in 2010 accumulated almost $3 trillion and bought other U.S. financial obligations. This makes the financial health of the United States dependent, at least in theory, on decisions made by the party leadership in Peking. Chinese military expenditures rose by a factor of eight during the 2000s, reaching $78 billion in 2010, and they continue to grow. It has the second largest military budget in the world. Of course, the U.S. military budget is about eight times bigger, but China has the resources to increase its spending even more. Security experts point to China's ambitions to control the seas around it. What would Washington do if China decides one day to take Taiwan by force?

Liberal economists dismiss these arguments. Chinese economic progress, liberals argue, has brought hundreds of millions in China out of poverty. Hundreds of millions of consumers all over the world benefit from the low price of Chinese goods. During the 2000s China became the engine of economic growth elsewhere as well, as China invested in Africa, America, and Southern Asia (Zoellick, 2012). By this logic, Chinese society will gradually evolve as a large middle class pushes for political reform. If China practices neo-mercantilism, that is no more than necessary at this stage to provide stability (McKinnon, 2010).

China increasingly complies with international organizations and international norms of behavior. After all, it does not want to contest the basic rules of the liberal international order (Ikenberry, 2011a, 2011b). Fears of China's financial takeover may be mistaken. After all, China provides American consumers with affordable goods in exchange for "pieces of paper." The dollar reserves accumulated by the Bank of China are the savings of Chinese people—the fruits of their hard work. No Chinese leadership would risk ruining the U.S. Treasury by "failing" the dollar. Liberals write about the United States and China as mutually dependent—although some of them admit that China benefitted from this dependency much more than its trade partner (Ferguson, 2010).

From the constructivist view, too, China is unlikely to become a global adversary. China has never pushed for world domination. After decades of poverty and suffering, China developed a very different national purpose—achievement and excellence—as an economic, not political superpower. This may explain China's extraordinary efforts to modernize everything from airports and superhighways to high-speed trains. The Chinese government turned the 2008 Summer Olympics in Beijing into a demonstration of national pride but also modernity. The legitimacy of the party rests ultimately not on ideology or political promises but rather on economic improvements and growing consumption. Per capita income in China is barely one-tenth of America's (which is close to $50,000). But consumption and living standards grow every year. In 2009, China became the world's largest market for automobiles.

World systems theorists believe that China is bent on replacing the United States in a few decades as the core of the global capitalist system. Manufacturing is moving to China from the developed North, and financial resources have already begun to follow suit. The result could be the replacement of the "Washington consensus," based on a neoliberal model of free trade, by a "Beijing consensus" based on state-run capitalism. These assumptions echo postcolonial studies, which would expect former colonies to demand an end to Western global domination (Arrighi and Lu Zhang, 2011). The global financial crisis gave more credibility to such views. The crisis hit the West; China's GDP in 2009 grew by 8.7 percent, largely because the Bank of China provided a $587 billion stimulus package to the domestic economy. Domestic consumption and construction soared. This was a fine example of Keynesian economic policies comparable to the Marshall Plan.

Millionaires take part in a social event at a hotel in Chengdu in 2012. China has shown a remarkable ability to generate wealth. But will China's state-run capitalism demonstrate its lasting ability to generate innovation? Will China's political system embrace openness?

Liberal economists argue back that China's state-run capitalism still has to demonstrate its lasting ability to generate innovation. If the West declines, they argue, then China's export would either decline or turn to domestic consumption. Chinese salaries would grow—meaning that China would become more "Americanized." Chinese Communist authorities may yet run up against the global trend toward openness and individualism. Already, China is trying to reduce its brain drain by offering incentives to its citizens who return to China after studying in the West. Moreover, top Chinese leaders are reportedly in training to learn more about world economic trends (Pin-Lin, 2010, 10).

In the absence of political opposition, and with a monopoly on power, party leaders can make decisions with relative ease. Their real challenge is to keep economic growth going. And, as history teaches, nothing lasts forever.

CONCLUSION

Economic theories rise and fall with the tides of history. Global interdependence challenges past theories, formed when a few wealthy states could define economic and financial policies for others as well. For decades, free-market principles worked well in Western Europe, Japan, and North America. In the twenty-first century, many Asian countries have adopted free-market policies too. However, "one size fits all" free-market policies can often damage rather than help countries with their unique financial, governmental, and social institutions. For example, India and China did not simply turn to liberal democracy, and Russia's attempts to shift rapidly to both a free-market economy and liberal democracy cost it dearly; its productive capacities declined dramatically and the population suffered. Today's experience suggests that sound economic policies require knowledge of each country's political, social, and cultural conditions.

CHAPTER SUMMARY

- International political economy focuses on how politics and economics interact in an international context. Political economists analyze such activities as production, consumption, finances, and trade taken in international contexts.

- Mercantilism calls for the accumulation and protection of resources in the name of the state, which should maintain a positive balance of trade. Mercantilism is often linked with realism, as well as with imperialism and colonialism.

- Economic liberalism assumes that only open trade and economic cooperation can lead to a peaceful and prosperous world. An early argument in defense of economic liberalism comes from the principle of comparative advantage, which explains why it is beneficial for two countries to trade with each other instead of relying on their own domestic markets.

- According to Keynesian economics, governments can spend more money than their revenues allow to decrease unemployment by putting money into the economy. Economic liberalism inspired the creation of numerous international institutions to facilitate international trade and provide financial stability.

- Conflict theories, including Marxism and dependency theory, argue that the world's economic structure unfairly benefits a dominant social class or a few rich states while others remain poor.

- Dependency theory states that the world's economic and trade system has been set in a way beneficial for rich nations but not for others.

- The constructivist view emphasizes the importance of shared ideals and national identities in shaping economic policies.

- Many economic theories are tested on the level of microeconomics, which considers the behavior of individual consumers, companies, and industries.

- Domestic political factors affect a state's economic and financial policies, its international trade, its surplus-oriented or trade deficit-tolerant strategies, and the international situation.

- In times of peace and prosperity, economic liberalism gains strength. Dependency theory gained prominence in the postcolonial period, when young states were choosing their own path of economic development.

- The growth of international cooperation and financial transactions has led to greater economic and political interdependence. Critics of economic globalization and international institutions borrow from conflict and dependency theories. Supporters point to the importance of interdependence and the example of China, a major beneficiary of globalization.

KEY TERMS

Autarky 200
Balance of trade 185
Comparative advantage 192
Consumption 184
Currencies 185
Dependency theory 197
Economic climate 196
Economic liberalism 191
Economic sanctions 187
Fair trade 199

Fiscal policy 193
Gross Domestic Product (GDP) 184
International political economy (IPE) 183
Keynesian economics 192
Macroeconomics 192
Mercantilism 188
Microeconomics 200
National purpose 196

North (Global) 198
Outsourcing 204
Production 184
Protectionism 187
Regional trade agreements 194
South (Global) 197
Tariffs 187

Visual Review INTERNATIONAL POLITICAL ECONOMY

1. What do we study?

INTERNATIONAL POLITICAL ECONOMY
Interaction of politics and economics in an international context

KEY CONCEPTS
States' production, consumption, finances, and trade

2. How do we study it?

MERCANTILISM
- Accumulating resources
- Protecting domestic markets

ECONOMIC LIBERALISM
- Classical: Free production, trade, and consumption
- Keynesian: Governments should play an active role
- Reliance on international economic and financial institutions, as well as trade agreements

CONSTRUCTIVISM
Economic policies depend on the social, political, and cultural conditions in which these policies are implemented

OTHER THEORIES
- Marxism: The world is dominated by a ruling class, which owns the major means of production
- Dependency: Technology-driven developed nations have been receiving more benefits from international trade

3. How do we apply it?

THE INDIVIDUAL CONTEXT
- Political leadership affects economic choices
- Microeconomics: Behavior of individual consumers influences international markets

THE STATE CONTEXT
Domestic factors affect *surplus-oriented* and *trade deficit-tolerant* economic policies

THE GLOBAL CONTEXT
Global economic and financial co-operation has led to both greater economic and political interdependence and new tensions and conflicts

Critical Thinking

- Compare and contrast mercantilism and economic liberalism.
- Would economic liberals support international trade sanctions, and if so, under what circumstances?
- Why are tariffs harmful for international trade? Can tariffs be helpful, and who would benefit from them?
- Why are the International Monetary Fund and the World Bank often considered a tool of the global North to dominate the global South?

CHAPTER

7

Light beams in place of New York City's World Trade Center, which was destroyed in the terrorist attacks of September 11, 2001.

International Terrorism

All of us have had to pause, reflect, and sometimes change our minds as we studied these problems and considered the views of others. We hope our report will encourage our fellow citizens to study, reflect—and act. . . .
We learned about an enemy who is sophisticated, patient, disciplined, and lethal.

—FINAL REPORT OF THE NATIONAL COMMISSION ON TERRORIST ATTACKS UPON THE UNITED STATES, 2004.

LANCE CORPORAL FREDERIK E. VAZQUEZ, OF MELROSE PARK, ILLINOIS, DIED ON JULY 24, 2010, WHILE SUPPORT-ING COMBAT OPERATIONS IN HELMAND PROVINCE, Afghanistan. He was twenty years old. Mark Leijsen, a forty-four-year-old sergeant major from the Netherlands, was killed by a roadside bomb in Uruzgan province. Petty Officer Second Class Xin Qi, of Cordova, Tennessee, twenty-five years old, died on January 23, 2010, while supporting combat operations in Afghanistan. He was a medical caregiver. There are three thousand more names from thirty countries who died since 2001 in "Operation Enduring Freedom" in Afghanistan. More than two thousand are from the United States. More than four hundred and forty are from the United Kingdom. One hundred and fifty eight are from Canada. Forty are from Poland.

When you read these pages, the number of casualties may be up. What have all of them died for?

On September 11, 2001, a radical group called *al-Qaeda* carried out terrorist strikes against the United States. The group destroyed the World Trade Center in New York and a portion of the Pentagon near Washington, DC. The terrorists hijacked four civilian airplanes and flew them into their targets, dying along with their victims. One plane crashed in Pennsylvania. Fifteen of the hijackers were from Saudi Arabia, and four came from other Arab countries of the Middle East.

The attackers were trained in al-Qaeda camps in Pakistan, Sudan, and Afghanistan. The Bush administration issued an ultimatum to the Taliban government, the religious group that controlled Afghanistan at that time and gave refuge to al-Qaeda. The ultimatum called for immediate delivery of Osama bin Laden and his associates to an American court. The Taliban offered to try bin Laden in Afghanistan in an Islamic court instead. The White House rejected the offer, and U.S. and British troops launched a war in Afghanistan.

The allied troops quickly established control over the country yet failed to capture bin Laden and destroy the Taliban and al-Qaeda completely. In 2003 the United States sent troops to Iraq. Meanwhile, the Taliban, supported by militant groups in western Pakistan, began to regain control over Afghani territories. It took ten years to hunt down and kill Bin Laden in his hideout in Pakistan. The U.S. President Barak Obama pledged in 2012 to withdraw the U.S. troops from Afghanistan in two years.

FIGURE 7-1
Coalition casualties in Afghanistan, 2001–2012.
Source: http://www.icasualties.org

Country	Total	Country	Total
Albania	1	Lithuania	1
Australia	38	NATO	10
Belgium	1	Netherlands	25
Canada	158	New Zealand	11
Czech Republic	5	Norway	10
Denmark	42	Poland	35
Estonia	9	Portugal	2
Finland	2	Romania	19
France	86	South Korea	1
Georgia	11	Spain	34
Germany	53	Sweden	5
Hungary	7	Turkey	14
Italy	47	UK	432
Jordan	2	US	2,122
Latvia	3	Total	3,186

The military operations triggered by 9/11 had a profound impact on international relations. The United States and other countries committed enormous resources to these efforts. Some analysts compared it to the Vietnam War and predicted that terrorist groups would only embolden themselves for more attacks against the United States and other countries. Others, more recently, considered the antiterrorist campaign accomplished successfully, and urged to end on "the war on terror" and focus on more pressing problems of the economy and budget debt. Yet others argued that the struggle against terrorism should move to the nonmilitary phase when intergovernmental and nongovernment organizations turn to economic and social issues that spawn terrorism.

Which argument is stronger? How dangerous is international terrorism and how does it affect the world? In this chapter we will guide you through the theories explaining international terrorism and explore how states, international organizations, and the entire global system deal with the challenge.

After reading this chapter, you should be able to:

► define terrorism, explaining its logic, strategies, and methods;
► explain how states, international organizations, and the entire global system deal with the challenge of terrorism;
► distinguish among different views of terrorism and counterterrorist policies; and
► apply your knowledge about terrorism and counterterrorism at three levels of analysis.

Learning Objectives

What Do We Study?

Most states agree that problem of international terrorism needs immediate attention. They only disagree as to how terrorism can be defeated. Journalists and security experts debate definitions and policies to deal with terrorism. Governments and international organizations have committed huge resources to study, understand, and combat it. Thousands of people have died. Many areas of our lives, including public safety procedures and international travel, have been altered. In this chapter we will define terrorism, examine its historical roots, discuss counterterrorism, and critically examine various views of terrorism and counterterrorism.

Terrorism and Counterterrorism

Terrorism is violence by nonstate actors, such as individuals or groups, to achieve radical political goals. Terrorism is thus a form of *political radicalism*—ideas and methods to produce rapid, dramatic change in the social or political order. Terrorism can be state sponsored, in that a foreign government can provide financial, military, or logistical support to terrorists to further its policy goals. Yet in essence it remains a nonstate phenomenon.

As a means to achieve political goals, terrorism can be viewed as domestic or international. **Domestic terrorism** pursues domestic political goals such as the dismantling of a government or a change in state policies. This does not necessarily present a direct danger to other states or international organizations. **International terrorism**, which is the main focus of this chapter, challenges international stability by threatening one country or a group of states. It rejects international law and defies international organizations. It could be the act of a radical group secretly operating in several countries, and it has regional or global consequences. The distinctions between domestic and international forms are imprecise, however; some apparently domestic acts of terrorism have regional or even global consequences.

International terrorism differs from guerrilla warfare, gangsterism, or piracy. **Guerrilla warfare** is political violence by identifiable, irregular combat units, usually to seize state power, win autonomy, or found new states (see Chapter 4). *Gangsters* and *pirates* may practice random killing, extortions, and kidnappings, but their goal is not political: It is profit (Boot, 2009). International terrorism usually sets no limits on violence and targets civilians in the name of extreme political goals.

States and international organizations develop measures, called **counterterrorism**, to prevent and combat international and domestic terrorism. This is a government's policy, with a budget, conducted according to legal rulings, and exercised by a special agency in coordination with other offices, international organizations and alliances, NGOs, or independent contractors. In the United States many federal institutions are involved in counterterrorism, above all the Department of Homeland Security, the CIA, and the NSA (see Chapter 4). They gather information, pursue and eliminate terrorist groups, and disrupt their activities including their financial operations. Overall, more than 1,200 federal organizations and close to 2,000 private companies have worked recently on programs related to counterterrorism, intelligence, and homeland security in the United States alone (Priest and Arkin, 2010a). The price tag of their operations is measured in hundreds of billions of dollars.

Why Definitions are Important

There are serious consequences to the use of the labels *terrorism* or *terrorist*. The policy choices of states and international organizations often depend on how terrorism is defined. Also, violent individuals, groups, and governments

Armed police hold a railway bridge antiterrorist drill in Anhui Province, China, in 2012. China had nearly 100,000 commandos, police, and members of the military on standby up to and during the 2008 Beijing Olympic Games to respond to potential terrorist attacks.

typically avoid being associated with terrorism and often contest its definitions (Hoffman, 1998; Sloan, 2006).

LEGITIMIZATION OF MILITARY ACTIONS

Because terrorism is considered an illegal form of violence, countries may choose extreme measures to deal with it. By labeling a group an international terrorist organization or a violent act as an act of international *terror*, a government can establish a justification for violent countermeasures, just as in times of war. Even an invasion of foreign territory can be labeled self-defense if it targets terrorists. In the wake of September 11, 2001, there was evidence that the Afghani government provided asylum and created conditions beneficial to the al-Qaeda terrorists. This gave the United States a justification to send troops to Afghanistan, with full support of the international community (See Figure 7.1.) Notice that the decision to label an act as terrorism or an organization as terrorist remains a prerogative of governments. The U.S. Department of State maintains an official list of foreign terrorist organizations, which is regularly updated.

MOBILIZATION OF INTERNATIONAL LAW

International law generally favors cooperation against terrorist groups or states accused of sponsoring terrorism. In 1988, a terrorist act against civilian Pan Am Flight 103 over Lockerbie, Scotland, killed 270 people. When it was established that a Libyan official had been involved, Western countries imposed sanctions on Libya. Its leader, Muammar Qaddafi, was kept away from international meetings, including UN sessions. Only after Libya formally apologized and offered compensation to the victims' families were sanctions lifted (Bergman, 2008).

@ On the companion website, you will find links to terrorist designation lists, the National Consortium for the Study of Terrorism and Responses to Terrorism, and the RAND database of worldwide terrorist incidents.

Also according to international law, individuals suspected of terrorist acts are subject to *extradition*, or removal from one country to another (where they committed their violent acts) to face charges. Many states cooperate with one another and extradite suspects. In the summer of 2005, for example, the Italian government sent a suspect in a terrorist attack on the London underground back to the United Kingdom. Some governments revoke the travel passports of individuals accused of terrorist activities (Wright, 2006). Saudi Arabia chose to detain terrorism suspects in specially organized rehabilitation camps (J. Stern, 2010).

Overall, the need to combat international terrorism has created an unprecedented network of new bilateral and international military, economic, and intelligence sharing and financial agreements. In a word, the threat of terrorism changed international relations.

JUSTIFICATION OF OTHER POLICIES

Some states may use swift counterterrorist measures questionable from the viewpoint of international law. For example, after the assassination of Israeli athletes during the 1972 Olympic Games in Munich by Palestinian militants, the Israeli government set up a special squad to scout and kill the perpetrators. The squad frequently acted illegally, using almost the same violent means as the hunted terrorists. (It was the subject of the controversial film *Munich*, directed by Stephen Spielberg.) Countries may also unilaterally toughen domestic security laws including street surveillance, passenger screening at airports, and travel restrictions for foreigners. Some view any forms of counterterrorism as justifiable because terrorists are "outside the law" (Klein, 2005). Others disagree on legal grounds. After 9/11 many criticized the U.S. government for suspending normal juridical norms for suspects

The graves of five murdered Israeli athletes in Tel Aviv. Palestinian terrorists kidnapped and killed 11 Israeli athletes at the Munich Olympics in 1972 in a crime that shocked the world. Israel launched covert operations to retaliate for the murder.

DEBATE > THE TERRORISM LABEL CAN BE MISUSED

Because policies are frequently based on how terrorism is defined, the term is subject to misuse. First, some governments use the label to combat domestic opposition. The Chinese government used this tactic in Tibet to crush public protests against oppressive Communist rule. The Russian government did the same to subdue the separatists in Chechnya.

Second, governments may argue that international law does not apply when terrorism is at stake. For example, after 2001, U.S. authorities identified many suspected terrorists as "illegal combatants" and disregarded the Geneva protocols, which prohibit indefinite detention of prisoners of war. For years, prisoners were kept at a U.S. military base at Guantanamo. This precedent caused serious domestic and international criticism of both the George W. Bush and Obama administrations.

Third, governments could use the *terrorism* label to settle personal scores with political or business opponents. By accusing a group or individuals of terrorist activities, a government can delegitimize them in the eyes of the courts and public opinion.

WHAT'S YOUR VIEW?

Can you suggest other examples of the actual or potential misuse of the term *terrorism*? Did you see American civil liberties endangered by the federal government after 9/11?

@ Search the Web for "We are not terrorists" (in quotation marks). You will find an amazing diversity of quotes, speeches, and statements. Select five cases. What arguments do the authors of these statements use to separate themselves from terrorism? If they are not terrorists, what do they call themselves? Why do they need to defend their image, and to whom do they appeal?

in terrorism, keeping them in special prisons, such as at the U.S. base Guantanamo in Cuba, and even using torture to obtain information. Critics also claimed that the "Patriot Act," a set of domestic counterterrorist policies signed by President George W. Bush in October 2001, limit civic freedoms at home. In 2013, new facts ignited the debate about the government's role in a vast domestic surveillance program.

▶ Define political radicalism. Can political radicalism be nonviolent?
▶ How does terrorism differ from gangsterism and guerrilla warfare?

CHECK YOUR KNOWLEDGE

How Terrorism Works

When we ask how terrorism works, we should not only look at methods, such as suicide bombing. We should look at assumptions and supposed justifications of terrorists.

ASSUMPTIONS AND METHODS

Terrorists understand that they cannot defeat states and international coalitions in an open battle. Governments have intelligence, armed forces, and law-enforcement institutions. Therefore, they rely on unconventional methods to cause fear among the population of a targeted country or a group of states (Chaliand and Blin, 2007). They rely on secrecy and the ability to keep their cells invisible from the governments. The Internet becomes an asset to terrorist groups because governments have little control over it (Horgan, 2009, 2).

Terrorist groups are often extremely difficult to infiltrate. Most are in reality *networks*, or loose collectives. Members of one group may not know members from others. Instead of building a formal hierarchical structure, they rely on loyalty and mutual surveillance. Their sense of collective involvement is reaffirmed by spiritual and material rewards for devotion—and merciless punishments for betrayal (Gunaratna, 2002).

Terrorist groups use violence or threats of violence to influence governments or key decision makers. Government officials are not always the direct targets. Terrorists often target civilians, including children, using random killings, bombings in public places, and attacks on television stations or hotels (Nacos, 2009). Everyone is potentially vulnerable. In September 2004, in the southern Russian city of Beslan, a terrorist group took more than one thousand hostages, including seven hundred children. The group was demanding, among other things, Russia's military withdrawal from the ethnic enclave of Chechnya. Russian officials in Moscow refused. As a result of the hectic rescue operation, more than three hundred hostages, mostly children, died.

Future terrorist attacks may attempt to use weapons of mass destruction (WMD): nuclear, biological, or chemical weapons. A small suitcase nuclear device in the hands of a terrorist can destroy New York, Washington , Moscow, Tokyo, or London. Preventing nuclear proliferation and a leak of nuclear know-how to terrorist organizations, therefore, remains a priority for the international community (Howard and Forest, 2008; D. Hoffman, 2010). The Internet and other communication networks add the possibility of **cyberterrorism**—paralyzing attacks online on political, financial, and economic centers. Threats may range from significant theft of data and disruption of computer operations to more deadly attacks that destroy entire systems and physical equipment (Gertz, 2011). Cyberterrorism poses a significant threat to a country's military capabilities by threatening its logistics network, stealing its operational plans, or obstructing its ability to deliver weapons on target. Even when the cyberterrorist is identified, it is difficult to retaliate (Lynn, 2010). We will address these threats later in the chapter. Table 7-1 summarizes the most common methods of terrorism.

The face of international terrorism changed irrevocably after September 2001. Before, terrorists usually relied on **coercion** and **extortion** to get what they wanted from governments—while promising not to use coercion in the future if their demands are satisfied. Negotiations between states and terrorists were possible (Bueno de Mesquita, 2005). Bin Laden and his associates created a new brand of terrorism: They aimed to cause a moral and political defeat to the West and rejected negotiations. It is still not clear if the Taliban just want to coerce the United States and NATO to withdraw from Afghanistan—or has more extreme goals and methods.

Terrorists look for publicity or *public exposure*. By committing an act of violence, a radical group is likely to attract the attention of millions. This is

TABLE 7-1 Methods of Contemporary Terrorism

Methods	Examples
Attacks against civilians in public places	In 2005, a series of coordinated suicide attacks in London took the lives of fifty-six people. Prerecorded statements from the perpetrators claimed that the attacks were in response to UK participation in the wars in Iraq and Afghanistan.
Attacks against military targets	In October 2000, two suicide bombers killed seventeen U.S. sailors and damaged the Navy ship, USS *Cole,* in Aden Harbor in Yemen. The terrorist group al-Qaeda took responsibility for the attacks.
Hostage taking	On June 27, 1976, a plane on its way from Tel Aviv through Athens to Paris with 248 passengers was taken hostage and landed in Entebbe, Uganda. The terrorists demanded the release of their fellows— mostly Palestinians—from various prisons.
Cyberterrorism	In May 2007, Russian hackers became enraged by Estonia's decision to remove the monument to a Soviet soldier from World War II from a central square in Tallinn, the Estonian capital. A massive cyberattack paralyzed the Estonian government for days.

important for at least two reasons. First, the group may rapidly publicize its agenda to seek sympathy (Pape, 2003; Pillar, 2001). Second, public exposure often helps a terrorist group to recruit supporters, sponsors, and new members. Copycat terrorist acts may also follow (Coleman, 2004). Figure 7.2 summarizes the tactics of terrorism.

THE "LOGIC" OF TERRORISM

Most terrorist groups use relatively similar arguments to justify their violence. Terrorism is explained as a method of *last resort.* Terrorism is portrayed as a desperate response to an acute problem. Once the source of injustice is

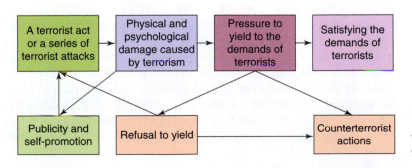

FIGURE 7-2 How terrorism and counterterrorism work.

DEBATE > TERRORISM AND GLOBAL INTERACTIONS

A local terrorist act may become a global problem in a connected world because fear can more easily spread. Terrorism can disrupt international communications, airways, tourism, business, commerce, and other global networks.

WHAT'S YOUR VIEW?

Do you think that globalization—including ease of international travel, internationalization of business, and stationing troops overseas—facilitates terrorism? If so, should states close their borders? After all, if no country has foreign entrepreneurs, tourists, and military forces abroad, terrorists no longer target those people. How would you decide?

 An article from *The Washington Post* argues that targeting travel is, unfortunately, effective. Also read the article about the influence of terrorism on international tourist activities in *European Journal of Social Sciences*. Find the links on the companion website.

---

removed, then violence will end. Terrorists often argue for *collective responsibility*. If civilians die in a terrorist act, it is claimed, they paid the price for being on the side causing injustice. Osama bin Laden, in his *Letter to America* in 2002, claimed that those who died in terrorist attacks on September 11, 2001, including Muslims, were guilty because they supported U.S. policies as taxpayers and consumers.

Finally, terrorism is justified as an act of *retaliation*. Terrorist groups often call their attacks a payback for grievances. The Marriott Hotel bombing in Pakistan in 2008 was an act of retaliation from local terrorist groups for Pakistan's cooperation with the United States. The two perpetrators of the 2013 terrorist act in Boston reportedly vented their grievances against U.S. foreign policy.

Terrorism: In the Name of What?

Before turning to terrorism, groups and individuals share certain goals. Such goals derive from *ideologies*, or comprehensive principles and beliefs. We briefly examine four major ideologies that inspired terrorists around the world: anarchism, radical Socialism, extreme nationalism, and religious fundamentalism. (See Table 7-2.)

ANARCHISM

As we saw in Chapter 2, anarchism seeks to create a borderless, peaceful society of free communes in which people generate and distribute wealth without government control. There are peaceful and violent types of anarchism. In the nineteenth and early twentieth centuries, violent anarchists have used political assassinations as a means to reach political goals. After an act of terrorism, they believed, people would rise against injustice and then turn to anarchism. This never happened, despite assassinations of many world leaders by anarchists. Anarchism has always been fragmented and poorly organized. A less dangerous form of anarchism today is the radical antiglobalization movement.

TABLE 7-2 Tactics and Goals of Terrorism Driven by Ideology

Ideology	Tactics of Terrorism	Goals of Terrorism
Anarchism	Acts against government officials and civilians to create panic and paralyze government and society.	Destruction of all state institutions. Creation of a self-governing society of free communes.
Extreme Nationalism	Acts against government officials and civilians of another nation to break their will. Acts against other ethnic groups.	Creation of a nation-state. The eviction of other ethnic groups.
Radical Socialism	Acts against governments, to unleash a revolution of masses.	A new society based on the abolition of private property and the destruction of privileged groups.
Religious Fundamentalism	Acts against those viewed as enemies of a religious order.	A religious revolution. A theocracy in one country or transnational religious order.

EXTREME NATIONALISM

In the context of international relations, **nationalism** is an ideology of terrorists trying to create a nation-state. Nationalist militants have used terrorist methods for many years. In July 1914, in the Bosnian city Sarajevo, Serbian nationalists assassinated Archduke Franz Ferdinand, heir to the Austro-Hungarian (Habsburg) throne and his wife Sophia, thus triggering a harsh response from Austria. The failure of European governments to resolve this crisis resulted in World War I. Nationalism-motivated terrorism was predominant throughout the twentieth century. In the twenty-first century this brand of terrorism declined. One of the most active radical groups remains the PKK (Kurdistan Workers' Party). It continues its violent struggle (including terrorism) against the Turkish government to create a sovereign Kurdistan.

RADICAL SOCIALISM

Radical Socialism seeks to destroy capitalism and liberal democracy in the name of social and economic equality (see Chapters 3 and 6). Radical Marxist groups used terrorist methods early in the twentieth century. During decolonization in the 1950s and 1960s, many radical Socialist groups in Latin America and Africa used terrorism and targeted authoritarian governments, which often relied on Western support. Ernesto Che Guevara (1928–1967), an Argentinean doctor, believed that random acts of deadly violence would spark revolutions across Latin America. Another Socialist, Abimael Guzmán, a former university professor in Peru, formed a radical Maoist group called Shining Path (*Sendero Luminoso*) that began a bloody campaign of terror against government

Masked supporters demonstrate by waving various PKK flags and images of jailed Kurdish rebel leader Abdullah Ocalan, left, in the Turkish city of Diyarbakir, 2013. The group is responsible for one of the world's bloodiest resistances, lasting nearly 30 years and costing tens of thousands of lives.

institutions and officials (Burt, 2009). Government forces in Bolivia tracked down, captured, and killed Guevara in 1967. Guzmán was captured and imprisoned for life in Peru in 1992.

In the 1970s another spike of Marxism-inspired terrorism occurred in Europe: the *Red Army Faction* (RAF) in West Germany and the Red Brigades (*Brigate Rosse*) in Italy targeted bankers and government officials to create instability and chaos. In 1978, Italian terrorists kidnapped and killed former prime minister Aldo Moro. Gradually, the wave of terrorism abated. Some of its leaders, including RAF's founder Ulrike Meinhof, committed suicide. Others were killed or captured. Only a few Socialist groups today use terrorism as a method of struggle against capitalism.

RELIGIOUS FUNDAMENTALISM

Religious fundamentalism is a set of beliefs and behaviors based on strict adherence to religious principles. Fundamentalist groups have had a long history of terrorism in India and Pakistan. Many terrorist organizations are inspired by radical and politicized interpretations of religion. A number of Islamic groups have organized terrorist acts to advance their political agenda—the creation of an Islamic state. In recent years, Salafism, a radical version of Islam, has inspired anti-Russian guerrillas in Northern Caucasus (Hahn, 2012). *Al-Qaeda*, an international underground network, wants the establishment of a global Muslim state governed by the Sharia law (Desai, 2007). *Jemaah Islamiyah* is a Southeast Asian radical organization attempting to establish an Islamic state to include Brunei, Malaysia, Singapore, Indonesia, and the southern Philippines. The *Taliban* is a Sunni political movement operating primarily in Afghanistan and Pakistan and using both terrorism and insurgency to build an Islamic state in Afghanistan. *Hamas* is a political movement in Palestine hoping to create an independent Islamic Palestine; it is still formally committed to destroy Israel as a state. This group, especially its military wing, has been engaged in violence and terrorism. *Hezbollah* is a Shiite group operating from Lebanon and targeting Israel and its supporters. (Both Sunnis and Shiites are different branches of Islam.) Radical groups inspired by Buddhism appeared in Myanmar (Beech, 2013).

This brief classification does not exhaust the long list of beliefs that can motivate terrorists. Even a belief in the need to protect nature can move some individuals to violence, or "ecoterrorism" (as we will see in Chapter 8).

▶ Explain the strategic goals of anarchism, Socialism, nationalism, and religious fundamentalism, especially Islamist groups. Can their goals be achieved by peaceful means?

CHECK YOUR KNOWLEDGE

DEBATE > ASSUMPTIONS AND MISCONCEPTIONS ABOUT TERRORISM, RADICALISM, AND VIOLENT GROUPS

Labels can be misleading. Test yourself on these claims: true or false?

"Almost every fundamentalist or radical group supports terrorism." *False*. Many fundamentalist groups reject violence. Most nationalist or Socialist groups also categorically rejected terrorist methods.

"Radical groups disagree about the methods they use." *True*. It is important to distinguish moderate and nonviolent wings in any movement from more radical wings.

"Violent groups don't change." *False*. Some groups abandon terrorism for the sake of international legitimacy. Nationalists often shift from violence to negotiations if they see their ultimate goal, the creation of a nation-state, acknowledged by the international community.

WHAT'S YOUR VIEW?

Do your own investigation and provide examples of political radicalism and fundamentalism that reject violence.

@ Go to the companion website to learn about the Hezbollah, or the Party of God, and discuss whether terrorist organizations change over time—and if so, how.

How Do We Study It?

The Realist View of Terrorism

Understanding international terrorism has been a challenge to realists. First, the main focus of realism is not on informal networks, but on power relations among sovereign states. Second, realism's models for decision-making often do not take into account the ideological or religious motivations that drive terrorist networks. Still, realism's framework of *power balance* and *asymmetrical threats* is useful in explaining international terrorism. Also, realism justifies the preventive use of force to neutralize terrorist threats.

POWER BALANCE

Nonstate actors can disrupt the balance of power much like states. Inaction in response to terrorism, realists argue, may weaken a targeted state's power and encourage terrorist groups to strike again. Terrorism may thus be used as a powerful tool of international destabilization.

Let's return to the 1914 Sarajevo assassination. The Serbian nationalists who killed Archduke Ferdinand did not act officially on behalf of Serbia, and the Serbian government condemned the terrorist act. However, the Austrian government in Vienna should have taken swift action to punish the Serbs because otherwise it would have encouraged Serbia, and its ally Russia, to reduce the influence of Austria-Hungary in Europe and in the Balkans. So Vienna made the fateful decision to declare war on Serbia. An unstable power balance in Europe, divided into two blocs, contributed to the decision of other countries—Russia, then Germany, and then France and the United Kingdom—to join the war. A nonstate group of nationalists had interfered in an international power balance and achieved an extraordinary result.

ASYMMETRICAL THREATS AND PREVENTIVE ACTIONS

Realism teaches that in a stable world, there is a *symmetry*, or balance of forces and threats: An attack by one state could cause a response from other states, and a balance is restored. Terrorism, however, poses an **asymmetrical threat** to sovereign states (Cordesman, 2002). Because terrorists do not represent a state, countries may find it difficult to identify the perpetrators and retaliate effectively. Terrorist groups therefore try to provoke governments to overreact or launch futile responses. Some say that the U.S. reaction to the 9/11 attacks was also exaggerated and led to a costly "war on terror" without any definite outcome.

International terrorism may destabilize a balance of forces in unpredictable ways: as you can see, the Serbian terrorists provoked European states to go to war that destroyed the existing international order. Realism maintains that

DEBATE > POWER BALANCE AND TERRORIST ATTACKS IN 1914 AND 2001

Terrorist acts in Sarajevo in 1914 and on September 11, 2001, in The United States are nearly a hundred years apart yet they seem to share some similarities in terms of their international dynamics and consequences. In both cases, nonstate groups committed extraordinary acts of violence. Both Austria-Hungary and the United States went to war against the countries (Serbia and Afghanistan, respectively) harboring terrorists. Both wars disrupted the power balance: in Europe and in the Persian Gulf. After the United States destroyed Saddam Hussein's Iraq, Iran remained the only regional power. We can see why states use military power in response to terrorist acts but also why the result of their actions is often unpredictable.

WHAT'S YOUR VIEW?

Do you think that the United States' government responding to the terrorist attacks of 2001 cared about global balance of power? Would the U.S. standing in the world have weakened if it had not gone to war against the Taliban?

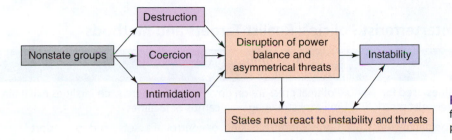

FIGURE 7-3 Terrorism from the realist perspective.

responses to a terrorist act can drag various forces into a wider conflict, as in Europe in 1914. (See Figure 7.3.)

In the context of asymmetrical threats, the key realist idea of international security based on deterrence (Chapter 4) becomes essentially ineffective. Because states cannot effectively retaliate against terrorism in "an eye for an eye" fashion, they should instead engage in preventive and punishing measures. States should use force preventively, whenever a verifiable evidence of an imminent terrorist threat emerges. Such realist logic influenced decision-making of the Bush Administration when it decided to attack Iraq in 2003. The United States has failed to find WMD in Iraq and has not discovered a connection between Saddam Hussein and terrorist networks. Still, the realist logic prevailed in guiding Washington's actions. The UN High-Level Panel on Threats, Challenges and Change, appointed by the General Secretary Kofi Annan, also reported in 2004 that countries may conceivably justify the use of force, "not just reactively but preventively and before a latent threat becomes imminent" (United Nations, 2004).

COUNTERTERRORISM

Realist strategies for counterterrorism include *monitoring* and *prevention*. Intelligence gathering ranges from electronic monitoring to infiltration into terrorist organizations. In the United States, more than eight hundred information technology companies were not long ago involved in counterterrorism intelligence (Priest and Arkin, 2010b; 2011). These policies also include elaborate measures to prevent terrorist groups from acquiring sophisticated military technologies, including WMD.

Other policies are *preemptive* and *punitive*. **Preemptive policies** take action against terrorists before they strike. These policies range from the physical elimination of groups to the disruption of their financial operations. Since 2001 scores of al-Qaeda militants have been detained or killed—mostly by unmanned aerial vehicles (UAV), commonly known as drones. From the realist viewpoint, such actions do not violate other countries' sovereignty for two reasons. First, governments often secretly grant permission for such actions. Second, some governments, such as in Pakistan, Sudan, or Afghanistan, do not exercise full control over their territory.

Another set of policies is called *homeland security*, after the American example. The September 11 attacks required a costly refurbishing and expansion of the U.S. government. New government structures were created to increase

TABLE 7-3 Counterterrorist Policies: Realist Targets and Methods

Targets	Methods: Monitoring, Preemption, and Homeland Security
Camps and other facilities used for training or to stage a terrorist attack	Political pressure on governments where such facilities exist; direct military strikes against camps or facilities
Financial assets of suspected terrorists	Confiscation, blocking, or control of assets used to support international terrorism
Terrorist networks and cells	Search and surveillance; operations against the existing networks; tougher immigration policies
Weapons of mass destruction and delivery systems	Safeguarding the sites where WMD are stored; protection of technologies to prevent their use by terrorists; ensuring nonproliferation of WMD beyond current nuclear states

the control of borders and immigration, screen millions of visitors, monitor electronic communications, and investigate suspects. After 2001 and particularly after the 2004 bombing in Madrid and the 2005 bombing in London, most governments of the European Union implemented tougher immigration policies, deportation procedures, and other legal restrictions to monitor the flow of people through EU borders. These policies were aimed at individuals and organizations suspected of helping terrorist organizations, particularly in the Middle East and Central Asia. (See Table 7-3.)

A bus destroyed by the July 2005 terrorist attack in London. This attack along with others in the London underground took the lives of more than 50 people. The British government soon tightened security and immigration procedures, most of which are still in place today.

In summary, realism assumes that states identify and eliminate the physical and organizational infrastructure of international terrorism. Realists also stand for punitive military operations against states that harbor terrorists. There should be pressure on states that provide financial and political support to terrorism. The combination of preventive measures and force should take incentive from the terrorist hands and eventually weaken them.

How can we measure the effectiveness of realist policies? Most obviously, the absence of new terrorist attacks may indicate that these policies have worked. There are, however, both obvious and hidden side effects. These include the high financial costs of counterterrorism, its impact on the economy, loss of individual freedoms, and the impact on democratic governance itself. We will address these issues later in this chapter.

The Liberal View of Terrorism

To understand terrorism, liberalism argues, we have to examine the conditions that breed political radicalism. Terrorism cannot be defeated by military means alone. It takes understanding the causes of terrorism and using legal means of international cooperation to defeat it. States combating terrorism are likely to succeed when they act together to create a better international environment and engage international institutions and nonstate actors.

UNDERSTANDING CAUSES OF TERRORISM

A key question is why terrorism takes place. Liberalism treats terrorism as a complex phenomenon exploiting acute social and political problems. This view finds support in a 1977 UN resolution stating that economic and social problems cause some people to turn to terrorism. This was not a justification of terrorism, but an attempt to explain it.

The logic of liberalism is straightforward: People turn to terrorism for a reason, even if it appears to be a distorted one. Corruption and nepotism in high offices, chronic unemployment, the injustices of daily lives, and profound inefficiency in addressing social problems all contribute to radicalism. Foreign occupation is another serious cause. From the liberal point of view, policies that address these causes can dry up the reservoir of violent radicalism and isolate terrorists from the rest of the population that may justify the terrorists' activities. It takes time and patience to implement such policies.

CRIMINALIZING TERRORISM

In a liberal point of view, in what is called the **criminalization of terrorism**, a democratic society should not apply one set of legal rules for its own citizens and another set for groups labeled terrorists. The main point is that illegal violent actions should not cause illegal counteractions. International law can be used in addition to domestic laws to qualify terrorist actions as crimes and deal with them using a broad domestic and international consensus (Schultz, 2004). If legal rules are not in place, they have to be set. Inside their countries, governments should not limit the rights of law-abiding citizens and should draw a clear line between monitoring terrorist activities and the surveillance of people's daily activities. They should coordinate their policies and rely on

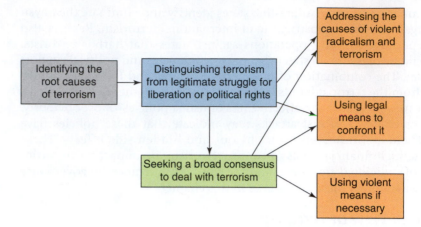

FIGURE 7-4 Terrorism from the liberal perspective.

international law against terrorist groups and their sponsors. The rule of law, in the end, is the best way to confront the lawlessness that is the breeding ground of radicalism and terrorism. (Figure 7.4 shows the steps in analyzing terrorism from the liberal perspective and choosing the appropriate counter-terrorism option).

LIBERALISM AND COUNTERTERRORISM

Supporters of the liberal view do not promise quick results. Rather, they em-phasize gradual improvements. They do not reject military actions against known terrorist groups and individuals. The difference between the liberal

TABLE 7-4 Fighting International Terrorism: The Liberal Perspective

Target	Method of Handling International Terrorism
Violent radical groups	Deterrence by propaganda and legal policies. Differentiation and marginalization of extremists. Attempts to negotiate with others.
Conditions and root causes of terrorism	The improvement of social and economic conditions of the population, reduction of potential social support for radical groups.
Terrorist propaganda, justified by nationalist and other legitimate goals	International condemnation of terrorism, outlawing groups that resort to terrorist methods. Support of national liberation and other legitimate causes through international organizations.
Anti-Western radicalism, especially Islamic fundamentalism	Educational campaigns. Cooperation with nonextremist Islamic and other religious organizations. Coordination of policies with local authorities.

and realist approaches is in the priorities they assign to negotiations, legal means, and the use of force.

Any action against terrorist groups should be strictly legitimate. It must be conducted in accordance with international law and include, whenever possible, international cooperation. Counterterrorist measures should be a combination of negotiations, law-enforcement operations, and military actions (if necessary)—all under the guidance of local and international rules. Such policies should legitimize counterterrorism.

Counterterrorism should include strategic cooperation between states, international organizations, and NGOs (Cronin, 2002). *Public diplomacy*, or the achievement of policy goals by engagement with the local communities and elements of civil society, should become an efficient form of counterterrorism. Public diplomacy seeks to separate terrorist and other radical organizations from their popular base (Simon and Martini, 2004).

Recent American experience with counterinsurgency (COIN) in Iraq and Afghanistan in 2006–2013 provided additional facts and new arguments for the liberal approach. In Iraq a combination of military power and public diplomacy eventually lead to the end of a civil war between the Sunnis and the Shiites. Foreign terrorist groups were either destroyed or driven away with the help of local communities. At the same time, in Afghanistan, COIN operations essentially failed. The Taliban was a homegrown movement and its fighters had a safe haven in neighboring Pakistan. Abject poverty and rampant corruption played a negative political role. Finally, the mountainous terrain was too difficult to control (Kaplan, 2012). These facts suggest that the liberal principles should not be applied without considering the actual social, cultural, and geographical factors.

Can democratic peace theory help in explaining terrorism and counterterrorism? It is obvious that developed democracies do not become "breeding grounds" of terrorists. Most of the al-Qaeda fighters came from the authoritarian and corrupt Middle East societies, above all Saudi Arabia, Yemen, and Egypt. Yet we still do not know how exactly democratization helps in defeating terrorism. It may be, as the critics of democratic peace theory maintain (see Chapter 2) that the process of democratic transition may actually lead to the temporary growth of discontent, ideological clashes, and terrorism. We will discuss this argument in more detail later in this chapter.

▶ What is public diplomacy in combating terrorism?
▶ What is the main point of the criminalization of terrorism?

CHECK YOUR KNOWLEDGE

The Constructivist and Other Views of Terrorism

Other approaches focus on different interpretations of terrorism's causes and suggest new approaches to counterterrorism. These include constructivism and conflict theories.

CASE IN POINT > *Northern Ireland*

International attempts to deal with the sources of terrorism in Northern Ireland demonstrate a potential and limitation of the liberal approach. Northern Ireland, a division of the United Kingdom, suffered for decades from a conflict between Roman Catholic and Protestant groups. The Irish Republican Army (IRA) and its successors sought to remove British influence from Northern Ireland and used terrorist acts to achieve this goal. Patient negotiations, mediation from other governments, the involvement of religious and secular groups, a referendum, legal reforms, and economic assistance seemed to bear fruit. In the 1990s, the British and Irish governments, with the help of Washington, reached a series of agreements that Ireland (the Republic of Ireland *and* Northern Ireland) could be unified only by peaceful means—and only if the majority of Northern Ireland voted for it. In 2005 the IRA promised to lay down its arms for good. Yet international agreements could not resolve the problem completely: Violent nationalist passions go beyond economic interests and legal reforms. They can flare up at any moment and require a very long time to pass away.

CRITICAL THINKING

What means helped to bring sectoral violence and terrorism in Northern Ireland under control? Can we apply the successful experience of Northern Ireland in other places like Afghanistan, Iraq, and Syria? Why? Why not? Explain your opinion.

IRA terrorist volunteers at a camp near Dublin in 1966. After decades of violence, it appears that terrorism is finally eradicated in Northern Ireland. Can other countries learn from this case?

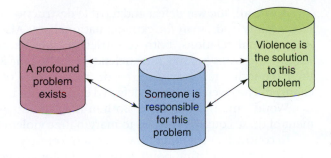

FIGURE 7-5 The constructivist view: The three pillars of terrorism.

THREE PILLARS OF TERRORISM

States and organizations, supporters of constructivism claim, define terrorism and conduct antiterrorist policies based on their perceptions. As perceptions change, so do policies. Counterterrorism is a product of social construction: It is based on ideological beliefs, the quality of information available to the decision makers, and the way they interpret it. Above all, constructivism attempts to understand the motivations of terrorists, their identities, and their ideas.

Violent radical groups pursue many different political goals and hold diverse creeds. Yet the choice of terrorism has three basic motives. We can call them the *three pillars of terrorism*. (See Figure 7.5.)

1. *"We see a profound problem."* Terrorists generally believe that some profound injustice has occurred or is occurring now. It might be a foreign occupation, ethnic or religious oppression, social and economic exploitation, imprisonment of certain individuals, or a devastating military defeat of their country.

2. *"We know who is responsible."* Terrorists see their targets as solely responsible for this injustice. They may identify the source of the injustice as their own government, a foreign state, a political regime, or the international order in general. In an ethnic conflict, for example, they see one side as an innocent victim and the other as a villain. There are no gray areas.

3. *"Violence is the solution."* Terrorists believe that only violence can direct attention to the injustice or even put an end to it. In their eyes, violence should destroy the source of the injustice, force others to deal with it, and awaken public attention. Most radical groups pay less attention to what they are going to do politically after the violent act is "successful" and their goal of destruction is achieved.

IDEOLOGY, IDENTITY, AND INTERNATIONAL CONTEXT

Constructivists argue that not every case of perceived injustice produces terrorism. Without a powerful ideology justifying random violence and individual sacrifice, terrorism cannot exist. The rise and fall of these ideologies should be regarded in an international context. Consider Japan and Germany after their defeat in World War II. The United States and other powers occupied both countries for years, and the Japanese and German people never resorted to terrorism. Why not?

Above all, the war defeat and terrible destruction undermined any support in Germany and Japan for extreme nationalism. Also, from the viewpoint of international relations, both countries quickly became allies of the United States: Americans became their defenders against the Soviet Union and assisted their economic recovery. As a result, the identity of those countries rapidly changed: They were no longer defeated enemies but instead became part of "the free World" and the U.S. allies. Both military defeat and international realignment of these countries helped to marginalize violent nationalist identities.

In contrast, at the end of the twentieth century, the societies of the Middle East became a meeting point between ideological versions of Islam and the people who looked for violent identities. The radical versions of Islam, funded by Saudi Arabia—*Wahhabism* and *Salafism*—sought to shape the identity of people in Afghanistan, Pakistan, and the Northern Caucasus in the 1980s–2000s. The al-Qaeda ideologues, including bin-Laden, used the wars in Afghanistan and Iraq to promote an extremely violent type of Islamic identity. They argued that there was a centuries-long war between "Crusaders" from the West and the forces of Islam. They regarded the Soviets in Afghanistan in 1980–88, and then the Americans in Saudi Arabia after 1991, as the "Crusaders" and were determined to defeat them at any cost.

DEBATE > ON MORAL RELATIVISM AND TERRORISM

The 1972 attack on Israeli athletes and coaches during the Olympic Games was considered in the West a barbaric terrorist act. Heads of most countries condemned it. Yet others refused to do so. The bodies of the five Palestinians participating in the Munich massacre were flown to Libya, where they were buried with full military honors.

In 1994, Baruch Goldstein, an Israeli citizen, walked into a mosque in Hebron and killed twenty-nine Palestinian worshipers. Although the Israeli government condemned the massacre, Goldstein's tomb has become a place of worship for many Jews. The tombstone reads: *Here lies the saint, Dr. Baruch Kappel Goldstein, blessed be the memory of the righteous and holy man, may the Lord avenge his blood, which devoted his soul to the Jews, Jewish religion, and Jewish land. His hands are innocent and his heart is pure. He was killed as a martyr of God.*

Have you heard the expression, "Your *terrorists* are our *freedom fighters*"? Moral relativists even use the constructivist argument that terrorists can be either villains or heroes based on one's point of view. Now try to challenge this moral relativism. At least two options are possible. One is to reject any kind of political violence. In this case, every terrorist act becomes unacceptable and immoral. The other option is to name conditions under which some forms of violence are acceptable. In this case, you will justify specific violent acts but not others.

WHAT'S YOUR VIEW?

Is violence ever acceptable, for example, in self-defense? Why or why not and under what circumstances? Return to the definition of terrorism in the beginning of this chapter. In your view, are there conditions under which terrorism is acceptable?

Read more about the events leading up to the 1983 attack in Lebanon: "Chapter 6: Lebanon: 1982–1984," by John H. Kelly, from *U.S. and Russian Policymaking with Respect to the Use of Force* (1996), edited by Jeremy Azrael and Emil A. Payin. Read the *New York Times* article about the aftermath of the 1994 Hebron attack: "WEST BANK MASSACRE: The Overview; Rabin Urges the Palestinians to Put Aside Anger and Talk," by Clyde Haberman, March 1, 1994. See the companion website for links.

CONFLICT THEORIES

Conflict theories explain terrorism as a form of political struggle against oppressors. Classical Marxism generally supported terror against the class of capitalists, supporters of the capitalist system, and governments representing it. However, disagreements among Marxists persisted about specific policies. Lenin and the Bolsheviks (see Chapter 3) supported mass terror against "class enemies" in Russia and in other countries, but not individual acts of terror. Other disagreements existed between the Soviet Union and newly formed Socialist countries, such as Cuba in the 1960s and Kampuchea or Ethiopia in the 1970s. The Soviets did not endorse random killings, kidnappings, and other terrorist acts committed by radical Communist groups. At the same time they did not condemn them publicly and supported some of the terrorist groups financially. Today's Marxists do not endorse terrorism by Islamic radical groups but do see it as a reaction to unjust policies. Those who regard international relations in terms of "North vs. South" may regard terrorism as an inevitable consequence of the structural inequality in the world; for them, only radical distribution of resources to the more poor regions can help to reduce terrorist activities.

> ▶ Name and explain the three pillars of terrorism.
> ▶ How do moral relativists view terrorism?

CHECK YOUR KNOWLEDGE

How Do We Apply It?

No approach fully explains terrorism. No single theory offers universally effective methods of counterterrorism. Realism emphasizes security and power politics but overlooks ideology, social causes, and individual motivations of terrorists. Liberalism pays attention to terrorism's causes but often overrates the chances for cooperation with radical groups. Constructivism helps to understand terrorists' motivations and identities, but often lacks practical solutions. The individual, state, and global contexts allow us to compare the applications of different theoretical approaches.

The Individual Context

How well do theories and hypotheses work to explain the behavior of individual terrorists and terrorists groups? Let's summarize the most significant findings. At the end of this chapter, we will return for a historical perspective to the case of al-Qaeda.

THE TERRORIST'S PROFILE

Do terrorists share common behavioral features? Law-enforcement professionals have long used behavioral profiling of criminal behavior. Can something similar be done with terrorism?

The answer is not encouraging. Attempts to create a single universal profile of the terrorist have so far been unsuccessful. Terrorists come from different backgrounds and are influenced by many different circumstances. What about liberal assumption that poverty is the main source of terrorism? Actually, studies based on statistical analyses have found a complicated correlation between a country's economic conditions and individual motivation of terrorists (Krueger, 2007; Abadie, 2006). Most organizers and leaders of terrorist networks never lived in poverty and even came from well-to-do families (Bernstein, 2009). At the same time, their "foot soldiers" are still likely to be poor (Pape, 2003).

Studies also contest a popular assumption that most terrorists are deeply disturbed. Although extreme violence such as suicide attacks seems irrational, terrorists believe that they act with complete rationality (Crenshaw, 2000; 2010). An individual's decision to commit a terrorist act appears rational within its social context: Injustice must be eliminated (Asal and Blum, 2005). Terrorists tend to believe that their actions have a deeper personal and spiritual meaning. (See Table 7-5.)

Theories of group influence also find empirical support. Mark Sageman (2004) examined the biographies of members of radical violent organizations. They were strongly influenced by *group pressure* from peers. Other studies show that individuals join extremist groups for the same reasons that people join gangs—to gain a sense of belonging. Only later do they acquire extremist views (Horgan, 2009). Refugee camps around Israel and in other parts of the world are a recruiting ground for terrorism because young people there develop an overwhelming sense of unity and a desire to fight together for a common goal.

TABLE 7-5 Is There a Terrorist Profile?

Factor	Findings
Age	Rank-and-file terrorists tend to be younger individuals. Globally, younger people commit most violent crimes of any nature.
Gender	Terrorists are mostly males. Yet women join their ranks frequently and for a variety of reasons.
Occupation	There are no direct links between a person's occupation and terrorism. Unemployment, however, is a factor.
Poverty	There is no direct correlation between a country's economic conditions and terrorism. However, poor people in areas with high levels of unemployment are more vulnerable to recruitment by radical groups.
Mental illness	No evidence exists for elevated rates of mental illness among terrorists. Partial evidence exists for low self-esteem, depression, and stress-related problems that affect an individual's search for glory and martyrdom.
Group pressure	Evidence exists for group pressure as a factor contributing to terrorism.
Radical ideology	Most terrorists are radicalized in their choice of action. However, radicalization is often a result of group pressure, not the other way around.

Sources: Crenshaw, 2010; Horgan, 2009; Post, 2004; 2008.

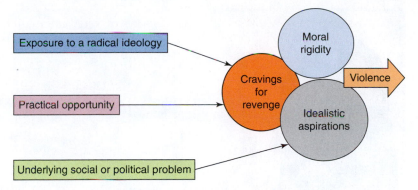

FIGURE 7-6 The inner world of a terrorist. A young person often grows up under relatively ordinary circumstances. Then comes a humiliating experience. It may lead to the shocking realization of society's injustices. As this individual becomes increasingly alienated from society, he or she contemplates action to address the perceived injustice. A group or individual then appears suggesting a radical solution, and violence becomes a moral duty, with an expected spiritual or other reward (Sageman, 2004).

Casualties among members of these groups only contribute to greater solidarity (Post, 2004).

The constructivist three pillars of terrorism seem to be valid. An individual is deeply convinced that violence should be committed to address a perceived injustice. A group or organization then provides the necessary tools and means to satisfy the craving for destruction and self-sacrifice. (See Figure 7.6.)

REHABILITATION AS COUNTERTERRORISM

The destruction of terrorists and their networks has been a major task of counterterrorism. But what do we know about **rehabilitation**, the process of assisting someone engaged in radical acts to return to the community? Is it possible to re-educate and change former radicals? Supporters of liberalism, in theory, believe in rehabilitation methods, but do they have facts to back their assumptions?

Special "de-radicalization" government centers in Saudi Arabia and Iraq (run by American Task Force 134) bring cautious but optimistic results. Such centers base their work on the assumption that many individuals had been radicalized despite having little knowledge of Islam, politics, and history. With education and psychological counseling, these people can change their political views. Others simply need to find jobs (Stern, 2010). How effective are such rehabilitation programs? Of 120 Saudi nationals who have been repatriated back to their country from the Guantanamo detention center, about 80 percent went back to normal life (Boucek, 2009). Others, however, returned to terrorist activities in Afghanistan and elsewhere. Of course, time and studies are needed to know more.

The State Context

Terrorism is influenced by a variety of domestic factors. In turn, the threat of terrorism compels countries to amend their policies. We have already seen in

U.S. Presidents George W. Bush and Barack Obama on the day of Obama's first inauguration, January 20, 2009. Were there differences in their views on terrorism? How were these views shaped by their life experiences?

earlier chapters how Presidents Bush and Obama were influenced by domestic politics. Let's see how the state context helps understand the complexity of counterterrorism as well as terrorists' motivations.

DOMESTIC COSTS OF COUNTERTERRORISM

After 2001, the United States committed considerable resources to enhance national security. The debates continue about how much the counterterrorism activities cost the American taxpayers. In September 2011, *The New York Times* put the price tag at $3.3 trillion. Independent estimates ranged from $3 trillion to $5 trillion (Stiglitz, 2011). These calculations included the cost of new government institutions and practices, such as the Department of Homeland Security and airport security checks, but also the cost of military and nonmilitary engagements in Iraq and Afghanistan—and even future medical expenses of the veterans of these wars.

The debates about the cost of counterterrorism bring us back to the discussion of asymmetrical responses to terrorism. The main goal of international terrorism, as you remember, is to weaken the international order. Terrorists also hope to trigger excessive and costly reactions from the countries they attack. Critics of U.S. counterterrorist policies claim that international terrorism in the twenty-first century is succeeding because of the cost Americans pay to combat it. The attacks of September 11 and the fear they generated caused long-term damage not only to the American budget but to the economy as well. Excessive airport security and visa scrutiny also diminished tourism to the United States for several years. The aftermath of the attacks brought a fundamental change to national priorities and policies. Without this shift, American government would not have fought two costly wars and could have invested more into its own infrastructure, research, and education.

TERRORISM AS A MEANS TO GAIN STATE POWER

Both realist and liberal commentators rightly mention that not every radical or fundamentalist group becomes a threat to international security (Cooper, 2004). Nationalist-driven terrorism tends to focus on domestic goals: gaining autonomy, independence, or establishing a new state. Once the goal is achieved, the reasons for further violence no longer exist. A study of four hundred terrorist groups in the twentieth century found that 124 of them eventually established ties to legitimate political parties (Weinberg and Pedahzur, 2003). In the past thirty years, many formerly radical political groups in Latin America have renounced violence. In Jordan, the Muslim Brotherhood, which had renounced violence, gained about one-third of the seats in parliament. The moderate wing of the Muslim Brotherhood in Egypt also denounced the use of violence in 1971 (Herzog, 2006). However, nationalist movements could transform into terrorist groups pursuing fundamentalist agendas. The low-intensity conflicts fought since the 1990s in the North Caucasus transformed a secular struggle for independence from Russia into a holy war to establish an Islamist state (Saradzhyan, 2010).

DEMOCRATIC GOVERNANCE AND TERRORISM

We already mentioned democratic peace theory and its possible implications for terrorism. Another issue for discussion is effectiveness of democracies in combatting terrorist threats. It may appear that authoritarian states can be more effective: They have fewer constraints than democracies in using harsh measures against terrorists. Yet history shows that authoritarian regimes cannot defeat terrorism: They just drive terrorists underground. Authoritarian states may also use the threat of terrorism as an excuse to attack the political opposition. For instance, the Chinese government to this day cites the threat of global terrorism to justify its crackdown on separatist forces in Xinjiang, a predominantly Muslim region, and Tibet.

Liberal democracies appear more vulnerable to terrorism than authoritarian regimes because of their openness and decentralization. Democracies often lack a political consensus on how to fight terrorism. We already mentioned that after 9/11 critics of the Bush administration claimed that its policies expanded government prerogatives at the expense of civil liberties. The phones of terrorism suspects were tapped, their Internet correspondence was monitored, and habeas corpus (the right to be brought before a judge) was suspended (Ignatieff, 2004). The challenge is to create effective counterterrorist policies without compromising democratic governance and freedoms.

Yet in the long run democracies tend to resist radical violence more successfully than nondemocratic regimes. Democratic means create legitimacy

Volunteers carry an injured child to safety after soldiers stormed a school seized by heavily armed terrorists near Chechnya in 2004. More than 300 hostages died, including 156 children, amid explosions and machine gun fire. What caused such a high number of casualties? We can blame the terrorists, but the counterterrorism operation by the Russian government was arguably inept.

and help gain popular support for counterterrorism. The decline of the IRA in Northern Ireland and the defeat of the Red Brigades in Italy and the RAF in Germany in the 1970s showed that democratic states could overcome terrorism without compromising their democratic principles.

Emerging democracies may be most vulnerable to terrorism because they lack effective institutions and a functioning civil society. They also are likely to suffer from corruption, nepotism, and tribalism. Some members of the police, the security services, and the public may actually sympathize with terrorist causes. For instance, in Pakistan both democratically elected leaders and the military dictators there had a poor record of dealing with terrorist groups. Officials from the Pakistani secret service (SIS) have long supported radical Islamists in Afghanistan and India. Pakistani domestic politics remain vulnerable to radical Islamism (Rashid, 2008).

CHECK YOUR KNOWLEDGE

▶ Which factors are commonly analyzed in the "terrorist profile"?
▶ If the main goal of terrorist groups is political, why don't most of them participate in the legitimate political process?

The Global Context

Assessments of terrorism and counterterrorist policies must also take into account their global impact. That includes terrorist strategies and the effectiveness of global counterterrorism. At the same time the global context allows us to see how international terrorism challenges or promotes international interdependence—political and economic.

THREATS TO THE GLOBAL ORDER

Do terrorists achieve their goals? Is terrorism effective in disrupting the global order? The conclusions are mixed. Particularly when the demands of violent groups are specific and limited, governments tend to cooperate. Sometimes they even pay ransom money for hostages. Most of the time, however, states and international organizations refuse to negotiate with terrorist groups, which do not achieve their political goals. In fact, terrorism is likely to delay the solutions of international conflicts or social problems:

- The anarchist movement, even at the height of its activities in the nineteenth and early twentieth century, failed to destroy government institutions or establish direct democracy. To the contrary, after World War I, new and powerful authoritarian states arose.
- Socialist radicalism of the 1960s and 1970s attained only limited success. A global alternative to liberal capitalism never materialized, and "red terrorism" abated.
- Terrorism has also delayed the resolution of many legitimate claims for national sovereignty including statehood for Palestinians.

The effectiveness of international Islamic terrorism deserves some discussion. As we already mentioned, the damage of the September 11 attacks was considerable and lasting. Terrorism and its threats affected the lives of hundreds of millions of people. At the same time, al-Qaeda and similar groups did not even come close to achieving their global goals. Polls show that religiously motivated terrorism, because of the destruction it caused for several decades, had alienated the majority of Muslims even in the areas where it had initially won many sympathizers (J. Horowitz, 2009). Fundamentalist Islamic movements did not overthrow the authoritarian regimes in the Middle East targeted by al-Qaeda. Surprisingly, the major threat to these regimes emerged during the "Arab Spring" of 2011, a series of mass protest actions in many Arab countries. Islamic groups, like "Muslim Brotherhood" in Egypt, may eventually come to share power as a result of the Arab revolutions—yet it means that they begin to be responsible for economic problems and social injustice, not just to react to it with violent means. Finally, influence of al-Qaeda and similar radical groups have been in decline all around the Islamic parts of the world (Husain, 2005; Pew Research Center, 2011).

Neorealists, liberals, and constructivists concur that terrorism will remain a difficult challenge. However, the international system today is generally more resilient than in the past, and terrorists cannot trigger a global calamitous war, like they had done in 1914. From neorealist perspective, there is a concert of great powers to act internationally against terrorist threats, even when some great powers may differ on specific details. Liberals correctly point to the role of the United Nations and its numerous institutions, as well as a host of nongovernment organizations: Terrorists may temporarily overwhelm weak or failing states, yet with the help of international cooperation—not excluding international intervention—these states no longer remain safe and lasting havens for terrorists. And constructivists argue that putting aside militant Islamic fundamentalism, there is a general decline of violent ideologies around the world. We can only hope that this trend continues.

GLOBAL WAVES

Are there distinct tides and ebbs of terrorism around the world? As we saw earlier, anarchism motivated a wave of terrorism in the late 1800s. A second wave, inspired by anticolonialism and nationalism, began in the 1920s and lasted for several decades. The late 1960s witnessed the birth of the terrorist attacks of radical Communist groups in Europe as well as Sri Lanka, Peru, and Colombia. This wave dissipated by the end of the last century, but a new wave, mainly religious terrorism, had already begun in the 1980s (Rapoport, 2001; Post, 2005a).

The willingness of some terrorist groups, particularly Islamists, to embrace religious martyrdom is a frightening development. In addition, terrorism has embraced new technologies, including the Internet. Instead of revolvers and dynamite, terrorists today use sophisticated explosives, civilian aircraft, ships, and high-speed trains to cause maximum damage to people and infrastructures. A miniaturized nuclear device could have catastrophic consequences anywhere at any time. There are serious concerns that Iran, after it develops nuclear weapons, will pass them on to terrorist organizations. In addition, unstable states, such as Pakistan, may not be able to maintain effective controls over their nuclear facilities.

Will it be another wave of terrorism? Where will it come from? Should we prepare for a series of nuclear attacks or anticipate a cyber assault against

In Buenos Aires, Argentina, in 2008, demonstrators hold up a sign that reads in Spanish "No more terrorism, no more violence, no more kidnapping, no more FARC." FARC is a radical terrorist organization from Colombia.

financial institutions and communication networks? Preventive policies may include the use of force. Yet most important, they will need coordinated policies of all responsible states and international organizations.

▶ Is terrorism an effective tactic of political change?
▶ Name three waves of terrorism in history.

CHECK YOUR KNOWLEDGE

GLOBAL COUNTERTERRORISM

September 11, 2001, marked a turning point for global counterterrorism. At the same time, as a result of the wars in Iraq and Afghanistan, the public mood in democratic countries may have swung in the opposite direction. People become tired of precautions and fear of terrorists. The experience and wisdom, however, demands that the structures and institutions of global terrorism should be made more efficient, not dismantled.

Significant international efforts will be needed to strengthen central authority in some countries. Both realists and liberals accept the view that failing states provide a breeding ground for terrorism. Yemen and Afghanistan are two examples. Building a stronger state becomes a counterterrorism policy (Boucek, 2010). Another important policy is pressure on political regimes, such as Iran, suspected of supporting international terrorism.

Part of the solution must come from within countries and regions that breed radicalism. For example, many Islamic scholars today denounce the ideology of violence, which, in their view, has nothing to do with Islam and its basic values. Killing terrorists, as liberals argue and as the U.S. government learned in Afghanistan and Iraq, will not end the problem of radical violence because it feeds on ideologies rooted in deep social and political problems.

Effective policies should combine several interconnected strategies. One is the reasonable and multilateral use of force to change the perceptions of the regional or global balance of power. Another is persistent attention to social and economic problems that provide mass backing for terrorist radicals. Serious work should be done to reappraise international law and law-enforcement procedures to criminalize terrorism. There must be coordinated information policies to encourage others not to glorify violence. Some of these policies may be ineffective, and tactical corrections will be necessary (Post, 2005b).

Another important issue in global antiterrorism policies is moral. Are deadly strikes against known terrorists acceptable if innocent people die as a "collateral damage"? The New America Foundation (NAF, 2012) estimates that of all people killed by U.S. drones in Pakistan, from 5 to 10 percent could be innocent bystanders, including children. This number was higher a few years earlier when the aerial attacks began.

Effective counterterrorism depends on knowledge of its ultimate targets. Are we fighting against specific individuals or against the ideologies that inspire them? Will the physical elimination of a potent radical group solve the problem of terrorism? To approach these questions, we turn to the case of al-Qaeda. Understanding its motivations and actions in the past is crucial for building effective defense, security, and foreign policies of the future.

Past, Present, and Future: Al-Qaeda

The name *al-Qaeda* ("the base") is forever linked to the terrorist attacks of 9/11. Al-Qaeda is an international terrorist network rooted in fundamentalist Islamic principles. It fights to create a global Islamic state, or **caliphate**. An effective way to understand al-Qaeda is to look at the careers and views of its founders—above all, at Osama bin Laden (1957–2011), who was born and grew up in Saudi Arabia. His father, born in Yemen, became a prominent real estate and commercial developer who made hundreds of millions of dollars on government construction projects in Saudi Arabia and elsewhere. This wealth and status helped bin Laden to become a leader. Despite opportunities presented to him by his high social status, bin Laden grew increasingly frustrated with the Saudi society. From his late teens, the main point of his frustration was that the society was progressively distancing itself from the fundamentalist principles of Islam (Bodansky, 2001). Contemporary music, dance, entertainment, mass media, ideas of democracy and equality between men and women—all bothered him immensely (Dennis, 2002).

Among those who strongly influenced bin Laden and his future al-Qaeda associates was an Egyptian fundamentalist thinker Sayyid Qutb (1906–1966), a member of the Egyptian organization *Muslim Brotherhood*. Qutb traveled in the United States and returned home a virulent enemy of American society and Western cultural influences. He was especially disgusted by social equality between men and women (Qutb, [1964] 2007):

• A true and just social system can be created only on the basis of the Sharia, or Islamic law. Islam knows only two kinds of societies, Islamic and un-Islamic, or *Jahiliya*. This inferior society—which cares for neither Islamic beliefs, values, laws, morals, nor manners—is, according to Qutb, the contemporary world.

• A true Islamic society would have no rulers because Muslims need neither judges nor police to obey divine law. Any secular authority or legal system must be repulsive to Muslims. Any secular system—authoritarian or democratic, nationalist or Communist, the free market or a planned economy—is illegitimate unless it follows the Sharia.

• Muslims should use preaching and *Jihad*, the duty to wage a holy war to overthrow secular governments—even if they are ruled by Muslims. As a result, people will be free from their servitude to other men and ready to serve God.

• The present Muslim generation had laid down its spiritual arms defeated by secularism.

From Qutb, the young bin Laden and other founders of al-Qaeda learned about offensive Jihad, which is the right and duty to inflict violence to advance spiritual and political beliefs (Coll, 2009).

KEY FORMATIVE EVENTS

The Soviet invasion of Afghanistan in 1979 gave a number of young educated and radical Saudis, including bin Laden, their first battlefield. They began to raise money and volunteer to fight against the Soviets. This new Jihad, against foreign invaders supporting the Communist Afghani regime, launched a "brotherhood" of militants. When the Soviet Union withdrew from Afghanistan in 1988, these militants considered it their historic victory over "the Satan." At this point bin Laden met with Ayman al-Zawahiri, an Egyptian doctor. Born in 1951 to a prominent family, he also was influenced by the ideas of Sayyid Qutb. Around 1988, al-Zawahiri and bin Laden formed a group, which a decade later became known as al-Qaeda. Al-Zawahiri provided ideas for its organizational structure and trained members; bin Laden supplied ideas and money. This group already aimed beyond the Soviet Union and against the "Great Satan"—the United States (Wright, 2006).

Bin Laden and his associates interpreted the Gulf War of 1991, in which the international coalition led by the United States evicted Iraqi troops from Kuwait, as another "crusade" of the West against Islam. They vowed to expel American troops from the "sacred land" of Saudi Arabia. Bin Laden grew increasingly critical of the Saudi royal family and government, to the point of mutual hostility. He had to leave Saudi Arabia and founded a new training base for al-Qaeda militants in Sudan. After 1996, the Taliban movement seized power in Kabul, and bin Laden and Al-Zawahiri moved their base to Afghanistan. From Afghanistan, they planned the attack on the United States.

GOALS AND METHODS

The National Commission on Terrorist Attacks upon the United States (known commonly was the 9/11 Commission) aptly summed up the essence of al-Qaeda's goals and methods: "The enemy rallies broad support in the Arab and Muslim world by demanding redress of political grievances, but its hostility toward us and our values is limitless. Its purpose is to rid the world of religious and political pluralism, the plebiscite, and equal rights for women. It makes no distinction between military and civilian targets. Collateral damage is not in its lexicon." (National Commission on Terrorist Acts, November 27, 2002).

The main goal of the founders of al-Qaeda is the creation of a global Islamic state. As you will remember, nationalist groups also pursue the creation of sovereign states. Yet their goals are quite different from al-Qaeda's. To achieve a global Islamic state, the entire global order must be destroyed. In their plan, nation-states will disappear, and a new stateless uniform Muslim society

Al-Qaeda leader Osama bin Laden in Afghanistan, from which he planned his attacks against targets in the United States. What places might another wave of anti-Western terrorism come from?

will emerge. (Compare this with anarchism's goals.) In the process, several regional caliphates will unify Muslims living in Europe, Africa, and Eurasia. In particular, caliphates could unify Arab states in the Middle East, North Africa, the Caucasus, Pakistan, Afghanistan, Indonesia, and Southeast Asia.

The most significant obstacle to these goals, al-Qaeda believes, is Western civilization, especially its individualism, materialism, secularism, and gender equality. Followers believe that Western societies are decadent and weak; they can therefore be terrorized, undermined, and eventually overwhelmed.

This second enemy is the Jews. Al-Qaeda beliefs borrow heavily from the old conspiracy theories about the Jewish "world dominance," including their control of the world's economic and financial system. Key is the Palestinian problem, and to solve it the state of Israel must be eliminated; and Israel's main supporter, the United States, must be undermined. In speeches, bin Laden and his associates frequently referred to their enemies as "Jews and Crusaders."

The third obstacle is corrupt regimes in Muslim countries. Their grip on power must be weakened and their secular governments eventually abolished. Although it is a daunting task, enemies can be weakened and defeated with the right methods.

Al-Qaeda leaders became convinced that, despite America's strength, the country was built on a weak secular foundation. Methods of terror could bring Western civilization down. Terror attacks by suicide bombers (a terrorist tactic frequently attributed to al-Zawahiri) must strike the West and its allies repeatedly and in the most vulnerable places. "We will use your laws against you," bin Laden boasted. A weakened West would not be able to support Israel, and the global system would crumble.

LESSONS

Based on what we know about al-Qaeda, what conclusions and recommendations can we form related to counterterrorism?

Although some reports portrayed bin Laden as a typical political player who simply despised America's policies (Hamud, 2005), most viewed him as uncompromising and obsessed. In the past, such individuals as Che Guevara or Guzmán (described earlier in this chapter) were rigid in their judgments and inflexible in their actions. They were ready to sacrifice their lives for the sake of an ideological agenda. As for bin Laden, Washington followed the realist logic. It concluded that talks were counterproductive, and President Obama ordered him killed on May 2, 2011, in a bold operation by U.S. Special Forces. This decision sparked debates. Should bin Laden have been put on trial? Such a trial would have brought justice. Yet it would also have given bin Laden a chance to continue his propaganda. It could have encouraged al-Qaeda to perpetrate new terrorist attacks in attempts to set its leader free.

The appeal of bin Laden's extremist views has been diminishing steadily. (See Figure 7.7.) A 2007 study found that over 80 percent of Pakistanis thought of al-Qaeda and similar groups as threats to national security—a rise of more than 40 percent over just a few years (Stern, 2010).

The struggle against terrorism will not be over, even if al-Qaeda's new leaders are imprisoned or killed. Increasingly, al-Qaeda has turned into a loose

Country/Year	2003	2005	2006	2007	2008	2009	2011
Indonesia	59	36	35	41	37	25	26
Pakistan	46	52	38	38	34	18	—
Jordan	56	61	24	20	19	28	13
Nigeria	44	—	61	52	58	54	—
Turkey	15	5	4	5	3	2	3
Palestinian Territories	72	—	—	57	—	52	34

Sources: Horowitz, 2009; Pew, 2011.

FIGURE 7-7 The declining influence of Osama bin Laden before his death in 2011. *Source: Juliana Horowitz (2009) and Pew Research Center (2011).*

network sharing some goals and methods but also finding new ones. Terrorism is too complex a social and political problem to simply go away. Much depends on the outcome of the "Arab Spring," the transformations in the Middle East Arab countries that began in 2011. If these transformations, for all their setbacks, generate better economic and social conditions, and encourage an educated youth, then al-Qaeda will be history. If corruption and injustice prevail, then the Islamic fundamentalism might inspire new legions of international terrorism.

CONCLUSION

The global struggle against terrorism cannot succeed if it is not supported by the international community, nongovernment organizations, and public opinion. In their counterterrorism policies, states should combine a variety of methods—including military action, surveillance, public diplomacy, economic sanctions, economic aid, law enforcement, education, training, and international law. It is also necessary to address the causes of terrorism, including unsettled territorial disputes, rampant poverty, injustice, and discrimination. This is a task not only for government but for all of us.

CHAPTER SUMMARY

- Terroriszm is a form of violent political radicalism by nonstate actors. States, international organizations, and NGOs develop long-term policies and short-term measures called counterterrorism to prevent and combat international and domestic terrorism.
- Definitions are important. By labeling a group an "international terrorist organization" or a violent act an "act of international terror," a government can establish legal, political, and moral justification for counterterrorist policies.
- Terrorist groups use physical violence and threats of violence to influence governments and decision makers. They also impose fear on communities.

- Before turning to terrorism, groups and individuals share certain unifying goals. Such goals derive from *ideologies*, or comprehensive principles, to justify their objectives, expectations, and actions. These ideologies include anarchism, radical Socialism, nationalism, and religious fundamentalism.
- From the realist point of view, terrorism is mainly an attempt to disrupt international security and balance of power by asymmetrical threats.
- Liberalism interprets terrorism as a by-product of cultural, political, and social causes and conditions that breed political radicalism.
- Constructivism stresses the importance of ideological and religious beliefs in the formation of terrorist identity. These factors can lead to terrorist behavior even when the causes of social and economic discontent are removed.
- Conflict theories explain domestic and international terrorism as a political struggle of the oppressed.
- There is no a typical social profile of a terrorist, but most terrorists share cravings for revenge, moral rigidity, and idealistic aspirations.
- Terrorism has roots in domestic politics, social structure, and the economy. In turn, the threat of international terrorism compels many states to amend their policies and laws.
- The effectiveness of terrorism and counterterrorism is measured in various contexts. Global efforts based on interdependence should improve counterterrorism's effectiveness.

KEY TERMS

Anarchism 228
Asymmetrical threat 232
Caliphate 250
Coercion and extortion 226
Counterterrorism 222

Criminalization of terrorism 235
Cyberterrorism 226
Domestic terrorism 222
Guerrilla warfare 222
International terrorism 222

Nationalism 229
Preemptive policies 233
Rehabilitation 243
Religious fundamentalism 230
Terrorism 222

1. What do we study?

KEY CONCEPTS

- Terrorism: A form of violent political radicalism by non-state actors

- Counterterrorism: Policies and measures to prevent and combat international and domestic terrorism

KEY STRATEGIES OF TERRORISM

- Intimidation

- Coercion and extortion

- Public pressure and exposure

KEY IDEOLOGIES OF TERRORISM

- Anarchism

- Radical socialism

- Nationalism

- Religious fundamentalism

2. How do we study it?

REALISM

- Terrorism disrupts the power balance

- Asymmetrical threat

- Counterterrorism involves monitoring and prevention

LIBERALISM

- To fight terrorism one should better understand its causes

- Criminalization of terrorism

- Emphases on broad international cooperation and public diplomacy

CONSTRUCTIVISM AND OTHER APPROACHES

- Terrorism is based on beliefs, available information and interpretations

- Motives: a problem, an assigned responsibility for the problem, and absence of non-violent choices

- Conflict approaches explain terrorism as a form of political struggle against oppressors

3. How do we apply it?

THE INDIVIDUAL CONTEXT

- No universal profile of a terrorist, yet most crave revenge, display moral rigidity, and have idealistic aspirations

- Terrorists' motivations may change

- Political leaders differ in how they understand terrorism and counterterrorism

THE STATE CONTEXT

- Terrorism is influenced by a variety of domestic factors, including its perceived cost

- Terrorism may be considered as a means to gain power

- Democracies and non-democracies are affected by and respond to terrorism differently

THE GLOBAL CONTEXT

- Terrorism as a method has a mixed record of accomplishing its goals

- There are several global "generations" of terrorism

- Global efforts should improve counterterrorism's effectiveness

Critical Thinking

- Compare and contrast terrorism and guerrilla warfare. Give examples.
- Explain why terrorism is an asymmetrical threat.
- Provide examples of preemptive but not violent counterterrorist policies.
- Suggest arguments for and against criminalization of terrorism.
- How and why have the tactics of terrorism changed over time?
- Is it possible to eradicate terrorism completely? Why or why not?

CHAPTER

8

A woman wears a face mask as she walks in Beijing, China, in 2012. Pollution has been a major problem in many Chinese cities. Can this country resolve the pollution problem alone?

Environmental Problems and International Politics

Nature provides a free lunch, but only if we control our appetites.
—WILLIAM RUCKELSHAUS

DO YOUR HAIRSPRAY AND REFRIGERATOR HAVE ANY-THING TO DO WITH INTERNATIONAL POLITICS? BELIEVE IT OR NOT, THEY DO. SCIENTIFIC RESEARCH HAS SHOWN that certain chemicals in air conditioning and cooling units, known as aerosol spray propellants, dangerously affect the atmosphere. With improving living standards and increased consumption in the second half of the past century, hundreds of millions of people began to use cooling and heating devices and aerosol sprays. Slowly, the protective ozone layer of the atmosphere began to deplete, and the sun's radiation increased, thus causing skin cancer and many other dangerous consequences. In 1985, twenty leading industrial countries signed the Vienna Convention for the Protection of the Ozone Layer to regulate some dangerous chemical substances used in sprays and coolants. In 1987, forty-three countries signed the Montreal Protocol to stop production of specific chemicals or reduce them substantially by 1999. Industries received incentives to phase out old chemicals and develop new, cleaner products.

Today's world faces an overwhelming range of environmental challenges. Coal and oil remain key sources of energy contributing to dangerous atmospheric pollution. These dangers are acknowledged not only by scientists but also by the vast majority of governments around the world. The international community launched new programs and initiatives. A whole new dimension of international relations has emerged.

The agreements on the ozone layer were successful because several powerful countries agreed to act together. Agreements for today's environmental problems appear to be more difficult to reach. Many proposed actions are vigorously contested. Finding and implementing global environmental policies may be one of the greatest challenges of our century.

In this chapter, we will discuss how environmental problems and the debates around them affect international relations and policies of countries, international organizations, and NGOs.

Learning Objectives

After reading this chapter, you should be able to:

▶ identify today's key environmental problems and major policies to address them;
▶ explain how environmental problems and the debates surrounding them affect international relations;
▶ understand similarities and differences among several approaches to environmental problems; and
▶ apply your knowledge to analyze individual decisions, state policies, and global developments on environmental problems.

What Do We Study?

Environmental problems and policies are a relatively new subject in international relations. For many years, the consensus was that sovereign governments had full authority to deal with the land, water, air, and natural resources of their countries as they pleased. Countries reached agreements on the environment mostly to get more profits from the extraction and sale of mineral resources. Even today, states usually do not ask for permission from others to drill for oil or to burn forests. During the last decades, however, the attitudes of international organizations and many states toward environmental problems began to change fundamentally.

Environmental politics includes the activities of political leaders, parties, NGOs, scientific laboratories, and others to influence environmental policy. These policies address at least two types of problems: *contamination* and *depletion*. **Contamination** is any by-product of human and nonhuman activities affecting the air, water, and soil. **Depletion** is the serious reduction of essential elements of the environment, such as loss of fresh water, clean air, or entire species. As we will see in this chapter, climate change is mainly caused by one form of contamination called greenhouse gases. At the same time, even ordinary garbage can be another source of contamination. Natural processes and natural disasters may cause contamination and depletion as well. (See Figure 8.1.)

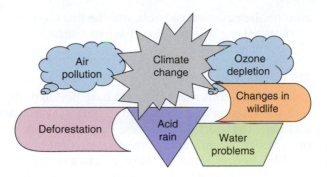

FIGURE 8-1 Main environmental problems.

Environmental Problems

ACID RAIN

Acid rain is caused by high contents of *sulfur dioxide, nitrogen oxides*, and other pollutants in the atmosphere. It can be caused by volcanic activities or biological processes in the soil, swamplands, and oceans. Gas emissions in major industrial and urban areas also contribute to the problem. Acid rain pollutes lakes and rivers, killing many small life forms, damaging buildings and historic monuments, corroding metal constructions, and affecting crops: A higher content of oxides in food is dangerous to our health.

Early negotiations regarding acid rain began in the 1970s between the United States and Canada. Other countries soon signed treaties leading to

---

CASE IN POINT > *A Disappearing Sea*

In the 1960s, the Soviet Union began an ambitious construction project. To irrigate cotton plantations and other agricultural projects, the government partially diverted two rivers that bring fresh water into the Aral Sea, a body of water shared by Kazakhstan and Uzbekistan, two former Soviet republics. The result was depletion, as the water supply to the sea declined significantly, and shallow streams quickly evaporated. By the 1980s, the fishing industry in the Aral Sea was in serious decline; today it is almost destroyed, being only 10 percent of its original size.

The vast area around the Aral Sea including river deltas is covered with salt and toxic substances as the result of receding water and pesticide runoff. Thousands of square miles of dry land have appeared, contributing to dust storms and damaging the environment of the region even further. The people living in the area experience a shortage of fresh water and suffer from respiratory and other health ailments.

CRITICAL THINKING

Who should be responsible for the disappearing sea? The territory of the Aral Sea is shared by Kazakhstan and Uzbekistan. Kazakhstan is attempting to save the northern part of the sea, already separated from the rest of the sea. Uzbekistan will not stop the irrigation of its cotton plantations and is more interested in searching for oil and gas on the exposed seabed. The depletion of the sea continues. What role could the international community play in this crisis, and what political and economic means can it use? Is this environmental battle worth fighting?

automobile emission controls and the filtration of factory emissions. Because of these efforts, the problem has diminished in urban areas but persists in many industrial regions.

AIR POLLUTION

Volcanic eruptions and forest fires have polluted the atmosphere for centuries. Industrialization and the growth of cities created new sources of pollution—including coal-burning factories, massive garbage dumps, animal wastes, and open sewer systems. Smog, an obvious form of air pollution, became unmistakable in Europe and the United States in the nineteenth century and later appeared in big cities all over the world. Not long ago, soot from burning was detected even in the ices of Greenland and high in the Himalayas (*Economist*, 2010).

In the twenty-first century, the largest sources of air pollution are power plants using coal: They produce almost a quarter of the pollution worldwide. The second largest cause is deforestation, or loss of forests due mostly to human activities. Transportation (including planes, ships, and cars), a third source, produces about 14 percent of emissions. (See Figure 8.2.)

Air pollution causes many respiratory problems, especially in urban and industrial areas. In 2010, massive forest fires in Russia produced heavy smog that lasted for weeks over large metropolitan areas; in Moscow alone millions suffered from heat and smog. Air pollution may also produce more serious long-term health consequences.

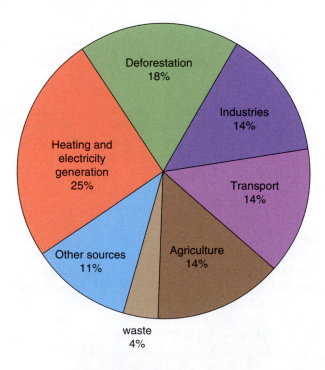

FIGURE 8-2 Sources of air pollution in the world. *Sources: EIA, World Resources Institute.*

OZONE DEPLETION

The ozone layer is a part of the atmosphere that protects humans and animals from the sun's deadly ultraviolet radiation. Scientists have registered a steady decline in the total amount of ozone in the earth's stratosphere—an estimated 3 percent per decade since the 1980s. This is called **ozone depletion**. Ozone "holes" have appeared over Antarctica and Australia. Research and coordinated international actions have significantly slowed the process by focusing on a major cause of ozone depletion, the chemicals that are produced naturally by marine organisms and are used in air conditioning and cooling units, as aerosol spray propellants, and for cleaning electronic equipment. No country can create a "shield" to guard its own atmosphere, which makes ozone depletion a global issue (Roan, 1989). As you will remember from the introduction to this chapter, the Vienna Convention and the Montreal Protocol limited production of certain chemicals contributing to ozone depletion.

CLIMATE CHANGE

Climate change is a significant and lasting alteration of global weather patterns (Gerrard, 2007). It most often means *global warming*—it means above all the rising temperatures, but also increasingly frequent abnormalities in climate conditions, such as frequent storms and devastating heat waves. It has been the most debated environmental problem of the past twenty years.

The earth's average temperatures have always fluctuated to some degree. The earth's history has included four major "ice ages" as well as warmer periods, when flora and fauna flourished. For the last thirty to forty years, however, temperatures have been steadily and rapidly rising, reaching the warmest level in

Government ministers in scuba gear held an underwater meeting of the Maldives' Cabinet in 2009. The purpose was to highlight the threat global warming poses to the lowest-lying nation on earth. Do such symbolic actions make any difference?

twelve thousand years. Glaciers have lost up to 10 percent of their mass over just the last decade, and ice that for centuries blocked northern seas is retreating. As the earth warmed in the last half of the twentieth century, one thousand seven hundred plant, animal, and insect species moved closer to the poles, at about four miles per decade (Parmesan and Yohe, 2003).

When did debate over global climate change begin? In 1896 a Swedish chemist and physicist, Svante Arrhenius, was one of the first to establish a connection between global temperatures and human activities. He calculated that air pollution from factories could double CO_2 levels in the atmosphere in three thousand years, warming the planet significantly. In 1938, Guy Callendar, a British engineer, also predicted a global rise in the world's temperature because of CO_2. Yet those projections were dismissed by the scientific community and essentially forgotten. Only by the start of the environmental movement in the early 1970s, the attitudes began to change. The first public hearings on global warming in the U.S. Congress took place in the mid-1970s. The policy makers, the scientific community, and ordinary people continue to debate climate change, its causes, and policies to address it.

What causes climate change? According to the widely accepted hypothesis, climate change is caused by the *greenhouse effect*, as the sun's radiation becomes trapped by the atmosphere, much as in a greenhouse. Instead of the glass ceiling of a greenhouse, however, this absorption results from pollutants in the atmosphere, including carbon dioxide (CO_2), methane (CH_4), and other so-called greenhouse gases. These gases affect an atmospheric layer that traps some of the sun's heat that warms the planet. Burning of fossil fuels caused the levels of CO_2 to increase by approximately 30 percent since the eighteenth century. At present, a few industrial countries emit more CO_2 than do all developing countries together. (See Figure 8.3.)

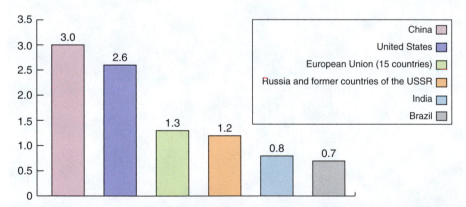

FIGURE 8-3 **Assessment of gas emissions in 2025 (projected, if no major changes take place); billions of tons or carbon equivalent.** Greenhouse emissions are the by-products of burning to produce energy, heat homes, cook food, and make machines work. In the 1850s, the burning of wood generated almost 90 percent of the world's energy. At the start of 20th century, coal produced 70 percent of the world's energy; in the 1950s, oil and coal each had about a 40 percent share. In the 21st century, oil still generates 40 percent of greenhouse gas emissions, followed by natural gas (25 percent), coal (25 percent), and nuclear reactions (about 5 percent). *Sources: EIA, World Resources Institute*

Skeptics argue that global warming is caused by a combination of factors, including not just human activities but also natural processes taking place in space, on the sun, in the atmosphere, and in the oceans (Jacques, 2009). Skeptics acknowledge the alarming signs of the major environmental changes but discount the scope and severity of the consequences. But even skeptics agree that changes in the ecosystem can have global effects. In the Little Ice Age of the fifteenth century, the earth's average temperature dropped by just 1°F (approximately 5°C). The Thames River in England froze, and Alpine glaciers touched villages as far south as modern Austria and Switzerland.

Although other factors may impact the temperature, the greenhouse hypothesis has received support from many authoritative scientists. What are the consequences of climate change? The most dramatic forecasts predict a 10°F (5.5°C) climb in global temperatures during this century and a 39-inch (1 m) rise in global ocean levels due to melting ice. Even more moderate forecasts project a rise of 3 inches (8 cm). Any scenario would have catastrophic consequences for low-level inhabited territories. New Orleans, London, Amsterdam, and many other cities would have to build storm-surge defenses to avoid flooding. Experts also project more frequent climatic abnormalities including heat waves, hurricanes and typhoons, as well as severe winters in some typically warm areas. Prominent politicians supported scientists' call for the urgency of addressing climate change.

DEFORESTATION

Deforestation is the massive removal or disappearance, thinning, changing, and elimination of trees, bushes, and other vegetation (Williams, 2006). Fires and flooding have caused deforestation throughout history, but these losses were replenished by natural growth. Humans too contributed to deforestation for centuries, but during the last fifty years the destruction of forests has increased significantly, as a consequence of agriculture and construction, including some of the earth's largest forested areas—in Brazil, Equatorial Africa, and Indonesia. In Brazil, the huge Amazonian forests have been shrinking rapidly since the 1950s because of cutting and burning. Over the past decade, according to the United Nations, an area the size of England was converted each year to other uses, mostly agriculture.

Deforestation contributes to greenhouse gas pollution, soil erosion, and **desertification**—the expansion of deserts into places previously available for agriculture. Desert expansion contributes to illness, hunger, and poverty (Johnson et al., 2006; Rechkemmer, 2004).

LOSS OF WILDLIFE

Deforestation, urban development, tourism, mining, and commercial hunting and fishing threaten animal life. Hunters kill rare species of monkeys, tigers, turtles, and rhinoceros for pleasure or souvenirs. Climate change also affects animals globally, and many of them cannot adapt to the changing natural conditions (Schellnhuber et al., 2006). In the last decade, more than sixteen thousand species were threatened with extinction. If current trends continue, between 15 percent and 37 percent of species will disappear by 2050 (Thomas et al., 2004).

LOSS OF CLEAN WATER

Chronic droughts, industrial and agricultural activity, and overpopulation can all lead to water shortages. Today approximately one billion people have no access to clean running water. Hundreds of millions drink unclean water directly from nearby rivers. The most troubling problems persist in India, China, and Mexico. Worldwide, agriculture is the main consumer of water, and the world's population is growing. By 2050, if trends continue, the demand for water for agriculture will double relative to 2000. Another problem comes from climate change. If the warming trend remains, more ice will melt. The disappearance of glaciers in the Tibet-Himalaya area may lead to substantial losses of river water for all neighboring countries. Because of changes in weather patterns, the Mediterranean region can expect a drop in precipitation of 25 to 30 percent by the middle of the century (N. Stern, 2007).

Water pollution is another major by-product of human activity, including sewage from towns and farms, discharges from power stations, and industrial silt. Rivers, lakes, and even seas are threatened by chemical waste. Especially dangerous are toxic heavy metals (such as mercury, lead, and cadmium) and oil spills. Unclean water contributes to serious illnesses in humans and kills living organisms in rivers, lakes, and oceans (Black, 2011; Pearce, 2007). China's rapid industrial development has dumped significant waste into major rivers, thus creating significant health hazards (Economy, 2010b).

Disasters and Accidents

Natural disasters, such as earthquakes or erupting volcanoes, can have devastating impacts. Yet man-made accidents, too, can have catastrophic environmental consequences. Natural disasters cannot be prevented, but their damaging consequences can be diminished through effective preparations, international assistance, and cooperation. For instance, the 2004 tsunami caused a significant loss of human life in many Asian countries because the affected countries had almost no early warning systems and lacked many adequate preparations. The governments could not rescue many victims. Medical help was often limited. Fresh water was absent, because saltwater and sewage infiltrated many water reservoirs (Helm, 2005). Although international forces (including the United States Navy) provided prompt and effective relief efforts, the local governments were often inefficient.

Accidents or human-created disasters are chemical leaks, radioactive leaks, and oil spills. In December 1983 in the Indian city of Bhopal, almost fifteen thousand people died and tens of thousands were injured by toxic gas leakage from a chemical refinery owned by a U.S. company, Union Carbide. At least one million people suffered serious health consequences. Union Carbide, which settled the case with the Indian government, continues to insist that the disaster was not an accident but a deliberate act of sabotage (D'Silva, 2006).

The most devastating leak of radioactive materials took place at the Chernobyl nuclear plant in the former Soviet Union in 1986. The largest series of oil spills in history took place during the Iraq's takeover of Kuwait in August 1990 and the Persian Gulf War in January 1991 between the United States and Iraq. Retreating Iraqi troops destroyed Kuwait's oil rigs, setting fires and

---

@ The International Program on the State of the Ocean (IPSO) is a consortium of scientists and other experts to identify problems and develop workable solutions to alter the degradation trajectory of the world's oceans. Find out more on the companion website.

@ The Historical Incidents database project funded by the National Oceanic and Atmospheric Administration's Environmental Services Data and Information Management Office includes the most significant oil-spill disasters since 1978. Find the link on the companion website.

Reporters wearing protective suits and masks visit the troubled Fukushima No. 1 nuclear power plant of the Tokyo Electric Power Co. in Okuma, Fukushima Prefecture, in 2012. Even wealthy Japan needed international help to deal with the consequences of the tsunami.

creating giant oil lakes. Between six and eight million barrels of oil spilled into the Persian Gulf. The biggest marine oil spill in history took place in the Gulf of Mexico in 2010, when an explosion in an oil platform operated by British Petroleum took the lives of eleven workers. From three to five million barrels of oil went into the water, causing serious damage to wildlife and contaminating the U.S. coastline. The economic impact was estimated at between $3 billion and $12 billion.

> ▶ What lesson did the 1985 Vienna Convention and the 1987 Montreal Protocol provide for today's governments and international organizations?
> ▶ Which environmental problem does the Aral Sea case illustrate?
> ▶ When and where did the largest series of oil spills in history take place?

CHECK YOUR KNOWLEDGE

Environmental Policies Today

Efforts to protect the environment include regulations and restrictions, green investment, and more comprehensive policies. Financial regulations, taxation, economic incentives, and legal directives all play a role.

RESTRICTION AND REGULATION

In 1900 the Lacey Act banned trade in wildlife, fish, and plants that have been illegally obtained, transported, or sold. This act is effective to this day, and the last amendment to it in 2008 prohibited import of illegal timber to the United States. Other policies in many countries regulate legal business activities that may be environmentally harmful. To reduce deforestation, for example, nearly 40 percent of the Amazon River basin is legally protected, including approximately 25 percent in private hands. Owners must keep 80 percent of their land forested. These are examples of **conservation**—regulatory policies to protect and preserve natural resources, plant and animal species, and their habitat. After the 1970s, a growing number of countries including the United States, Canada, Australia, Sweden, and many others adopted legal measures to protect hundreds of species on their territories. In 1986 the International Whaling Commission banned commercial whaling.

Taxation and other financial incentives for environmental protection have gained recognition as well (Nordhaus, 2008). An example is *emissions trading* to limit pollution. Here companies and countries receive "credits," giving them the right to emit a pollutant, but only up to a limit. Those who cannot cut pollution that far are required to buy additional credits from others that pollute less. According to the UN Climate Change Secretariat, emissions trading could generate up to $100 billion per year for developing countries to invest in their economies if they reduce their pollution (Fusaro and James, 2006). (See Figure 8.4.)

The United Nations took up a major initiative to globalize policies on climate change. In June 1992 the international meeting in Rio de Janeiro, commonly known as the Earth Summit, produced the UN Framework Convention on Climate Change (UNFCCC). The goal of this treaty was to stabilize greenhouse gas concentrations in the atmosphere. Since then, UN conferences on climate change have met periodically. A milestone was the conference in Kyoto, Japan, in 1997, when the participants signed the **Kyoto Protocol** to the UNFCCC. Most industrial countries agreed to reduce greenhouse gas emissions by an average of 6 to 8 percent below 1990 levels from 2008 through 2012. Later governments agreed to extend the Protocol to 2020.

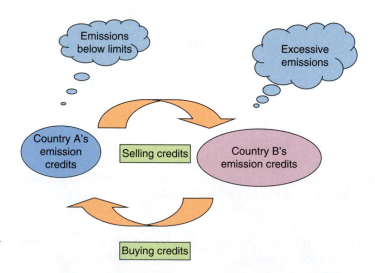

FIGURE 8-4 Emissions trading: Countries that limit their emissions can receive financial rewards; Countries that fell short of cutting their emissions pay a penalty.

Some countries, small and big, do not participate in the Kyoto Protocol. Some are ready to cut their emissions but would not participate in emission trading. Canadian officials argued it was too expensive for Canada to contribute $7 billion per year—the price of carbon credits for this country—at a time of economic recession (van Loon, 2011). The U.S. Congress during the Clinton, Bush, and Obama administrations did not ratify the Kyoto Protocol, and China refused as well. A major objection was that the required emission cuts would hurt these countries' economic situation. Without the participation of the world's biggest polluters, the UN effort was incomplete.

GREEN INVESTMENTS

Green investments are business ventures in which companies are involved in activities reducing contamination and depletion. Typically, green investments require governmental policies to stimulate private business. In most cases, these are investments in environmentally friendly technologies, business methods, and agricultural practices. Green investments go beyond simple restrictions. Many countries, for example, invest in reforestation to make up for lost trees and other vegetation. In China and Costa Rica, policies are being set for agriculture: The fewer trees farmers cut, the more trees farmers plant, the more money they get in form of subsidies. In the same way, **geo-engineering** aims at technological solutions of environmental problems (Victor et al., 2009). One strategy for reducing the existing accumulation of greenhouse gases involves releasing particles into the air to reflect more sunlight back into space. Another strategy includes collection and storage of carbon gases from coal plants. Germany, for example, draws new carbon capture and storage laws

Wind-powered electricity generators have become common in many countries. In Denmark, 26 percent of the electricity comes from wind-powered generators. In Germany, the figure is 9 percent. In the United States, according to the Department of Energy, it is only 3 percent. Why does the United States lag behind?

(CCS) to allow companies to store CO_2 indefinitely in underground storage facilities. Regions that host such facilities would receive financial compensation (German Energy Blog, 2012).

Unlike coal or oil, **renewable energy** is replaced naturally as fast as it is consumed (Kemp, 2006). It draws on such alternative sources as wind, the sun, tides, and geothermal power—the natural heat within the earth. Wind-powered electricity generators, solar thermal plants, and photovoltaic power stations are examples of new technologies producing renewable energy. Between 2005 and 2015, British Petroleum pledged to invest up to $8 billion in "renewables." General Electric's growth strategy, called *ecomagination*, commits the company to using wind power, diesel-electric hybrid locomotives, new efficient aircraft engines and appliances, and advanced water-treatment systems. Another area of investment is *biofuels*, made from plants, vegetables, or celluloid (Soetaert and Vandamme, 2009). Brazil has reduced its dependence on oil and gas by producing biofuels from sugarcane. The Chinese government makes significant investments in wind technology and electric cars. India's recently created National Solar Mission is working to increase dramatically the use of the sun's energy. The government is providing up to 90 percent support for setting up solar power plants. One of the specific goals is to install twenty million solar lights around the country.

The costs associated with this "green revolution" are still considered to be prohibitively high for many countries, especially poor ones. The International Energy Agency estimated that to reduce global oil consumption by a quarter and cut global greenhouse gas emissions in half by 2050, the world would need to invest $50 billion to $100 billion each year in clean-energy technologies, compared to about $10 billion a year spent recently (Levi et al., 2010). Even within the European community only the most prosperous countries, such as Germany and the Netherlands, can afford to spend significant funds on renewables. Newer members of the community—Bulgaria, Rumania, Poland, Latvia, Estonia, and Lithuania—have asked for assistance.

Usually the poorer the country is, the less inclined it is to invest in geo-engineering and renewables. That places increasing pressure on wealthy countries to provide financial support through loans or grants (Esty and Winston, 2006). The **Global Environment Facility (GEF)**, created in 1991, provides funds for projects in six areas: climate change, biodiversity, pollution in international waters, land degradation, ozone depletion, and persistent *organic pollution*—such natural contaminants as fish and animal waste (French, 1994). From the start, the GEF has supported almost two thousand environmental initiatives in countries that otherwise would not have had the financial resources. About 20 percent of the funding is distributed through nongovernmental organizations.

Without coordinated international efforts, the green revolution would be ineffective. Yet China, Japan, and the United States for many years refused the leadership role in environmental policies, citing the threat of economic slowdown. The European Union remains the most active actor in international environmental politics (see next section).

India has its own Ministry of New and Renewable Energy. Find the link on the companion website. What are the ministry's main accomplishments?

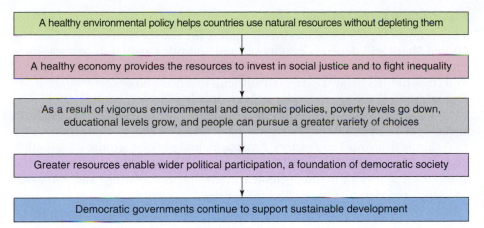

A healthy environmental policy helps countries use natural resources without depleting them

↓

A healthy economy provides the resources to invest in social justice and to fight inequality

↓

As a result of vigorous environmental and economic policies, poverty levels go down, educational levels grow, and people can pursue a greater variety of choices

↓

Greater resources enable wider political participation, a foundation of democratic society

↓

Democratic governments continue to support sustainable development

FIGURE 8-5 Main conclusions of the *Our Common Future* report.

COMPREHENSIVE POLICIES

A more comprehensive policy is **sustainable development** that meets the needs of the present without sacrificing the ability of future generations to meet their needs. This policy is about stimulating economic growth while at the same time protecting the environment and natural resources (Victor, 2006; P. Rogers et al., 2007). The idea of sustainable development emerged partly in response to a 1987 report, *Our Common Future.* Prepared by the UN-sponsored World Commission on Environment and Development, it argued that helping local economies, protecting natural resources, and ensuring social justice for all people are not contradictory but rather complementary goals. (See Figure 8.5.)

The European Union is the world's leader in designing and implementing comprehensive environmental policies. Starting in the 1970s, many environmentalist groups began to have a significant impact on Europe's political life. From the 1990s, practically all discussions of the EU's economic development focused on the environment and sustainable development.

In 2008, the EU Climate Change program established the 20-20-20 targets: 20 percent of the energy consumed in Europe must come from renewable sources, and countries must reduce gas emissions by up to 20 percent by 2020. To accomplish these ambitious goals, the EU will have to impose tougher pollution restrictions, encourage low-emission vehicles, expand emissions trading, and invest in public transportation and low-energy construction. The main problem is a lack of resources to meet these targets, especially after the 2008 through 2011 financial crisis and economic slowdown. Skeptics also argue that, even if the 20-20-20 targets are met, their impact on climate change will be insignificant.

Many unresolved issues remain. It is unclear whether key developing countries—Brazil, India, and China—will cooperate with UNFCCC initiatives. It is also unclear how to combine comprehensive, global environmental policies with many countries' desire for financial security, economic growth, and guaranteed employment.

POLICY IMPLEMENTATION

Environmental policies often run up against the realities of everyday life. The United States still depends heavily on coal and oil; a switch to renewables is impossible without a long transitional period and huge investments. Federal and trade deficits make it extremely difficult to pay for more costly alternatives to coal and oil. Sweden, despite a three-decade-long ban on nuclear plants, cannot close its nuclear facilities because there are no realistic and environmentally friendly replacements. A growing demand for energy forces the country to continue using nuclear reactors. Environmental policies require imagination and innovation, but there are limits. People continue to buy cars that run on gasoline—and they are becoming more efficient and less polluting, and, compared to hybrid and electric cars, still less expensive.

CHECK YOUR KNOWLEDGE

▶ Define renewable energy. If the benefits of renewable sources of energy are obvious, why haven't all countries switched to renewables?

▶ What is sustainable development? Why do the 20-20-20 EU targets appear as an example of sustainable development?

How Do We Study It?

Realism

States traditionally struggled for natural resources and considered nature as an asset to conquer and exploit. Experts and politicians trained in realpolitik acknowledged the environmental issues but still treated them as marginal. In their view, states maintain **environmental sovereignty**—the right to use and protect their environment and natural resources. At the core of environmental sovereignty is a country's pursuit of its interests, in light of domestic politics. After the 1970s, however, realists began to connect the problems of depletion and contamination to national interests and security threats. It became clear that uncontrolled use of national resources and inattention to environmental problems could undermine international stability.

ACCIDENTS, DISASTERS, AND SECURITY

Natural and human-created disasters are serious events affecting security and military policies, especially if they cause massive casualties and significant environmental damage. In turn, governments now accept a greater responsibility than ever for dealing with the consequences. After the 2004 tsunami in Asia and the earthquake in Haiti in January 2010, several countries committed their military forces to the rescue operations, and U.S. naval vessels delivered humanitarian assistance. However, any deployment of foreign troops in another country, regardless of their mission, can become a source of security concerns, and international tensions can easily arise.

Environmental disasters may quickly worsen existing social problems, especially in poor countries like Haiti, triggering political violence and instability.

A titanium capsule with the Russian flag, planted on the Arctic Ocean seabed under the North Pole in 2007. Two Russian mini-submarines descended to the ocean floor to claim much of the Arctic's oil-and-mineral wealth. Which countries were most anxiously observing Russia's geopolitical move?

(We discuss similar cases in the next chapter). Conversely, wars and political turmoil may have catastrophic consequences for the environment, as the Gulf War in 1991 demonstrated. Terrorist groups seeking to cause significant damage may focus on nuclear reactors, chemical plants, hydroelectric stations, or dams (Levi, 2009). Their protection thus becomes part of a government's environmental security policies.

Depletion of natural resources is a potential cause of conflict. Realists argue that the constantly increasing demands for natural resources, clean water, and agricultural lands could become a major source of local and regional conflicts. Scarcity of natural resources is often a security issue (Le Billon, 2006). Israel, for example, controls most freshwater reservoirs, including underground aquifers, in the Gaza and the West Bank. While Palestinians demand full access, Israel considers water a strategic asset and uses it to put pressure on the other side. In the 1980s, Turkey began to construct hydroelectric dams using water from the Euphrates River to rotate turbines to produce electricity. These dams reduced the water flow in Syria, Iran, and Iraq, which was protested (Homer-Dixon, 1991). More recently, China's similar projects in Tibet caused serious concerns in India and other neighboring countries (Economy, 2010b).

GLOBAL COMMONS

The **global commons** includes areas not under any one country's sovereign control, such as the open ocean, the seabed, the atmosphere, the outer space, and Antarctica. The idea of the global commons has found global support.

However, commons have also emerged as potential sites of conflict around the world (Nonini, 2007). Without international restrictions, private companies or predator states could endanger the environment in the global commons and deplete its resources. And without international agreements, disputes over environmental and other policies in the global commons are likely (Grover, 2006). One of such areas is the Arctic: The polar seas began to thaw, thus allowing countries to navigate in the area during summer and explore natural resources there (Zellen, 2009; Borgerson, 2008). International agreements have long protected global commons from hostile takeovers and depletion. This policy has become a strategic priority for the United States and other developed democratic states.

The 1959 Antarctic Treaty prohibits any economic exploration and military operations, including nuclear tests, on the sixth continent. No country may claim a territory in Antarctica. Additional agreements regulate research, economic, and military activities on the continent. For example, the 1991 Madrid accord bans coal mining and oil exploration in Antarctica for fifty years. Some business activities such as tourism are allowed, so long as they are regulated and the profits are shared. In the realist view, denying privileged access to Antarctica benefits international security because it maintains the existing balance of power.

CHECK YOUR KNOWLEDGE

▶ What is environmental sovereignty? Give an example.
▶ What are global commons? Give examples.

In sum, supporters of realism acknowledge the importance of environmental policies and international environmental cooperation. At the same time, realism continues to view environmental issues in the context of security interests and the balance of power.

Liberalism

Liberal models treat environmental issues as requiring a sustained and coordinated international effort. Unlike realism, liberal internationalism treats environmental policies as a central feature of modern-day international relations. As you will remember from earlier chapters, many liberals claim that the destructive nature of contemporary wars should make them obsolete as a policy option. Similarly, the depth and scope of today's environmental problems should change the traditional, power-driven approach to international politics. Liberals strongly believe in environmental agreements, institutions, and the involvement of nongovernment organizations (Harris, 2004).

INTERNATIONAL TREATIES AND ORGANIZATIONS

An early wave of environmental treaties came in the 1970s. They were mostly regional, signed by countries with shared concerns about contamination, conservation, and the protection of endangered species. The Amazon Cooperation

Treaty of 1978 provided guidelines to eight Latin American countries for water use, transportation, environmental research, tourism, and commercial developments in the Amazon region. In Western Europe, with the help of newly formed green parties, Environmental Action Programs (EAP) were launched. Governments allocated funds for massive cleaning efforts in rivers and lakes. In one successful international action, countries banned chloro-fluorocarbons (CFCs) in aerosol spray cans and refrigerators in response to ozone depletion.

From the very start, the most ambitious goal of environmental advocates was to develop a global policy framework under the UN umbrella. In 1973, the United Nations Environment Programme (UNEP) was founded, with its head-quarters in Nairobi, Kenya. Its activities covered protection of the atmosphere and global ecosystems, the promotion of environmental science and educa-tion, and an early warning and emergency response system in cases of environ-mental disasters. UNEP has developed guidelines and treaties on international trade in harmful chemicals, cross-border air pollution, and contamination of international waterways (UNEP, 2010). In 1988, the United Nations funded the Intergovernmental Panel on Climate Change (IPCC) to evaluate the most recent science and human activities related to climate change. During the 1990s, the agenda of international environmental politics broadened. Now it included global environmental agreements. We have already discussed the 1992 UN Conference that created the UNFCCC. For the first time, a true global environmental institution was formed, with 172 countries participating. Ten years later, the Earth Summit of 2002—the World Summit on Sustainable Development—took place in South Africa.

The signing of the Kyoto Protocol in 1997 was a shining moment for global environmental politics (McGovern, 2006). More than 190 countries later ratified this agreement and pledged to reduce their emissions of carbon dioxide and five other greenhouse gases. Many countries considered emissions trading. The next decade, however, was largely disappointing for environmentalists and their sup-porters. Powerful forces in the United States, China, Canada, and other countries began to view emerging environmental policies as a threat to their countries' economic interests. Skeptics attacked the environmental movement, warning that climate control would end in a global bureaucratic regime and huge expen-ditures without effect (Lomborg, 2010).

Despite the global financial crisis and recession of the past decade, global environmental politics has not waned—just the contrary. In April 2009 the leaders of the United States, China, the European Union, India, Russia, and twelve other major economic powers, as well as the United Nations and Denmark, created the Major Economies Forum on Energy and Climate (MEF). The group made a strong effort to boost the UNFCCC negotiations, culminat-ing in a December 2009 conference in Copenhagen. The Copenhagen Accord set several important goals. First, the countries pledged to keep global tem-peratures from increasing to more than 2°C (3.6°F) above preindustrial levels. Next, they promised to allocate up to $100 billion a year by 2020 to help developing countries deal with climate change. They also promised *transparency*: assured methods so that others could verify whether they are cutting emissions.

Finally, the accord required that all but the poorest countries produce specific plans for curbing emissions (Levi, 2010a).

The 2010 Cancun Agreement by 193 countries confirmed the key goals established by the Copenhagen Accord. To achieve those goals, industrialized countries would have to cut their emissions between 25 and 40 percent compared with 1990 levels by 2020. These cuts would be voluntary and subject to international inspection. A new Green Climate Fund under UN auspices was established, to manage billions of dollars in support of climate action (Levi, 2010b). The major problem remains: Facing financial and economic difficulties of the past several years, countries remained reluctant or unable to cut their emissions when significantly faced with domestic political and economic pressures.

You can access descriptions of the Kyoto Protocol, the Copenhagen and Cancun Agreements, and assessments of their impact on policies and the environment on the companion website.

NONGOVERNMENT ORGANIZATIONS

Environmental NGOs first emerged to advocate environmental policies in areas neglected by the public or the government. Some, like Greenpeace, choose provocative and attention-grabbing strategies (see the concluding case). Others, like the Sierra Club and The National Audubon Society, focus on education. The Centre for Science and Environment (CSE) is named after a successful media campaign against air pollution in large Indian cities. Partly because of this group's pressure, the government decided to use compressed natural gas as the main fuel in the capital city's buses and taxis. Still other NGOs focus on funding. The GEF, for one, provides grants to developing countries for projects that benefit the global environment and promote sustainable developments in local communities. The GEF helps countries address such problems as biodiversity, greenhouse gas emissions, pollution in international waters, land degradation, the ozone layer, and persistent organic pollutants.

Visit the companion website to learn more about nongovernment environmental organizations that have appeared during the last decade.

NGOs, according to liberal theories, advance democratic governance and represent a wide range of interests and opinions not represented in large bureaucratic structures. They also monitor environmental policies and reveal problems that governments often overlook or ignore. NGOs enhance awareness about environment problems, educate and influence the public, and launch direct actions. At the same time, some environmental NGOs developed a controversial reputation. See the concluding case of "Greenpeace" at the end of this chapter.

PUBLIC AWARENESS

In a democratic society, public opinion should affect policy-making, and education can shape public opinion. The more people know and care about the environment, the more supportive they are of environmental policies. The liberal view thus favors sustained educational efforts and public discussions about the environment.

Global public opinion despite fluctuations is generally warming up to environmental issues. In a 2009 Pew global survey, majorities in twenty-three of twenty-five surveyed countries agreed that protecting the environment should

The mall of the Emirates in Dubai, UAE, includes an artificial mini ski resort and is a shopping and recreational paradise. Critics admit that this mall consumes too much energy to entertain just a few consumers. How should governments of countries labeled "environmental offenders" address the criticism?

be given priority, even at the cost of slower economic growth and job losses. Many were willing to pay higher prices to address climate change—54 percent of those surveyed in Canada, 41 percent in the United States, and 88 percent in China (Pew, 2009). In the United States, according to Gallup surveys, in 2012, 55 percent of Americans worried a great deal or a fair amount about global warming; 45 percent worried "only a little" or "not at all" (Gallup, 2012). Specific economic circumstances, however, affect public opinion. During an economic slowdown, most Americans prioritized economic growth (54 percent) over environmental protection (36 percent; J. Jones, 2011).

DEBATE > "ENVIRONMENTAL OFFENDERS"

The World Wildlife Fund (WWF) assesses consumption habits in different countries and publishes a list of "environmental offenders." The residents of the United Arab Emirates (UAE) top the list. Each person in the UAE needs 12 hectares (30 acres) of biologically productive land and sea to sustain life—area needed for the production of vegetables, fish, fruit, or rice and to absorb waste. The United States was the second-worst "offender," with a requirement of 9.6 hectares. The average global requirement, according to the WWF, is 2.2 hectares per person, but the available supply is only 1.8 hectares.

WHAT'S YOUR VIEW?

What is the main point of such a list, and how effective is the publication of the list? If you reduce your personal consumption habits, will it affect the environment in any measurable way? Why or why not?

 Go online to learn more about the World Wildlife Fund.

CHECK YOUR KNOWLEDGE

▶ What are the key differences between realist and liberal views of environmental policies?
▶ The Kyoto Protocol obliged their participants to do what?
▶ In which ways would public awareness affect environmental polices of governments?

Constructivism

Why did international environmental politics emerge only in the last decades of the twentieth century and not earlier? Policies stem from social and political debates and reflect people's changing values and identities and new awareness of the environment.

Mastery values encourage individuals to exercise control over nature and exploit its resources. **Harmony values** encourage a different attitude—one of preservation and care (Smith and Schwartz 1997). In the constructivist view, both harmony and mastery values affect the environmental policies of different countries and in different periods.

For centuries, mastery values dominated politics. They were behind policies of rapid industrialization and the extraction of natural resources in the twentieth century. Market competition and mass consumption reinforced mastery values in democratic societies, but these values influenced Communist countries as well. Harmony values, in contrast, encourage conservation and environmental protection. They are attached to concerns for the common good inherent in liberal democracy.

International environmental policies are most effective when they adjust to local political, social, and cultural contexts and address local concerns. Environmentalism is strong in the Canadian province of Quebec, which generates eco-friendly hydroelectricity that it sells it to other provinces and the United States. Elsewhere, environmental policies often run into local resistance. In Indonesia, many African countries, and Brazil, peasants oppose attempts to ban *slash-and-burn* farming—a method of farming that contributes to deforestation and air pollution—because they desperately need new farmlands. To stop slashing and burning, the structure of the local economies must change. New jobs for local farmers are needed, which requires significant investment. Other countries can help if they face no serious economic problems themselves. But during a recession, investments decrease.

Strong resistance to environmental policies in the United States is a more complicated case, but it too points to the connections among politics, values, and economic interests. Power companies and carmakers are not thrilled about policies limiting gas emissions because they may limit profits. The Bush and the Obama administrations allowed the use of new technologies like hydraulic fracturing. "Fracking" may be questionable from the environmental point of view, but it could make the United States self-sufficient in terms of oil and gas in a few years. Environmental policies are even more difficult to implement in countries exporting oil, gas, and coal. Saudi Arabia, Russia, and other oil and

@ Visit the companion website to learn more about intellectual movements in philosophy, art, sociology, and science that reflect harmony and mastery values: utilitarianism, progressivism, romanticism, and others.

gas producers are genuinely interested in having other states dependent on these energy sources. A reduction in oil consumption due to environmental policies will mean a loss of profit.

Constructivism argues that changing the structure of economic incentives should go hand in hand with enhancing environmental education and awareness. However, changing values could be a more complicated task than introducing new taxes or restructuring the Latin American agriculture.

Alternative and Critical Views

For conflict theories, economic discrimination is embedded in today's international environmental politics. **Environmental discrimination** refers to actions and policies by wealthy countries of the global North that sustain the contamination and depletion of the environment of the global South. Facing tough environmental policies at home, corporations continuously moved their industrial facilities to less-developed countries and shipped toxic waste there for inexpensive recycling (Grossman, 2007). Most climate control efforts contribute to global inequality. Rich countries can afford to slow production, cut emissions, and adopt tough conservation measures. However, poor countries would suffer from tough new regulations, which would depress their economies. These countries were not given a chance to develop in the past because of colonialism. Environmental policies imposed by the North would have a similar effect.

Critics of imperialism and colonialism argue that, for centuries, powerful Western nations ignored environmental policies while depleting the natural resources of the rest of the world. Today, the disparity in consumption of energy between the rich North and the poor South is staggering. The United States has less that 5 percent of the global population, but it consumes almost 25 percent of the world's energy. On average, U.S. residents consume six to ten times as much energy as do people in rapidly developing countries like India and China—and twenty times as much as people in poor states like Bangladesh.

What would be a solution? There should be global *environmental justice* based on the equal protection from environmental problems and a fair distribution of environmental benefits (Walker, 2009). The main investment in global environmental policies should come from the North (Roberts and Parks, 2006). Because wealthy countries remain the main consumers of energy and the chief global polluters, they should cut their emissions first. This should allow less-developed states to increase energy consumption and develop their economies. Some scholars argue that such policies will be impossible to implement unless major structural changes take place. Today's environmental problems, they maintain, have their root in the inability of the capitalist system to address the accelerating threat to life on the planet (Magdoff and Foster, 2011).

▶ Compare mastery and harmony values. Can it be a compromise between these two sets of values?

▶ What is slash-and-burn farming? Could you suggest an alternative to it?

CHECK YOUR KNOWLEDGE

How Do We Apply It?

The Individual Context

In the United States, former senator and vice-president Albert Gore received the Nobel Peace Prize for his global environmental advocacy. Yet the president of the Czech Republic, Vaclav Klaus, openly criticized "global warming hysteria." What makes political leaders strong defenders or entrenched skeptics of environmental policies?

ENVIRONMENTALISM AND SKEPTICISM

Views of the environment can be understood as a continuum. (See Figure 8.6.) On the one side of this continuum is **environmentalism,** the belief in the necessity of urgent and comprehensive actions to protect the environment. Environmentalists support conservation of natural resources, push for measures against contamination, and endorse sustainable development. They believe that many environmental problems are urgent, and the earth's natural resources are limited (Cullen, 2010). Commercial activities harmful to the environment should be regulated or banned. Environmentalism is associated with harmony values and a belief in growth through preservation. Environmentalism is also rooted in *progressivism,* or the belief in deliberate social action for the sake of the common good. This social action must be ecologically sound. Environmentalists also insist that the world should do significantly more to protect the environment (Davis, 2007).

At the other end of the continuum is **environmental skepticism.** Skeptics are likely to adopt mastery values and to believe that environmental policies require a more cautious, balanced approach (Lomborg, 2004; 2007). They support conservation on a smaller scale and believe in the priority of business and market forces over government regulations (Walley and Whitehead, 1994). Skeptics maintain that other serious problems including genocide, diseases, and hunger should receive more urgent care than the environment.

Political leaders' education, family experiences, and other circumstances contribute to their choices. Al Gore's concern for nature was enhanced by his experience as a student, when one of his professors made him aware of rising global temperatures, and as a father, when his son was hit by a car and recovered

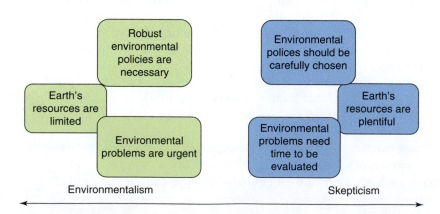

FIGURE 8-6 The spectrum of attitudes: Environmentalism and environmental skepticism.

Former German Foreign Minister Joschka Fischer presents his new book in Berlin, Germany, in 2011. He was the leader of the Alliance '90/The Greens when this movement grew into an even more powerful political force in Europe.

CASE IN POINT > *Alarming and Skeptical Voices*

Contemporary environmental discussions resemble the longtime debate between *cornucopians* (a reference to the "cornucopia," or horn of plenty), who believed that natural resources are practically limitless, and neo-Malthusians, the followers of the nineteenth-century British scholar Thomas Robert Malthus (1766–1834), who predicted that the inevitable depletion of natural resources would generate conflicts (Homer-Dixon, 1991).

James Lovelock, a British environmental scientist, drew wide attention for his *Gaia hypothesis*, named after a Greek goddess. Every grain of sand, drop of water, or breath of air is a particle in this immense, interdependent structure—a structure whose disturbance could lead to disaster. In fact, Lovelock believes that if nothing is done during the next fifty years, global warming will make most of the planet uninhabitable, and civilization will perish. Lovelock proposes, among other things, urgently switching to nuclear energy and building giant pipes to transfer carbon dioxide from the atmosphere to the ocean.

Bjørn Lomborg, a Danish political scientist, calls himself a "skeptical environmentalist." In *Cool It* (2007), he admits that the environment is under serious stress, but more research and thinking are needed before launching multibillion-dollar projects. If the European Union adopts all the policies it wants to control noxious emissions, he says, it would cost taxpayers $250 billion, but the results would be negligible (Lomborg, 2010). His organization, the Copenhagen Consensus Center, supports cost-efficient environmental policies.

CRITICAL THINKING

This debate, like the debate between the neo-Malthusians and the cornucopians, appeals to both emotions and common sense, but it is not always based on solid research. Academics and mainstream environment experts hesitate to support Lovelock's doomsday scenarios, and they question Lomborg's expertise. Still, the publications of both authors continue to attract great public attention. Why do you think this is happening? Where do you personally stand in this debate?

only after a coma. Environmentalism often finds reinforcement in religious values. *Evangelical environmentalism* treats environmental problems and climate change in particular as a serious moral issue. Many members of all religions believe people have a spiritual duty to protect the environment (Jenkins, 2008).

Scientists and politicians often disagree about the gravity of environmental problems. They also argue about which policies should be launched to deal with these problems. However, it is incorrect to portray environmental debates as a battle between government bureaucrats—old, conservative, and uneducated "dinosaurs" eager to ignore environmental problems—and young, progressive, and talented activists. In fact, over the past twenty years, there has been a significant change in environmental attitudes: State leaders are increasingly susceptible to the arguments and demands of environmental groups. Individual leaders may change their views, too. Large and small countries alike are more likely to conduct robust environmental policies because of a major shift today from mastery to harmony values among ordinary people and the governing elites. Education has sparked awareness and brought changes in the ways both regular people and politicians see the environment. The political climate is warming toward environmental issues even faster than the global temperature is rising.

A SENSE OF MISSION AND LEADERSHIP

The success of international environmentalism testifies to the role of individual scientists, activists, and political leaders. When Rachel Carson published *Silent Spring* in 1962, warning about the use of pesticides in agriculture, the book became an immediate sensation, affecting the views of millions. Some, like the Canadian ecologist Bill Darnell, came to environmentalism because of their opposition to nuclear war and nuclear testing. Darnell came up with a powerful combination of words, *green* and *peace*, and cofounded one of the most famous environmental organizations, Greenpeace.

Many student radicals of the 1960s saw environmental protection as society's next frontier, and many of them later became prominent politicians. Brice Lalonde, leader of the French National Union of Students, established Friends of the Earth. Daniel Cohn-Bendit and Joschka Fischer, prominent European politicians and legislators, helped in 1981 to write the political agenda for the Green Party in Germany. In the United States, President Jimmy Carter became a convinced environmentalist because of his experience as an engineer on a nuclear submarine and a farmer in Georgia. In May 1977, he proposed a host of environment policies, ranging from conservation to new energy research. To set an example, Carter installed solar panels on the roof of the White House to heat some of its water boilers. At the dedication ceremony in 1979, he predicted that these panels would supply "cheap, efficient energy" twenty years later (Biello, 2010).

In Europe, environmental policies have had support from conservative and liberal political leaders; in the United States, personal views have mattered more. When Ronald Reagan came to power, many of Carter's environmental programs were discontinued. The solar panels on the White House were dismantled in 1986 and sold at auction. After Al Gore became vice-president in the Clinton administration in the 1990s, he did much to revive a federal environmental agenda. When George W. Bush was in the office, he was unenthusiastic about the Kyoto Protocol and treated the UNFCCC with strong reservations. President Obama attempted to return to a more active environmental agenda after 2009 but later redirected his priorities due to the country's economic problems (Tumulty, 2011).

The State Context

Why do political leaders in Germany and Sweden enact proactive environmental policies, regardless of the political party in office? Why do China and the United States frequently appear not to do enough? Domestic politics plays a strong role, including political institutions and political behavior (Economy, 2010b; Kamieniecki and Kraft, 2007).

NATIONAL PURPOSE AND PARTISAN POLITICS

Sometimes countries reduce their sovereignty in exchange for financial benefits. They agree, for example, on **debt-for-nature swaps.** These are international deals allowing a financially struggling state to designate an area for environmental conservation in exchange for, say, a reduction in its foreign debt. The World Wide Fund for Nature pioneered the idea of building national parks in exchange for financial incentives. In Guatemala, the $24-million debt-for-nature swap should protect the tropical forest for many years. Guatemala's debt to the United States was invested in conservation efforts (ENS, 2006).

The environment's place in a country's priorities depends on how that country sees its *national purpose*. For three decades, starting in the late 1940s, China defined its national purpose in terms of industrial development and rapid economic growth. Chinese Communists believed the environment must be put into the service of the revolution. Forests had to be felled, mountains leveled, and rivers reversed in their courses (Shapiro, 2001). As a result, the Chinese government did not consider depletion or air and water pollution to be urgent problems. More recently, the Chinese Communist Party changed its environmental strategies. It initiated a plan to become 20 percent more energy efficient by 2010 and continue beyond that target (Dutta, 2005). To date, the results of this policy are inconclusive.

The United States has gone through policy cycles, depending on national purpose and priorities. This "seesaw" environmental history can be explained not only by individual presidents but also by the ideological polarization between the two major political parties—especially after the 1980s. The Republicans have defined national purpose primarily in terms of economic liberalism and rejected most federal intervention. They argue that strict environmental regulations could weaken American businesses and make the United States less competitive with other countries (McGovern, 2006). In contrast, the Democrats see national purpose in terms of economic regulation and robust environmental policies. They argue that green policies will create jobs and help to avoid serious future problems. There is no bipartisan agreement on environmental policies in Washington, and none is likely to emerge any time soon. At the same time, as we have mentioned, both Bush and Obama

Police block a large crowd at the scene of environmental protests in the town of Haimen, China, in 2011. Citizens protested against a coal-fired power plant they claimed was a health hazard.

administrations agreed to support new methods of drilling for oils and gas. Such methods promise energy self-sufficiency.

Partisan divides on environmental issues are associated with ideology and politics. In democratic societies, parties associated with social-democratic programs tend to support environmentalism to a greater extent than conservative groups. In many European countries, Green Parties have gained strength and won seats in legislatures. Meanwhile parties supporting industrial interests are usually skeptical about environmentalism. Agricultural parties maintain a mixed position: They support environmental protection but oppose costly regulations. The balance in partisan politics can shift considerably, depending on a country's economic situation: With high unemployment and a stagnant economy, environmental concerns are often put aside. Economic prosperity allows more people to support dynamic environmental policies.

THE DEMOCRATIC CONTEXT

Democratic context can be favorable or unfavorable to environmental policies. Already in the 1970s, when the international environmental movement emerged, its opponents called it "elitist." The majority of voters may not understand adequately the scientific arguments behind environmental policies, but immediately see that they are expensive. In times of economic and financial recession, the general public tend to vote for their pockets more and listen less to the warnings of environmental scientists.

In democracies, policies that require state appropriations also require support from voters. A major problem is a gap between the knowledge gathered by environmental scientists on the one hand and general public on the other (McCarthy, 2011). And there are too many interest groups that doubt environmental studies and criticize their conclusions as either unreliable or exaggerated. Also the high cost of the proposed international environmental actions alienates many voters who fear losing their jobs or do not want to pay for these policies from their own pocket (I. Murray, 2008).

In non-democracies, environmental activism faces significant problems including censorship and suppression. In 1995, the Nigerian military government executed "Ken" Beeson Saro-Wiwa, a prominent activist who exposed environmental abuse committed in his country by oil companies. This reminds us that environmental activities, protected and even encouraged in democratic countries, may be dangerous in authoritarian and corrupt states. In democracies, where the media and public opinion carry more weight, environmental policies are debated more openly than in countries run by authoritarian regimes. Highly publicized public protests and petition campaigns halted the construction of nuclear power plants in many European countries. In the 1980s, media-driven public pressure against the use of CFCs in refrigerators and aerosol sprays influenced governmental regulations and international agreements and forced companies to look for more environmentally friendly technologies. In the 1990s, opposition prompted several governments to keep genetically engineered foods off the market or to require proof that these products are safe. (See Figure 8.7.)

The Global Context

Environmental policies face at least three challenges at the global level. The first is the need to balance environmental policies and economic development. The second is the necessity for sustained global effort by governments and NGOs. The third is the need for new effective strategies to deal with the consequences of climate change if current policies fail.

THE ENVIRONMENT AND BUSINESS

Supporters of environmentalism generally argue they are not against business interests but only against greed and ignorance that the free market cannot

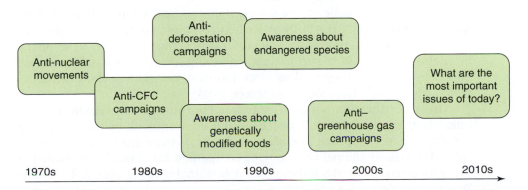

FIGURE 8-7 Environmental activism: A few examples.

A member of Nigeria's Ogoni community hails the trial of the Royal Dutch Shell oil company in 2009. Shell was charged with complicity in the death of Nigerian activist Ken Saro-Wiwa, who had reported environmental abuses by oil companies.

control. Supporters of businesses say that they want to protect the earth but oppose harsh regulations that halt economic growth (Pielke, 2010). Can environmentalism and economic interests be reconciled?

Realists point out that, as long as oil and coal remain the least expensive sources of energy, countries will continue to use them. Renewables are simply too expensive. According to the International Energy Agency, in the United States electricity from new nuclear power plants is 15 to 30 percent more expensive than electricity from new plants using coal. Wind power is more than twice as expensive as coal, whereas solar power costs about five times as much. In other countries, like China, renewables cost even more compared to coal (Levi et al., 2010). And global demands for energy are rising. In response, supporters of realism and liberalism may agree: Governments and the private sector must invest more in cleaner energy sources.

One way to reconcile business and environmental interests is **socially responsible investing** (SRI), a business strategy combining the pursuit of the social good, environmental protection, and profits—all at the same time. Today, many businesses support SRI as part of their marketing strategies. National parks are an example of SRI. They tend to spark tourism, stimulate environmental research, and create jobs (Gaston and Spicer, 2004).

Green certification is another way to merge business and environmental interests. Companies that pursue responsible environmental policies receive a certificate that is supposed to make their products more attractive to consumers and thus more competitive. Logging companies, for example, are invited to apply for green certificates if they promise sustainable development. The Forest Stewardship Council, an NGO based in Germany, has drawn up rules for sustainable forestry.

THE NEED FOR GLOBAL EFFORTS

How will all these programs be financed, and how will they fit into strategies for global development? Massive environmental investment in the least-prosperous countries must play a major part in any international effort. The 2009 UN climate conference in Copenhagen pledged to set aside $30 billion a year to help the world's poorest countries deal with climate change. Rich countries also agreed, as we have seen, to allocate $100 billion per year and to direct funds from the global North to the global South to pay for emissions reduction (Levi, 2010a; Levi, 2010b). Many projects will be ambitious and expensive but also necessary. Desertec, an initiative backed by German firms, plans to build by 2050 one hundred solar power plants and scores of wind farms in northern Africa at a total cost of $552 billion. The project that started in 2009 will sell, if everything goes well, much of the electricity generated to Europe. In the end, consumers will pay for clean energy, and African countries will benefit economically (Desertec, 2012).

Support for new environment-friendly technologies can also take place on a global scale, and research and implementation will both benefit from multilateral efforts. Renewables, for example, supplied around 15 percent of world energy in the first decade of the 2000s, and this share is going up. Wind power is booming in Europe and the United States thanks to private investment and government subsidies.

Enforcement of environmental policies, too, shows the need for global efforts. As realists argue, international agreements remain useless unless they are enforced. For example, the 1976 Convention on International Trade in Endangered Species (CITES) prohibited trading in rhino horn. More than 170 countries joined the treaty, including the countries most involved in horn importing—China, Japan, Vietnam, and Yemen. Unfortunately, trade simply moved onto the black market, and hunters continue to kill these rare animals.

Last, global solutions may help where government bureaucracies are slow to respond (Ebrahim, 2006). After the 2004 tsunami in the Indian Ocean killed so many, UNESCO took leadership, and in 2005 an international agreement with twenty countries was reached to create the Indian Ocean Tsunami Warning System, emulating the U.S. system in the Pacific. It is hoped that such a system would be able to prevent many negative consequences of natural disasters in the future.

New environmentally friendly technologies and other innovations have difficulty moving from the research laboratory to the market. Multibillion-dollar funding itself often creates problems. Instead of pursuing long-term environmental policies, countries frequently create their own arbitrary "wish lists" of projects to be funded by international organizations (Spector, 2005). The main goal is to control the money. Take, for example, water policies. The Consultative Group on International Agricultural Research showed that small, direct investments in projects designed to help regions lacking water are very effective. However, many governments insist on large investments under *their* control. This strengthens liberal claims for the importance of NGOs and independent activism in keeping pressure on decision makers.

GLOBAL POLICIES

Global cooperation is needed to address climate change and other environmental challenges. A single, even economically advanced, country cannot produce the clean-energy innovation for the world. Countries must cooperate to sustain policies that are environmentally just and do not benefit the wealthiest countries only (Walker, 2012). Different countries' efforts can build on one another. The United States can learn from China and Germany about clean-coal technologies. U.S. labs can help India with its massive solar energy projects. Brazil will need the research of European chemical labs to increase its production of biofuels from sugar cane (Levi et al., 2010).

The responsibility of major industrial powers for greenhouse emissions is obvious. However, cutting emissions in the North and allowing them to climb in the South is probably not a good idea. The world should turn more to renewable technologies and sustainable development.

But what if the world is slow to turn to renewables and fails to address climate change? What if its consequences become inevitable? Heat waves will become more frequent and harsh. Desertification will affect already dry places. Rains will fall harder in other places, thus increasing flooding. Many more species will be endangered. More ice will melt and sea levels will keep rising. New global policies have to be implemented to adjust to severely worsening conditions. Three major strategies should be implemented. Countries will have to take responsibility for creating a safe infrastructure, including dams, housing insulated against heat and cold, and reliable communications. Every wealthy country will be responsible for its own environmental security, but poorer countries should be helped. Food security—the guaranteed availability of food—will be another challenge in poor agricultural regions. The right to sufficient, healthy, and nutritious food must be satisfied regardless of environmental and social constraints (McDonald, 2011). Some parts of the planet will face significant depopulation, while others will become overcrowded. To avoid massive social problems, coordinated immigration and population policies may be needed, challenging traditional conceptions of state sovereignty. The world also needs coordination between global environmental and energy policies (Levi, 2013). But the most far-reaching global environmental policy will also sustain economic growth, provide opportunities, and improve social conditions around the world.

▶ Explain environmentalism and skepticism. Can these points of view be reconciled?

▶ What is a country's national purpose referring to the environment? Give examples.

▶ Explain green certification.

CHECK YOUR KNOWLEDGE

Past, Present, and Future: Greenpeace

Over the past forty years, Greenpeace has drawn support from all over the world and inspired enthusiastic critics. Many admire its dramatic style of environmental activism. Others see it as dubious and self-promoting. To achieve its goals, Greenpeace often chooses confrontational and controversial methods. What, then, is the real Greenpeace?

THE ROOTS OF GREENPEACE

Greenpeace traces its roots to 1971, when several young people grew increasingly frustrated over nuclear testing. Early "green peaceniks" sailed on an old fishing boat from Vancouver, Canada, to Amchitka, a small island near Alaska's west coast, with the hope of disrupting underground nuclear testing. The protesters were intercepted and the nuclear testing went on. However, many copycat groups have emerged.

In the 1970s, such groups launched a worldwide campaign against commercial whaling and seal hunting, sparking public condemnation and political pressure against the whaling industries. In 1986 the International Whaling Commission banned commercial whaling. Meanwhile other activists were turning against toxic waste and pollution.

In the late 1970s regional groups formed Greenpeace International to oversee the goals and operations of regional organizations. Other groups chose to remain independent but to tackle similar environmental problems. Greenpeace today is a global NGO, with its headquarters in the Netherlands and offices in more than forty countries. The organization receives hundreds of millions of dollars in donations from almost three million individual supporters and grants.

METHODS AND GOALS

Greenpeace activists use nonviolent protest to raise the level and quality of public debate about the environment. The group promotes harmony values (Greenpeace, 2013). Two of its methods are direct action and public education.

Activists disrupt business activities by picketing, blocking roads, jamming communications, or staging sit-ins. They also aim to raise awareness of environmental issues by sponsoring lectures, research, and educational programs. Greenpeace uses litigation and scientific research to back up its claims. In the 1980s, it pushed for a global moratorium on radioactive waste dumping at sea. In 2003, intense

Nuclear expert Heinz Smital of Greenpeace Germany measures radiation in a playground in Fukushima, Japan, in early 2013.

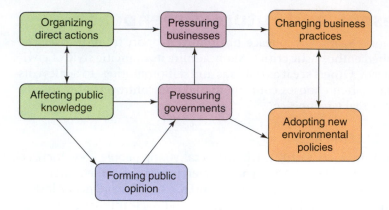

FIGURE 8-8 Methods of Greenpeace.

lobbying efforts by Greenpeace resulted in the UN sanctions on Liberia for illegal logging. In 2005, Sony Ericsson under pressure from Greenpeace and other groups began to phase toxic chemicals out of its products. In 2010, after years of lobbying by Greenpeace, food giant Nestlé agreed to stop purchasing palm oil, the production of which destroys Indonesian rainforests. Greenpeace sponsors research in the area of renewable energy. It also develops its own technologies, such as Greenfreeze—a refrigerator free of chemicals that contribute to ozone depleting and global warming. Greenpeace currently sponsors a global campaign to stop deliberate deforestation by 2020. Not long ago, its website also asked visitors to sponsor *Green Warrior*, a sailboat that would block coal shipments at sea, track illegal shipments of timber, and spot unlawful fishing operations. (See Figure 8.8.)

Critics acknowledge Greenpeace's role in environmental activism but question the significance of its efforts. Realists argue that governments are unlikely to support environmental policies that threaten their core interests. Greenpeace almost certainly exaggerated the success of its antinuclear campaign. The United States, the Soviet Union, and France stopped nuclear testing in the atmosphere and underground, but not necessarily because of pressure from environmentalists; these countries had changed their long-term strategic nuclear plans for other reasons. U.S. nuclear policies, for example, were influenced mainly by negotiations with the Soviet Union. Greenpeace also claims that its relentless efforts to oppose nuclear waste shipments from France to Russia ended in victory, but Russia has said Greenpeace had little to do with its decision. Nestlé agreed not to buy palm oil from questionable sources, but these deals already accounted for less than 1 percent of the global trade of palm oil. Finally, is passing an environmental law enough? Monitoring this law's implementation is a difficult and tedious task that many environmental groups didn't focus on much in the past.

Greenpeace sometimes chooses form over substance, flashy labels over serious efforts to educate. Its promotional materials speak of "dirty energy," "deadly fuels," the "oil fuels war," "climate destroying oil and coal companies," and "genetic pollution" (Greenpeace, 2011). Greenpeace sometimes, as critics say, chooses the wrong battles. Some activists claim that the real source of environmental problems is capitalism itself. Yet they may be most effective in the market societies, where they can express their opinions freely and influence politics by a wide range of lawful means. In authoritarian countries, where governments regulate and control business, environmental groups are ignored, their actions suppressed, and their activists jailed. This does not mean that capitalism eagerly embraces environmental values. Environmental policies are the product of long and difficult battles for hearts, minds, and pockets.

IN THE END, VALUES

From the first, Greenpeace embraced the tactics of the peace campaign and civil rights movement of the 1960s, including individual acts of disobedience and appeal to moral foundations. Yet it has also evolved. Not many people thirty years ago understood Greenpeace, its ideology, or its methods. It took a generation to attract supporters globally. Today Greenpeace relies on help from lawyers and scientists to function effectively within democracy. Online fundraising is a key to its success as well.

Greenpeace's evolution reflects broader political and cultural changes as well. It began its journey by fighting for causes that many people then opposed or misunderstood—from radioactive waste dumping at sea to illegal logging, genetically modified foods, and sustainable agriculture. All these causes are increasingly acceptable. Greenpeace's tactics in the past probably alienated many more people than they attracted. But where Greenpeace once had just a few members, it can now draw on the energy of tens of thousands of volunteers, researchers, and lawyers and a multimillion-dollar budget. Greenpeace and other groups have changed many of their tactics and targets, but they remain loyal to the goal of environmental protection. (See Figure 8.9.)

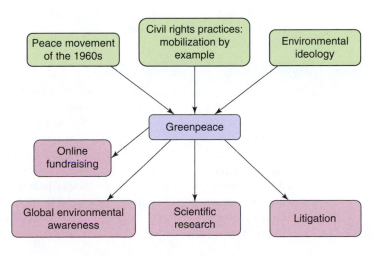

FIGURE 8-9
Greenpeace: Sources and actions.

CONCLUSION

In *The Tragedy of the Commons*, published in *Science* in 1968, the prominent ecologist Garrett Hardin argued that even the most rational individuals acting independently from one another will eventually deplete a limited resource they share together. Our global environment is truly a limited resource, and to secure our future countries must act together. The opening of this chapter illustrated how a collective effort and mutual compromises solved one serious environmental problem twenty-five years ago. But are countries today ready to cooperate and sacrifice even more? The debates about global environment and environmental policies will continue to reflect who we are and what we stand for socially and politically. Action must follow, but it is up to you what kind of action that will be.

CHAPTER SUMMARY

- The world faces a seemingly endless list of environmental problems, ranging from global climate change and acid rain to water shortages and human-created disasters.
- In response to such urgent environmental problems as contamination and depletion, states, international institutions, and NGOs must all contribute to policies ranging from short-term actions to long-term global projects.
- Realists emphasize environmental sovereignty—a country's right to use its natural resources in accord with its core interests. Liberal internationalists believe that the scope and urgency of environmental problems supersede states' sovereignty and requires efforts of the global community.
- Constructivists maintain that environmental policies are socially constructed and reflect values such as national purpose as well as interests. Some conflict theories emphasize the different impacts of environmental problems on the global North and global South.
- Political institutions, partisanship, and individual convictions all affect environmental policies. In democracies, environmental policies are debated openly. Authoritarian governments are more likely to regulate environmental debates or ban them altogether.
- Environmental policies face at least three challenges on the global level—the need to balance environmental policies and economic development, the need for sustained global efforts, and the need for new strategies should global temperatures continue to rise.

KEY TERMS

Acid rain 259
Climate change 261
Conservation 266
Contamination 258
Debt-for-nature swaps 281
Deforestation 263
Depletion 258
Desertification 263
Environmentalism 278

Environmental politics 258
Environmental
  skepticism 278
Environmental
  sovereignty 270
Global commons 271
Global Environment Facility
  (GEF) 268
Green certification 285

Harmony values 276
Kyoto Protocol 266
Mastery values 276
Natural disaster 264
Ozone depletion 261
Socially responsible investing
  (SRI) 284
Sustainable development 269
Water pollution 264

1. What do we study?

ENVIRONMENTAL PROBLEMS

Interconnected threats to ecosystems, including climate change, deforestation, loss of wildlife, and loss of clean air and water

DISASTERS

Natural calamities and man-made accidents that may have catastrophic environmental consequences

ENVIRONMENTAL POLICIES

- Two major categories of problems: contamination and depletion

- Regulations and restrictions, green investment, and more comprehensive policies

2. How do we study it?

REALISM

- Environmental policies should not undermine state sovereignty

- Some environmental problems can become security threats

- Countries should cooperate regarding global commons

LIBERALISM

- Environmental policies are a central feature of IR

- International organizations and treaties play a key role in policies

- Nongovernment organizations' role should increase

- Public awareness brings change

CONSTRUCTIVISM

- Environmental policies are socially constructed and reflect values as well as interests

OTHER THEORIES

- Conflict and dependency theories: Rich countries must accept a greater responsibility for the environmental problems they have created

3. How do we apply it?

THE INDIVIDUAL CONTEXT

- Individual values, education, and leadership affect leaders' choices in their environmental policies

THE STATE CONTEXT

- Political institutions and partisanship

- In democracies, environmental policies are debated openly

- Authoritarian governments tend to regulate environmental debates or ban them altogether

THE GLOBAL CONTEXT

- Countries try to balance environmental policies and economic development

- They continue sustained global efforts and seek new strategies

Critical Thinking

- Using an empirical case of your choice, analyze a depletion problem that has led or might lead to an international conflict.
- Realists argue that governments are unlikely to support environmental policies that threaten their core interests. Discuss this argument from a constructivist view, focusing on countries' "core interests."
- How important are renewable energy strategies? Should governments have a separate ministry in charge of these issues, such as in India?
- Should developing countries have the right to pollute to catch up with the industrialization process? Discuss.

CHAPTER

9

Refugees cross from the Democratic Republic of the Congo into Uganda in 2008. Ethnic and political conflicts continue to devastate several African countries. What could other countries do to alleviate the suffering of civilians victimized by war?

Humanitarian Challenges

The decision to intervene in any country or crisis [must be] based solely on an independent assessment of people's needs—not on political, economic, or religious interests.
—DOCTORS WITHOUT BORDERS

I N APRIL 1994, AN EXPLOSION OF MASS VIOLENCE SHOOK THE REPUBLIC OF RWANDA, A SMALL AFRICAN COUNTRY OF ELEVEN MILLION PEOPLE. GERMANY AND THEN BELGIUM HAD ruled this country as colonial powers for decades, but in 1962 it became an independent state. Unfortunately, political and ethnic tensions brewing for many years grew into a civil war in 1990. Rwanda comprised three ethnic groups—the Twa, the Hutu, the Tutsi—of which the Hutu are in the distinct majority. After Rwanda gained independence from Belgium, a conflict between the Hutus and the Tutsis began. Dormant for decades, it degenerated into genocidal killings. Most victims were Tutsi men, women, and children pursued by Hutu militia and violent mobs. Some terrified Tutsis fled to the marshlands, where their rivals found them and killed them with machete knives. In a matter of weeks, an estimated eight hundred thousand Tutsi were brutally killed. The surviving women were raped. Overall, four million civilians fled to refugee camps in neighboring Burundi, Tanzania, Uganda, and Zaire.

Meanwhile, the world was watching from the distance. There were French paratroopers in Rwanda on a peacekeeping mandate, but they did next to nothing to prevent the carnage. Why did leading world powers fail to act? Only the appeals of the neighboring African states flooded by refugees—mostly the Hutus who feared revenge—triggered action from the international community. It comes down to complacency and a lack of political will.

Rwanda's tragedy highlights a core question of international relations. When one country faces a tragic loss of life, do other states have the obligation to intervene? Should the U.N peacekeeping troops use force in a country without an expressed permission of its government? A consensus has grown among Western powers that the use of force is necessary to save civilian lives. As President Obama said in 2011, "Some nations may be able to turn a blind eye to atrocities in other countries. The United States of America is different. And as president, I refused to wait for the images of slaughter and mass graves before taking action." These words explained the U.S. military action in 2011, when it joined other NATO states in support of rebels in Libya. Yet some other states, including Russia and China, were quick to criticize these policies claiming that they were illegitimate. Which position was right?

This chapter is dedicated to international efforts to stop massive human suffering. We shall see that these actions raise both moral and political questions.

Learning Objectives

After reading this chapter, you should be able to:

▶ identify and explain major humanitarian challenges and their causes;
▶ discuss humanitarian policies to address these challenges;
▶ outline similarities and differences among key approaches to humanitarian challenges; and
▶ explain leaders' choices, countries' political conditions, and global contexts affecting humanitarian challenges and policies.

What Do We Study?

Suffering is inseparable from human existence. However, many forms of suffering are preventable and can be alleviated. At this very moment, millions of people suffer from political and ethnic violence, natural disasters, persistent food shortages, acute infectious diseases, and forceful migration. These are **humanitarian crises**—incidents or continuing problems threatening the health, safety, security, and well-being of many, usually in a distinct geographic area. A conflict causing massive civilian deaths, like the one in Rwanda, is a

humanitarian crisis. Rapidly spreading infectious diseases, acute water shortages caused by a drought, or massive hunger as a result of a flood or earthquake
are other examples.

Countries, as well as international and nongovernment organizations,
plan, develop, and conduct policiesto deal with these crises. Humanitarian
policies are based on three fundamental principles: humanity, impartiality,
and independence. *Humanity* means that policies first of all must save lives and
alleviate suffering. *Impartiality* means no preferences for any political leader,
country, or group. *Independence* means that humanitarian policies are not
guided by open or hidden political, economic, or military objectives of participating states (United Nations, 2011; Young, 2010). (See Figure 9.1.)

Humanitarian interventions are the actions of foreign powers in a humanitarian crisis with or without the approval of a legal authority controlling
the area (Roberts, 2000). Besides bringing relief, humanitarian interventions
also attempt to eliminate the sources of the crisis, especially human causes.
Some interventions involve armed forces. In cases of natural catastrophes, governments usually welcome foreign aid and rescue groups. However, when political disputes or ethnic-religious strife are involved, states are much more
reluctant to invite foreign countries to intervene. Countries also choose to participate or not get involved in international humanitarian actions.

By international law, all countries have **humanitarian sovereignty**—the
right to accept or reject humanitarian interventions on their territories. The UN
Charter of 1945 states in article 2(7) that "nothing . . . shall authorize the
United Nations to intervene in matters which are essentially within the domestic jurisdiction of any state. . . ." Humanitarian sovereignty (which is a facet
of state sovereignty) is an essential principle of international relations restricting interventions. However, as we shall see, this principle faces practical as well
as moral limitations.

Types of Humanitarian Challenges

Many humanitarian crises affect large groups of people and spread across borders. They quickly become regional and even global problems.

PANDEMICS AND INFECTIOUS DISEASES

Infectious diseases are maladies caused by biological agents such as viruses, bac-
teria, or parasites. Outbreaks of infectious diseases in a large population are called
epidemics. An epidemic spreading over a continent or globally is a **pandemic**.

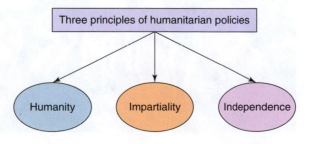

FIGURE 9-1 **Three
principles of humani-
tarian policies.** Alleviate
suffering first (human-
ity), play no favoritism
(impartiality), and do
not allow self-interested
agendas (independence).

For centuries, our ancestors were practically defenseless against pandemics. In the 1300s the Black Death killed almost a quarter of Europe. Around the same time, a pandemic killed millions in China, Central Asia, and India. Infectious diseases brought to America by European colonizers also caused the deaths of Native Americans five hundred years ago. Between 1918 and 1920, the Spanish flu killed from fifty to one hundred million people, including five hundred thousand in the United States, four hundred thousand in Japan, two hundred thousand in Great Britain, and over seventeen million in India.

The Ebola virus outbreak in Africa in the 1970s, the cholera epidemic in Latin America, and the plague in India in the 1990s are just a few recent examples of pandemics (Lakoff, 2010). The World Health Organization recognizes today more than fourteen hundred infectious diseases. Among the deadliest are lower respiratory infections; HIV/AIDS; and infections causing diarrhea, tuberculosis, malaria, and measles. These illnesses cause the death of some ten to twelve million people each year. Malaria alone kills an estimated 1.2 million people a year, mostly African children. When deadly forms of influenza appeared, such as SARS in 2002 and H5N1 (Avian flu) in 2009, states took costly measures out of fear that the illness would spread (Karesh and Cook, 2005).

Epidemics and pandemics are clearly international problems. First, they cause significant global disruptions. They can directly affect the functioning of governments and the preparedness of armed forces, firefighters, paramedics, and the police (Stewart, 2006). Second, without international cooperation, governments may overreact to a rapidly developing pandemic. As a disease spreads, death tolls rise, and medication runs low, and governments could close international borders and stall trade. Finally, many governments lack the resources or

In Washington, DC, in 2012, AIDS activists from around the world participated in a march to demand rights and resources to deal with HIV/AIDS globally. Do such rallies make an impact on policies?

proper management to protect their populations from preventable diseases. International involvement could save millions of lives (Wolfe, 2011).

AIDS

AIDS is a disease of the immune system characterized by increased vulnerability to infections. The *human immunodeficiency virus* (HIV) is its cause. Although AIDS develops much more slowly than influenza, it is a pandemic. According to the UNAIDS and the World Health Organization, the total number of people infected by HIV in the second decade of the century could be between thirty-five and forty-eight million. Nearly twenty-five million people have died from AIDS. Around four hundred thousand children are infected with HIV each year, most of them in Africa. Every day, approximately eight thousand people die of AIDS-related illnesses, and more than fourteen hundred of them are children, according to *Doctors Without Borders*. HIV infection rates reached 25 percent in some areas of southern and eastern Africa. In some countries the rate is declining; yet in central Asia and Eastern Europe the rate is growing. (See Map 9.1.)

AIDS is a serious global problem, but it is generally preventable and treatable with international cooperation. Wealthy countries have been able to stop the rapid spread of the HIV infection and provide medication for the infected. Globally, deaths due to AIDS have declined since 2007. Approximately $16 billion is spent on AIDS prevention and treatment every year in low-income countries; half the money is foreign aid. Yet people in countries without efficient health systems continue to suffer ("A Strategic Revolution in HIV," 2011). Poor hygiene and unsafe sex practices contribute to the problem.

CHRONIC STARVATION AND MALNUTRITION

Malnutrition is a severe medical condition resulting from constant food shortages. Chronic malnutrition leads to hunger and *starvation*. The last devastating **famine**—severe food scarcity—in Western Europe, in the 1840s, caused mass

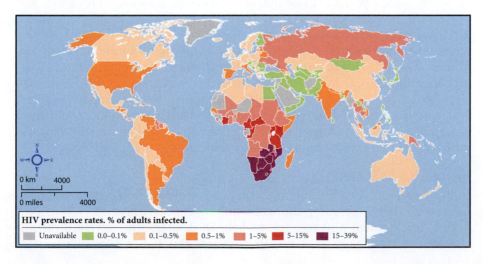

MAP 9-1 Worldwide HIV prevalence rates. *Source: The United Nations*

HIV prevalence rates. % of adults infected.

| Unavailable | 0.0–0.1% | 0.1–0.5% | 0.5–1% | 1–5% | 5–15% | 15–39% |

deaths and a wave of immigration to the United States, particularly from Ireland and Scotland. In the twentieth century, famine continued to break out in less-developed countries: in India, Russia, and China in the first half of the century; in some African countries (such as Nigeria, Ethiopia, and Angola) in the second half. According to the UN Food and Agriculture Organization (FAO), from seven hundred million to one billion people suffer from malnutrition at this very moment. In Ethiopia alone in 2011, according to the UN World Food Programme (WFP), approximately six million people depend on food aid simply to stay alive. The problem of malnutrition relates not only to the availability but also to the quality of food. The balanced diet largely available in industrially developed nations is out of reach for at least three billion people, who do not receive proper protein, vitamins, and minerals.

ACUTE SUFFERING

The Rwanda genocide of 1994 was an extreme example of acute suffering. Sub-Saharan Africa is particularly susceptible to this type of humanitarian catastrophe (see Chapter 5). In the Democratic Republic of Congo, where multiple political factions for years have been fighting for control of the territories and resources, civilians are the easiest targets. Those fleeing violence are forced to spend months and years in crowded camps under constant fear of death and physical harm. Civilians in combat zones also live with the persistent threat of violence, and many develop stress-related disorders. Women and children remain the most vulnerable groups. Rape is particularly devastating, because along with physical injury it brings long-lasting and demoralizing psychological trauma (Ritchie et al., 2005; Shiraev and Levy, 2013). In many places, children are forced into slavery. According to some reliable accounts, more than twenty million people have endured slavery in the first decade of this century (Bales et al., 2009). Without proper international action, millions could suffer for years.

Learn more on the companion website about the humanitarian crisis in Rwanda and other parts of the world.

Causes of Humanitarian Crises

"When it rains, it pours." Humanitarian crises often have multiple causes, and one serious problem can lead to another. The earthquake in Japan in March 2011, the worst in a century, produced a disastrous tsunami that destroyed entire towns and killed thousands of people. A quarter of a million people lost homes. The tsunami also damaged the Fukushima nuclear plant, causing a significant radioactive threat. Although Japan is a wealthy country with an efficient government, the disaster was devastating. In less-developed countries and regions, natural disasters can lead to infectious diseases, hunger, and other acute suffering. Mismanagement, a lack of resources, rampant corruption, and political violence worsen humanitarian problems and delay their solution.

NATURAL DISASTERS

In the twentieth century alone, an estimated seventy million people died from natural disasters, including droughts, floods, and earthquakes. Today, economic development and technology help in dealing with severe droughts. However, earthquakes, tsunamis, hurricanes, and floods continue to pose grave danger, especially in less-developed countries. In 2004 the Indian Ocean tsunami killed over two hundred thirty thousand people because regional early warning systems failed or were absent. The Haitian earthquake in January 2010 cost two hundred twenty-two thousand lives, mostly because many buildings were constructed in violation of anti-seismic standards. By contrast, in the Japanese earthquake of 2011, most dwellings remained intact and only the tsunami caused significant casualties.

In the immediate aftermath of a natural disaster, most social services are absent or in short supply. Natural health hazards continue to bring devastation to millions of people, especially in remote or overpopulated regions. Some countries provide effective care, whereas others do not; and so international assistance plays an crucial role (Woods and Woods, 2007).

MISMANAGEMENT

In today's world, a drought should not cause mass suffering: A state can always purchase food from abroad or ask for assistance. Indian economist Amartya Sen, winner of the 1998 Nobel Prize in economics, showed that the main cause of famine in today's world is inefficient bureaucracy. In 1942, for example, a cyclone hit a vast area of Bengal and Orissa (now territories of Bangladesh and India) and destroyed virtually all rice harvests. Although food supplies remained significant, the incompetence and inaction of corrupt authorities took almost three million lives (Sen, 1981).

Weak and collapsing state structures can be a serious cause of mismanagement. When its central state collapsed, Somalia fell into the hands of warlords. A fragile order was preserved by brutal force or by tribal loyalties (Mohamoud, 2006), but major elements of the social infrastructure disintegrated, including health care services. The United Nations estimated in 2010 that there were only four doctors and twenty-eight nurses or midwives for every one hundred thousand people.

Corruption and fraud also contribute to humanitarian problems. Emergency food supplies often end up in the hands of criminals, and money meant for medication is often used to buy weapons. Although effective anti-malarial drugs are available on the market, many Africans have very limited access (Singer et al., 2005).

In this information age, mismanagement in failing states, just like genocidal killings, sooner or later becomes an issue on the agenda of intergovernment institutions and NGOs.

POLITICS

Political leaders may deliberately cause acute suffering for their own purposes. In the twentieth century, the Soviet Union and China caused the largest human-made famines in modern history. During the Soviet campaign of collectivizing the peasantry from 1929 through 1932, authorities seized land and property, including horses and cattle, and forced peasants to join *collective farms*. When the farms failed to meet unrealistically high quotas for delivery of agricultural products to the state, the government seized all food. Troops blockaded many agricultural areas, particularly in the Ukraine, preventing

Filipino children wait in line to receive porridge during a free food program organized by a local NGO in Quezon City, Philippines, in 2012. Poverty afflicts about a third of the Philippines' 94 million people.

starving peasants from fleeing to cities where food could still be found. The resulting famine killed from five to seven million in the Ukraine, southern Russia, Kazakhstan, and other parts of the former Soviet Union (Martin, 2001; Khlevniuk, 2008). Another human-made famine arose in Communist China from 1960 to 1962 when the authorities forced peasants into agricultural labor communes and seized their crops. About thirty million people, mostly in the countryside, died from harvest failures and starvation (Becker, 1998).

From 1967 to 1970, the central government blockaded Biafra in southeast Nigeria to prevent it from declaring independence. As food supplies failed to reach the region, famine and violence spread. Although from two to three million people died, there was no international humanitarian intervention. Some countries in fact supported the Nigerian government, while others remained neutral. France supported an independent Biafra but could not help its population. Only later, when photographs shocked world opinion, did the crisis spark heated debates about the moral responsibility of the world community to stop humanitarian disasters.

MASS VIOLENCE

War or an ongoing political conflict can also lead to a humanitarian crisis. Civilians caught up in the conflict zone are typically deprived of medical care or humanitarian aid. When Sri Lanka launched an all-out military assault on Tamil Tiger rebels in 2009, the fighting caused massive civilian casualties. Civilians from two of India's northeastern states, Assam and Manipur, suffered from recurring ethnic and religious violence for years. Tens of thousands fled to crowded refugee camps, where malaria, measles, and other infectious diseases became widespread. As you will remember, international law allows humanitarian interventions to stop genocidal violence and to take legal action against the perpetrators.

EXTREME POVERTY

About one billion people live today in **extreme poverty**, defined by the World Bank as $1.25 per person per day. One billion and a half live on no more than $2 per day. For most of the twentieth century, the world was divided into the richer North and the poorer, underdeveloped South. Although extreme poverty is now rare in Europe, the United States, Canada, and Japan, where taxpayers support generous welfare systems, almost 40 percent of sub-Saharan Africa is extremely poor. The rise of China improved the situation with poverty in the global South dramatically. Still, one-fourth of the world's poor live in India, the most populous democratic country.

As a group, the extremely poor are also the most defenseless against disease, starvation, and physical and psychological abuse. Of all economic groups they face the highest risk of injury or death. Poverty is a social trap, and the extremely poor are the most likely victims of a humanitarian crisis (Sachs, 2005). (See Map 9.2.)

OVERPOPULATION

Overpopulation is a high concentration of people within a region threatening its *subsistence*, or the minimum conditions to sustain a reasonable quality of life. Around 1800, the world population was close to one billion. It grew to 1.6 billion in 1900 and to three billion by 1960 (United Nations Population Division, 2004). It is about seven billion now and projected to grow to eight billion by 2025. (See Figure 9.2.)

Overpopulation can lead to serious health, environmental, and social problems, as in the city of Lagos in Nigeria. The population of this industrial and commercial center has reached twenty million, and thousands of new job seekers arrive each month. Lagos became a giant agglomeration of slums

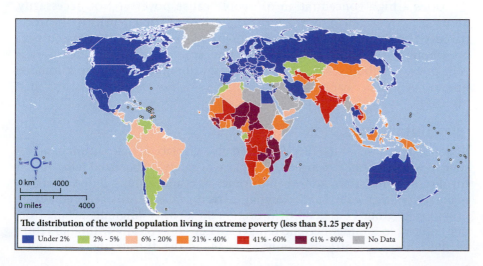

The distribution of the world population living in extreme poverty (less than $1.25 per day)

| Under 2% | 2% - 5% | 6% - 20% | 21% - 40% | 41% - 60% | 61% - 80% | No Data |

MAP 9-2 The distribution of the world population living in extreme poverty (less than $1.25 per day). *Source: The United Nations*

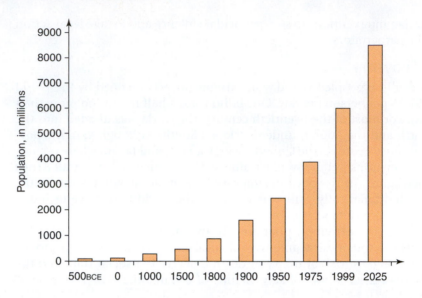

FIGURE 9-2 Global population growth.

lacking parks, recreational areas, plumbing, and modern health facilities. Although the vast majority has access to electricity, running water is limited and its quality is very poor. Human waste is commonly disposed of by the drainage of rainwater into open ditches. Many overpopulated areas are also prone to social instability, violence, and environmental problems (Angus and Butler, 2011).

A rapid concentration of people does not automatically lead to overpopulation, especially in economically advanced countries. New York City, London, Sydney, Tokyo, Shanghai, Hong Kong, and Moscow do not suffer from the lack of resources. On the contrary, they attract greater resources and attain greater economic success (J. Cohen, 2005). However, where high density and poverty coexist, problems occur.

Does a high concentration of people cause poverty? Not necessarily. Monaco, a country in Europe, has the highest population density in the world (twenty-three thousand people per square kilometer), and yet its citizens are among the wealthiest. At the same time, scarcely populated areas can be very poor. Cambodia has only seventy-eight people per square kilometer but an average per capita GDP of just $2,400—twenty-six times less than Monaco's.

INVOLUNTARY MIGRATION

Violence, hardship, or the threat of it can also displace people within or across state borders in search of *asylum*, or a place of safety. This forced relocation is **involuntary migration**, and when it comes to ethnic groups, authorities may make it a political goal. *Ethnic cleansing* is the forced removal or outright extermination of groups based on their origin and identity. Migrants fleeing from one country to another become **refugees**. They are typically willing to return to their home country, but only as soon as the threats there diminish.

International help in these cases is essential. In 2008 alone, the United Nations ran approximately three hundred refugee camps around the world with six million people. Half of these people were from Africa (Agier, 2010).

Internally displaced persons (IDP) are involuntary migrants who do not cross international borders. They unwillingly leave their homes or region under threats of death, starvation, or imprisonment (Phuong, 2010). Recently there were over twenty million IDPs, most of them in Columbia, Sudan, Democratic Republic of the Congo, Iraq, and Azerbaijan. (See Table 9-1.)

Human trafficking is the illegal international trade in human beings for the purposes of exploitation. The U.S. Department of State (2013) estimates that that as many as 27 million men, women, and children are trafficking victims at any given time. Half are minors, and more than 80 percent are girls

TABLE 9-1 Illustrations of Involuntary Migration

Time, Place	Events and Consequences
1915 The Ottoman Empire	The Ottoman government, abetted by extreme nationalists, began to resettle 1.5 million Armenians from Anatolia to Palestine. Many of them died on the way from starvation and brutality.
1922 Turkey-Greece	Millions of Greeks and Turks from the former Ottoman Empire were forced to relocate from the places where they lived for centuries.
1939–1949 The Soviet Union	Soviet dictator Joseph Stalin forcibly relocated about 3 million people from the Baltic states, Western Ukraine and Belarus, the Crimea and Southern Caucasus into Siberia and Kazakhstan.
1941–1945 Germany and Territories Under Its Occupation	German dictator Hitler forcibly relocated nearly 6 million people in various parts of Europe. When Germany lost the war, almost 13 million Germans were forcibly relocated; many of them died along the way.
The 1980s Afghanistan	Two million Afghan refugees established temporarily settlements in Pakistan and Iran during the Soviet occupation in the 1980s.
1995 Rwanda	1.7 million ethnic Hutus, fearing reprisals from the ethnic Tutsis, fled from Rwanda into Zaire and Tanzania.
1999 Serbia	About 700,000 Kosovo Albanians fearing the Serbian military crossed the Yugoslav border into Albania and Italy.
2006 Central African Republic	As a result of an ongoing political conflict, approximately 150,000 Central Africans remained internally displaced, and more than 70,000 have fled into neighboring Chad and Cameroon.
1983–2009 Sri Lanka	During the course of the civil war, many hundreds of thousands of people became internally displaced; tens of thousands remained refugees after the end of the war.
2010 Kyrgyzstan	About 100,000 ethnic Uzbeks fled from southern Kyrgyzstan to neighboring Uzbekistan to escape deadly clashes with ethnic Kyrgyz that left 2,000 dead. Another 300,000 remained internally displaced for months.

Sources: Naimark, 2002; Ramet, 2005; Benvenisti et al., 2007; Hitchcock, 2008; Muller, 2008

DEBATE > PREVENTING MIGRATION

Governments also restrict migration. During the Cold War, most Communist countries did not allow their citizens to emigrate permanently and restricted even short-term travel abroad (Munz, 2003). The governments of Cuba and North Korea maintained such rules for more than fifty years. China enforces *hukou*, regulating migration within the country, especially from rural to urban areas. Many human rights groups criticize such policies. You too may see restrictions on migration as a violation of human rights. But sovereign states have the right to conduct their own migration policies. Western countries, for example, have restricted immigration, especially facing the financial crisis after 2008 (Art, 2011). China and Japan too limit immigration.

WHAT'S YOUR VIEW?

Could you name the conditions when a restrictive migration policy—within as well as between countries—becomes a humanitarian problem?

 Read more on the companion website about China's restrictive domestic migration policy.

and women. People are trafficked for sexual purposes, marriage, and labor exploitation. Some are ordered to beg on the streets or steal for money. Others, especially children, become soldiers. Yet others are sacrificed for their organs. The vast majority of victims are poor and uneducated. They have no means to resist injustice and cruelty. Human trafficking is one of the fastest growing global crimes. The international criminal groups use fraud, extortion, and bribery of officials to move people across the borders (Shelley, 2010).

INTERCONNECTED PROBLEMS

One humanitarian challenge almost inevitably leads to another. Approximately one billion people today, according to the United Nations, lack access to running water. For another billion, 75 percent of the water comes from nearby rivers without proper filtering. Unclean water contributes to epidemics, and hunger worsens their deadly impact. Unhealthy populations living in poverty are especially vulnerable. Violent conflicts in a natural disaster area add to food shortages and massive starvation. Chronic suffering also contributes to disabilities.

Take AIDS, for example. A middle-class individual in a developed country today may live with AIDS for thirty to forty years or more, thanks to early diagnosis and treatment. Poverty and corruption shorten the lives of AIDS patients in other countries. In Africa, half of poor infants diagnosed with HIV die before the age of two. In the sixty-eight poor countries with the most AIDS-related childhood deaths, only 22 percent of mothers had access to treatment that prevents mother-to-child transmission of the virus ("A Strategic Revolution," 2011). Malnutrition often makes effective AIDS treatment nearly impossible because medications do not work properly in a body weakened by hunger.

The complexity of humanitarian problems not only makes international assistance imperative, but also raises questions. What kind of assistance can be most effective—and who should be responsible, individual states or international organizations? How far can international actors go, and should they always have consent from the states affected by the problems?

Environmental pollution and trash scattered in the crowded Makoko neighborhood of Lagos, Nigeria. Although megalopolises grow rapidly, in the countries where governments are inefficient and economic infrastructure is poor, acute environmental problems are inevitable.

▶ Define a humanitarian intervention.
▶ What is a pandemic?
▶ Who are the *internally displaced*?
▶ What is human trafficking?

CHECK YOUR KNOWLEDGE

Humanitarian Policies

There are three types of humanitarian polices. First, international interventions may remove the immediate cause of suffering or a potential threat. Second, relief efforts can help victims of a humanitarian disaster. Third, preventive measures may avert future crises. These policies, of course, frequently overlap. They can be unilateral or multilateral, depending on the involvement of states, NGOs, and intergovernmental organizations. They can also be non-military or armed.

HUMANITARIAN INTERVENTION

Humanitarian intervention, as we mentioned in the introduction on the Rwanda case, is the most controversial of these policies. In **peacekeeping**, the armed forces of one or several countries cross state borders in response to genocidal violence. This intervention has two goals: to stop violence (peace-making) and to create the conditions for lasting peace (peace building) (Bellamy and Williams, 2010). The UN Security Council can authorize peacekeeping operations if all five permanent members agree. UN peacekeeping is

@ You can find
out more
about UN-sponsored
peacekeeping operations
on the companion
website.

guided by three basic principles: consent of the involved governments and groups, impartiality, and the use of force only in self-defense. In 2013, there were sixteen peacekeeping missions worldwide including Haiti, Kosovo, Afghanistan, Timor, Mali, Liberia, South Sudan, and Democratic Republic of the Congo.

After Rwanda, the U.S. and British politicians began to argue that humanitarian intervention should not stop before a massive use of military force and a violation of formal state sovereignty. On the basis of this argument, in Yugoslavia in 1999 and Libya in 2011, NATO forces acted against the Serbian leader Slobodan Milošević and the Libyan leader Muammar Qaddafi. Russia and China, both permanent members of the UN Security Council, objected, citing violation of the principle of state sovereignty and other principles of peacekeeping. Critics also claim that NATO humanitarian interventions tend to target some regimes and some countries but not others.

How does humanitarian intervention and peacekeeping warfare differ from aggressive warfare? First, the states involved do not plan to occupy permanently or annex another state's territory. Neither do they pursue, in most cases, regime change in another country or act solely on behalf of their own strategic interests. Second, humanitarian interventions aim at political forces that use deadly violence against a population or pose an immediate threat of violence. And finally, such interventions require legitimacy, in the form of an international mandate—such as a UN Security Council resolution (Welsh, 2004). In a civil war, UN resolutions do not authorize directly targeting any of the feuding factions and do not sanction the removal of political authorities. The UN admits that success in peacekeeping is difficult to guarantee because peacekeeping missions go to the most difficult social and political environments.

How can we balance respect for a country's sovereignty with the urgent need to stop a humanitarian disaster? The question remains much debated in the theory and practice of humanitarian interventions and peacekeeping missions.

RELIEF EFFORTS

Relief efforts provide immediate aid to a country without violating its sovereignty and usually with its cooperation. After the 2004 tsunami destroyed coastal communities in Sri Lanka, Indonesia, and elsewhere, U.S. military personnel delivered 2.2 million pounds of emergency supplies. Twenty-five ships and ninety-four aircraft participated in the effort. After a 2005 earthquake, hundreds of relief workers arrived in Pakistan (Kashmir) bringing food, medical supplies, tents, and blankets. Governments welcomed the assistance and helped to distribute the supplies.

Private companies and influential individuals contribute to international humanitarian efforts too. The American Relief Administration (ARA), led by Herbert Hoover, gave help to European countries, including Russia, early in the twentieth century, after the devastation of World War I. The ARA shipped more than four million tons of relief supplies, saving millions of lives. In the 1960s, a group of young French physicians, dismayed by the world's inaction in Biafra, started Doctors Without Borders. Since 1971, this organization has delivered aid in more than seventy countries affected by armed conflict, epidemics, and disasters (Bortolotti, 2006). It sent more than two hundred medical volunteers after the 2004 tsunami disaster alone. In the United States, private companies and individuals also gave over $500 million in humanitarian assistance to the victims of the tsunami. Immediately after the 2011 tsunami in Japan, more than 130 countries contributed money and sent teams of search and rescue specialists, emergency medical personnel, and engineers to devastated regions.

CRISIS PREVENTION

Most infectious diseases are preventable. Well-off countries have practically eradicated malaria, for example, by eliminating large bodies of standing water—the most common breeding grounds for the single-celled parasites that cause the illness. In countries with well-organized and well-funded medicine, medication to treat malaria is easily available as well. But less economically advanced countries need significant help—and a coordinated global effort.

The **World Health Organization** (WHO) finances the development and distribution of preventive vaccines, along with educational materials. For more than sixty years WHO has monitored influenza worldwide (Garrett, 2005). Because many infectious diseases are easily spread from animals to humans, the WHO collaborates with the UN Food and Agriculture Organization (FAO), as well as the World Organisation for Animal Health (WOAH), to track disease outbreaks in animals. These organizations advise governments on animal commerce, quarantines, and vaccination.

Individual countries—often acting in accord—also contribute to disease prevention. Consider international initiatives in the fight against AIDS. In 2006, leaders of the most economically developed nations (the G-8) announced that, by the end of the first decade of the twenty-first century, AIDS medication should be available to all who need it. The UN has also set an ambitious target—to halve the number of cases of sexual transmission of HIV by 2015, to ensure that no child will be born with HIV, and to get fifteen million more people onto treatment ("A Strategic Revolution," 2011). And the Global Fund to Fight AIDS, Tuberculosis, and Malaria (GFATM) has committed over $22 billion in 150 countries to fight these three diseases.

NGOs play an increasing role in disease prevention. The Bill & Melinda Gates Foundation, founded in 2000, is the major charitable organization in the world today, attracting tens of billions of dollars in donations. The foundation conducts HIV and agricultural research, conducts sanitation programs, and coordinates testing of new vaccines (Peters et al., 2010).

 Go online to read about the Bill & Melinda Gates Foundation. How effective are the foundation's initiatives? Also read about the WHO and GFATM. Where have AIDS prevention policies succeeded? What are the remaining difficulties?

POPULATION POLICIES

Several policies deal with overpopulation (P. Brown, 2006). Some aim at improving living conditions—constructing new homes, providing access to running water, building sanitation systems, and offering health care. Others focus on education, to help men and women plan their families. These policies help people learn about the physiology of pregnancy, childbirth, and contraceptives. They educate and empower women to play a greater role in family planning,

The skyline of Shanghai, China, population 23 million (and growing) as of the 2011 census. The Chinese government considers overpopulation a serious problem and uses legal means to limit births.

and they teach families about their rights and responsibilities. The logic of family planning is straightforward: As the United Nations Population Fund insists, families with few children are better off economically than families with many.

Critics argue that family planning promotes abortion. Even more controversial are state-mandated policies of birth control, most notably in China.

CASE IN POINT > *Population Control in China*

In 1979 China, facing out-of-control overpopulation, launched the **one-child policy**. Each family was permitted to have no more than one child, and married couples with more than one child must pay substantial fees. Exceptions do exist. Parents in rural areas and several big cities, including Beijing, may have two children. Some ethnic minorities and couples with advanced college degrees are also exempt—but even they are allowed no more than two children

(Fong, 2006). These measures have slowed population growth in China, which now has approximately three to four hundred million fewer people than it could have had otherwise (China has overall 1.34 billion people). There are many controversies and drawbacks, however. As a result of its one-child policy, China is aging rapidly: Fewer people enter the labor force and more people retire. Many Chinese families preferring boys turned to selective abortion

of female fetuses. As a result, according to the Chinese Academy of Social Sciences, some twenty-four million Chinese men of marrying age will find themselves lacking wives in 2020.

CRITICAL THINKING
Discuss other economic and social problems China could face in the near future due to the one-child policy. In your view, should China modify this policy and if yes, in which way? Explain your opinion.

ANTIPOVERTY POLICIES

Experts continue to argue about the causes of poverty and the most effective policies to reduce it (Banerjee and Duflo, 2011). Some advocate international trade and development strategies; they hope that cheap labor in poor regions will attract private investments from wealthy countries. Others ask for greater investment in poor regions. Still others suggest a global redistribution of wealth from the rich countries to the poor ones. In some areas, particularly in Africa, people lack any education and skills to break out of total misery. Displaced people, refugees lack any food, clothing, and medicine (Kapuscinski, 2002). So, direct economic assistance remains the most common policy. The United States, the UK, Germany, and France all provide direct help to dozens of countries. The UN FAO funds assistance projects, conducts negotiations to stimulate trade, and distributes funds to help developing countries modernize agriculture and fishing.

Meanwhile, as many argue, direct assistance is a short-term remedy, it makes people dependent on outside help and does not attack the roots of poverty. Since the start of the twenty-first century, global poverty rates are in steady decline. Yet hundreds of millions in China, India, Brazil, and Turkey have risen above the poverty level not because of Western help, but because of the success of their economies. Still, market reforms alone can deepen inequality without eradicating poverty. A combination of economic aid, long-term investments, and economic reforms is probably the best way to approach the issue of global poverty.

The Grameen Bank, founded in Bangladesh, is an innovative approach to help the chronically poor. This bank makes small loans to the needy. Called *microcredit*, such loans are given without requiring *collateral*—property or valuable items that traditional banks take over if a loan is not repaid (and that most loan applicants in Bangladesh don't have). But money is not given away either. Each loan must be paid back with interest. How does the bank operate without "solid" financial guarantees? It turns to communities. Every borrower must belong to a local group, which provides support and helps its members pay back their loans. Most of the bank's loans go to women—who still, compared to men, have fewer opportunities to generate an income or to obtain a commercial bank loan. In 2006, the founder of the bank, Muhammad Yunus, and his organization, received the Nobel Peace Prize.

Read more about Grameen Bank and Foundation on the companion website. Did you notice that the vast majority of the bank's clients are women? Why does the bank maintain this policy?

REFUGEE POLICIES

States, IGOs, and NGOs provide temporary sanctuaries for refugees until they can safely return back to their homes (Agier, 2010, 36). Some sanctuaries are temporary, such as shelters for flood victims. Others exist for decades, under protection from governments or international organizations. Some refugee camps even become integrated into their communities.

The UN High Commissioner for Refugees, established in 1950, coordinates international policies to protect refugees. The agency has helped tens of millions to find temporary asylum or resettle. It also has a mandate to help refugees without citizenship (UN High Commissioner for Refugees, 2012).

Every country has its own refugee policies. In the United States and most European nations, asylum was long granted to people who are already in the country and unable or unwilling to return home because of a well-founded fear of persecution. Several years ago, however, some European states began to introduce admission tests, quota systems, and other legal barriers to asylum (Hainmueller and Hiscox, 2007).

CHECK YOUR KNOWLEDGE

▶ How does peacekeeping differ from aggressive warfare?
▶ When did China introduce its one-child policy and why?
▶ Which approach did the Grameen Bank introduce related to loans?

How Do We Study It?

Realism

In the realist view, states have primary responsibility for resolving humanitarian crises within their territory. Realists do not reject humanitarian intervention as a policy option. They recognize the need for international relief efforts and preventive measures. However, they argue that states should always put their national interests first. (See Figure 9.3.)

Realists see humanitarian interventions as warranted in two cases. First, a country may intervene if a foreign humanitarian crisis directly affects its sovereignty or security (Holzgrefe and Keohane, 2003). In 1971, India sent its military to East Pakistan, struck by a natural disaster, after about ten million refugees moved from there to India. Second, states may intervene in humanitarian crises if they cause regional destabilization. During the crisis around Biafra in the 1970s, the United Kingdom helped the central government in Nigeria. London wanted to prevent a chain of tribal secessions in Africa.

Realists warn that humanitarian interventions may create security dilemmas (see Chapter 4) and even contribute to instability and new wars. India's

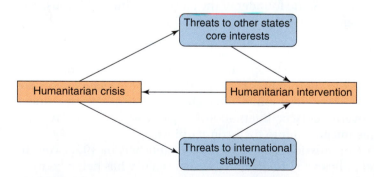

FIGURE 9-3 The realist view of humanitarian interventions. A country, realists argue, may intervene in a foreign humanitarian crisis if it directly affects the country's sovereignty or security. States may intervene in other countries' humanitarian crises if they cause significant regional destabilization.

humanitarian intervention in East Pakistan led to a war between India and Pakistan, producing an international crisis that drew attention from the United States, China, and the Soviet Union. The balance of power in the region changed in India's favor, when India won the war and helped set up the new state of Bangladesh in place of East Pakistan. In 1979, the Vietnamese invasion of Cambodia removed from power the genocidal government of Pol Pot. Yet it also provoked China to attack Vietnam in retribution. The tension in Southeast Asia lasted a decade, until Vietnam agreed to pull out its troops.

Other actions, too, have drawn criticism from realists. In barely a decade, these included the military operations of NATO in Yugoslavia on the side of the Kosovo Albanians in 1999, the U.S. intervention in Iraq in 2003, and the NATO actions in Libya in 2011. Realists argued that those operations had nothing to do with international stability or security, and humanitarian reasons alone could not justify war. In Yugoslavia, they feared, an independent Kosovo could destabilize the entire Balkans and produce new humanitarian problems. In Iraq, realists point out, the fall of Saddam shifted the balance of power in the Persian Gulf in favor of Iran, which was not in the interests of the West. Will Libya after Qaddafi become a beacon to African democracy or merely a failed state—a source of instability and new refugees (Rose, 2011)? Time will tell.

Liberalism

Liberalism emphasizes not just dangers but opportunities in humanitarian interventions. Liberals believe that preventing genocides and curbing genocidal autocrats must be a priority. This policy should strengthen an international community based on law, interdependence, and peaceful cooperation. Even state sovereignty can be put aside for the sake of humanitarian principles. (See Figure 9.4.)

THEORETICAL PRINCIPLES

The liberal approach draws on a rich intellectual and legal tradition. The **humanitarian tradition**, or *humanitarianism*, states that human beings, regardless

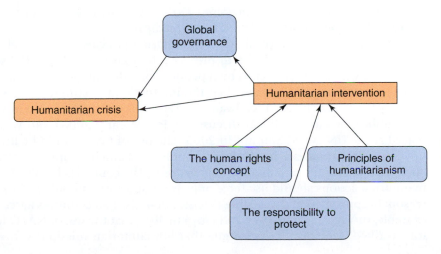

FIGURE 9-4 The liberal view of humanitarian interventions. The principles of humanitarianism, human rights, and the responsibility to protect justify humanitarian interventions.

Hollywood actress Demi Moore and Nepalese activist Anuradha Koirala with children at a rehabilitation center in Kathmandu, Nepal, for victims of human trafficking in 2011. Between half a million and one million people are trafficked across international borders each year.

of their origin and social status, are morally responsible to help those who suffer (Festa, 2010). Applied to international relations, this means that states have the responsibility to protect their citizens from the consequences of natural disasters, mass violence, starvation, or infectious diseases. Humanitarianism also claims that countries have the moral right to intervene for humanitarian reasons and not just out of strategic or security considerations (Power, 2002). Liberals criticize policy that puts state interests above morality (A. Buchanan, 2003; 2010).

Human rights (discussed in Chapter 6) provide a second intellectual and legal foundation for the liberal view. The 1948 UN Universal Declaration of Human Rights stated these rights broadly, and disagreements exist about specific rights. Are human rights limited to individual safety and physical integrity (Weiss, 2007)? Or are there additional *civil and political rights*, such as protection against discrimination and repression? Do individuals have a right to food, clothing, housing, health, and education (Madigan, 2007)?

The third foundation of liberal humanitarian policies is a relatively new legal concept, the **responsibility to protect** (often known as **R2P**). If a sovereign country does not protect its own people from identifiable causes of death and acute suffering, R2P states, then the international community must act. Military forces may be used (G. Evans, 2009). This concept appeared in scholarly publications and political discussions in the early 2000s and was embraced at the UN World Summit in 2005. The use of force should be limited, however. Humanitarian intervention should be launched only in cases of large-scale loss of life or a manifest danger of it. The countries involved in humanitarian actions should use force only as a last resort and only if they have reasonable prospects of succeeding (Weiss, 2004). Not all countries agreed, for example, in Yugoslavia in 1999 and Libya in 2011 that the use of NATO forces was justified. Moreover, critics argue that humanitarian missions can easily bog down in guerrilla warfare. For this reason humanitarian interventions should avoid the use of ground troops.

GLOBAL GOVERNANCE

Another new concept may provide still more room for effective humanitarian policies (Rosenau et al., 2005). **Global governance** is global cooperation with little or no power to enforce compliance. This means that humanitarian issues should be addressed voluntarily and collectively, through a sustained international effort (Forsythe et al., 2004; Keck and Sikkink, 1998).

Global governance is not a world government that would substitute for individual countries in addressing poverty, infectious diseases, or human trafficking. Global governance does not create a system of mandatory policies and practices. It uses existing structures, such as the United Nations or other international organizations (Rosenau, 1999). Participating states have equal status when it comes to decision-making, but NGOs are particularly important. According to the UN Development Program (UNDP), the number of humanitarian NGOs reached thirty-seven thousand (Polman, 2010, 10). The more power international law gives them, liberals argue, the more effective they become. *Universal jurisdiction* and *extraterritoriality* (discussed in Chapter 5) are thus essential.

No single formula or ideology, liberals insist, can solve all humanitarian problems. Each country has a unique history and politics. Free markets and strict government regulations each have their place. (See Tables 9-2 and 9-3.)

Constructivism

Humanitarian policies, constructivists argue, depend on perceptions. Humanitarian policies played an increasing role in international relations during the last century as many societies became more open, democratic, and interconnected. A country's interests are more often shaped not only by fear or aspirations for power, as realists often argue, but by concern for humanity as a whole. Relatively small countries, such as Norway and Canada, are commonly the most active in humanitarian policies. In public opinion polls, Canadians

TABLE 9-2 Some Features of Global Governance

Mutual Interdependence	Humanitarian issues should be addressed collectively.
Universal Jurisdiction	Global humanitarian aid, when necessary, is justified by the legal principles of extraterritoriality.
Equality among States	Equality and fairness apply, with no single international authority such as a state or a small group of states.
An Increasing Role for Nongovernmental Organizations	NGOs can address some local humanitarian problems more efficiently than states.
Pragmatism and Flexibility in Finding Solutions	No single formula or ideology can solve all humanitarian problems. Local conditions must be considered.

TABLE 9-3 Global Compact as an Element of Global Governance

Global Concerns	Governance Principles
Human Rights	Principle 1. Businesses should respect human rights. Principle 2. They must not be complicit in human rights abuses.
Labor Standards	Principle 3. Businesses should respect freedom of association and the right to collective bargaining. Principle 4. Compulsory labor must be eliminated. Principle 5. Child labor should be abolished. Principle 6. Discrimination in employment and occupation must end.
Environment	Principle 7. Businesses should support a precautionary approach to environmental challenges. Principle 8. They should promote greater environmental responsibility. Principle 9. They should encourage green technologies.
Anticorruption	Principle 10. Businesses should work against all forms of corruption, including extortion and bribery.

Source: United Nations Global Compact: www.unglobalcompact.org

see themselves as more caring, less individualistic, and less selfish than their neighbors in the United States (Carrière et al., 2003). Russia and China are more cautious when it comes to foreign humanitarian initiatives. This reflects their values and identities, including their mistrust of the West.

Perceptions, in turn, are inseparable from the international context. During the Cold War, humanitarian actions were largely subordinate to geopolitical interests—above all the strategic interests of the United States and the Soviet Union (Weiss, 2007, 31). The superpowers also provided humanitarian assistance to build positive images of their countries (Westad, 2007). Immediately after the Cold War, attention to humanitarian policies diminished.

CASE IN POINT > *Global Compact*

United Nations Global Compact attempts to bring companies together with UN agencies and nongovernmental organizations to address humanitarian and social challenges. (See Table 9-3.) Participation is voluntary. Business leaders join Global Compact because they believe that traditional solutions to humanitarian problems may not work. Corruption, abuse, and neglect linger. Global Compact supports new labor, environmental, and anticorruption standards.

CRITICAL THINKING

Do you agree that a joint effort by corporations and NGOs can make a significant impact on the international system? Or do you think this is just another initiative that produces few significant results? Why? What other international policies or agreements should be implemented to make this effort work?

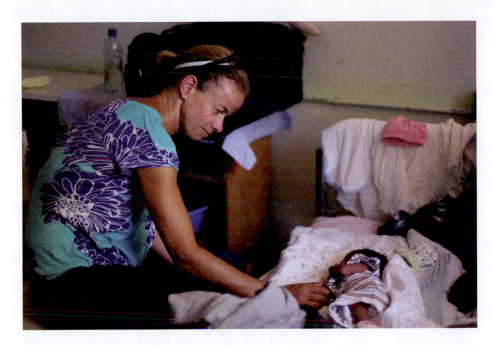

A Canadian aid worker checks on a baby she helped deliver the previous day at a hospital in Haiti in 2011. Historically, Canada has actively participated in humanitarian actions overseas. Some countries are very active in humanitarian missions, whereas others are not.

A country's elites tend to react to international events selectively, constructivism contends, in line with their identity, their interests, and their emotions. Political leaders and elites consider the plight of people of their own race, ethnicity, or religion as more compelling and important than the suffering of others (Finnemore, 2004). During the war in Bosnia in the early 1990s, the Arab media focused on atrocities committed against Bosnian Muslims, whereas the Russian media emphasized atrocities against the Christian Serbs (Sobel and Shiraev, 2003).

The evolution of societal norms helps governments and international organizations mobilize public support for humanitarian missions. So does, hopefully, the diminishing power of racism and xenophobia. Still, it is often difficult for political leaders to argue for massive humanitarian assistance to countries that do not evoke public sympathy.

Conflict Theories

Conflict theories maintain that inequality is the most important cause of humanitarian problems. "Inequality" means the lingering gaps between social groups, rich and poor, or wealthy countries and the rest of the world. Rescue operations and emergency aid are necessary, but no short-term act can address the structural issues.

Conflict theories also prescribe policies to rectify structural problems. In *The Wretched of the Earth* (2005), Frantz Fanon rejected European humanism as a model for the Third World. The victims of suffering in poor countries, Fanon wrote, must rise up and fight for their own security and prosperity. Others insist that the world needs global affirmative action. Wealthy nations must restructure their relations with the rest of the world. These prescriptions, you should remember, represent the *dependency theory* of international relations (Chapter 6). Take hunger, for example. Most countries could feed their own people, but international trade and finance compel them to export food instead. Paradoxically, food-exporting poor states depend on the financial assistance of food-importing rich powers (Lappe et al., 1998). To change this unfair order, the world's richest states must allow all countries to exercise sovereignty.

Some theorists believe that Western states use humanitarian intervention not just to address suffering, but rather to advance their strategic interests. Capitalist countries are commonly accused of wrapping expansionist designs in humanitarian rhetoric (Weiss, 2007; Bass, 2009). The global governance proposed by liberals is criticized as a way for powerful institutions and countries to impose their rules and interests on the rest of the world.

Feminism notes that humanitarian problems disproportionally affect women, and yet they do not receive due attention from the international community. Women over the past several years were also the most common victims of the HIV pandemic. Women and girls are targets of mass atrocities, human trafficking, and sexual assault. Rape is a form of intimidation and humiliation during violent conflict. This can also be a type of genocide when it is deliberately and systematically used against a particular ethnic or religious group. Sexual violence against women has long been widespread and underreported. It was widespread during the Armenian massacre in 1915; the partition of India in the 1940s; in armed conflicts in Latin America in the 1970s; and in African conflicts in Angola, Liberia, Sierra Leone, Rwanda, Somalia, and Sudan. Wars in East Timor, Sri Lanka, and Myanmar involved mass rape of civilians. Rape was also rampant during the war in Bosnia, a European country, in the 1990s (Leatherman, 2011). Feminism encourages scholars and politicians to expand their traditional state-centered view of international security (see Chapter 4) and focus more on the security concerns and protection of the individual, including women (Kuehnast et al., 2011).

CHECK YOUR KNOWLEDGE

▶ Explain global governance.
▶ What does R2P mean?

How Do We Apply It?

We can apply theories of international relations to humanitarian problems only if we take into account the complexity of world politics. Which theories provide a road map to more efficient policies? What are the proper roles of institutions, structures, and culture in all this?

The Individual Context

Humanitarian policies and their acceptance are often based on the choices of individuals. Political leaders may act out of conviction, ideology, or personal interest.

LEADERS' CHOICES

Some leaders are actively involved in humanitarian issues because of their deep-seated convictions. Kofi Annan from Ghana was devastated by the UN failure to stop genocide in Rwanda in 1994. Later, as UN secretary general from 1997 to 2006, he became an advocate of the responsibility to protect (R2P). Moral intentions and political calculations are often interconnected. Former British prime minister Tony Blair supported the U.S. invasion of Iraq in 2003 for humanitarian reasons. At the same time, he believed his support would consolidate the alliance between the United States and the United Kingdom (Blair, 2010).

United Nations Secretary-General Kofi Annan in 1997. After the UN failed to stop the genocide in Rwanda in 1994, Annan became an advocate of the responsibility to protect (R2P).

Circumstances may alter a leader's choice. President Clinton failed to stop the genocide in Rwanda but used force to stop the ethnic cleansing in Kosovo several years later. President Bush rejected a humanitarian intervention in Darfur because the United States was already involved in wars in Iraq and Afghanistan. President Obama stated in 2011 that he was using force in Libya only because he had no other choice. Historically, stronger powers tend to insist on their right to interfere in humanitarian issues, whereas officials from less powerful countries choose caution (Bass, 2009).

Leaders also may accept or reject humanitarian aid out of ideological conviction. In 2003, Iran suffered a massive earthquake, killing more than twenty-six thousand people. The government of Tehran accepted help from more than forty countries but refused aid from Israel.

DENYING OR HIDING PROBLEMS

Leaders of the Soviet Union and other Socialist states were concerned for building a positive image of Communism. They were thus reluctant to admit to devastating problems in their own countries. They censored reports of natural disasters, epidemics, and human rights violations. During the 1930s and 1940s, Stalin effectively covered up massive hunger in the Soviet Union and rejected international assistance. Many years later, in the twenty-first century, Communist governments in Cuba and North Korea blocked information about serious humanitarian problems in their countries.

Authoritarian leaders facing little opposition at home tend to underemphasize the severity of problems in their countries. President Robert Mugabe of Zimbabwe often criticized international humanitarian efforts to help his country as imperialist ploys. Ideology or preoccupation with their country's prestige caused several African leaders to interfere with attempts to fight the AIDS epidemics there. These leaders also accused the international community of using the AIDS crisis as a pretense to expand Western domination.

The State Context

Humanitarian policies are based in part on a country's domestic politics, including competition among political parties, media coverage, and lobbying efforts.

THE POLITICAL CLIMATE

When the public in a democratic country is not interested in a crisis overseas, then the government is under less pressure to intervene. Politicians may in fact use public opinion to justify inaction. During the genocidal violence in Bosnia in the 1990s, European leaders at first refrained from intervention. In the United States, the Bush and then Clinton administration also used public opinion as a reason not to intervene (Sobel, 2001).

At the same time, political elites can change the policy climate. From 1995 to 1999 the Clinton administration helped convince Americans that the United States should intervene in Bosnia, where violence had already cost one hundred thousand lives. Politicians in France, Germany, the Netherlands, and the UK also grew frustrated over the inaction of their governments. NGOs and the media argued for a moral duty to launch a humanitarian military action. Finally, in 1995, a military coalition intervened.

The refugee policies of Europe's political parties reflect humanitarian principles but also electoral concerns. Parties of the left traditionally support generous immigration policies, particularly for the victims of repression (Sniderman et al., 2004). The left also recruits heavily from immigrant communities. Moderate social democratic parties, with their reliance on middle and lower middle class members, tend to support refugees so long as they do not threaten jobs. Parties of the political center support immigration by those with job skills, especially in the professions, but not the open-door immigration policies of the European Union. Parties on the right try to limit immigration for ideological reasons. They also point to the tight job and housing markets and the need to preserve a distinct European or national identity. Libertarians generally believe in a universal right to travel and settle in the country of one's choice so long as one accepts that nation's rules and customs.

FAVORABLE CONDITIONS

Why are some humanitarian missions more effective than others? Effective humanitarian assistance requires favorable social and economic conditions, the absence of violence, local customs, and low levels of corruption and fraud. Securing these, however, is difficult. In countries such as Afghanistan and Somalia, humanitarian missions are much more difficult. Armed forces may stop violence, but they often contribute to local conflicts and may even bring new violence (Young, 2010).

Much of sub-Saharan Africa has long lacked the conditions for successful humanitarian missions. Weak and corrupt institutions in these countries usually support traditional customs and biases, not seek to change them. When it comes to AIDS, for example, most women have little control over their sex lives and many suffer from abuse. Married women who are faithful to their husbands are at risk of contracting HIV, too, because men often have multiple sex partners. Local leaders tend to resist attempts to promote contraceptives, insisting that abstinence is the only proper preventive behavior. As a result, not long ago women were close to 60 percent of adults living with HIV (Patterson, 2006).

Some policies can be effective simply because they are imposed on the population. China's one-child policy is an example. Why did this policy succeed even though it targeted the most deep-seated values and cultural practices? It was effective because the Communist Party controlled the school system, the media, and local party networks. Particularly after the 1960s, the Chinese government began to shape a younger generation's beliefs. Opposing views were not allowed.

The Global Context

A more global world is likely to face a range of old and new humanitarian problems. Will future problems affect more people than ever? What are the main lessons of past policies, and how can the future be better?

NEW AND EVOLVING CONCERNS

Globalization brings new opportunities. However, globalization may also create new problems or deepen existing ones. Consider just a few developments—travel, migration, and climate change. Feel free to add your own ideas.

Global travel creates new health risks. Take infectious diseases as an example. With international travel expanding, people can carry a dangerous infectious disease to the far side of the world before the first symptoms appear. Insects and small animals can spread disease as well. Trade in animals and animal products now includes hundreds of species of wildlife (Wolfe, 2011; Karesh and Cook, 2005).

Global migration also brings new problems and deepens old ones. Whereas wealthier families tend to move to comfortable and less-crowded places, new megacities in the developing world attract millions of migrants from poorer areas. Natural disasters and epidemics find most of their victims in such crowded places. Globally, the poor remain the most vulnerable to threats to their health and safety.

Global climate change (see Chapter 8) may lead to more frequent floods and droughts. Wealthy countries and regions may adjust to these changes, but others—and there will be hundreds of millions of them—will suffer.

Most people in developed countries are accustomed to a stable income, a good education, medical care, and generous social benefits. Their comfortable lives may leave them more open to considering the suffering of others. The recent global recession, however, may have changed that. To many people, a country torn apart by tribal violence may appear more distant and their problems less significant. Others may lose their faith in the possibility of solving problems—including humanitarian problems. The temptation to turn away is not new (Power, 2002). Calls for humanitarian action often come from a few leaders and a handful of activists who face widespread indifference. And that indifference may well increase.

POLICY ARGUMENTS

Recall from the start of this chapter the principles behind humanitarian intervention—humanity, impartiality, and independence. Although these principles have international recognition, debates continue about how to apply them. Many question the legitimacy of intervention for humanitarian reasons without another country's consent (Chandler, 2006; Rieff, 2006). Realists and liberals may agree on the need to enforce the rule of law and to save lives. But, they insist, sovereignty can be suspended only temporarily and only as part of a sustained international effort (Keohane, 2003). Because the United Nations tends to apply R2P to humanitarian crises, there is a growing need for international enforcement. But because the United Nations has no armed forces, countries with strong militaries are likely to remain the global "enforcers."

Another challenge to R2P is the blurring boundary between humanitarian assistance and military intervention to achieve political goals (Orbinski, 2009). Critics insist that R2P is just a cover for Western interference (Weiss, 2004). The debates flared up again in the spring of 2011, when France and Britain, supported by the Obama administration, led the attacks against the dictatorial regime in Libya. They acted to protect Libya's population from slaughter and had UN Security Council authorization. Yet critics, including Russia and China, argued that the military strikes violated a UN mandate prescribing neutrality in a civil war. Humanitarian interventions continue to split the international community.

EFFICIENCY OF AID

By recent estimates, humanitarian aid is now close to $160 billion each year (Polman, 2010). Is it effective, and how can we measure its effectiveness? With all the praise heaped on NGOs, criticism has become increasingly audible.

One issue is global coordination. A dozen large NGOs control the majority of nongovernmental humanitarian funding (Agier, 2010, 35). Unfortunately, their efforts may duplicate one another. They also do not coordinate their programs effectively with the Red Cross, Red Crescent, and other UN-funded organizations.

Medical officers from the U.S. Navy hospital ship *Comfort* provide medical care and humanitarian assistance to Haitians in 2011. The field of humanitarian medicine is concerned with diseases that primarily affect the poorest countries, where the public health infrastructure is in dire condition or nonexistent.

Another problem is accountability. American NGOs have spent hundreds of millions of dollars on humanitarian assistance in Iraq and Afghanistan—but how effective was it? How much of each dollar is spent on humanitarian aid, and how much is wasted, owing to corruption and fraud? This is not easy to judge. NGOs are usually audited in their countries of origins, but aid recipients are often not audited at all. Fighting factions often use financial aid to continue the violence. The BBC found that Ethiopian warlords used millions of dollars in Western aid meant for victims of the famine of 1984 and 1985 to buy weapons. The rebels posed as merchants and met with charity workers to obtain relief money (BBC, 2010). Some warlords also manipulate donors for personal enrichment (Polman, 2010). Transparent bookkeeping does not always solve the problems of corruption.

SUSTAINABILITY OF SUCCESS

Short-term interventions alone cannot solve today's humanitarian problems. Rather, successful term policies must be *sustainable*. What, then, are the ingredients for long-term success in a global world?

One feature of successful policies is a *participatory approach*. NGOs, for example, can act as effective lobbyists for humanitarian actions. Ordinary people, too, can contribute money and become volunteers. The Web and social media have become effective mobilization tools as well.

Transparency and accountability are another feature. Without addressing corruption, humanitarian aid programs are ineffective. Again NGOs and other independent participants are important.

Wealth creation is another feature of successful humanitarian policies. For example, the creation of a stable market economy can help combat poverty. The experiences of Chile, Botswana, India, or South Korea show that private enterprise can deliver essential goods, food, and services. As poverty rates go down, the middle class grows, and the quality of social services improves. The decline in fertility rates in the world's poorest regions since the 1960s is probably linked to improving living standards.

New international policies will probably emerge. Disease prevention is also a security issue, but *global health security* requires a serious global effort. Some countries have already begun to care for the health of other nations ("International Health Regulations," 2007). For example, countries have started sharing information about new viruses and infectious diseases. *Humanitarian medicine* is a new field concerned with diseases that affect primarily the poorest countries, where the public health infrastructure is in dire condition or non-existent. It brings today's diagnostic and pharmaceutical tools to people who otherwise wouldn't get treatment (Lakoff, 2010, 60).

Effective humanitarian policies are also linked to the development of international law (A. Buchanan, 2010), to legitimize efforts to fight pandemics, hunger, or the consequences of civil wars. Once again, the role of NGOs and international organizations can only increase (Ayittey, 2005). What the world needs right now is a strong collective effort.

▶ Explain the debates around R2P policy.
▶ Why was China's one-child policy relatively successful?
▶ What is humanitarian medicine?

CHECK YOUR KNOWLEDGE

Past, Present, and Future: Celebrity Activism

Fridtjof Nansen (1861–1930), a Norwegian scientist and bold Arctic explorer, made headlines more than a century ago, but many still discuss his voyages. Fewer recall that he later received the Nobel Prize for his humanitarian efforts. In 1921 the League of Nations appointed Nansen as high commissioner for refugees. He helped millions of victims of World War I, the Russian Civil War, and other conflicts. He proposed a temporary certificate to allow residence in countries where refugees were not citizens. These "Nansen passports," recognized by over fifty countries, helped millions to find a new home and survive mass violence. Nansen led the life of a celebrity while directing the world's attention to the fate of prisoners of war, refugees, and famine victims. He became one of the first humanitarian activists.

Celebrity activism is the involvement of famous individuals—primarily from the arts, science, or entertainment—in humanitarian action. In the past, celebrities came from privileged groups. They raised money and organized hospitals during wartime to aid soldiers of their own countries. Today's celebrities deal with different problems, including poverty, human trafficking, land mines, AIDS, hunger, and human rights. They are also not from the aristocracy but rather "media darlings" who can attract global attention almost instantly—far more quickly, in fact, than politicians. When actress Angelina Jolie traveled to Cambodia, she reminded the world of the plight of refugees and the victims of land mines—legacies of the lethal Pol Pot regime. When Bono, the singer from U2, met with top British and U.S. officials to discuss Africa, the events made headlines. When Natalie Imbruglia, the Australian singer, went to Nigeria to campaign for better treatment of *fistula*—a childbirth-related illness— reporters, photographers, and filmmakers accompanied her everywhere.

UN High Commissioner for Refugees Special Envoy Angelina Jolie meets with Syrian refugees at the Zaatari refugee camp in Jordan in 2012. When can high-profile individuals be more effective than governments in solving humanitarian issues?

Thanks to Twitter, Facebook, and hundreds of blogs, celebrity activism is always "breaking news." But does it make a difference? Consider several arguments.

Celebrities routinely give away tens of thousands of dollars to schools, hospitals, refugee camps, and rehabilitation centers all over the world. Joey Cheek, the Olympic speed skater, donated $40,000 of his prize money to refugees in Darfur. A fashion show generated $170,000 for the Rainforest Foundation, founded by the British singer Sting. Angelina Jolie gave $500,000 to the National Center for Refugee and Immigrant Children foundation, to pay for legal care of orphaned asylum-seekers. Together with Brad Pitt, she gave $1 million to relief efforts in Haiti after the deadly earthquake there. Actor Nicolas Cage pledged $2 million to help former child soldiers and exploited kids. Bob Geldof, an Irish singer and songwriter, organized six free concerts in Europe and in North America involving Elton John, Madonna, Faith Hill, Stevie Wonder, Paul McCartney, Coldplay, U2, and Bon Jovi to raise money for Africa. Bono had a role in powerful nations' joint decision to write off $40 billion of debt owed by eighteen countries, mostly in sub-Saharan Africa.

Often celebrities are excellent fundraisers. Many of the wealthy (and not so wealthy) reach for their wallets. Some are moved by the eloquent appeals of singers and actresses. Others donate for the privilege of meeting them or simply joining them in a common cause.

Celebrities also raise public awareness by helping to educate and mobilize public opinion. Years ago, actress Audrey Hepburn began her engagement with the United Nations International Children's Emergency Fund (UNICEF). At that time, not many people knew about the fund or her involvement in it. These days, eight out of ten young Britons said they learned about the Make Trade Fair campaign from Chris Martin, a singer from *Coldplay*. Today's celebrity appearances can draw the instant attention of hundreds of millions of viewers. Celebrities themselves blog or go on Twitter to organize grassroots campaigns. A global campaign cofounded by Bono, known as One, calls on "citizens, voters, and taxpayers" to tell their governments to help Africa defeat poverty, malaria, and AIDS and to restructure its debts. One of its goals is to make sure that no child is born in Africa after 2015 with AIDS.

You can learn about the One campaign on the companion website.

More celebrities see their role as promoting awareness for specific causes. The Creative Coalition even offers training to prepare the rich and famous for public roles as social advocates. Supermodel Heather Mills, like Angelina Jolie and the late Princess Diana, was engaged in the campaign against land mines. George Clooney and Ashley Judd work for AIDS education; Woody Harrelson, Josh Lucas, and Leonardo DiCaprio chose environmental issues. Because of Angelina Jolie, many people learned about refugee camps from Sierra Leone to Tanzania; Thailand to Ecuador; Kosovo to Kenya, Sri Lanka, Northern Russia, Jordan, Chad, Darfur, India, and Cost Rica.

Celebrities make humanitarian organizations and their efforts more recognizable and, probably, more effective. Actor Robin Williams participated in the activities of Doctors Without Borders, and P. Diddy (Sean Combs) contributed to the World Wildlife Fund. Many other humanitarian groups need more international attention, which famous individuals could provide instantaneously.

Some celebrities have access to national political leaders and top government offices. Over the years, Bono visited the heads of state of a dozen of the most influential nations. Producer Bob Geldof reportedly could get an appointment with former British prime minister Tony Blair in a matter of days.

Critics maintain that celebrity activism, despite its success, is not always what it appears to be. Most of celebrity activists have tens or hundreds of millions of dollars in assets. A team of "advisers" and lawyers monitors a star's every financial move. They recommend charitable donations that make sense financially. Tax incentives, especially in the United States, encourage celebrities to contribute to humanitarian causes. Celebrities also use their humanitarian activities and the media attention they generate to promote their products. A foreign trip can help advertise a forthcoming album or film.

Even if celebrities are true altruists, and profits or lower taxes are not their top priority, their activities can evoke criticism. They often want to see the immediate effects of their work, but humanitarian problems require a sustained effort. It takes years to achieve real, not superficial, change in the struggle against poverty and disease. Celebrities may also lack sufficient expertise. They may believe that their opinions on social and political issues are valuable simply because *they* express them. And what if they display "celebrity activism complex"—a desire to do something important simply because it feels good? Sure, celebrities make people listen to what they sing and say. But their actions could be misguided. For example, substantial sums of money generated by rock concerts went to organizations under the control of corrupt governments.

People who live in the spotlight are easy to admire or to criticize. Liberals may criticize celebrity activism for its flashy style and inattention to the deeper social causes of humanitarian problems. Others may disapprove of celebrities for advocating controversial philosophies. Yet in some cases celebrity activism indeed brings public attention to serious problems faster and more efficiently than governments do. Humanitarian aid provided by famous people makes a difference. Food for the starving, shelters for the refugees, medications for children—they all matter. In the end, why celebrities donate their money and time is less significant than the results.

CONCLUSION

Overall, global awareness of real and potential humanitarian problems has advanced. So have humanist values in foreign policy and international law. In the end, the most effective humanitarian policies will allow people to develop their full potential and lead dynamic and peaceful lives in accord with their needs, cultural demands, and communities. A strong moral case remains for forceful humanitarian intervention in desperate cases. Would the world still do nothing if it had a second chance to avert genocide in Rwanda? From the Balkans to Liberia and from Sierra Leone to Kosovo, armed interventions have, on balance, helped to end or forestall catastrophes.

We began the chapter with questions. When one country faces a tragic loss of life, do other states have the obligation to intervene? When hunger strikes, is there a right or responsibility to help? When people face the overwhelming and destructive forces of nature, they must do everything they can to help. But who should protect people from the mismanagement, neglect, and abuses of their fellow human beings—and how? And what should be done to diminish global poverty? The global jury is still out.

CHAPTER SUMMARY

- Humanitarian problems include infectious diseases such as AIDS, chronic starvation and malnutrition, and acute suffering. They are caused by natural disasters, mismanagement, damaging policies, mass violence, extreme poverty, overpopulation, and involuntary migration. Humanitarian problems are usually interconnected, and so are their causes.

- Humanitarian policies are based on three principles: humanity, impartiality, and independence. These policies may include international interventions to remove an immediate cause of massive suffering or a potential threat to a population, relief efforts to help victims of a humanitarian disaster, and preventive measures against future crises. Particular policies may address overpopulation, poverty, and refugees.

- Besides bringing relief, humanitarian interventions also attempt to eliminate the sources of the crisis, especially if they are human made. Sovereignty is an essential principle of international relations restricting interventions.

- Realism recognizes the need for international relief efforts and preventive measures to avoid humanitarian problems. However, realists argue that states should put their national interests first.

- Liberalism recognizes that preventing genocides and curbing genocidal autocrats must be the higher priority of foreign policy. The liberal approach draws on a rich intellectual and legal tradition. It also takes into account such new concepts as the responsibility to protect and global governance.

- Constructivists argue that humanitarian policies are based on interests and perceptions inseparable from a broader international context. Conflict theories maintain that the most important cause of humanitarian problems is inequality—between social groups, the rich and the poor, or wealthy countries and the rest of the world.

- Circumstances increase or limit leaders' choices. Some leaders are actively involved in humanitarian issues out of deep-seated conviction. Others may act out of necessity.

- A country's humanitarian policies are based on competition among political parties, media coverage, and lobbying efforts. Effective humanitarian assistance requires favorable social and economic conditions, the absence of violence, local customs, and low levels of corruption.

- Globalization—including travel, migration, and climate change—may create new humanitarian problems or deepen existing ones. Efficiency, transparency, and accountability remain significant challenges. Debates continue regarding the humanity, impartiality, and independence of humanitarian interventions.

KEY TERMS

1. What do we study?

KEY ISSUES

- Incidents or continuing problems threatening the health, safety, security, and well-being of many
- Pandemics, chronic starvation and malnutrition, other forms of acute suffering

CAUSES OF HUMANITARIAN PROBLEMS

- Environmental disasters and accidents
- Politics, mismanagement, neglect, and mass violence
- Mostly interconnected

HUMANITARIAN POLICIES

- Intervention: the actions of foreign powers in a humanitarian crisis with or without the approval of a legal authority controlling the area
- Relief efforts: aid to a country without violating its sovereignty
- Prevention

2. How do we study it?

REALISM

- A country may intervene if a foreign humanitarian crisis directly affects its sovereignty or security
- States may intervene in humanitarian crises if they cause regional destabilization

LIBERALISM

- Policies rooted in three principles: humanitarianism, responsibility to protect, and human rights
- Emphasis on international cooperation and global governance

CONSTRUCTIVISM

- Countries build their humanitarian policies on their evolving values, perceptions, and their concern for humanity as a whole

OTHER THEORIES

- Conflict theories: economic and political inequality is the key cause of humanitarian problems
- Feminism: humanitarian problems disproportionally affect women, yet women do not receive due attention

3. How do we apply it?

THE INDIVIDUAL CONTEXT

Leaders' choices are rooted in values or affected by individual circumstances that affect humanitarian policies

THE STATE CONTEXT

Humanitarian policies are connected to a country's domestic politics, including competition among political parties, media coverage, and lobbying efforts

THE GLOBAL CONTEXT

- Global challenges such as migration, travel, and climate change affect humanitarian problems and policies to alleviate them
- Efficiency and sustainability of global humanitarian efforts remain key challenges

Critical Thinking

- Discuss the pros and cons of humanitarian interventions.
- What conditions, in your view, are necessary for global governance to succeed?
- Should global governance allow some authoritarian means to address the most acute humanitarian problems? Under what circumstances?
- Does celebrity activism make a difference in the global efforts to fight illness, poverty, violence, or injustice? If so, in what way? If not, why not?

Conclusion: Forecasting the World of 2025

T HE SCIENCE OF INTERNATIONAL RELATIONS IS LIMITED IN ITS PREDICTIVE POWER. BECAUSE SO MANY FACTORS (BOTH KNOWN AND HIDDEN) INFLUENCE WORLD POLITICS, it is very difficult to make accurate forecasts. For example, few experts anticipated the implosion of Communism in 1989. Very few predicted the global financial meltdown in 2008 in the United States and the crisis of the Eurozone in 2011–12. And virtually no one could foresee the revolutionary turmoil in the Arab world that started in 2011. It is so easy today to miss new trends of tomorrow. Yet we shouldn't be discouraged. There are ways of making reasonably reliable forecasts in international relations. Every event has specific causes and every development is set in a context. Wars, revolutions, treaties, economic miracles, and great alliances—they all have precedents. Their lessons can be thoroughly studied and applied. The key for success is your knowledge and a measure of imagination.

It is time for a final exercise for you and your class. Using this book as a guide, try to make a few predictions. Use the key concepts and theories from Chapters 1 and 2, and then utilize other chapters that can be relevant for your forecasts. Your task is to discern certain patterns in international relations and creatively extrapolate them into the future.

We will begin with the international system, its main actors, and its stability.

- **While protecting stability, how will the strong states treat the weak states?**

States differ in their ability to deliver essential functions—such as to collect taxes, enforce the law, maintain stability, and protect the population—as measured by the *index of state capability*. By this measure, the United States or some countries of the European Union are fairly strong states. In contrast, in many areas of Africa and Asia, states are either weak or very weak. They are failing. Unstable and filled with tensions, they often need urgent international

Opposition supporters react as they hear the official presidential election results in Caracas, Venezuela, in April 2013. Hugo Chavez's hand-picked successor, Nicolás Maduro, won a razor-thin victory in a special presidential election, edging out the opposition's leader.

assistance simply to survive. Somalia and Afghanistan have long been regarded as failing states.

What will happen to the relationship between the strong and the weak states in the next ten years? Will the strong states like the United States continue to maintain international stability? What will prevent them from simply taking over the weak and unstable states and imposing on them their rules? History knows several successful precedents of such actions (see Chapter 1). Or maybe the world will forever be divided on wealthy and stable states on one hand and poor and unstable on the other? Looking for clues, use Chapter 2 on sovereignty, state power, and international institutions, and Chapter 5 on international law. After reading this book and learning many facts and theories, do you believe more or believe less in a possibility of a stable world in 2025?

- **Global order: Will a powerful coalition emerge to challenge the United States?**

Supporters of Realism argue that the United States is unlikely to remain an unchallenged global power for a long time. A coalition of states is likely to emerge to test America's supremacy. Other Realists disagree and contend that these threats are exaggerated because the United States' hegemony is "stable" (Chapter 2). They believe that we live in the world where the most powerful, democratic states such as United Kingdom, France, Germany, and Japan have no interest in challenging Washington's power and supremacy. Partly as a result of America's relatively good historical record, many countries prefer Washington's hegemony to that of their neighbors (Walt, 2005b). Other experts think states like Russia and China are simply incapable of throwing a serious challenge either now or in the near future.

Which one of these two arguments do you see as more plausible than the other? To answer, browse the pages from Chapters 2 and 3 referring to state power, power balancing, multipolarity and unipolarity, identity, and security regimes.

Now consider three hypothetical scenarios. How probable are they to you?

1. To challenge the United States' domination, China, Russia, India, and Brazil in 2018 form the *Transcontinental Economic Alliance*. Its members control prices for most manufactured goods, establish economic sanctions against the United States, and start a new global currency to compete against the dollar.
2. Iran, Kazakhstan, China, and Russia, accompanied by several Central Asian states, build a new political and military pact called the *Eurasian Alliance*. Its key goal is to resist the "export of democracy" from Washington to Eurasia. They also keep American companies in Eurasia under control, keep Western NGOs out, and act jointly in the United Nations to advance their global interests. The United States agrees in 2018, under political pressure from its allies, to coordinate all its Eurasian policies with the Eurasian Alliance.
3. Several oil-producing authoritarian countries such as Saudi Arabia, Venezuela, Nigeria, and Iran form the *New Energy Alliance* and drastically reduce their oil shipments to the United States and Western Europe. Most oil tankers in 2018 are redirected to Asia and Africa instead. The alliance calls for a "fair" distribution of global energy resources and refuses the United States' and British oil companies to operate in its countries.

Which of these scenarios do you consider plausible, somewhat probable, and barely possible? Are there in your opinion other plausible alliances to emerge in several years, and will they be successful?

• **In which areas will NGOs replace governments?**

Supporters of liberal internationalism (Chapter 2) argue that NGOs are becoming the most significant and capable actors in international relations. NGOs use vast networks of volunteers and highly skilled professionals, and are often more efficient than government agencies. NGOs are usually more transparent than the large bureaucratic institutions. They also work closely with local populations and often have firsthand knowledge about the countries and regions in which they operate. Acting as global "whistleblowers" and "watchdogs," they can more effectively discover problems and attract immediate international attention.

In your view, in which areas of international relations would NGOs be getting most influence? Will it be international security (Chapter 4), international trade (Chapter 5), environmental protection (Chapter 8), humanitarian aid (Chapter 9), or some other areas? In which areas do you think states and coalitions of states would retain their superior decision-making power?

• **How would new media change the world?**

Supporters of liberalism (see Chapters 2 and 9) also believe that today's innovations in electronic communications should help in weakening authoritarian governments globally. The more access people have to the information exposing corrupt and abusive governments, the less authority and legitimacy these governments have. Not long ago, people in the Philippines, Ukraine, Lebanon, Tunisia, and Egypt were using smart phones and the Internet to organize resistance and push their corrupt governments out of power. Do you believe that free information means democratization? Authoritarian governments can certainly push back.

Supporters of constructivism (Chapter 3) think the actual results of the ongoing technological changes are not that clear. True, the global informational revolution changes international relations. Yet these changes are not necessarily advancing democracy. For instance, during the political turmoil in the Middle East and North Africa in recent years, the "Twitter revolution" benefited in the end political Islam and not necessarily liberal democracy. Authoritarian governments in Iran, Zimbabwe, and China seek to control Internet and Web-based social networks. Moreover, in China, the Web allows nationalists to express their anger against the West and Japan, as well as hostility toward Tibetans, Muslim Uighurs, and other ethnic minority groups. Violent separatist and terrorist groups use the Web and mobile devices to launch attacks and threaten international security (see Chapters 4 and 7).

Five years down the road, what would be the key political outcomes of the global "media revolution"? Will radical groups and authoritarian governments use the new media to go on the offensive and bring democracy down in their countries? Or do you rather see more openness and transparency forming a new political culture, thus leading to democratization and peace around the world? Explain your choices referring to Chapters 3 and 9.

• **Who would benefit from the globalization of the economy? Will poverty end?**

Supporters of world systems and dependency theories (Chapters 3 and 6) have long maintained that the North (particularly Western Europe and the United States) draws the most benefits from the emerging global economy, whereas the South gets only what is left. Most recently, certain theorists started to speak about the "Chinese miracle." In this view, China has learned to benefit from the international economic system, and the United States appears to be a loser. Supporters of economic liberalism (Chapter 6) disagree with these conclusions. Their argument is that in today's global economy both the United States and China, along with many other countries, should benefit from economic openness and trade.

In your view, which countries would benefit the most in an emerging economic order? Will the North–South divisions persist in ten years and how deep will they remain?

A new technological revolution may change a global economic forecast and thus affect international relations in general (Evans-Pritchard, 2011). Consider *3D printing*, a technology that "copies" three-dimensional objects from a digital file. In a few years, giant assembly lines and big factories may no longer be needed: many goods will be produced on demand, locally. This means that 3D printing may undermine the manufacturing capacity of countries, such as China and India. They manufacture and sell cheap products relying mostly on low-wage labor. 3D printing should challenge the whole global economic situation. Which countries will benefit the most? Which would lose? Can every country benefit?

Which scenario for the global economy do you envision, and why?

• **A democratic peace—will it actually be "peaceful"?**

Liberalism embraces the idea that democracies do not fight one another (Chapter 2). More democracy means more peace and international security. We learned in Chapter 1 that Japan and Germany transformed into wealthy and peaceful democracies after they had been occupied by the United States. During the Cold War, NATO encouraged its members, including Greece and Turkey, to become more democratic to avoid war with each other.

However, democratization is a very complicated process. Realists and constructivists argue that far away from Washington or Paris, the political outcome of democratic transitions becomes even more complicated. The experiences of Iraq, Afghanistan, and some other countries show that democratization does not necessarily stop violence (Chapter 7). Democratic reforms do not rapidly end pervasive poverty (Chapter 6). A quick transition away from authoritarianism often produces ethnic or religious clashes and constant violence. Free elections may bring to power religious fundamentalists or ultra-nationalists, sworn enemies of liberal democracy (Chapter 3). Moreover, some emerging democracies tend to be more war prone than authoritarian states.

We also should not overlook the threat of international terrorism. If democratization continues to spread around the world, some groups may continue to use terrorism and other forms of violence to achieve their political goals. As we know the early attempts at building democracy in Iraq led to sectarian ethnic violence, which inspired terrorist groups including al-Qaeda. The removal of the authoritarian regime in Libya had several unintended consequences for Algeria and Mali, where violent groups unleashed terrorism against governments.

Will the world in ten years be more democratic or less democratic? Will the world become more stable and have fewer military conflicts if most countries become democratic? Do you anticipate that the West will support an authoritarian but stable Middle East and Africa, or will it instead support democratic yet unstable governments there? What is your reasoning?

Scenarios

What will the world be like in future decades? Let's look at some scenarios for 2025. Based on what you have learned in this course, how plausible does each of these seem to you?

Beijing, China. *A new chairperson of the Microsoft Corporation, Shen Yang, said during today's press conference that the company needed to restore the confidence* *of its customers. To stay on the path of innovative research and development, it needs new ideas. After a new generation of Japanese "wallpaper computers" that transform our entire surroundings reached the market, Microsoft nearly lost its global competitiveness. It has therefore agreed to become a state corporation owned by Chinese government. The company will close some factories in Asia and build new ones in the United States and Canada, where labor is cheaper.*

New York. *The incoming UN Secretary General, Evo Morales, former president of Bolivia, said that his top priority would be expanding the permanent membership of the UN Security Council. A longtime advocate of the inclusion of a country from Central America, he favors the candidacy of Cuba, which had its first multiparty elections last year. Radical reform of the United Nations should continue, he added, with elimination of the veto power of Security Council members. The UN will have its armed forces permanently stationed in all continents. Following the example of Canada and Sweden, countries should amend their constitutions to comply with the decisions of the United Nations and other international organizations.*

Ankara. *Top government delegations from Turkey and Iran have signed a mutual protocol on nuclear energy, as well as on educational, scientific, and professional exchanges between the two countries. For the first time in history, female leaders represent the Turkish and Iranian governments. They both studied in the United States and received their advanced degrees in international affairs.*

Moscow. *Russian President Vladimir Putin met with the leaders of the New European Alliance, formed just last year and including three former republics of the Soviet Union: Russia, the Ukraine, and Belarus. Putin underscored that the alliance is not hostile to NATO but an alternative to it. He also promised to return to multilateral negotiations concerning Russia's recent takeover of the vast area of the Arctic Ocean.*

Pyongyang. *The new capital of the unified Korea is rapidly becoming a booming modern metropolis. Using electric cars and solar-driven public transportation, Pyongyang has managed to avoid the traffic and pollution problems that beset the old capital, Seoul, for decades. The Korean Green Party in Parliament, which includes a number of former Communist officials, is urging a comprehensive ban on the use of gasoline-driven vehicles in five years.*

What do you think about these fictional news stories? Make your own assessment of how probable these developments are. Glance back at this book's table of contents to identify the pages that would be most helpful in assessing each of these hypothetical events. Will the UN be seriously reformed in a decade and in which way? Will North and South Korea merge without a conflict? Will China emerge as the second superpower? Will the United States keep its global economic leadership? Will Moscow be able to significantly challenge Washington's foreign policy? Could Iran radically reform its regime and open the doors to the West? None of us has a crystal ball, yet some developments are more likely than others.

Careers in International Relations

STUDYING INTERNATIONAL RELATIONS IS INTELLECTUALLY CHALLENGING AND EMOTIONALLY REWARDING. IT ALSO BROADENS YOUR CAREER POSSIBILITIES BY DEVELOPING your knowledge base and critical-thinking skills. A comprehensive knowledge of international relations and a sincere desire to understand other points of view are two pre-requisites for contributing to the foundation of a stable, safe, and prosperous world.

Careers in IR can take many paths, several of which we explore below. At minimum, a bachelor of arts is required for careers in diplomacy, international business, intelligence analysis, and defense or foreign policy. A graduate degree is strongly recommended and may be required; it is an important way to advance your knowledge, develop your skills, and expand your employment opportunities. In addition, your success will depend on your individual skills, professional knowledge, integrity, volunteer and research experience, and ability to work with others.

Diplomacy

Diplomatic work has traditionally been one of most attractive fields of employment in international relations. In this field, you might remain within your own country in its foreign-policy offices, or you could be sent overseas to work on a diplomatic mission. Diplomatic work is highly competitive, and the selection process is rigorous. Although the rules may be changing, most people applying for diplomatic work in the United States have to pass a special comprehensive exam (the Foreign Service Officer Test) and go through a difficult interview process, which requires additional studying and training.

NGOs, IGOs, and Think Tanks

Working for nongovernmental organizations (NGOs), international governmental organizations (IGOs), and think tanks is becoming increasingly important and popular. As in diplomatic fields you might remain in your home country or move abroad for some time. You could work on projects ranging from conducting research and teaching, to delivering humanitarian aid, to guiding negotiations and settling ethnic or religious tensions in local communities.

Defense and Security

Many people pursuing a military or national security career also need training in political science and international relations. Conducting humanitarian and peacekeeping operations, gathering military intelligence, analyzing regional and local conflicts—all these and many other activities of today's military offices require advanced knowledge of IR theory and practice. There are also many jobs within the government and private organizations requiring analytical skills and knowledge of foreign policy, policies of foreign countries, international law, the nature of ethnic conflicts, and negotiation strategies.

Law

Working as an attorney, you may specialize in cases involving international consulting or litigation, such as family affairs, business, commerce, or investments. You could also be an immigration lawyer. If you develop expertise in international law, you may work for government and international institutions. Many students who apply to law or business school study international relations to advance their knowledge in world affairs.

Teaching and Research

A Ph.D. is typically required for teaching international relations at colleges and universities in the United States and Canada. Recipients of this degree may also seek out research or consulting positions in government or nongovernmental organizations. Teaching at a university frequently becomes a springboard to various fields of policymaking. President Obama taught at the University of Chicago, and many U.S. secretaries of state have taught political science or international relations at the college level, including Condoleezza Rice, Madeleine Albright, George Shultz, and Henry Kissinger.

Journalism

Working as a journalist also requires advanced knowledge of international issues and regional conflicts, a deep understanding of very complex information, and the ability to explain it to thousands or even millions of viewers, readers, or listeners. International reporters today have to be proficient in two or more languages. As a journalist, you should know the history and current status of international relations, understand various IR theories, and be familiar with their contemporary applications.

Online Resources

Career opportunities and internships in IGOs:
   The United Nations: https://careers.un.org
   UNESCO: http://www.unesco.org/new/en/unesco/join-us/
   UNICEF: http://www.unicef.org/about/employ
   The World Bank: www.worldbank.org/jobs
   The European Union: http://www.eu-un.europa.eu
   NATO: www.nato.int

Career opportunities and internships in NGOs and think tanks:
   The Woodrow Wilson Center: http://www.wilsoncenter.org/opportunities
   The Brookings Institution: http://www.brookings.edu/about/employment
   The Chicago Council on Global Affairs: http://www.thechicagocouncil.org/files/AboutUs/Career_Opportunities/
   The Washington Center for Internships and Academic Seminars: http://www.twc.edu/
   Arms Control Association (Washington, D.C.): http://www.armscontrol.org/internships
   ECPAT-USA: http://ecpatusa.org/who-we-are/internships-and-volunteers/
   Greenpeace: http://www.greenpeace.org/usa/en/about/jobs/
   The World Wildlife Fund – United States: http://worldwildlife.org/internships
   Doctors Without Borders: http://www.doctorswithoutborders.org/work/

U.S. government career opportunities and internships (general search):
   USAJOBS: http://www.usajobs.gov

U.S. government career opportunities and internships (selected departments and agencies):
   The U.S. Department of State: http://www.careers.state.gov/
   The Central Intelligence Agency: https://www.cia.gov/careers/index.html
   The U.S. Environmental Protection Agency: http://www.epa.gov/internships/
   The U.S. Department of Homeland Security: http://www.dhs.gov/student-opportunities
   The U.S. Department of Defense: http://www.whs.mil/HRD/Apply/

See more options on the companion website

Glossary

Accessibility bias In cognitive theories, the rule that a leader tends to pick the option that is most easily available.

Acid rain The accumulation of acids in clouds, rain, snow, sleet, and, subsequently, lakes and rivers owing to sulfur dioxide, nitrogen oxides, and other pollutants in the atmosphere.

Aggression An attack by a state aiming at retribution, expansion, or conquest.

Analogy The comparison of a new situation to a familiar one. Analogies may provide quick answers in place of a more lengthy discussion.

Analysis Breaking down a complex whole into smaller parts to understand its essential features and their relationships.

Anarchism An ideology and movement sought to create a borderless, peaceful, self-governing society of free, local communes in which people generate and distribute wealth without government control.

Anarchy Applied to realism, the lack of any executive power above individual states capable of regulating their behavior.

Antiglobalization (see **globalization**) Resistance to globalization, or an active return to traditional communities, customs, and religion.

Asymmetrical threat The danger imposed by terrorism because a state cannot effectively retaliate and restore a balance of power.

Atlanticism The belief that the relationship between the United States and Europe is a focus of national interest.

Autarky A long-term policy of national self-sufficiency and rejection of imports, economic aid, and cooperation.

Autocratic rulers Leaders who use unlimited power and who follow international and domestic law only if it suits them.

Balance of trade The difference between the size of exports and imports of a country.

Bipolar order A type of world organization based on two centers of power or influence..

Bureaucratic bargaining The process by which political groups and institutions express their interests and make trade-offs and compromises.

Caliphate A global Islamic state (one of ultimate goals of al-Qaeda).

Climate change A significant and lasting alteration of global weather patterns (Gerrard, 2007). It most often means *global warming*, or the rising temperatures and increasing number of abnormal and unseasonable climatic phenomena such as devastating storms and heat waves.

Coercion and **extortion** The use of force and threats of force to compel others to comply with their demands.

Cognitive maps Models of information processing and decision-making.

Cold War (1946–1989) The state of tensions and competition between the Soviet Union and its allies on one side, and on the other, the Western world, including the United States, Western Europe, and their allies.

Collective security An arrangement in which the security of one country becomes the concern of others as well.

Communism A classless political and social order free from oppressive government.

Comparative advantage A theory that explains why it is beneficial for two countries to trade with each other instead of relying on their own domestic production.

Competitive authoritarianism A hybrid political culture with a competitive electoral system in which a single leader or party dominates. They use the state power to defeat opposition and mobilize public opinion

Complex interdependence The condition among states when anarchy is replaced by cooperation among states as the main feature of international relations

Conflict theories Approaches that emphasize economic, social, and political inequality as a source of contradictions and tensions among social groups. Conflict theories highlight the role of social classes, ruling elites, and other dominant groups in shaping global affairs.

Conflict An actual or perceived antagonism between states and international or nongovernment organizations.

Conservation A policy of protecting and preserve natural resources, including plant and animal species and their habitats.

Consistency bias In cognitive theories, the rule that the human mind operates so as to keep beliefs, opinions, and ideas consistent.

Constructivist view (or constructivism) An approach to international relations that assumes that state actions and policies are based on how leaders, bureaucracies, and societies interpret, or *construct*, information.

Consumption The selection, adoption, use, disposal, and recycling of goods and services.

Contamination The byproducts of human and non-human activities in air, water, and soil.

Content analysis A research method that systematically organizes and summarizes both what was actually said or written and its hidden meanings (the manifest and latent content).

Conventional war Conducted by regular armies that clash in pitched battles usually along recognizable frontlines.

Cooperation A foreign policy that addresses other states' concerns for their security.

Core In dependency theory, economically developed states that exercise their hegemonic power.

Counterterrorism Long-term policies and specific short-term measures to prevent and combat international and domestic terrorism.

Criminalization of terrorism Considering terrorism a form of criminal behavior in the context of domestic and international law.

Critical thinking A strategy for examining, evaluating, and understanding international relations on the basis of reasoning and valid evidence.

Culture A set of values, behaviors, and symbols shared by a group of people and communicated from one generation to the next.

Currencies The physical component of a country's money supply, comprising coins, paper notes, and government bonds.

Customary law Law derived from the past practices of sovereign states in the absence of repeated objections from other states.

Cyberterrorism Paralyzing attacks online on political, financial, and military centers.

Debt-for-nature swaps Agreements to designate an area for environmental conservation in exchange for a reduction in the country's foreign debt.

Deforestation The massive removal or disappearance of forests, owing to the thinning, changing, and elimination of trees, bushes, and other vegetation.

Democratic leaders Leaders who treat the letter and spirit of the law as the core of their domestic policy and, in most circumstances, foreign policy.

Democratic peace theory The theory that democracies are not likely to fight one another.

Dependency theory The belief that the world economic order is based on the flow of resources from a "periphery" of poor states to a "core" of wealthy states.

Depletion The serious reduction of essential elements of an ecosystem, such as loss of forests, fresh water, or entire species.

Desertification The expansion of deserts into the places previously available for agriculture.

Diplomacy The management of international relations through negotiations.

Domestic terrorism Terrorism to achieve domestic political goals, such as dismantling a government or a change in policies.

Domino theory An American view during the Cold War that a seizure of power by Communists in one country will produce a chain reaction of Communist takeovers in other countries allied with the West.

East African Community (EAC) An economic and political union between five countries (Tanzania, Uganda, Burundi, Kenya, and Rwanda).

Economic climate A set of values and practices, such as the level of trust, transparency, and corruption that encourages or discourages economic investments.

Economic liberalism The belief and theory that only free market, free trade, and economic cooperation can lead to a peaceful and prosperous world.

Economic sanctions The deliberate, government-driven withdrawal, or threat of withdrawal, of customary trade and financial relations in an effort to change another country's policies.

Environmental politics The activities of political leaders, parties, NGOs, scientific laboratories, and others to influence environmental policy.

Environmental skepticism A questioning of environmentalism from the point of view of science or practicality.

Environmental sovereignty The right of states to use and protect their environment and natural resources.

Environmentalism Belief in the necessity of urgent and comprehensive policies to protect the environment.

Epidemic An outbreak of infectious disease in a large population.

Experiment A research method that puts participants in controlled testing conditions. By varying these conditions, researchers can examine the behavior or responses of participants.

Extraterritoriality Exemption from the jurisdiction of local law.

Extreme poverty A profound lack of resources and the inability to gain access to them.

Eyewitness accounts Descriptions of events by individuals who observed them directly.

Failing state A state in which the government is incapable of exercising their major functions, defending borders, or making key decisions.

Fair trade (also known also as trade justice) Initiatives arising from a belief that free trade alone cannot solve such lingering problems as chronic poverty, diseases, and environmental troubles.

Famine Severe food scarcity causing malnutrition, starvation, disease, and increasing mortality.

Feminist theories Theories that argue that men's political domination and their oppression of women shape international relations.

Fiscal policy The use of government spending or revenue collection to influence the economy, jump-start it out of recession, or create jobs.

Focus group methodology A survey method involving small discussion groups used intensively in foreign-policy planning, conflict resolution analysis, and academic research.

Food and Agriculture Organization (FAO) A UN agency that coordinates international efforts to overcome hunger.

Foreign policy A complex system of actions involving official decisions or communications related to other nation states, international institutions, or international developments in general.

Freedom of the seas The principle that countries have the right to travel by sea to and trade with other countries; each state's sovereignty ends with its territorial waters.

Fundamentalism A point of view or social movement distinguished by rigid adherence to principles rooted in tradition (typically religious tradition) and often by intolerance of individual rights and secularism.

General principles of law Cross-cultural principles of morality and common sense.

Genocide The deliberate extermination or prosecution of racial, ethnic, religious, and other social groups, whether in war or in peacetime.

Geopolitics The theory and practice of using geography to achieve political power or seek security.

Global commons Geographical areas not under any nation's sovereign control.

Global Environment Facility (GEF) An independent financial organization established in 1991 that provides grants to developing countries for projects that benefit the global environment and promote sustainable development.

Global governance The global cooperation of international actors with little or no power of enforcing compliance. This approach is based on the mutual interdependence of nations, the idea that global issues should be addressed by a collective effort, and the assumption that there is no single formula for solving all humanitarian problems.

Globalization The growing irrelevance of state borders, the growing importance of international exchanges of goods and ideas, and increased openness to innovation.

Graduated reciprocation in tension-reduction (GRIT) Small goodwill steps by one or two sides in an international conflict help to build trust and reduce international tensions.

Green certification The grant of certificates to companies that pursue responsible environmental policies to make their products more competitive in the market.

Gross domestic product (GDP) The total market value of all the goods and services produced within the borders of a state during a specified period.

Group pressure In political psychology, the ability of other people to alter individual decisions.

Guerrilla warfare Political violence by identifiable, irregular combat units, usually to seize state power, win autonomy, or found new states.

Harmony values The view that the environment should be preserved and cherished rather than exploited.

Hegemony One state's overwhelming power in relation to other states.

Human rights Fundamental rights with which all people are endowed regardless of their race, nationality, sex, ethnicity, religion, or social status.

Human trafficking The illegal trade in human beings for purposes of exploitation.

Humanitarian crisis Threatens to the health, safety, security, and well-being of many people, usually in a single geographic area.

Humanitarian intervention Assistance with or without the use of military force to reduce the disastrous consequences of a humanitarian crisis.

Humanitarian sovereignty A country's responsibility for its own humanitarian policies and the right to accept or reject humanitarian interventions.

Identity The characteristics by which a person is recognizable as a member of a cultural group, such as a nation, an ethnic group, or a religion.

Imperial overreach A hegemonic state's exhaustion of economic resources, erosion of political will, and the weakening of imperial ideology.

Imperialism (Lenin's theory of) A global struggle among international corporations and banks for territories and resources.

Infectious diseases Serious maladies caused by a biological agent such as a virus, bacterium, or parasite.

Intelligence Information about the interests, intentions, capabilities, and actions of foreign countries, including government officials, political parties, the functioning of their economies, the activities of nongovernmental organizations, and the behavior of private individuals.

Intergovernmental organization (IGO) An organization composed of sovereign member-states.

Internal affairs Matters that individual states consider beyond the reach of international law or the influence of other states.

Internally displaced persons Those who involuntarily leave their home and region under threats of death, starvation, or imprisonment.

International law Principles, rules, and regulations concerning the interactions among countries and other institutions and organizations in international relations.

International mandate Legal permission to administer a territory or enforce international law.

International order The established system of the world's organization and functioning.

International political economy (IPE) The interactions between politics and economics in an international context.

International politics The political aspects of international relations. The emphasis on politics suggests the prime focus of these studies: power-related interests and policies.

International relations The study of interactions among states as well as the international activities of nonstate organizations.

International security Mutual security issues involving two or more states.

International terrorism Terrorism that involves international groups, interaction between countries, or international organizations, often with regional or global consequences.

International treaties Written agreements between nations (also called agreements, charters, pacts, covenants, and conventions).

Interventionism A policy of interference in other states' affairs or international conflicts without regard for their consent.

Involuntary migration Relocation within or across state borders due to violence, hardship, severe suffering, or a significant threat of these.

Isolationism A policy of nonparticipation in international alliances; freedom to act or not to act in international conflicts.

Jurisdiction The right and authority to make decisions and apply justice.

Keynesian economics The principle that national governments should conduct expansionary fiscal and monetary policies whenever necessary to ease the undesirable effects of economic recessions.

Kyoto Protocol A 1997 international agreement to limit air pollution and reduce global warming.

Laws of war Common principles that states should follow in case of an armed conflict.

Liberal institutionalism The belief that international institutions allow more efficient international relations than power politics.

Liberal interventionism A broader approach to security that mandates military action by a coalition of states and IGOs, when all nonviolent means are exhausted.

Liberalism A school of thought based on the rejection of power politics, the need for international cooperation, distribution of shared interests, and the role of nonstate actors in shaping state preferences and policy choices. Liberalism opposes realist explanations, which emphasize cost–benefit analysis and state security interests.

Lobbying Activities with the goal of influencing public officials in support of legislation or policies.

Log rolling A concession made by one party to the other party on domestic issues in exchange for their support on foreign policy.

Macroeconomics The study of the structure and performance of the entire economy, including the interrelationship among diverse sectors.

Malnutrition A medical condition resulting from famine or chronic food shortages.

Marxism A social, political, and economic theory that interprets international relations as a struggle between states representing ruling elites interested in control over territories, people, and resources.

Mastery values The view that individuals may exercise control over and exploit natural resources.

Mercantilism The economic view that emphasizes the accumulation of resources and capital by states as well as state regulation of trade.

Microeconomics The field of economics that considers the behavior of individual consumers, companies, and industries.

Militarism A tendency to rely on military force in response to foreign threats.

Multilateralism Coordination of foreign policy with allies; participation in international coalitions, blocs, and international organizations.

Multipolar order A world with multiple centers of power or influence.

Nation A large group of people sharing common cultural, religious, and linguistic features and distinguishing themselves from other large social groups. A nation may also refer to people who have established sovereignty over a territory and set up international borders recognized by other states.

National purpose In the constructivist view, a major economic goal that political and business elites want to achieve for their country.

National security A state's need to protect its sovereignty, territorial integrity, and vital interests.

Nationalism Individual and collective identification with a country or a nation. Nationalism also can become the belief in a nation's special role. Often, it is the belief that an ethnic group has the right to form an independent state.

Natural disaster A natural hazard such as an earthquake or a volcano eruption with devastating impact on the ecosystem.

Neoliberalism A theoretical position postulating that state interests remain a main subject of analysis in international relations, yet that these interests are realized in the context of interdependence among states.

Nongovernment organizations (NGOs) Public or private groups unaffiliated formally with a government and attempting to influence foreign policy, to raise international concerns about a domestic problem or domestic concerns about a global issue, and to offer solutions.

North (Global) In dependency theory, predominantly rich and technology-driven countries that benefit from the raw materials and cheap labor of the (Global) South.

Nuclear deterrence Maintaining nuclear weapons with the intention not to use them but to deter others from nuclear attack.

Nuclear proliferation The spread of nuclear weapons, material, information, and technologies to create nuclear weapons.

One-child policy China's policy initiated in 1979 limiting the number of children that a family can have.

Outsourcing The practice of moving business and jobs to other countries and regions where labor costs are lower.

Overpopulation A high concentration of people within a region threatening its subsistence, or the minimum conditions to sustain a reasonable quality of life. It can cause serious environmental and social problems.

Ozone depletion Steady decline in the amount of ozone in the stratosphere, allowing the sun's damaging ultraviolet radiation to reach the earth.

Pandemic An international epidemic that spreads across national borders.

Parochialism A worldview limited to the small piece of land on which we live or to the narrow experience we have.

Peace psychology The study of the ideological and psychological causes of war to develop educational programs to reduce the threat.

Peacekeeping Military or nonmilitary intervention to stop violence (peacemaking) and to create the conditions for lasting peace (peace building).

Pearl Harbor syndrome Attitudes and policies designed to avoid sudden and devastating attack.

Periphery In dependency theory, former colonies, underdeveloped, and chronically poor states.

Political culture A set of values and norms essential to the functioning of international and national political institutions, including the attitudes of states toward each other and individual citizens.

Political psychology The study of the interactions between political and psychological factors in individual and group behavior.

Political socialization The study of how individuals acquire their political knowledge and beliefs.

Postcolonial studies The critique of Western domination in postcolonial Africa, Asia, and Latin America.

Power The ability of a state to protect its own security and impose its will on other states and actors.

Preemptive policies Action against terrorists before they strike.

Preemptive war A war launched to destroy the potential threat of an enemy when an attack by the adversary is imminent.

Preventive war A war started states to protect themselves if they believe that other states might threaten them in the future.

Production The process of creating goods and services with market value.

Proletarian internationalism The duty to support Communist movements around the world.

Protectionism Economic restrictions by the state to discourage imports and encourage domestic production including "import substitution."

Proxy war Armed conflict orchestrated by other, more distant countries using substitute forces to avoid a direct confrontation with each other.

Rational model In political psychology, the view that politicians act, for the most part, logically, to maximize positive outcomes and to minimize negative outcomes.

Realism A school of international relations that focuses on power, security, and state interests.

Realpolitik Policy rooted in the belief that the foundation of a nation's security is power and the threat of its use.

Refugees Involuntary migrants under threats of political or religious persecution or ethnic and religious violence.

Regional trade agreements Mutual commitments that bind several neighboring countries to pursue common economic and financial policies.

Rehabilitation Helping someone return to the community after being involved in radical or terrorist group.

Religious fundamentalism A set of beliefs and behaviors based on strict adherence to religious principles.

Resistance bias In cognitive theories, the rule that leaders resist changing their ideas about international relations.

Responsibility to Protect (R2P) The principle that if a sovereign country does not protect its own people from identifiable causes of death and acute suffering, then other countries and the international community must take action.

Revisionist (predator) state A state conducting policies of systematic disregard for international rules and turning to belligerent actions in the international arena.

Security community A group of countries united by mutual security interests, arrangements, and common liberal values.

Security dilemma A situation in which one state's efforts to improve its security cause insecurity in others.

Security regime A region in which a powerful country provides protection to other states in exchange for their cooperation.

Separatism The advocacy of or attempt to establish a separate nation within another sovereign state.

Socially responsible investing (SRI) A business strategy combining the pursuit of the social good, environmental protection, and profits.

Soft power A state's ability to influence other states by example, through economic and social success.

Sources of international law International treaties, international customary law, and general principles of law recognized by civilized nations.

South (Global) Predominantly agricultural countries that are dependent on the rich and technology-driven (Global) North.

State government An institution with the authority to formulate and enforce its decisions within a country's borders.

Status quo state A state that observes and protects the established rules of international behavior.

Supranationalism The delegation of authority to institutions or organizations that may supersede the authority of individual states by their consent.

Survey The investigative method in which groups of people answer questions on a certain topic.

Sustainable development A comprehensive policy that meets the needs of the present without sacrificing the ability of future generations to meet their own needs. This policy is about stimulating economic growth while at the same time protecting the environment and natural resources.

Tariffs Taxes or financial charges imposed on imported goods.

Terrorism Random violence conducted by nonstate actors, such as individuals or groups, against governments or their citizens to achieve political goals.

Theory A general concept or scheme that one applies to facts to analyze them.

Tribalism A way of thinking and a movement identifying itself not with nation-states but rather with a religious or ethnic group.

Two-level game theory A model in which states react to both domestic and international politics.

Tyrant A ruler who uses unlimited power to oppress the people of the ruler's country or its foreign possessions.

Unilateralism Reliance on a state's own resources rather than support from others; acting alone in foreign policy.

Unipolar order A world with only one center of power or influence.

Universal jurisdiction The principle that the perpetrators of certain crimes cannot escape justice by moving to another country and invoking its sovereign immunity.

War An organized violent confrontation between states or other social and political entities, such as ethnic or religious groups.

Water pollution The by-products of human activities that are harmful to rivers, lakes, seas, and underground water.

Weapons of mass destruction Nuclear, chemical, and biological weapons can quickly and indiscriminately kill tens of millions of people.

Xenophobia Fear and contempt of foreign countries and foreigners, helping politicians and regimes to mobilize public opinion, defeat political opposition, win elections, neutralize critics, or justify war.

References

A Strategic Revolution in HIV and Global Health (Editorial). 2011. *The Lancet* 377 (9783) June 18: 2055.

Aaronson, Susan Ariel. 2010. Is China Killing the WTO? *International Economy*, Winter.

Abadie, Alberto. 2006. Poverty, Political Freedom, and the Roots of Terrorism. *American Economic Review* (Papers and Proceedings) 96 (2): 50–56.

Abdelal, Rawi. 2001. *National Purpose in the World Economy.* Ithaca, NY: Cornell University Press.

Abrams, Irwin. 1957. The Emergence of the International Law Societies. *Review of Politics* 19 (3): 361–380.

Adamsky, Dima. 2010. *The Culture of Military Innovation: The Impact of Cultural Factors on the Revolution in Military Affairs in Russia, the US, and Israel.* Stanford, CA: Stanford University Press.

Adler, Emanuel and Michael Barnett, eds. 1998. *Security Communities.* Cambridge, UK: Cambridge University Press.

Adler, Emanuel. 2008. The Spread of Security Communities: Communities of Practice, Self-Restraint, and NATO's Post-Cold War Transformation. *European Journal of International Relations* 14 (2): 195–230.

Agier, Michel. 2010. Humanity as an Identity and Its Political Effects. *Humanity* 1 (1): 29–46.

Akçam, Taner. 2007. *A Shameful Act: The Armenian Genocide and the Question of Turkish Responsibility.* New York: Picador.

Alamgir, Jalal. 2008. *India's Open-Economy Policy: Globalism, Rivalry, Continuity.* London: Routledge.

Allison, Graham and Philip Zelikow. 1999. *Essence of Decision: Explaining the Cuban Missile Crisis.* 2nd edition. New York: Longman.

Allison, Graham. 1971. Allison, Graham (1971). *Essence of Decision: Explaining the Cuban Missile Crisis.* 1st edition. New York: Little, Brown, and Company.

Almond, Gabriel and Sidney Verba. 1963. *The Civic Culture.* Boston: Little, Brown and Company.

Anderson, Kym, ed. 2005. *The World's Wine Markets: Globalization at Work.* London: Edward Elgar.

Angell, Norman. 1910. *The Great Illusion: A Study of the Relation of Military Power in Nations to Their Economic and Social Advantage.* London: Heinemann.

Angus, Ian and Simon Butler. 2011. *Too Many People?: Population, Immigration, and the Environmental Crisis.* Chicago: Haymarket Books.

Arrighi, Giovanni and Lu Zhang. 2011. Beyond the Washington Consensus: A New Bandung. In *Globalization and Beyond: New Examinations of Global Power and its Alternatives*, eds. Jon Shefner and Patricia Fernandez-Kelly. University Park: Pennsylvania State University Press.

Arrighi, Giovanni. 1994. *The Long Twentieth Century: Money, Power, and the Origins of Our Times.* New York: Verso.

Art, David. 2011. *Inside the Radical Right: The Development of Anti-Immigrant Partied in Western Europe.* Cambridge, UK: Cambridge University Press.

Asal, Victor and Andrew Blum. 2005. Holy Terror and Mass Killings? Reexamining the Motivations and Methods of Mass Casualty Terrorists. *International Studies Review* 7 (1): 153–155.

Ayittey, George B. N. 2005. *Africa Unchained: The Blueprint for Africa's Future.* New York: Palgrave Macmillan.

Ayman, Roya and Karen Korabik. 2010. Why Gender and Culture Matter. *American Psychologist* 65 (3): 157–170.

Baldoni, John. 2004. *Great Motivation Secrets of Great Leaders*. New York: McGraw-Hill.

Bales, Kevin, Zoe Trodd, and Alex Williamson. 2009. *Modern Slavery: The Secret World of 27 Million People*. London: Oneworld.

Banerjee, Abhijit and Ester Duflo. 2011. *Poor Economics: A Radical Rethinking of the Way to Fight Global Poverty*. New York: Public Affairs.

Barner-Barry, Carol and Robert Rosenwein. 1985. *Psychological Perspectives on Politics*. Prospect Heights, IL: Waveland.

Bass, Gary. 2009. *Freedom's Battle: The Origins of Humanitarian Intervention*. New York: Vintage Books.

BBC. 2010. Ethiopia Famine Aid "Spent on Weapons." March 3. Online at http://news.bbc.co.uk/2/hi/8535189.stm (accessed September 25, 2012).

Beck, Barbara. 2011. All Aboard: Women Will Get a Lift to the Top. *The Economist*. November 17. Special edition: The World in 2012, 99.

Becker, Jasper. 1998. *Hungry Ghosts: Mao's Secret Famine*. New York: Owl Books.

Beech, Hannah. 2013. The Face of Buddhist Terror. *Time*, July 1. Online at http://ti.me/10zStLO (accessed July 17, 2013).

Bellamy, Alex and Paul Williams. 2010. *Understanding Peacekeeping*. Cambridge, UK: Polity.

Benvenisti, Eyal, Chaim Gans, and Sari Hanafi, eds. 2007. *Israel and the Palestinian Refugees*. Berlin: Springer.

Beres, Louis R. 2008. On Assassination, Preemption, and Counterterrorism: The View From International Law. *International Journal of Intelligence and CounterIntelligence* 21 (4): 694–725.

Bergman, Ronen. 2008. *The Secret War with Iran: The 30-Year Clandestine Struggle Against the World's Most Dangerous Terrorist Power*. New York: Free Press.

Bergsten, C. Fred. 2005. Rescuing the Doha Round. *Foreign Affairs* 84 (7). Special WTO edition. Online at http://bit.ly/1bFXKUt (accessed July 17, 2013).

Bernstein, Richard. 2009. Upper Crust Is Often Drawn to Terrorism. *The New York Times*. December 30. Online at http://nyti.ms/6S5b73 (accessed June 25, 2013).

Betts, Richard. 2008. *Conflict after the Cold War: Arguments on Causes of War and Peace*. 3d edition. New York: Longman.

Betts, Richard. 2011. Institutional Imperialism. *The National Interest*. May–June: 85–96.

Bhagwati, Jagdish. 2004. *In Defense of Globalization*. New York: Oxford University Press.

Biello, David. 2010. Where did Carter White House's Solar Panels Go? *Scientific American Blog*, September 10. Online at http://www.scientificamerican.com/article.cfm?id=carter-white-house-solar-panel-array (accessed September 25, 2012).

Black, Richard. 2011. World's Oceans in "Shocking" Decline. *BBC News*. June 20. Online at http://www.bbc.co.uk/news/science-environment-13796479?print=true (accessed September 25, 2012).

Blair, Tony. 2010. *A Journey: My Political Life*. New York: Knopf.

Blanchard, William. 1996. *Neocolonialism American Style, 1960–2000*. New York: Praeger.

Blight J. G., B. J. Allyn, and D. A. Welch. 1993. *Cuba on the Brink: Castro, the Missile Crisis, and the Soviet Collapse*. New York: Pantheon Books.

Blustein, Paul. 2009. *Misadventures of the Most Favored Nations: Clashing Egos, Inflated Ambitions, and the Great Shambles of the World Trade System*. New York: Public Affairs.

Bodansky, Yossef. 2001. *Bin Laden: The Man who Declared War on America*. Roseville, CA: Prima Lifestyles.

Boot, Max. 2007. Another Vietnam? *Wall Street Journal*. August 24. Online at http://www.cfr.org/publication/14083/another_vietnam.html (accessed July 18, 2013).

Boot, Max. 2009. Pirates, Then and Now: How Piracy Was Defeated in the Past and Can Be Again. *Foreign Affairs* 88 (4): 94-107.

Booth, Ken and Nicholas Wheeler. 2007. *The Security Dilemma: Fear, Cooperation and Trust in World Politics*. New York: Palgrave Macmillan.

Borah, Rupakjyoti. 2011. BRICS: The New Great Game. *ISN Insights*. June 23. Online at http://bit.ly/12QmLUU (accessed July 19, 2013).

Borch, Fred and Gary Solis. 2010. *Geneva Conventions*. New York: Kaplan Publishing.

Borgerson, Scott G. 2008. Arctic Meltdown. The Economic and Security Implications of Global Warming. *Foreign Affairs* 87 (2) March/April.

Bortolotti, Dan. 2006. *Hope in Hell: Inside the World of Doctors Without Borders*. Buffalo, NY: Firefly Books.

Boucek, Christopher. 2009. Saudi Detainee-Rehab Program Mostly Successful. NPR's *All Things Considered*. December 31. Source: http://bit.ly/12Hel2h (accessed June 30, 2013).

Boucek, Christopher. 2010. Al Qaeda in 2010. *The Diane Rehm Show*. January 5. Online at: http://bit.ly/15QPRqj (accessed July 18, 2013).

Bricmont, Jean. 2006. *Humanitarian Imperialism: Using Rights to Sell War*. New York: Monthly Review Press.

Brown, Paul. 2006. *Notes from a Dying Planet, 2004–2006: One Scientist's Search for Solutions*. Lincoln, NE: iUniverse, Inc.

Bryce, Robert. 2009. *Gusher of Lies: The Dangerous Delusions of "Energy Independence."* New York: PublicAffairs.

Buchanan, Allen. 2003. Reforming the International Law of Humanitarian Intervention. In *Humanitarian Intervention: Ethical, Legal, and Political Dilemmas*, eds. J. L. Holzgrefe and Robert Keohane. New York: Cambridge University Press, 130–74.

Buchanan, Allen. 2010. *Human Rights, Legitimacy, and the Use of Force*. New York: Oxford University Press.

Bueno de Mesquita, Ethan. 2005. Conciliation, Counterterrorism, and Patterns of Terrorist Violence. *International Organization* 59 (1): 145–176.

Bull, Hedley, ed. 1988. *Intervention in World politics*. New York: Oxford University Press.

Bull, Hedley. 1977. *The Anarchical Society: A Study of Order in World Politics*. New York: Columbia University Press.

Burt, Jo-Marie. 2009. Guilty as Charged: The Trial of former Peruvian President Alberto Fujimori for Grave Violations of Human Rights. *International Journal of Transitional Justice* 3 (3): 384–405.

Burt, Jo-Marie. 2010. *Political Violence and the Authoritarian State in Peru: Silencing Civil Society*. New York: Palgrave Macmillan.

Buzan, Barry and Lene Hansen. 2009. *The Evolution of International Security Studies*. New York: Cambridge University Press.

Caprioli, Mary and Mark Boyer. 2001. Gender, Violence, and International Crisis. *Journal of Conflict Resolution*, 45 (4): 503–518.

Carpenter, Ted. 2006. *America's Coming War with China: A Collision Course over Taiwan*. New York: Palgrave Macmillan.

Carr, Edward H. 1969. *Twenty Years' Crisis, 1919–1939: An Introduction to the Study of International Relations*. 2nd edition. New York: Palgrave Macmillan. Originally published in 1939.

Carrière, Erin, Marc O'Reilly, and Richard Vengroff. 2003. "In the Service of Peace": Reflexive Multilateralism and the Canadian Experience in Bosnia. In *International Public Opinion and the Bosnia Crisis*, eds. Richard Sobel and Eric Shiraev. Lanham, MD: Lexington Books, 1–32.

CARSI. 2010. The Central America Regional Security Initiative. U.S. Department of State. Bureau of Public Affairs. Online at http://www.state.gov/documents/organization/145956.pdf (accessed September 25, 2012).

Carson, Rachel. 1962. *Silent Spring*. New York: Houghton Mifflin.

Chakrabarty, Dipesh. 2007. *Provincializing Europe: Postcolonial Thought and Historical Difference*. Princeton, NJ: Princeton University Press.

Chaliand, Gerard and Arnaud Blin. 2007. *The History of Terrorism: From Antiquity to Al Qaeda*. Berkeley: University of California Press.

Chan, Steve. 1997. In Search of Democratic Peace: Problems and Promise. *Mershon International Studies Review* 41 (1): 59–91.

Chandler, David. 2006. *From Kosovo to Kabul and Beyond: Human Rights and International Intervention*. Ann Arbor, MI: Pluto Press.

Chappel, Louise. 2008. The International Criminal Court: A New Arena for Transforming Justice. In *Global Governance: Feminist Perspectives*, eds. Shirin Rai and Georgina Waylen. New York: Palgrave Macmillan.

Checkel, Jeffrey. 1998. The Constructivist Turn in International Relations Theory. *World Politics* 50 (2): 324–348.

Chernyaev, Anatoly. 2000. *My Six Years with Gorbachev*. Translated and edited by Robert D. English and Elizabeth Tucker. University Park: Pennsylvania State University Press.

Cholett, Derek and James Goldgeier. 2002. The Scholarship of Decision-making: Do We Know How We Decide? In *Foreign Policy Decision-Making*, eds. Richard Snyder, H. W. Bruck, and Burton Sapin. Originally published in 1962, "revisited" by eds. Valerie Hudson, Derek Cholett, and James Goldgeier in 2002. New York: Palgrave Macmillan.

Cholett, Derek and James Goldgeier. 2008. *America Between the Wars: From 11/9 to 9/11: The Misunderstood Years between the Fall of the Berlin Wall and the Start of the War on Terror*. New York: PublicAffairs.

Christison, Bill. 2002. Former CIA Officer Explains Why the War on Terror Won't Work. *Counterpunch* (an online magazine) March 45. Online at http://bit.ly/14bei54 (accessed July 14, 2013).

Cohen, Joel E. 2005. Human Population Grows Up. *Scientific American* 293 (3): 48–55. Online at http://bit.ly/OUTbgQ (accessed July 15, 2013).

Cohn, Carol. 1987. Sex and Death in the Rational World of Defense Intellectuals. *Signs* 12 (4): 687–718.

Coleman, Loren. 2004. *The Copycat Effect: How the Media and Popular Culture Trigger the Mayhem in Tomorrow's Headlines*. New York: Pocket.

Coll, Steve. 2009. *The Bin Ladens: An Arabian Family in the American Century*. New York: Penguin Press.

Cooper, Barry. 2004. *New Political Religions, or An Analysis of Modern Terrorism*. Columbia: University of Missouri Press.

Copeland, Dale. 1996. Economic Interdependence and War. *International Security* 20 (4): 5–41.

Cordesman, Anthony. 2002. *Terrorism, Asymmetric Warfare, and Weapons of Mass Destruction: Defending the U.S. Homeland*. Westport, CT: Praeger.

Costigliola, Frank. 2000. "I Had Come as a Friend": Emotion, Culture, and Ambiguity in the Formation of the Cold War. *Cold War History* 1 (1) August: 103–128.

Cottier, Thomas and Manfred Elsig, eds. 2011. *Governing the World Trade Organization: Past, Present and Beyond Doha*. New York: Cambridge University Press.

Crane, George and Abla Amawi. 1997. *The Theoretical Evolution of International Political Economy: A Reader*. New York: Oxford University Press.

Crawford, Michael and Jami Miscik. 2010. The Rise of the Mezzanine Rulers: The New Frontier for International Law. *Foreign Affairs* 89 (6) November/December: 123–132.

Crenshaw, Martha. 2010. *Explaining Terrorism: Causes, Processes, and Consequences*. New York: Routledge.

Cronin, Audrey. 2002. Behind the Curve: Globalization and International Terrorism. *International Security* 27 (3) Winter: 30–58.

Cronin, Audrey. 2010. The Evolution of Counterterrorism: Will Tactics Trump Strategy? *International Affairs* 86 (4): 837–856.

Cronin, Bruce. 1999. *Community under Anarchy: Transitional Identity and the Evolution of Cooperation*. New York: Columbia University Press.

Cullen, Heidi. 2010. *The Weather of the Future: Heat Waves, Extreme Storms, and Other Scenes from a Climate-Changed Planet*. New York: Harper.

Cutler, Robert. 1981. Decision Making and International Relations: The Cybernetic Theory Reconsidered.*Michigan Journal of Political Science* 1 (2): 57–63. Online at http://bit.ly/1aqXjeY (accessed July 16, 2013).

D'Silva, Themistocles. 2006. *The Black Box of Bhopal: A Closer Look at the World's Deadliest Industrial Disaster*. Victoria, BC:Trafford Publishing.

D'Souza, Dinesh. 2010. *The Roots of Obama's Rage*. Washington, DC: Regnery Publishing.

Davis, David H. 2007. *Ignoring the Apocalypse: Why Planning to Prevent Environmental Catastrophe Goes Astray*. Westport, CT: Praeger.

Davis, Mike. 2011. Spring Confronts Winter. *New Left Review* Online at http://newleftreview.org/II/72/mike-davis-spring-confronts-winter (accessed July 15, 2013).

Debs, Alexandre and H. E. Goemans. 2010. Regime Type, the Fate of Leaders, and War. *American Political Science Review* 104 (3): 430–445.

http://www.cato.org/pub_display.php?pub_id=1288 (accessed September 25, 2012).

Dennis, Anthony. 2002. *Osama bin Laden: A Psychological and Political Portrait*. Lima, OH: Wyndham Hall.

Der Spiegel. 2010. Staff. Beijing's High-Tech Ambitions: The Dangers of Germany's Dependence on China. Online at http://bit.ly/12kRVsf (accessed July 16, 2013).

Desai, Meghnad. 2007. *Rethinking Islamism: The Ideology of the New Terror*. New York: Palgrave Macmillan.

Desertec. 2012. Online at http://www.desertec.org/ (accessed July 19, 2013).

Deutsch, Karl W., Sidney A. Burrell, and Robert A. Kann. 1957. *Political Community and the North Atlantic Area: International Organization in the Light of Historical Experience*. Princeton, NJ: Princeton University Press.

Deutsch, Morton and Robert Krauss. (1962). Studies of Interpersonal Bargaining. *Journal of Conflict Resolution* 6 (1): 52–76.

Donnelly, Jack. 2009. Realism. In Theories of International relations, ed. Scott Burchill, et al. New York: Palgrave Macmillan.

Doremus, Paul N., William W. Keller, Louis W. Pauley, and Simon Reich. 1998. *The Myth of the Global Corporation*.Princeton, NJ: Princeton University Press.

Dower, John. 2000. *Embracing Defeat: Japan in the Wake of World War II*. New York: Norton.

Doyle, Michael. 1986. Liberalism and World Politics. *American Political Science Review* 80 (4): 1151–1169.

Dueck, Colin. 2010. *Hard Line: The Republican Party and US Foreign Policy Since World War II*. Princeton, NJ: Princeton University Press.

Dutta, Manoranjan. 2005. *China's Industrial Revolution And Economic Presence*. Hackensack, NJ: World Scientific Publishing Company.

Easterly, William. 2001.*The Elusive Quest for Growth: Economists Adventures and Misadventures in the Tropics*. Cambridge, MA: MIT Press.

Easterly, William. 2006. *The White Man's Burden: Why the West's Efforts to Aid the Rest Have Done So Much Ill and So Little Good*. New York: Penguin Press.

Ebrahim, Alnoor. 2006. *NGOs and Organizational Change*. Cambridge, UK: Cambridge University Press.

Economy, Elizabeth. 2010a. The Game Changer: Coping with China's Foreign Policy Revolution. *Foreign Affairs* 89 (6) November/December: 142–152.

Economy, Elizabeth. 2010b. *The River Runs Black: The Environmental Challenge to China's Future*. Ithaca, NY: Cornell University Press.

Eisenhower, Dwight. 1960. Public Papers of the Presidents, Dwight D. Eisenhower. 1035–1040. Online at http://www.h-net.org/~hst306/documents/indust.html (accessed July 16 25, 2013).

Ekelund, Robert B., Jr. and Robert F. Hébert. 2007. *A History of Economic Theory and Method*. Long Grove, IL: Waveland Press.

English, Robert D. 2000. *Russia and the Idea of the West: Gorbachev, Intellectuals and the End of the Cold War*. New York: Columbia University Press.

Enloe, Cynthia. 2000. *Bananas, Beaches, and Bases. Making Feminist Sense of International Politics*. Berkeley: University of California Press.

Enloe, Cynthia. 2007. *Globalization and Militarism*. New York: Rowman & Littlefield.

ENS. 2006. U.S. Swaps Guatemalan Debt for Forest Conservation. *Environmental News Service*. October 3. http://bit.ly/197W7PT (accessed July 19, 2013).

Erikson, Erik. 1969. *Gandhi's Truth: On the Origins of Militant Nonviolence*. New York: W.W. Norton.

Esty, Daniel and Andrew Winston. 2006. *Green to Gold: How Smart Companies Use Environmental Strategy to Innovate, Create Value, and Build Competitive Advantage*. New Haven, CT: Yale University Press.

Eurobarometer. 2011. Migrant Integration: Aggregate Report. Conducted by TNS Qual+ at the request of Directorate General Home Affairs. Online at http://bit.ly/noM7CG (accessed June 16, 2013).

Evangelista, Matthew. 1999. *Unarmed Forces: The Transnational Movement to End the Cold War*. Ithaca, NY: Cornell University Press.

Evans, Gareth. 2009. *The Responsibility to Protect: Ending Mass Atrocity Crimes Once and for All*. Washington, DC: Brookings Institution Press.

Evans, Peter. 1998. Transnational Corporations and Third World States: From the Old Internationalization to the New. In *Transnational Corporations and the Global Economy*, eds. Richard Kozul-Wright and Robert Rowthorn. New York: St. Martin's Press, 195–224.

Evans-Pritchard, Ambrose. 2011. World Power Swings Back to America. *Telegraph*. October 23. Online at http://bit.ly/ptenjk (accessed September 25, 2012).

Fanon, Frantz. 2005. *The Wretched of the Earth*. New York: Grove Press. Originally published in French in 1961.

Fearon, James and David Laitin. 2003. Ethnicity, Insurgency, and Civil War. *American Political Science Review* 97 (1): 75–90.

Fearon, James. 1995. Rationalist Explanations for War. *International Organization* 49 (3): 379–414.

Fearon, James. 1998. Bargaining, Enforcement, and International Cooperation. *International Organization* 52 (2): 269–306.

Ferguson, Niall. 2010. The End of Chimerica: Amicable Divorce or Currency War? Testimony before the Committee on Ways and Means U.S. House of Representatives, March 24. Online at http://belfercenter.ksg.harvard.edu/publication/20029/end_of_chimerica.html (accessed September 22, 2012).

Festa, Lynn. 2010. Humanity without Feathers. *Humanity* 1 (1): 3–27.

Finnemore, Martha. 1996. *National Interests in International Society*. Ithaca, NY: Cornell University Press.

Finnemore, Martha. 2004. *The Purpose Of Intervention: Changing Beliefs About The Use Of Force* (Cornell Studies in Security Affairs). Ithaca, NY: Cornell University Press.

Fong, Vanessa L. 2006. *Only Hope: Coming of Age Under China's One-Child Policy*. Palo Alto, CA: Stanford University Press.

Forsythe, David, Roger Coate, and Thomas Weiss. 2004. *The United Nations and Changing World Politics*. Boulder, CO: Westview Press.

Fouskas, Vassilis. 2003. *Zones Of Conflict: U.S. Foreign Policy in the Balkans and the Greater Middle East*. Sterling, VA: Pluto Press.

French, Hilary. 1994. GEF replenishment. *World Watch* 7 (4): 7.

Friedrich, Hans-Peter. 2011. An Interview of German Interior Minister. *Der Spiegel*, August 9. Online at http://bit.ly/oz01L0 (accessed July 17, 2013).

Fromkin, David. 2009. *The Peace to End All Peace*. New York: Henry Holt.

Fukuyama, Francis. 2011. *The Origins of Political Order: From Prehuman Times to the French Revolution*. New York: Farrar, Straus, and Giroux.

Fursenko, Aleksandr and Timothy Naftali. 1997. *'One Hell of a Gamble.' Khrushchev, Castro, and Kennedy, 1958–1964*. New York: W. W. Norton.

Fusaro, Peter C. and Tom James. 2006. *Energy & Emissions Markets: Collision or Convergence*. Hoboken, NJ: Wiley.

Gaddis, John Lewis. 1982. *Strategies of Containment: A Critical Appraisal of Postwar American National Security Policy*. New York: Oxford University Press.

Gaddis, John Lewis. 2006. *The Cold War: A New History*. New York: Penguin Books.

Gallup. 2012. Americans' Worries About Global Warming Up Slightly. March 30. Online at http://bit.ly/18p98lj (accessed July 17, 2013).

Gang, Ding. 2011. War's Legacy Still Tints Vietnam's View of US. *Global Times*, July 6. Online at http://bit.ly/nH5USI (accessed July 15, 2013).

Gangale, Thomas. 2009. *The Development of Outer Space: Sovereignty and Property Rights in International Space Law*. Westport, CT: Praeger.

Garrett, Laurie. 2005. The Next Pandemic? *Foreign Affairs* 84 (4) July/August.

Gartzke, Erik. 2007. The Capitalist Peace. *American Journal of Political Science* 51 (1): 166–191.

Gaston, Kevin and John Spicer. 2004. *Biodiversity: An Introduction*. Malden, MA: Blackwell Publishing.

Gates, Nathaniel, ed. 1998. *Race and US Foreign Policy During the Cold War*. New York: Routledge.

Gause, F. Gregory. 2005. Can Democracy Stop Terrorism? *Foreign Affairs* 84 (5): 62–76.

Gelpi, Christopher and Peter Feaver. 2002. Speak Softly and Carry a Big Stick? Veterans in the Political Elite and the American Use of Force. *American Political Science Review* 96 (4): 779–793.

George, Alexander. 1969. The "Operational Code": A Neglected Approach to the Study of Political Leaders and Decision-Making. *International Studies Quarterly* 13 (2): 190–222.

Gereffi, Gary and Korzeniewicz, Miguel, eds. 1993. *Commodity Chains and Global Capitalism*. New York: Praeger.

German Energy Blog. 2012. Online at http://www.germanenergyblog.de/?page_id=3061 (accessed September 23, 2012)

Gerrard, Michael, ed. 2007. *Global Climate Change and U.S. Law*. Chicago, IL: American Bar Association.

Gertz, Bill. 2011. Computer-Based Attacks Emerge as Threat of Future, General Says. *The Washington Times*, September 13. Online at http://bit.ly/mYp915 (accessed Juluy 17, 2013).

Glad, Betty. 2009. *An Outsider in the White House: Jimmy Carter, His Advisors, and the Making of American Foreign Policy*. Ithaca, NY: Cornell University Press.

Goemans, Henk E., Kristian Skrede Gleditsch, and Giacomo Chiozza. 2009. Introducing Archigos: A Data Set of Political Leaders, 1975–2003. *Journal of Peace Research* 46 (2): 269–283.

Goldfrank, Walter. 2000 Paradigm Regained? The Rules of Wallerstein's World-System Method. *Journal of World-Systems Research* 6 (2): 150–195.

Goldgeier, J. and P. Tetlock. 2001. Psychology and International Relations Theory. *Annual Review of Political Science* 4: 67–92.

Goldgeier, James. 1999. *Not Whether but When: The U.S. Decision to Enlarge NATO*. Washington, DC: Brookings.

Gong, Sasha. 2009. Those Uppity Peasant Workers: The End of the Era of Cheap Chinese Labor. *The International Economy* Winter: 10–11, 83.

Goodman, Mel. 2008. *Failure of Intelligence: The Decline and Fall of the CIA*. New York: Rowman & Littlefield.

Gottlieb, Gidon. 1994. Nations without States. *Foreign Affairs* 73 (3) May/June.

Graber, Doris. 2005. *Mass Media and American Politics*. 7th edition. Washington, DC: CQ Press.

Gray, Colin. 1982. *Strategic Studies: A Critical Assessment*. Westport, CT: Greenwood Press.

Greenpeace International. 2013. About Greenpeace. Online at http://www.greenpeace.org/international/en/about/ (accessed July 17 2013).

Grimmett, Richard. 1999. Foreign Policy Roles of the President and Congress. U.S. Department of State. Online at http://fpc.state.gov/6172.htm (accessed September 25, 2012).

Grossman, Elizabeth. 2007. *High Tech Trash: Digital Devices, Hidden Toxics, and Human Health*. Washington, DC: Island Press.

Grotius, Hugo. 2005. *The Freedom of the Seas*. New York: Adamant Media Corporation.

Grover, Velma, ed. 2006. *Water: Global Common and Global Problems*. Enfield, NH: Science Publishers.

Gruber, Lloyd. 2000. *Ruling the World: Power Politics and the Rise of Supranational Institutions*. Princeton, NJ: Princeton University Press.

Guérot, Ulrike. 2010. The Yalta System Falls Apart and Germany Is Still Undecided Where to Go Next. Online at http://www.aicgs.org/expert/dr-ulrike-guerot/ (accessed September 2, 2011).

Haaretz Service. 2010. Germany's Deutsche Bank Divests from Israel Firm Linked to West Bank

Separation Fence. May 30. Online at http://bit.ly/ccUg5s (accessed July 17, 2013).

Haas, Ernst B. 1958. *The Uniting of Europe: Political, Social, and Economic Forces, 1950–1957*. Stanford, CA: Stanford University Press.

Haberman, Clyde. 1994. West Bank Massacre: The Overview; Rabin Urges the Palestinians to Put Aside Anger and Talk. *The New York Times*. March 1. Online at http://nyti.ms/15RT6Qw (accessed July 19, 2013).

Hahn, Gordon. 2012. Global Jihadism Comes to Russia's North Caucasus. *Fair Observer*. Online at http://bit.ly/RYJK0I, July 12 (accessed July 12, 2013).

Hainmueller, Jens and Michael Hiscox. 2007. Educated Preferences: Explaining Individual Attitudes Toward Immigration in Europe. *International Organization* 61 (2): 399–442.

Hamud, Randall, ed. 2005. *Osama Bin Laden: America's Enemy in His Own Words*. San Diego, CA: Nadeem Publishing.

Hanson, Victor. 2001. *Carnage and Culture: Landmark Battles in the Rise of Western Power*. New York: Doubleday.

Hardin, Garrett. 1968. The Tragedy of the Commons. *Science* 162 (3859): 1243–1248.

Harris, Frances. 2004. *Global Environmental Issues*. West Sussex, UK: Wiley.

Harrison, Selig and Clyde Prestowitz, Jr. 1990. Pacific Agenda: Defense or Economics? *Foreign Policy* 79 (Summer): 60.

Hart, Paul. 1991. Irving L. Janis' Victims of Groupthink: A Psychological Study of Foreign Policy Decisions and Fiascoes. *Political Psychology* 12 (2): 247–278.

Hartman, Laura and Patricia Werhane. 2009. *The Global Corporation: Sustainable, Effective and Ethical Practices, A Case Book*. New York: Routledge.

Hayek, Friedrich. 2007. *The Road to Serfdom*. Chicago: University of Chicago Press. Originally published in 1944.

Heider, Fritz. 1959. *The Psychology of Interpersonal Relations*. New York: Wiley.

Held, David. 2007. *Globalization/Anti-Globalization: Beyond the Great Divide*. Cambridge, UK: Polity.

Helm, Dieter, ed. 2005. *Climate Change Policy*. Oxford, UK: Oxford University Press.

Hemmer, Christopher. 1999. Historical Analogies and the Definition of Interests: The Iranian Hostage Crisis and Ronald Reagan's Policy toward the Hostages in Lebanon. *Political Psychology* 20 (2) June: 267–289.

Henig, Ruth. 2010. *The League of Nations: The Makers of the Modern World*. London: Haus Publishing.

Herrmann, Richard K. and Richard Ned Lebow, eds. 2004. *Ending the Cold War: Interpretations, Causation, and the Study of International Relations*. New York: Palgrave Macmillan.

Herzog, Michael. 2006. Can Hamas Be Tamed? *Foreign Affairs* 85 (2) March/April: 83–94.

Hinckley, Ronald. 1992. *People, Polls, and Policymakers: American Public Opinion and National Security*. New York: Lexington Books.

Hindmoor, Andrew. 2006. *Rational Choice* (Political Analysis). New York: Palgrave Macmillan.

Hiro, Dilip. 2010. *After Empire: The Birth of a Multipolar World*. New York: Nation Books.

Hirschman, Nancy. 2010. Choosing Betrayal. *Perspectives on Politics* 8 (1) March: 271–278.

Hitchcock, William I. 2008. *The Bitter Road to Freedom. A New History of the Liberation of Europe*. New York: Free Press.

Hitchcock, William I. 2010. The Marshall Plan and the Creation of the West, in: Melvyn P. Leffler and Odd Arne Westad, eds., *The Cambridge History of the Cold War*. Vol 1. Origins. London: Cambridge University Press, 154-174.

Hoekman, Bernard and Michel Kostecki. 2010. *The Political Economy of the World Trading System*. New York: Oxford University Press.

Hoffman, Bruce. 1998. *Inside Terrorism*. New York: Columbia University Press.

Hoffman, David. 2010. *The Dead Hand: The Untold Story of the Cold War Arms Race and Its Dangerous Legacy*. New York: Anchor.

Holsti, Ole. 1992. Public Opinion and Foreign Policy: Challenges to the Almond-Lippmann Consensus. *International Studies Quarterly* 36 (4): 439–466.

Holsti, Ole. 2004. *Public Opinion and American Foreign Policy*. Revised edition. Ann Arbor: University of Michigan Press.

Holzgrefe, J. L. and Robert O. Keohane, eds. 2003. *Humanitarian Intervention: Ethical, Legal, and Political Dilemmas*. Cambridge, UK: Cambridge University Press.

Homer-Dixon, Thomas. 1991. On the Threshold: Environmental Changes As Causes of Acute Conflict. *International Security* 16 (2): 76–116.

Hopkirk, Peter. 1994. *The Great Game: The Struggle for Empire in Central Asia*. New York: Kodansha International.

Horgan, John. 2009. *Walking Away from Terrorism: Accounts of Disengagement from Radical and Extremist Movements*. New York: Routledge

Houghton, David. 2008. *Political Psychology: Situations, Individuals, and Cases*. New York: Routledge.

Howard, Russell and James Forest, eds. 2008. *Weapons of Mass Destruction and Terrorism*. Dubuque, IA: McGraw-Hill.

Hudson, Valerie. 1999. Cultural Expectations of One's Own and Other Nations' Foreign Policy Templates. *Political Psychology* 20 (4): 767–801.

Hufbauer, Gary and Barbara Oegg. 2003. Beyond the Nation-State: Privatization of Economic Sanctions. *Middle East Policy* 10 (2): 126–134.

Hunt, Swanee. 2007. Let Women Rule. *Foreign Affairs* 86 (3): 109–120.

Huntington, Samuel. 1993. The Clash of Civilizations. *Foreign Affairs* 72 (3): 22–28.

ICJ (International Court of Justice). 2004. Legal Consequences of the Construction of a Wall in the Occupied Palestinian Territory. General List No. 131. July 9.

Ignatieff, Michael. 2004.*The Lesser Evil: Political Ethics in an Age of Terrorism*. Princeton, NJ: Princeton University Press.

Ikenberry, G. John. 2011a. The Future of the Liberal World Order. *Foreign Affairs* 90 (3) May/June: 56–68.

Ikenberry, G. John. 2011b.*Liberal Leviathan: The Origins, Crisis, and Transformation of the American World Order*. Princeton, NJ: Princeton University Press.

Ikenberry, G. John and Joseph M. Grieco. 2002. *State Power and World Markets: The International Political Economy*. New York: W. W. Norton & Co.

International Health Regulations: The Challenges Ahead (Editorial). 2007. *The Lancet* 369 (9575) May 26: 1763.

Iriye, Akira. 2002. *Global Community: The Role of International Organizations in the Making of the Contemporary World*. Berkeley: University of California Press.

Jackson, Robert. 2005. *Classical and Modern Thought on International Relations: From Anarchy to Cosmopolism* (Palgrave Macmillan History of International Thought). New York: Palgrave Macmillan.

Jacques, Peter. 2009. *Environmental Skepticism* (Global Environmental Governance). London: Ashgate.

Jarausch, Konrad. 2008. *After Hitler: Recivilizing Germans, 1945–1995*. New York: Oxford University Press.

Jenkins, Willis. 2008. *Ecologies of Grace: Environmental Ethics and Christian Theology*. New York: Oxford University Press.

Jervis, Robert. 1976. *Perceptions and Misperceptions in International Politics*. Princeton, NJ: Princeton University Press.

Jervis, Robert. 1982. Security Regimes. *International Organization* 36 (2): 357–378.

Jervis, Robert. 2002. Theories of War in an Era of Leading-Power Peace. *American Political Science Review* 96 (1): 1–14.

Joffe, Josef. 2009. The Default Power: The False Prophecy of America's Decline.*Foreign Affairs* 87 (5) September/October: 21-35.

Johnson, Pierre M., Karel Mayrand, and Marc Paquin, eds. 2006. *Governing Global Desertification: Linking Environmental Degradation, Poverty, and Participation*. London: Ashgate.

Kahler, Miles and David Lake, eds. 2003. *Governance in a Global Economy: Political Authority in Transition*. Princeton, NJ: Princeton University Press.

Kahneman, Daniel and Amos Tversky. 1979. Prospect Theory: An Analysis of Decisions under Risk. *Econometrica* 47 (2): 263–292.

Kahneman, Daniel, and Amos Tversky. 1972. Subjective Probability: A Judgment of Representativeness. *Cognitive Psychology* 3: 430–454.

Kahnemen, Daniel and Jonathan Renshon. 2007. Why Hawks Win. *Foreign Policy* 158: 34–38.

Kalyvas, Stathis and Laia Balcellis. 2010. International System and Technologies of Rebellion: How the End of the Cold War Shaped Internal Conflict. *American Political Science Review* 104 (3): 415–429.

Kamieniecki, Sheldon and Michael Kraft, eds. 2007. *Business and Environmental Policy: Corporate Interests in the American Political System* (American and Comparative Environmental Policy). Cambridge, MA: MIT Press.

Kane, Thomas. 2006. *Theoretical Roots of US Foreign Policy: Machiavelli and American Unilateralism*. New York: Routledge.

Kant, Immanuel. 2003. *To Perpetual Peace: A Philosophical Sketch*. Indianapolis, IN: Hackett Publishing. Originally published in 1795.

Kaplan, Robert. 2012. *The Revenge of Geography: What the Map Tells Us About Coming Conflicts and the Battle Against Fate*. New york: Random House.

Kapuscinski, Ryszard. 2002.*The Shadow of the Sun*. New York: Vintage.

Karesh, William and Robert Cook. 2005. The Human-Animal Link. *Foreign Affairs* 84 (4) July–August.

Keck, Margaret and Kathryn Sikkink, eds. 1998. *Activists Beyond Borders: Advocacy Networks in International Politics*. Ithaca, NY: Cornell University Press.

Kelly, John. 1996. Chapter 6: Lebanon: 1982–1984. In *U.S. and Russian Policymaking with Respect to the Use of Force*, eds. Jeremy Azrael and Emil Payin. Conference Proceedings. Rand Corporation. Online at http://bit.ly/16P1Fc6 (accessed July 18, 2013).

Kemp, William. 2006. *The Renewable Energy Handbook: A Guide to Rural Energy Independence, Off-Grid and Sustainable Living*. Tamworth, Canada: Aztext Press.

Keohane, Robert. 1989. *International Institutions and State Power*. London: Westview Press, Inc.

Keohane, Robert. 2003. Political Authority after Intervention: Gradation in Sovereignty. In *Humanitarian Intervention: Ethical, Legal, and Political Dilemmas*, eds. J. L. Holzgrefe and Robert Keohane. New York: Cambridge University Press, 275–298.

Kershaw, Ian. 2000. *The Nazi Dictatorship: Problems and Perspectives of Interpretation*. New York: Bloomsbury.

Keynes, Robert. 1965. *The General Theory of Employment, Interest and Money*. New York: Harcourt, Brace & World. Originally published in 1936.

Khlevniuk, Oleg. 2008. *Master of the House: Stalin and His Inner Circle*. New Haven, CT: Yale University Press.

Khong, Yuen Foong. 1992. *Analogies at War: Korea, Munich, Dien Bien Phu, and the Vietnam Decisions of 1965*. Princeton, NJ: Princeton University Press.

Kirkpatrick, Jeane. 2002. Convention on the Elimination of All Forms of Discrimination against Women. Testimony before the Senate Foreign Relations Committee, Washington, DC. June 13.

Kissinger, Henry. 2001. The Pitfalls of Global Jurisdiction. *Foreign Affairs* 80 (4) July/August: 86–96.

Klein, Aaron J. 2005. *Striking Back: The 1972 Munich Olympics Massacre and Israel's Deadly Response*. New York: Random House.

Koseki, Shoichi. 1998. *The Birth of Japan's Postwar Constitution*. Translated by Ray Moore. Boulder, CO: Westview Press.

Kosterman, Rick and Seymour Feshbach. 1989. Toward a Measure of Patriotic and Nationalistic Attitudes. *Political Psychology* 10 (2): 257–274.

Kowert, P. 1996. Where *Does* the Buck Stop?: Assessing the Impact of Presidential Personality. *Political Psychology* 17 (3): 421–452.

Krauthammer, Charles. 2008. Crooked Roads to Democracy. *The Washington Post*. January 4, A21.

Krueger, Alan. 2007. *What Makes a Terrorist: Economics and the Roots of Terrorism*. Princeton, NJ: Princeton University Press.

Krugman, Paul. 2009. Chinese New Year. *The New York Times*, December 31.

Kuehnast, Kathleen, Chantal de Jonge Oudraat, and Helga Hernes, eds. 2011. *Women and War: Power and Protection in the 21st Century*. Washington, DC: United States Institute of Peace Press.

Kydd, Andrew. 2005. *Trust and Mistrust in International Relations*. Princeton, NJ: Princeton University Press.

Lakoff, Andrew. 2010. Two Regimes of Global Health. *Humanity* 1 (1): 59–79.

Lappe, Frances M., Joseph Collins, and Peter Rosset. 1998. *World Hunger: Twelve Myths*. New York: Grove Press.

Larson, Deborah. 1985. *Origins of Containment*. Princeton, NJ: Princeton University Press.

Larson, Deborah. 1997. *Anatomy of Mistrust: U.S.-Soviet Relations During the Cold War*. Ithaca, NY: Cornell University Press.

Lauterpacht, Hersch. 2011. *The Function of Law in the International Community*. New York: Oxford University Press. Originally published in 1933.

Laver, Michael. 1979. *Playing Politics*. London: Penguin.

Laver, Michael. 1997. *Playing Politics: The Nightmare Continues*. New York: Oxford University Press.

Layne, Christopher. 1994. Kant or Cant: The Myth of the Democratic Peace. *International Security* 19 (2): 5–49.

Le Billon, Philippe. 2006. *Fuelling War: Natural Resources and Armed Conflicts*. New York: Routledge.

Leatherman, Janie. 2011. *Sexual Violence and Armed Conflict*. Cambridge, UK: Polity.

Leffler, Melvyn. 2007. *For the Soul of Mankind: The United States, the Soviet Union, and the Cold War*. New York: Farrar, Straus and Giroux.

Lenin, Vladimir. 1996. *Imperialism as the Highest Stage of Capitalism*. New York: Pluto Press. Originally published in 1916.

Levada Center. 2013. Online at http://bit.ly/19M6xlO (accessed July 17, 2013).

Lévesque, Jacques. 1997. *The Enigma of 1989: The USSR and the Liberation of Eastern Europe*. Berkeley: University of California Press.

Levey, David and Stuart Brown. 2005. The Overstretch Myth. *Foreign Affairs* 84 (2) March/April: 2–7.

Levi, Michael, Elizabeth Economy, Shannon O'Neil, and Adam Segal. 2010. Globalizing the Energy Revolution. *Foreign Affairs* 89 (6) November/December: 111–121.

Levi, Michael. 2009. *On Nuclear Terrorism*. Cambridge, MA: Harvard University Press.

Levi, Michael. 2010a. Beyond Copenhagen. *Foreign Affairs*. Postscript. February.

Levi, Michael. 2010b. Reinforcing Climate Promises in Cancun. An Interview. Council on Foreign Relations. November 24. Online at http://www.cfr.org/publication/23453/reinforcing_climate_promises_in_cancun.html?cid=rss-analysis-briefbackgroundersexp-reinforcing_climate_promises_i-112410 (accessed September 25, 2012).

Levi, Michael. 2013. *The Power Surge: Energy, Opportunity, and the Battle for America's Future*. New York: Oxford University Press.

Levitsky, Steven and Lucan Way. 2010. *Competitive Authoritarianism: Hybrid Regimes After the Cold War*. New York: Cambridge University Press.

Levy, David. 2009. *Tools of Critical Thinking: Metathoughts for Psychology*. Long Grove, IL: Waveland Press.

Levy, Jack. 1984. The Offensive/Defensive Balance of Military Technology: A Theoretical and Historical Analysis. *International Studies Quarterly* 28 (2) June: 219–238.

Liberman, Peter. 2006. An Eye for an Eye: Public Support for War against Evildoers. *International Organization* 60 (3) July: 687–722.

Lieven, Anatol and John Hulsman. 2006. *Ethical Realism: A Vision for America's Role in the World*. New York: Pantheon.

Lindkvist, Sven. 2007. *Terra Nullius: A Journey Through No One's Land*. New York: New Press.

Linklater, Andrew. 2009. The English School. In *Theories of International Relations*, ed. Scott Burchill et al. New York: Palgrave Macmillan, 86–110.

List, Friedrich. 2006. *National System of Political Economy. Volume 1: The History*. New York: Cosimo Classics. Originally published in 1841.

Lomborg, Bjørn, ed. 2004. *Global Crises, Global Solutions*. Cambridge, UK: Cambridge University Press.

Lomborg, Bjørn. 2007. *Cool It: The Skeptical Environmentalist's Guide to Global Warming*. New York: Knopf.

Lomborg, Bjørn. 2010. An Interview. *Financial Times*, December 9. Online at http://on.ft.com/18t3hPf (accessed July 15, 2013).

Loyola, Mario. 2010. Legality over Legitimacy. *Foreign Affairs* 89 (4) July–August. Online at http://fam.ag/13TtFQO (accessed July 18, 2013).

Lynn, William J. 2010. Defending a New Domain. The Pentagon's Cyberstrategy. *Foreign Affairs* 89 (5) September/October: 97-108.

MacNair, Rachel. 2003. *The Psychology of Peace: An Introduction*. Santa Barbara, CA: Praeger.

Madeley, John. 2009. *Big Business, Poor Peoples: How Transnational Corporations Damage the Global Poor*. London: Zed Books.

Madigan, Janet. 2007. *Truth, Politics, and Universal Human Rights*. New York: Palgrave Macmillan.

Magdoff, Fred and John B. Foster. 2011. *What Every Environmentalist Needs to Know about Capitalism*. New York: Monthly Review Press.

Mahbubani, Kishore. 2002. *Can Asians Think? Understanding the Divide Between East and West*. South Royalton, VT: Steerforth.

Mahler, Gregory. 2004. *Politics and Government in Israel: The Maturation of a Modern State*. Lanham, MD: Rowman & Littlefield.

Mak, Geert. 2008. *In Europe: Travels Through the Twentieth Century*. New York: Vintage.

Maoz, Zeev and Bruce Russett. 1993. Normative and Structural Causes of Democratic Peace, 1946–1986. *The American Political Science Review* 87 (3): 624–638.

Marrar, Khalil. 2008. *The Arab Lobby and US Foreign Policy*. New York: Routledge.

Marsh, Peter. 2012. *The New Industrial Revolution: Consumers, Globalization, and the End of the Mass Production*. New Haven, CT: Yale University Press.

Martin, Terry. 2001. *The Affirmative Action Empire: Nations and Nationalism in the Soviet Union, 1923–1939*. Ithaca, NY: Cornell University Press.

Marx, Karl and Friedrich Engels. 2011. *The Communist Manifesto*. SoHo Books. Originally published in 1848.

Mazower, Mark. 2000. *Dark Continent: Europe's Twentieth Century*. New York: Vintage.

McCarthy, Michael. 2011. Global Warning: Climate Sceptics Are Winning the Battle. *The Independent*, October 11. Online at http://ind.pn/oakpOW (accessed July 18, 2013).

McFaul, Michael. 2009. *Advancing Democracy Abroad: Why We Should and How We Can*. New York: Rowman & Littlefield.

McGovern, Joe. 2006. *The Kyoto Protocol*. Pittsburgh, PA: Dorrance Publishing Co.

McKinnon, Ron. 2010. A Reply to Krugman. *International Economy*, Winter.

McNamara, Robert. 1996. *In Retrospect: The Tragedy and Lessons of Vietnam*. New York: Vintage.

Mearsheimer, John and Stephen Walt. 2007. *The Israel Lobby and US Foreign Policy*. New York: Farrar, Straus and Giroux.

Mearsheimer, John. 2003. *The Tragedy of Great Power Politics*. New York: W. W. Norton & Company.

Miéville, China. 2006. *Between Equal Rights: A Marxist Theory of International Law*. Chicago: Haymarket Books.

Milgram, Stanley. 1963. Behavioral Study of Obedience. *Journal of Abnormal and Social Psychology* 67 (4): 371–378.

Mitzen, Jennifer. 2005. Reading Habermas in Anarchy: Multilateral Diplomacy and Global Public Spheres. *American Political Science Review* 99 (3): 401–417.

Mohamoud, Abdullah. 2006. *State Collapse and Post-Conflict Development in Africa: The Case of Somalia 1960–2001*. West Lafayette, IN: Purdue University Press.

Moravcsik, Andrew. 2001. Why Is the US Human Rights Policy So Unilateralist? In *Multilateralism and U.S. Foreign Policy,*eds. Stewart Patrick and Shepard Forman. Boulder, CO: Lynne Rienner.

Morgenthau, Hans J. 2006. *Politics among Nations: The Struggle for Power and Peace*. 7th edition, revised by Kenneth W. Thompson and W. David Clinton. New York: McGraw-Hill. Originally published 1948.

Morris, Ian. 2010. *Why the West Rules—for Now: The Patterns of History and What They Reveal about the Future*. New York: Farrar, Straus and Giroux.

Moyo, Dambisa. 2010. *Dead Aid: Why Aid is Not Working and How There Is a Better Way for Africa*. Vancouver, BC: Douglas & Mcintyre Ltd.

Mueller, John. 1989. *Retreat from Doomsday: The Obsolescence of Major War*. New York: Basic Books.

Muller, Jerry. 2008. Us and Them: The Enduring Power of Ethnic Nationalism. *Foreign Affairs* 87 (22) March/April: 18–35.

Munz, Rainer. 2003. *Diasporas and Ethnic Migrants: Germany, Israel and Russia in Comparative Perspective*. London, UK: Routledge.

Murray, Henry. 1943. *Analysis of the Personality of Adolf Hitler: With Predictions of His Future Behavior and Suggestions for Dealing with Him Now and After Germany's Surrender*. October. Cornell University Law Library. Online at http://bit.ly/gdkgGV (accessed July 15, 2013).

Murray, Iain. 2008. *The Really Inconvenient Truths: Seven Environmental Catastrophes Liberals Don't Want You to Know About—Because They Helped Cause Them*. Washington, DC: Regnery Publishing.

Nacos, Brigitte, Robert Shapiro, and Pierangelo Isernia, eds. 2000. *Decision-Making in the Glass House*. Boulder, CO: Rowman & Littlefield.

Nacos, Brigitte.2009.*Terrorism and Counterterrorism. Understanding Threats and Responses in the Post–9/11 World*. 3rd edition. New York: Longman.

NAF (New America Foundation). 2012. The Year of the Drone. An Analysis of U.S. Drone Strikes in Pakistan, 2004–2012. Online at http://counterterrorism.newamerica.net/drones (accessed August 8, 2012).

Naimark, Norman. 2002. *Fires of Hatred: Ethnic Cleansing in Twentieth Century Europe*. Cambridge, MA: Harvard University Press.

Narizny, Kevin. 2003. Both Guns and Butter, or Neither: Class Interests in the Political Economy of Rearmament. *American Political Science Review* 97 (2): 203–220.

Narlikar, Amrita. 2005. *WTO: A Very Short Introduction*. New York: Oxford University Press.

National Commission on Terrorist Acts upon the United States. 9-11 Commission Report. Online at http://www.9-11commission.gov/report/index.htm (accessed September 25, 2012).

Nau, Henry. 2002. *At Home Abroad: Identity and Power in American Foreign Policy*. Ithaca, NY: Cornell University Press.

Neumann, Iver. 1996. *Russia and the Idea of Europe: A Study in Identity and International Relations*. London: Routledge.

Newman, Edward, Ramesh Thakur, and John Tirman. 2006.. *Multilateralism Under Challenge?: Power, International Order, and Structural Change*. Tokyo: United Nations University Press.

Nonini, Donald, ed. 2007. *The Global Idea of "The Commons."* New York: Berghahn Books.

Nordhaus, Richard. 2008. *A Question of Balance: Weighing the Options on Global Warming Policies*. New Haven, CT: Yale University Press.

Nye, Joseph. 2002. *The Paradox of American Power: Why the World's Only Superpower Can't Go It Alone*. Oxford, UK: Oxford University Press.

Nye, Joseph. 2004. *Soft Power: The Means to Success in World Politics*. New York: Public Affairs.

O'Brien, Patrick Karl and Armand Clesse, eds. 2002. *Two Hegemonies: Britain 1846–1914 and the United States 1941–2001*. Aldershot, UK: Ashgate.

Olson, Mancur. 1971. *The Logic of Collective Action: Public Goods and the Theory of Groups* Cambridge, MA: Harvard University Press.

Oneal, John R. and Bruce M. Russett. 1997. Classical Liberals Were Right: Democracy, Interdependence, and Conflict, 1950–1985. *International Studies Quarterly* 42 (2) June: 264–294.

Oppenheim, Lassa. 2008. *Oppenheim's International Law*. 9th edition, eds. Robert Jennings and Arthur Watts. New York: Oxford University Press.

Orbinski, James. 2009. *An Imperfect Offering: Humanitarian Action for the Twenty-First Century*. New York: Walker & Company.

Our Common Future. Report of the World Commission on Environment and Development. 1987. Online at http://www.un-documents.net/wced-ocf.htm (Accessed July 15, 2013).

Owen, John M. 2005. Iraq and the Democratic Peace. *Foreign Affairs* 84 (6) November/December.

Page, Benjamin and Robert Shapiro. 1988. Foreign Policy and the Rational Public. *Journal of Conflict Resolution*. 32: 211-247.

Pant, Harsh. 2011. China and Pakistan: A New Balance of Power in South Asia. *ISN: International Relations and Security Network*. June 20. Online at http://bit.ly/QoKfiy (accessed September 25, 2012).

Pape, Robert. 2003. The Strategic Logic of Suicide Terrorism. *American Political Science Review* 97 (3): 343–361.

Parker, Kathleen. 2010. Obama, Our First Female President. *The Washington Post*, June 30. Online at http://wapo.st/cHTwjC (accessed July 15, 2013).

Parmesan, Camille and Gary Yohe. 2003. A Globally Coherent Fingerprint of Climate Change Impacts across Natural Systems. *Nature* 421: 37–42.

Patterson, Amy. 2006. *The Politics of AIDS in Africa*. Boulder, CO: Lynne Rienner.

Pearce, Fred. 2007. *When the Rivers Run Dry: Water—The Defining Crisis of the Twenty-first Century*. Boston, MA: Beacon Press.

Peerenboom, Randall. 2008. *China Modernizes: Threat to the West or Model for the Rest?* Oxford, UK: Oxford University Press.

Peet, Richard. 2009. *Unholy Trinity: The IMF, World Bank and WTO*. 2nd edition. London: Zed Books.

Pelligrini, Dominick, ed. 2010. *Nuclear Weapons' Role in 21st Century U.S. Policy*. Hauppage, NY: Nova Science.

Peters, Anny, Maja Micevska-Scharf, Francien Van Driel, and Willy Jansen. 2010. Where Does Public Funding For HIV Prevention Go To? The Case of Condoms versus Microbicides and Vaccines. *Globalization and Health* 6 (1): 23. Online at http://www.globalizationandhealth.com/content/6/1/23 (accessed September 25, 2012).

Pew Research Center. 2009. U.S. Seen as Less Important, China as More Powerful. December 3. Online at http://bit.ly/10Op1jG (accessed July 19, 2013).

Pew Research Center. 2010. Americans Spending More Time Following the News: Ideological News Sources: Who Watches and Why. September 12. Online at http://bit.ly/rlXOQ8 (accessed July 19, 2013).

Pew Research Center. 2011. Confidence in Osama bin Laden. Online at http://www.pewglobal.org/database/?indicator=20 (accessed July 16, 2013).

Phuong, Catherine. 2010. *The International Protection of Internally Displaced Persons*. New York: Cambridge University Press.

Pielke, Roger. 2010. *The Climate Fix: What Scientists and Politicians Won't Tell You About Global Warming*. New York: Basic Books.

Pillar, Paul. 2001. *Terrorism and U.S. Foreign Policy*. Washington, DC: Brookings Institution Press.

Pin-Lin, Chong. 2010. Can China Become the World's Engine for Growth? Symposium contribution. *International Economy*, Winter: 10.

Plokhy, S. M. 2010. *Yalta: The Price of Peace*. New York: Viking Adult.

Polman, Linda. 2010. *The Crisis Caravan: What's Wrong with Humanitarian Aid?* New York: Metropolitan Books.

Post, Jerrold. 1990. Explaining Saddam Hussein: a Psychological Profile. Presented to the House Armed Services Committee. December 1990. http://www.au.af.mil/au/awc/awcgate/iraq/saddam_post.htm

Post, Jerrold. 2004. *Leaders and Their Followers in a Dangerous World: The Psychology of Political Behavior* (Psychoanalysis and Social Theory). Ithaca, NY: Cornell University Press.

Post, Jerrold. 2005a. The New Face of Terrorism: Socio-Cultural Foundations of Contemporary Terrorism. *Behavioral Sciences and the Law* 23(4): 451-465.

Post, Jerrold. 2005b. When Hatred is Bred in the Bone: Psycho-cultural Foundations of Contemporary Terrorism. *Journal of Political Psychology* 26 (4): 615–636.

Post, Jerrold. 2008. *The Mind of the Terrorist. The Psychology of Terrorism from the IRA to al-Qaeda.* New York: Palgrave Macmillan.

Prebisch, Raúl. 1989. *Antología del pensamiento político, social y económico de América Latina* (In Spanish). Buenos Aires: Ediciones de Cultura Hispánica.

Priest, Dana and William Arkin. 2010a. A Hidden World, Going Beyond Control. *The Washington Post.* July 19, A7.

Priest, Dana and William Arkin. 2010b. National Security, Inc. *The Washington Post,* July 20, A1.

Priest, Dana and William Arkin. 2011. *Top Secret America: The Rise of the New American Security State.* Boston: Little, Brown, and Co.

Primakov, Evgeny. 2009. *Russia and the Arabs: Behind the Scenes in the Middle East from the Cold War to the Present.* New York: Basic Books.

Putnam, Robert. 1988. Diplomacy and Domestic Politics: The Logic of Two-Level Games, *International Organization* 42 (3): 427–460.

Qutb, Sayyid. 2007. *Milestones.* Chicago, IL: Kazi Publications. Originally published in 1964.

Ramet, Sabrina. 2005. *Thinking about Yugoslavia: Scholarly Debates about the Yugoslav Breakup and the Wars in Bosnia and Kosovo.* New York: Cambridge University Press.

Rankin, Jennifer. 2010. Rules on Unusual Food Heading to Arbitration. *EuropeanVoice.com.* July 1. Online at http://www.europeanvoice.com/article/imported/rules-on-unusual-food-heading-to-arbitration/68372.aspx (accessed September 25, 2012).

Rapkin, David P. and Jonathan R. Strand. 2006. Reforming the IMF's Weighted Voting System. *The World Economy* 29 (3): 305–324.

Rapoport, David. 2001. Modern Terror: The Four Waves. *Current History,* 419–425.

Rashid, Ahmed. 2008. *Descent into Chaos: The United States and the Failure of Nation Building in Pakistan, Afghanistan, and Central Asia.* New York: Viking Adult.

Reardon, Betty. 1985. *Sexism and the War System.* New York: Teachers College Press.

Rechkemmer, Andreas. 2004. *Postmodern Global Governance: The United Nations Convention to Combat Desertification.* Baden-Baden, Germany: Nomos Verlagsgesellschaft.

Renshon, Stanley. 2004. *In His Father's Shadow: The Transformations of George W. Bush.* New York: Palgrave Macmillan.

Renshon, Stanley. 2009. National Security in the Obama Administration: Reassessing the Bush Doctrine. New York: Routledge.

Renshon, Stanley. 2011. *Barack Obama and the Politics of Redemption.* New York: Routledge.

Reus-Smit, Christian. 2009. Constructivism. In *Theories of International Relations,* 4th edition, ed. Scott Burchill et al. New York: Palgrave Macmillan, 212–236.

Rey, Marie-Pierre. 2004. Europe Is Our Common Home. A Study of Gorbachev's Diplomatic Concept. *Cold War History* 4 (2): 33–65.

Rieff, David. 2006. *At the Point of a Gun: Democratic Dreams and Armed Intervention.* New York: Simon & Schuster.

Ritchie, Elspeth Cameron, Patricia Watson, and Mathew Friedman, eds. 2005. *Interventions Following Mass Violence and Disasters: Strategies for Mental Health Practice.* New York: The Guilford Press.

Roan, Sharon. 1989. *Ozone Crisis: The 15-Year Evolution of a Sudden Global Emergency.* Hoboken, NJ: Wiley.

Roberts, Adam. 2000. The So-Called "Right" of Humanitarian Intervention. *Yearbook of International Humanitarian Law* 3: 3–51.

Roberts, J. Timmons and Bradley Parks. 2006. *A Climate of Injustice: Global Inequality, North-South Politics, and Climate Policy.* Cambridge, MA: MIT Press.

Rogers, Peter, Kazi F. Jalal, and John Boyd. 2007. *An Introduction to Sustainable Development.* New York: Routledge.

Rogowski, Ronald. 1990. *Commerce and Coalitions: How Trade Affects Domestic Political Alignments.* Princeton, NJ: Princeton University Press.

Rose, Gideon. 2011. In Libya: How Obama Can End a Mission That Started Badly. *Washington Post.* March 25. Online at http://bit.ly/15tYCXA (accessed July 18, 2013).

Rosenau, James. 1961. *Public Opinion and Foreign Policy: An Operational Formation.* New York: Random House.

Rosenau, James. 1999. Toward an Ontology for Global Governance. In *Approaches to Global Governance Theory,* eds. Martin Hewson and Timothy J. Sinclair. Albany: State University of New York.

Rynning, Sren and Jens Ringsmose. 2008. Why Are Revisionist States Revisionist? Reviving Classical Realism as an Approach to Understanding International Change. *International Politics* 45 (1): 19–39.

Sachs, Jeffrey. 2005. *The End of Poverty: Economic Possibilities for Our Time.* New York: Penguin Press.

Sageman, Marc. 2004. *Understanding Terror Networks.* Philadelphia: University of Pennsylvania Press.

Said, Edward. 1994. *Culture and Imperialism.* New York: Vintage.

Sanford, George. 2009. *Katyn and the Soviet Massacre of 1940: Truth, Justice, and Memory.* New York: Routledge.

Sapolsky, Robert M. 2006. A Natural History of Peace. *Foreign Affairs* 85 (1) January/February: 104–120.

Saradzhyan, Simon. 2010. Chechnya: Divisions in the Ranks. *ISN: International Relations and Security Network.* August 11. Online at http://www.isn.ethz .ch/isn/Current-Affairs/Security-Watch/Detail/ ?lng=en&id=120017 (accessed September 20, 2012).

Sarkesian, Sam C., John Allen Williams, and Stephen J. Cimbala. 2007. *US National Security: Policymakers, Processes and Politics.* 4th edition. Boulder, CO: Lynne Rienner.

Sarotte, Mary. 2009. *1989: The Struggle to Create Post-Cold War Europe.* Princeton, NJ: Princeton University Press.

Sathasivam, Kanishkan. 2005. *Uneasy Neighbors: India, Pakistan and US Foreign Policy.* London: Ashgate.

Schein, Virginia E. 2002. A Global Look at Psychological Barriers to Women's Progress in Management. *Journal of Social Issues* 57 (4): 675–688.

Schellnhuber, Hans-Joachim, Gary Yohe, Wolfgang Cramer, Tom Wigley, Nebojsa Nakicenovic, eds. 2006. *Avoiding Dangerous Climate Change.* Cambridge, UK: Cambridge University Press.

Schlesinger, Stephen. 2003. *Act of Creation: The Founding of the United Nations; A Story of Superpowers, Secret Agents, Wartime Allies and Enemies and Their Quest for a Peaceful World.* Boulder, CO: Westview Press.

Schmidt, Gustav, ed. 2001. *A History of NATO—The First Fifty Years: Three-Volume Set.* New York: Palgrave Macmillan.

Schulte, Constanze. 2005. *Compliance with Decisions of the International Court of Justice.* New York: Oxford University Press.

Schultz, Richard. 2004. Showstoppers: Nine Reasons Why We Never Sent Our Special Operation Forces after Al Qaeda before 9/11. *Weekly Standard,* January 26, 25–33.

Schweller, Randall. 1997. New Realist Research on Alliances: Refining, Not Refuting, Waltz's Balancing Proposition. *American Political Science Review* 91 (4): 913–917.

Scott, Bruce. 2001. The Great Divide in the Global Village. *Foreign Affairs* 80 (1) January/February: 160-177.

Scully, Eileen. 2001. *Bargaining with the State from Afar.* New York: Columbia University Press.

Sears, David, Leonie Huddy, and Robert Jervis, eds. 2003. *Oxford Handbook on Political Psychology.* New York: Oxford University Press.

Sen, Amartya. 1981. *Poverty and Famines: An Essay on Entitlement and Deprivation.* Oxford, UK: Oxford University Press.

Shapiro, Judith. 2001. *Mao's War against Nature: Politics and the Environment in Revolutionary China.* New York: Cambridge University Press.

Sharp, Paul. 2009. *Diplomatic Theory of International Relations* (Cambridge Studies in International Relations Series). New York: Cambridge University Press.

Shelley, Louise. 2010. *Human Trafficking: A Global Perspective.* New York: Cambridge University Press.

Shepard, Todd. 2006. *The Invention of Decolonization.* Ithaca, NY: Cornell University Press.

Shiraev, Eric and David Levy. 2013. *Cross-Cultural Psychology: Critical Thinking and Contemporary Applications.* 5th edition. Boston: Allyn and Bacon.

Shiraev, Eric and Richard Sobel. 2006. *People and Their Opinions: Thinking Critically about Public Opinion.* New York: Longman.

Shiraev, Eric. 2013. *Russian Government and Politics.* 2nd edition. New York: Palgrave Macmillan.

Shirer, William. 1990. *The Rise and Fall of the Third Reich: A History of Nazi Germany.* New York: Simon & Schuster.

Shlapentokh, Vladimir, Eric Shiraev, and Eero Carroll. 2008. *The Soviet Union. Internal and External Perspectives on Soviet Society.* New York: Palgrave Macmillan.

Simon, Steven and Jeff Martini. 2004. Terrorism: Denying Al Qaeda its Popular Support. *The Washington Quarterly* 28 (1) Winter: 131–145.

Singer, Burt, Awash Teklehaimanot, Andrew Spielman, Al Schapira, and Yesim Tozan, eds., Jeffrey D. Sachs, series editor. 2005. *Coming to Grips with Malaria in the New Millennium.* London, UK: Earthscan.

Singer, Hans W. 1999. *Growth, Development and Trade: Selected Essays of Hans W. Singer.* Northhampton, MA: Edward Elgar Publishing.

Singh, Michael. 2010. Iran Re-Revolution: How the Green Movement Is Repeating Iranian HIstory. *Foreign Affairs.* July 26. Online at http://fam

.ag/aQJunk (accessed September 25, 2012). Registration is required. Another version is available online at http://bit.ly/1bwKeUK (accessed July 16, 2013).

Sjoberg, Laura, ed. 2009. *Gender and International Security: Feminist Perspectives*. New York: Routledge.

Sloan, Stanley. 2010. *Permanent Alliance?: NATO and the Transatlantic Bargain from Truman to Obama*. New York: Continuum.

Sloan, Stephen. 2006. *Terrorism: The Present Threat in Context*. London: Berg Publishers.

Smith, Adam. 1977. *An Inquiry into the Nature and Causes of the Wealth of Nations*. Chicago: University of Chicago Press.

Smith, Peter & Shalom Schwartz. 1997. Values. In *Handbook of Cross-Cultural Psychology* (3), eds. J. Berry, M. Segall, & C. Kagitcibasi. Boston, MA: Allyn & Bacon, 77–118.

Sniderman, Paul, Louk Hagendoorn, and Markus Prior. 2004. Predisposing Factors and Situational Triggers: Exclusionary Reactions to Immigrant Minorities. *American Political Science Review* 98 (1): 35–50.

Snyder, Jack. 2000. *From Voting to Violence. Democratization and Nationalist Violence*. New York: W. W. Norton.

Snyder, Jack. 2005. *Electing to Fight: Why Emerging Democracies Go to War*. Cambridge, MA: MIT Press.

Snyder-Hall, R. Claire. 2010. Third-Wave Feminism and the Defense of "Choice." *Perspectives on Politics* 8 (1): 255–261.

Sobek, David. 2008. *Causes of War*. Cambridge, UK: Polity.

Sobel, Richard and Eric Shiraev, eds. 2003. *International Public Opinion and the Bosnia Crisis*. Lanham, MD: Lexington Books.

Sobel, Richard. 2001. *The Impact of Public Opinion on U.S. Foreign Policy Since Vietnam*. New York: Oxford University Press.

Soetaert, Wim and Erik Vandamme, eds. 2009. *Biofuels*. West Sussex, UK: Wiley.

Soeters, Joseph. 2005. *Ethnic Conflict and Terrorism: The Origins and Dynamics of Civil Wars*. New York: Routledge.

Spector, Bertram, ed. 2005. *Fighting Corruption in Developing Countries: Strategies and Analysis*. Bloomfield, CT: Kumarian Press.

Spector, Stephen. 2008. *Evangelicals and Israel: The Story of American Christian Zionism*. New York: Oxford University Press.

Spivak, Gayatri Chakravorty. 1999. *A Critique of Postcolonial Reason: Toward a History of the Vanishing Present*. Cambridge, MA: Harvard University Press.

Stern, Jessica. 2010. Mind over Martyr: How to Deradicalize Islamist Extremists. *Foreign Affairs* 89 (1) January/February: 95-108.

Stern, Nicholas. 2007. *The Economics of Climate Change: The Stern Review*. Cambridge, UK: Cambridge University Press.

Stewart, William. 2006. *How to Prepare for a Pandemic and Other Extended Disasters*. Charleston, SC: BookSurge Publishing.

Stiglitz, Joseph. 2002. *Globalization and Its Discontents*. New York: W. W. Norton & Company.

Stiglitz, Joseph. 2011. The Price of 9/11. *Economist's View*. September 1. Online at http://economists-view.typepad.com/economistsview/2011/09/stiglitz-the-price-of-911.html (accessed September 24, 2012).

Stoddard, Abby. 2006. *Humanitarian Alert: NGO Information and its Impact on US Foreign Policy*. Bloomfield, CT: Kumarian Press.

Strand, Jonathan. 2013. *Regional Development Banks: Lending with a Regional Flavor* (Global Institutions). New York: Routledge.

Sweig, Julia. 2010. A New Global Player. Brazil's Far-Flung Agenda. *Foreign Affairs* 89 (6) November/December: 173–184.

Takiff, Michael. 2010. *A Complicated Man: The Life of Bill Clinton as Told by Those Who Know Him*. New Haven, CT: Yale university Press.

Taubman, William. 2004. *Khrushchev: The Man and His Era*. New York: W. W. Norton.

Tavares, Rodrigo. 2009. *Regional Security The Capacity of International Organizations*. New York: Routledge.

Tetlock, Philip, Richard Lebow, and Geoffrey Parker, eds. 2006. *Unmaking the West: "What If?" Scenarios That Rewrite History*. Ann Arbor: The University of Michigan Press.

Tetlock, Philip. 2011. In an interview to The Washington Post. Online at http://wapo.st/epJAG5 (accessed September 2012).

Theiss-Morse, Elizabeth. 2009. *Who Counts as an American?: The Boundaries of National Identity*. New York: Cambridge University Press.

Thomas, Chris D., Alison Cameron, et al. 2004. Extinction Risk from Climate Change. *Nature* 427: 145–148.

Thomas, Daniel. 2001. *The Helsinki Effect: International Norms, Human Rights, and the Demise of Communism*. Princeton, NJ: Princeton University Press.

Thompson, Nicholas. 2009. *The Hawk and the Dove: Paul Nitze, George Kennan, and the History of the Cold War*. New York: Henry Holt.

Thurow, Lester. 1992. *Head to Head: The Coming Battle among Japan, Europe, and America*. New York: William Morrow.

Tickner, Ann. 1992. *Gender in International Relations: Feminist Perspectives on Achieving Global Security*. New York: Columbia University Press.

Time to Call the Sweep? *The Economist*. November 18, 2010. Online at http://www.economist.com/node/17519770 (accessed September 25, 2012).

True, Jacqui. 2009. Feminism. In *Theories of International Relations*, ed. Scott Burchill et al. 4th edition. New York: Palgrave Macmillan, 237–259..

Tumulty, Karen. 2011. Will Obama Be Reelected? The Economy Could Hold the Answer. *The Washington Post*. August 5, A1.

U.S. Department of State. 2013 Trafficking Persons Report. Online at http://www.state.gov/j/tip/rls/tiprpt/2013/ (accessed June 29, 2013).

UN High Commissioner for Refugees. 2012. Online at http://bit.ly/atXDsz (accessed July 15, 2013).

UNEP, United Nations Environment Programme. 2010. *Annual Report*. New York: United Nations.

United Nations Population Division. 2004. *World Population Prospects: The 2004 Revision*. New York: United Nations.

United Nations. (2004). A More Secure World: Our Shared Responsibility. Report of the High-Level Panel on Threats, Challenges and Change. http://www.un.org/secureworld/report2.pdf

United Nations. 2011. Translating Principles into Practice: Humanitarian Policies. *Humanitarian Negotiations with Armed Groups: A Manual and Guidelines for Practitioners*. Online at http://ochaonline.un.org/humanitariannegotiations/Chapter3-4.htm (accessed September 23, 2012).

Van Evera, Stephen. 2001. *Causes of War: Power and the Roots of Conflict*. Ithaca, NY: Cornell University Press.

van Loon, Jeremy. 2011. Canada May Miss $6.7 Billion Carbon Offset Bill by Exiting Kyoto Protocol. *Bloomberg.com*. Online at http://bloom.bg/siU2bD (accessed July 16, 2013).

Vattel, Emerich de. 2001. *Law of Nations or Principles of the Law of Nature, Applied to the Conduct and Affairs of Nations and Sovereigns*. Holmes Beach, FL: Gaunt. Originally published in 1758.

Victor, David, Granger Morgan, Jay Apt, John Steinbruner, and Katharine Ricke. 2009. The Geoengineering Option: A Last Resort against Global Warming? *Foreign Affairs* 88 (2) March/April: 64-76.

Victor, David. 2006. Recovering Sustainable Development. *Foreign Affairs* 85 (1) January/February.

Volkan, Vamik and Norman Itzkowitz. 1984. *The Immortal Ataturk: A Psychobiography*. Chicago, IL: University of Chicago Press.

Walker, Gordon. 2009. Globalizing Environmental Justice: The Geography and Politics of Frame Contextualization and Evolution. *Global Social Policy* December (9): 355–382.

Walker, Gordon. 2012. *Environmental Justice: Concepts, Evidence and Politics*. New York: Routledge.

Wallechinsky, David. 2006. *Tyrants: The World's 20 Worst Living Dictators*. New York: Harper Paperbacks.

Wallerstein, Immanuel. 1979. *The Capitalist World-Economy*. Cambridge, UK: Cambridge University Press.

Wallerstein, Immanuel. 2004. *World-System Analysis: An Introduction*. Durham, NC: The Duke University Press.

Walley, Noah and Bradley Whitehead. 1994. It's Not Easy Being Green. *Harvard Business Review* 72 (3) May/June: 46–51.

Walt, Stephen. 1987. *The Origins of Alliances*. Ithaca, NY: Cornell University Press.

Walt, Stephen. 1991. The Renaissance of Security Studies. *International Studies Quarterly* 35 (2): 211–239.

Walt, Stephen. 1998. One World, Many Theories. *Foreign Policy* 110 Spring: 29–46.

Walt, Stephen. 2005a. The Relationship between Theory and Policy in International Relations. *Annual Review of Political Science* 8: 23–48.

Walt, Stephen. 2005b. Taming American Power. *Foreign Affairs* 84 (5) September/October: 105–120.

Wapner, Paul. 2002. Paradise Lost? NGOs and Global Accountability. *Chicago Journal of International Law* 3 (155): 155.

Ward, Martin. 1999. Who Are the Many? *The Ottawa Citizen*. August 2, B6.

Waylen, Georgina. 2010. A Comparative Politics of Gender: Limits and Possibilities. *Perspectives on Politics* 8 (1) March: 223–231.

Weinberg, Leonard and Ami Pedahzur. 2003. *Political Parties and Terrorist Groups*. New York: Routledge.

Weiss, Thomas. 2004. The Sunset of Humanitarian Intervention? The Responsibility to Protect in a Unipolar Era. *Security Dialogue* 35 (2): 135–153.

Weiss, Thomas. 2007. *Humanitarian Intervention: Ideas in Action*. Cambridge, UK: Polity.

Welsh, Jennifer M., ed. 2004. *Humanitarian Intervention and International Relations*. New York: Oxford University Press.

Wendt, Alexander. 1992. Anarchy Is What States Make of It: The Social Construction of Power Politics, *International Organization* 46 (2): 391–425.

Wendt, Alexander. 1999. *Social Theory of International Politics*. Cambridge, UK: Cambridge University Press.

Westad, Odd Arne. 2007. *The Global Cold War: Third World Interventions and the Making of Our Times*. New York: Cambridge University Press.

Whalley, John. 1997. Why Do Countries Seek Regional Trade Agreements? In *The Regionalization of the World Economy*, ed. Jeffrey Frankel. Chicago: The University of Chicago Press, 63–86.

Wibben, Annick. 2011. *Feminist Security Studies. A Narrative Approach*. New York: Routledge.

Williams, Michael. 2006. *Deforesting the Earth: From Prehistory to Global Crisis, An Abridgment*. Chicago: University of Chicago Press.

Wittkopf, Eugene and James McCormick, eds. 2004. *The Domestic Sources of American Foreign Policy: Insights and Evidence*. Lanham, MD: Rowman & Littlefield.

Wittkopf, Eugene. 1990. *Faces of Internationalism: Public Opinion and American Foreign Policy*. Durham, NC: Duke University Press.

Wohlforth, William C., ed. 2003. *Cold War Endgame: Oral History, Analysis, Debates*. University Park: The Pennsylvania State University Press.

Wolfe, Nathan. 2011. *The Viral Storm: The Dawn of a New Pandemic Age*. New York: Times Books.

Woodall, Pam. 2011. Hey Big Spenders. *The Economist*. Special Edition: The World in 2012, 140.

Woods, Michael and Mary Woods. 2007. *Droughts (Disasters Up Close)*. Minneapolis, MN: Lerner Publications.

Woods, Ngaire. 2007. *The Globalizers: The IMF, the World Bank, and Their Borrowers*. Ithaca, NY: Cornell University Press.

World Health Organization. 2012. Malaria. Key Facts. Online at http://bit.ly/b5frdR (accessed July 17, 2013).

World Trade Organization. 2012. Online at http://bit.ly/a8VhKw (accessed July 18, 2013)

Wright, Lawrence. 2006. *The Looming Tower: Al Qaeda and the Road to 9/11*. New York: Vintage Books.

Wrong, Michela. 2002. *In the Footsteps of Mr. Kurtz: Living on the Brink of Disaster in Mobutu's Congo*. New York: Harper Perennial.

Yankelovich, Daniel. 2005. Poll Positions. *Foreign Affairs* 84 (5) September/October: 2–16.

Yergin, Daniel and Joseph Stanislaw. 1998. *The Commanding Heights: The Battle Between Government and the Marketplace That Is Remaking the Modern World*. New York: Free Press.

Young, Michael. 2010. Development at Gunpoint? Why Civilians Must Reclaim Stabilization Aid. *Foreign Affairs*. December 19. Online at http://fam.ag/hqPHpb (accessed July 18, 2013).

Zahariadis, Nikolaos. 2008. *State Subsidies in the Global Economy*. New York: Palgrave Macmillan.

Zakaria, Fareed. 2008. *The Post-American World*. New York: W. W. Norton.

Zaslavsky, Victor. 2004. *Class Cleansing: The Massacre at Katyn*. New York: Telos Press Publishing.

Zelikow, Philip and Condoleezza Rice. 1995. *Germany Unified and Europe Transformed: A Study in Statecraft*. Cambridge, MA: Harvard University Press.

Zellen, Barry S. 2009. *Arctic Doom, Arctic Boom: The Geopolitics of Climate Change in the Arctic*. Westport, CT: Praeger.

Ziegler, Jean. 1981. *Switzerland Exposed*. New York: Schocken Books.

Zinn, Howard. 2002. *The Power of Nonviolence: Writings by Advocates of Peace*. Boston, MA: Beacon Press.

Zizek, Slavoj. 2009. Berlusconi in Tehran. *London Review of Books*, 31 (14), July 23: 3-7.

Zoellick, Robert. 2012. *Robert Zoellick on China 2030 report: Transcript of Media Questions and Answers*. Bejing, China, Februalry 27. Online at http://bit.ly/zHjAiy (accessed July 19, 2013).

Zubok, Vladislav. 2007. *A Failed Empire: The Soviet Union in the Cold War from Stalin to Gorbachev (The New Cold War History)*. Chapel Hill: The University of North Carolina Press.

Credits

PHOTO CREDITS

CHAPTER 1

p. xxxiv: AP Photo/Franklin Reyes; p. 5: AP photo/ Seth Wenig; p. 8: BEN STANSALL/AFP/Getty Images; p. 11: AP Photo/Alexander F. Yuan; p. 16: Mario Tama/ Getty Images; p. 19: Imaginechina via AP Images; p. 21: AP photo/Lennart Preiss; p. 26: AP Photo/ Department of State/HO; p. 30: AP Photo/Vahid Salemi; p. 33: AP Photo/Anja Niedringhaus; p. 37: AP photo/Seth Wenig; AP photo/Lennart Preiss; AP Photo/Vahid Salemi

CHAPTER 2

p. 38: Sipa via AP Images; p. 43: bpk, Berlin/The Congress of Berlin (closing session), 1892/Werner, Anton von (1843-1915)/Art Resource, NY; p. 45: LBJ Library photo by Yoichi Okamoto; p. 48: PRAKASH SINGH/AFP/GettyImages; p. 54: HOANG DINH NAM/AFP/GettyImages; p. 58: Copyright Bettmann/ Corbis/AP Images; p. 62: AP photo; p. 66: Copyright Bettmann/Corbis/AP Images; p. 70: Jose CABEZAS/ AFP/GettyImages; p. 72: AP Photo/Liis Treimann; p. 77: PRAKASH SINGH/AFP/GettyImages; HOANG DINH NAM/AFP/GettyImages; Jose CABEZAS/AFP/ GettyImages

CHAPTER 3

p. 78: AP photo/B.K.Bangash,File; p. 82: Albert Harlingue/Roger Viollet/Getty Images; p. 86: AP photo/Gemunu Amarasinghe; p. 90: AP photo/ Sayyid Azim; p. 94: AP photo/Lefteris Pitarakis; p. 96: BERTRAND LANGLOIS/AFP/GettyImages; JEWEL SAMAD/AFP/GettyImages; p. 101: AP photo/Vincent Yu, File; p. 106: AP photo/Alik Keplicz; p. 109: AP Photo/Misha Japaridze; p. 113: AP photo/Bill Allen;

p. 117: AP photo/Gemunu Amarasinghe; AP photo/ Sayyid Azim; p. AP photo/Alik Keplicz

CHAPTER 4

p. 118: The Yomiuri Shimbun via AP Images; p. 121: AP Photo/Yonhap, Choi Jae-koo; p. 124: AP photo/Abdel Meguid al-Fergany; p. 129: Copyright Bettmann/Corbis/AP Images; p. 132: photo by AFP/ Getty Images; p. 135: AP photo/Juan Karita; p. 137: Kyodo via AP Images; p. 140: AP photo/Tom Pennington, File; p. 142: AP photo/The Canadian Press, Darryl Dyck; p. 145: Copyright Bettmann/ Corbis/AP Images; p. 146: AP photo/Abdel Meguid al-Fergany; photo by AFP/Getty Images; Kyodo via AP Images

CHAPTER 5

p. 148: LEVINE/SIPA/1303021424 Sipa via AP Images; p. 151: AP Photo/Farah Abdi Warsameh; p. 154: SSPL/Getty Images; p. 158: AP photo/Francois Mori; p. 162: Frontpage of French newspaper Le Petit Journal Illustre, 1928- Leemage.; p. 164: AP Photo/ Abd Raouf; p. 167: AP photo/Musa Sadulayev, File; p. 169: AP photo/Anonymous; p. 172: AP photo/ POOL/Jerry Lampen; p. 176: Copyright Bettmann/ Corbis/AP Images; p. 180: AP photo/Francois Mori; AP photo/Musa Sadulayev, File; AP photo/ Anonymous

CHAPTER 6

p. 181: photo by Pictorial Parade/Getty Images; p. 185: AP Photo/Kostas Tsironis; p. 190: AP photo/ Mahesh Kumar A; p. 191: Copyright Bettmann/ Corbis/AP Images; p. 196: AP photo/Timur Nisametdinov, NIPA; p. 199: Marijan Murat/picture-alliance/dpa/AP Images; p. 203: CTK via AP

Images; p. 208: AP Photo/B.K. Bangash; p. 211: CATHERINE HENRIETTE/AFP/Getty Images; p. 215: Imaginechina via AP Images; p. 217: AP Photo/ Kostas Tsironis; AP photo/Mahesh Kumar A; Imaginechina via AP Images

CHAPTER 7

p. 218: Copyright © 2003-2012 Shutterstock Images LLC; p. 222: Imaginechina via AP Images; p. 224: © Alexandra Boulat/VII/Corbis; p. 230: AP Photo; p. 234: AP photo / Dylan Martinez, Pool; p. 238: Terrence Spencer/Time Life Pictures/Getty Images; p. 244: AP photo/Pablo Martinez Monsivais; p. 246: © VIKTOR KOROTAYEV/Reuters/Corbis; p. 248: AP photo/ Eduardo Di Baia; p. 251: AFP/Getty Images; p. 255: © Alexandra Boulat/VII/Corbis; Terrence Spencer/Time Life Pictures/Getty Images; p. Colombians protesting against FARC

CHAPTER 8

p. 256: Ed Jones/AFP/Getty Images; p. 261: AP photo/ Mohammed Seeneen; p. 265: The Yomiuri Shimbun via AP Images; p. 267: © Lunamarina | Dreamstime. com; p. 271: AP photo/Association of Russian Polar Explorers; p. 272: MARK RALSTON/AFP/Getty Images; p. 279: Sean Gallup/Getty Images; p. 282: MARK RALSTON/AFP/Getty Images; p. 284: AP photo/ Bebeto Matthews; Lars Nicolaysen/picture-alliance/ dpa/AP Images; p. 291: The Yomiuri Shimbun via AP Images; MARK RALSTON/AFP/Getty Images; AP photo/Bebeto Matthews

CHAPTER 9

p. 292: Sam Dcruz Copyright © 2003-2012 Shutterstock Images LLC; p. 296: Alex Wong/Getty Images; p. 300: AP photo/Aaron Favila; p. 305: Copyright Carlos Cazalis/Corbis/APImages; p. 308: Tim Graham/Getty Images; p. 312: PRAKASH MATHEMA/AFP/Getty Images; p. 315: Canadian Press via AP Images; p. 317: AP photo/Marty Lederhandler; p. 320: THONY BELIZAIRE/AFP/Getty Images; p. 322: AP Photo/Jason Tanner, UNHCR; p. 326: AP photo/Aaron Favila; PRAKASH MATHEMA/ AFP/Getty Images; THONY BELIZAIRE/AFP/Getty Images

CONCLUSION

p. 327: AP Photo/Fernando Llano

FIGURE CREDITS

CHAPTER 3

p. 88: Created by OUP based on data from the Inter-Parliamentary Union, 2011; Created by OUP based on data from Beck, 2011

CHAPTER 4

p. 126: Created by OUP based on data from Wittkopf, E. (1990). Faces of Internationalism: Public Opinion and American Foreign Policy. Durham, NC: Duke University Press; Sobel, R. (2001). The impact of Public Opinion on US Foreign Policy Since Vietnam. New York: Oxford University Press; Hinckley, R. (1992). People, polls, and policymakers: American Public Opinion and National Security. New York: Lexington Books.

CHAPTER 6

p. 205: Created by OUP based on data from Woodall, 2011; p. 209: Created by OUP based on data from The Economist, "The World in 2012," page 107

CHAPTER 7

p. 223: Created by OUP based on data from http:// www.icasualties.org; p. 243: Created by OUP based on data from Sagemen, 2004; p. 253: Created by OUP based on data from Juliana Horowitz and Pew Research Center (2009; 2011)

CHAPTER 8

p. 260: Created by OUP based on data from EIA, World Resources Institute; p. 262: Created by OUP based on data from EIA, World Resources Institute

CHAPTER 9

p. 297: Created by OUP based on data from The United Nations; p. 301: Created by OUP based on data from The United Nations

Index